London
2012

A SELECTION
OF **RESTAURANTS** & **HOTELS**

Commitments

*S*ince our first edition in 1900, our ambition has remained the same: to accompany you on your journeys and to help you choose the best establishments in which to stay or eat, whether that's a small and practical or a grand hotel, a local gastropub or a fine dining restaurant.

→ Anonymous inspections

Our inspectors make regular and anonymous visits to hotels and restaurants to gauge the quality of products and services offered to an ordinary customer. They settle their own bill and may then introduce themselves and ask for more information about the establishment. Our readers' comments are also a valuable source of information, which we can then follow up with another visit of our own.

→ Independence

Our choice of establishments is a completely independent one, made for the benefit of our readers alone. The decisions to be taken are discussed around the table by the inspectors and the editor. The most important awards are decided at a European level. Inclusion in the Guide is completely free of charge.

→ Selection & choice

The Guide offers a selection of the best hotels and restaurants in every category of comfort and price. This is only possible because all the inspectors rigorously apply the same methods.

→ Annual updates

All the practical information, the classifications and awards are revised and updated every single year to give the most reliable information possible.

Consistency: The criteria for the classifications are the same in every country covered by the Michelin Guide.

→ And our aim...

...to do everything possible to make travel, holidays and eating out a pleasure, as part of Michelin's ongoing commitment to improving travel and mobility.

Dear reader

*W*e are delighted to present the 2012 edition of the Michelin Guide for London.

All the restaurants within this guide have been chosen first and foremost for the quality of their cooking. You'll find comprehensive information on over 500 dining establishments, ranging from gastropubs and neighbourhood brasseries to internationally renowned restaurants. The diverse and varied selection also bears testament to the rich and buoyant dining scene in London, with the city now enjoying a worldwide reputation for the quality and range of its restaurants.

You'll see that Michelin Stars are not our only awards – look out also for the Bib Gourmands. These are restaurants where the cooking is still carefully prepared but in a simpler style and, priced at under £28 for three courses, they represent excellent value for money.

As well as the restaurants, our team of independent, full-time inspectors have also chosen 50 hotels. These carefully selected hotels represent the best that London has to offer, from the small and intimate to the grand and luxurious. All have been chosen for their individuality and personality.

We are committed to remaining at the forefront of the culinary world and to meeting the demands of our readers. As such, we are always very interested to hear your opinions on any of the establishments listed in our guide. Please don't hesitate to contact us as your contributions are invaluable in directing our work and improving the quality of the information we provide.

Thank you for your support and happy travelling with the 2012 edition of the Michelin Guide for London.

Consult the Michelin Guide at www.viamichelin.com
and write to us at themichelinguide-gbirl@uk.michelin.com

Contents

● Where to **eat**

How to use this guide

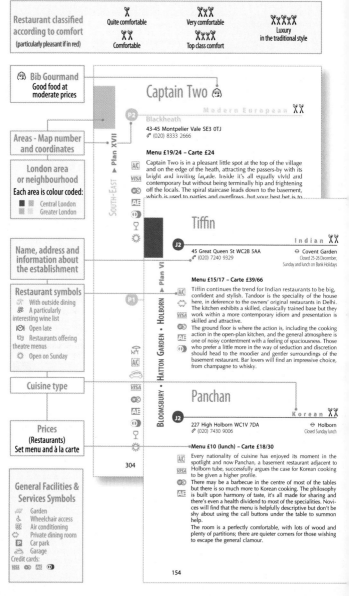

Restaurant classified according to comfort
(particularly pleasant if in red)

- X Quite comfortable
- XX Comfortable
- XXX Very comfortable
- XXXX Top class comfort
- XXXXX Luxury in the traditional style

Bib Gourmand Good food at moderate prices

Areas - Map number and coordinates

London area or neighbourhood
Each area is colour coded:
- Central London
- Greater London

Name, address and information about the establishment

Restaurant symbols
- With outside dining
- A particularly interesting wine list
- Open late
- Restaurants offering theatre menus
- Open on Sunday

Cuisine type

Prices (Restaurants)
Set menu and à la carte

General Facilities & Services Symbols
- Garden
- Wheelchair access
- Air conditioning
- Private dining room
- Car park
- Garage

Credit cards:

SOUTH-EAST ▶ Plan XVII

Captain Two

Modern European XX

P2 Blackheath

43-45 Montpelier Vale SE3 0TJ
(020) 8333 2666

Menu £19/24 – Carte £24

Captain Two is in a pleasant little spot at the top of the village and on the edge of the heath, attracting the passers-by with its bright and inviting façade. Inside it's all equally vivid and contemporary but without being terminally hip and frightening off the locals. The spiral staircase leads down to the basement, which is used to parties and overflows, but your best bet is to

304

BLOOMSBURY • HATTON GARDEN • HOLBORN ▶ Plan VI

Tiffin

Indian XX

J2

45 Great Queen St WC2B 5AA
(020) 7240 9329

Covent Garden
Closed 25-26 December, Sunday and lunch on Bank Holidays

Menu £15/17 – Carte £39/66

Tiffin continues the trend for Indian restaurants to be big, confident and stylish. Tandoor is the speciality of the house here, in deference to the owners' original restaurants in Delhi. The kitchen exhibits a skilled, classically trained base but they work within a more contemporary idiom and presentation is skilled and attractive.

The ground floor is where the action is, including the cooking action in the open-plan kitchen, and the general atmosphere is one of noisy contentment with a feeling of spaciousness. Those who prefer a little more in the way of seduction and discretion should head to the moodier and gentler surroundings of the basement restaurant. Bar lovers will find an impressive choice, from champagne to whisky.

Panchan

Korean XX

J2

227 High Holborn WC1V 7DA
(020) 7430 9006

Holborn
Closed Sunday lunch

Menu £10 (lunch) – Carte £18/30

Every nationality of cuisine has enjoyed its moment in the spotlight and now Panchan, a basement restaurant adjacent to Holborn tube, successfully argues the case for Korean cooking to be given a higher profile.

There may be a barbecue in the centre of most of the tables but there is so much more to Korean cooking. The philosophy is built upon harmony of taste, it's all made for sharing and there's even a health dividend to most of the specialities. Novices will find that the menu is helpfully descriptive but don't be shy about using the call buttons under the table to summon help.

The room is a perfectly comfortable, with lots of wood and plenty of partitions; there are quieter corners for those wishing to escape the general clamour.

154

Hotel classification according to comfort
(particularly pleasant if in red)

Quite comfortable

Comfortable

Very comfortable

Top class comfort

Luxury in the traditional style

Hotel symbols

39 rm Number of rooms
☲ Breakfast included (or not)
♦/♦♦ Prices for a single/ double room
⅋ Quiet hotel
⅋O With restaurant
⅃ Swimming pool
⊛ Spa
⅏ Sauna
⅍ Tennis
ƒ♭ Exercise room
⅌ Lift
⅊ Broadband connection
⅋♩ Wireless
▭ Satellite TV
⌆ Equipped conference room

Map coordinates

⊖ Underground station

Agatha's

I2

15 Charlotte St W1T 1RJ
℘ (020) 7806 2000

⊖ Goodge Street

44 rm – ♦£247/282 ♦♦£347, ☲ £19 – 8 suites
⅋O **Hercule** (See restaurant listing)

Le Petit François ✿✿

G3

French ✗✗✗✗

43 Upper Brook St W1K 7QR
℘ (020) 7408 0881

⊖ Marble Arch
Closed Christmas-New Year, Sunday, Saturday lunch and Bank Holidays – booking essential

Menu £48 – Carte £60/130

In today's rush for the new and the now, we sometimes forget about the jewels we already have. Le Petit François is guaranteed its own chapter when the history of British gastronomy is written and today, over forty years after it first opened in Chelsea, it's still maintaining its own high standards and respect for tradition. The service is unerringly professional: this is where any budding restaurateur should come if they want to learn how things are done 'properly' and one can observe the hierarchical structure from one's chair. The room retains a clubby and masculine feel but it also offers a palpable sense of history; those new to the restaurant are guided gently through its customs and politely reminded of its traditions.

The menu represents classic French cuisine and not just an English idea of French cuisine; a style of food which is becoming rarer by the day. A Soufflé Suissesse is rich enough to live on for days and the use of luxury items, from lobster to foie gras, would make Epicurus blanch. Those who prefer a lighter style, however, are not ignored.

First Course	Main Course	Dessert
• Hot foie gras and crispy duck pancake flavoured with cinnamon.	• Roast saddle of rabbit with crispy potatoes and parmesan.	• Bitter chocolate and praline 'indulgence'.
• Lobster mousse with caviar and champagne butter sauce.	• Whole roast John Dory with artichokes, olive oil and mashed potato.	• Iced amaretto nougat with cherries cooked in red wine syrup.

41

MAYFAIR • SOHO • ST JAMES'S ▶ Plan II

WESTMINSTER ▶ Plan V

...ion, within strolling distance of Soho, or ...own private screening room that attract ...n industry sorts and arty souls who have ...own, but the stimulating way in which it ...and the prevailing vibe.

...warehouse has been deftly transformed ...l and proves that comfort and design can ...and that something good has come from ...g a combination of abstract art, sculpture ...rtists of the neighbouring Bloomsbury set, ...be also quite English in tone. The drawing ...ress-free areas, in contrast to the bustle of ...restaurant.

...bedrooms are one-off pieces of furniture ...rawer fabrics and fittings, all supported by ...amme of virtually constant refurbishment. ...e enthusiastic and confident. The loft and ...l stir emotions of envy and desire or, if

373

Area - Map number

Stars for good cooking
✿ to ✿✿✿

✿
Starred restaurant symbol

Sample menu for starred restaurant

A culinary history of London

London, influenced by worldwide produce arriving via the Thames, has always enjoyed a close association with its food, though most of the time the vast majority of its people have looked much closer to home for their sustenance.

Even as far back as the 2nd century AD, meat was on the menu: the profusion of wildlife in the woods and forests around London turned it into a carnivore's paradise, thereby setting the tone and the template. Large stoves were employed to cook everything from pork and beef to goose and deer. The Saxons added the likes of garlic, leeks, radishes and turnips to the pot, while eels became a popular staple in later years.

What a lark!

By the 13th century, the taste for fish had evolved to the more exotic porpoise, lamprey and sturgeon, with saffron and spices perking up the common-or-garden meat dish. Not that medieval tastes would have been considered mundane to the average 21st century diner: Londoners of the time would think nothing about devouring roasted thrush or lark from the cook's stalls dotted around the city streets. And you'd have been unlikely to hear the cry "Eat your greens!" In the 15th century the vegetable diet, such as it was, seemed to run mainly to herbs such as rosemary, fennel, borage and thyme.

As commercial and maritime success burgeoned in the age of the Tudors, so tables began to groan under the weight of London's penchant for feasting. No excess was spared, as oxen, sheep, boars and pigs were put to the griddle; these would have been accompanied by newly arrived yams and sweet potatoes from America and 'washed down' with rhubarb from Asia. People on the streets could 'feast-lite': by the 17th century hawkers were offering all sorts of goodies on the hoof.

Full of beans

All of this eating was of course accompanied by a lot of drinking. Though much of it took place in the alehouses and taverns - which ran into the thousands - by the 18th century coffee houses had become extraordinarily popular. These were places to do business as well as being convenient 'for passing evenings socially at a very small charge'.

Perhaps the biggest revolution in eating habits came midway through the 19th century when the first cavernous dining halls and restaurants appeared. These 'freed' diners from the communal benches of the cook-house and gave them, for the first time, the chance for a bit of seclusion at separate tables. This private dining experience was an egalitarian movement: plutocrats may have had their posh hotels, but the less well-off were buttering teacakes and scones served by 'nippies' at the local Lyons Corner House.

Influenced by post-World War II flavours brought in by immigrants from Asia, the Caribbean and Africa, Londoners can now enjoy an unparalleled cuisine alive with global flavours, while the worlds of food and drink have fused remarkably well in recent years with the growing excellence of the gastropub, which had its roots in the creative maelstrom of the capital.

S.Vidler / Prisma/Age Fotostock

Practical London

ARRIVAL/DEPARTURE

If you're coming to London from abroad, it's worth bearing in mind that the capital's airports are (with one exception) a long way from the city itself. Better news is that they're all well served by speedy express train services; even better news is that if you travel by Eurostar you can go by train direct from the heart of Europe to the heart of London without having to worry about luggage limits, carousels and carbon footprints…

By air

Most people coming to London from overseas arrive via Heathrow (the UK's busiest) and Gatwick airports (more on both at www.baa.co.uk). You can catch the Heathrow Express rail service (www.heathrowexpress.co.uk) to Paddington (just west of the centre) every 15 minutes, and that's just about how long

the journey takes. Another alternative is to board the Piccadilly line tube train from Heathrow: it's cheaper, but the drawn-out travelling time can make it seem as if you've spent most of your holiday just getting into the centre. Gatwick is further out, south of London's M25 ring road, and the quickest way into the city is via the Gatwick Express rail service (www.gatwickexpress.co.uk), which takes half an hour to reach Victoria station. There are also frequent train services run by Southern (www.southernrailway.com) between Gatwick and Victoria, and Thameslink (www.firstcapitalconnect.co.uk), which connect with a host of central London stations, including London Bridge and King's Cross. The capital has three other airports: Stansted (www.stanstedairport.com), 35 miles northeast of the city; Luton (www.london-luton.com), 30 miles to the north, and London City Airport (www.londoncityairport.com), which is nine miles to the east, and connects to the centre via the Docklands Light Railway.

By train

The days of having to fly into London from abroad are long gone. Smart travellers from the Continent now jump on the Eurostar (www.eurostar.com) from Paris, Brussels or Lille, zip along at 186mph, and step onto the platform at St Pancras International in the time it takes to devour a coffee and a croissant (a big coffee, admittedly). From there, three tube lines from the adjoining King's Cross station whisk you into town. Book Eurostar far enough in advance (which isn't very far, by any means) and you can get tickets for just £59 return.

GETTING AROUND

By tube

First, the bad news: the tube can get hot and overcrowded; engineering works can close lines at weekends and the escalators are sometimes out of action. But the good news? Generally speaking, the tube is by far the quickest way to get around town. There are 12 lines, plus the Docklands Light Railway; these cover pretty much the whole city and are all clearly shown on the free map you can pick up at any tube station or London Travel Information Centre. Trains run from 5am to just past midnight Monday-Saturday, with a reduced timetable on Sundays. For details about the line you wish to use, check the Transport for London website www.tfl.gov.uk or phone the 24-hour Travel Information Service on + 44 (0)20 7222 1234.

By bus

They might move a bit slower than tubes, but when you ride on the top of a double-decker bus, you get the added bonus of an absorbing, tourist-friendly view to take in on the way. Though the world-famous Routemasters have now been all but phased out, the replacement buses with low-floors are accessible to passengers with buggies and wheelchair-users. There's a handy central London bus map which you can pick up at transport information centres at larger tube stations. Or you can plan your bus trip online by checking out the useful 'Journey Planner' to be found on the Transport for London website. Most Central London routes require that you buy tickets before you board; you can get these from machines by the bus stop. The flat fare is £2 and this includes travel across all zones (see also 'The Pearl that is Oyster', below).

By car

The best advice is not to drive in central London, not if you want your sanity preserved anyway. Roadworks and parking can be the stuff of nightmares, and that's before the Congestion Charge Zone, albeit now reduced in size, is even taken into consideration. This zone covers the central area and is clearly marked by the red 'C' signs painted on the road. It's in operation Monday-Friday 7am-6pm (weekends and holidays are free) and you'll need to register the car's number plate on a database (go to www.cclondon.com for details). If it all sounds a bit too much of a headache,

you always have the option of hailing a black cab – just stick out your hand when you see one with its taxi light illuminated.

By boat

'Taking to the water' has become increasingly popular over the last few years: the Thames offers some little-seen views of London, and cutting through the open expanse of river can certainly lay claim to being your most relaxing travel option. Most river services operate every 20 minutes to one hour, and there are piers all over the central area where you can jump on board, from Chelsea Harbour in the west to Woolwich Arsenal in the east. For more details go to www. tfl.gov.uk

The pearl that is oyster

Londoners on the move make sure they don't leave home without their Oyster. It's an electronic smartcard and it's the fastest and easiest way to pay for single journeys around town. You don't even have to take it out of your purse or wallet: you just zap it over a yellow reader to let you through tube gates or onto a bus. Oysters are charged with a pre-paid amount of credit and can cover a set period of time or be used to pay-as-you-go. You'll always pay less for a journey than on the equivalent Day Travelcard or Bus Pass. To check out the whole deal, visit www.tfl.gov.uk/oyster

LIVING LONDON LIFE

It almost goes without saying that visitors to the capital are spoilt for choice when it comes to having a good time. For instance, you could visit one of the city's 300 museums or galleries, many of which are free, or you could see for yourself why London's theatre scene is considered the best in the world. Come nightfall, choose from the vast number of restaurants, offering cuisines from all parts of the world, or from one of 5,000 pubs and bars. At the weekend, an interesting alternative to shopping or sports events is to browse one of the farmers' markets that have sprung up in recent years. On a Saturday, the best of the bunch can be found at Ealing, Notting Hill, Pimlico, Wimbledon and Twickenham. On Sundays, two of the favourites are in Marylebone and Blackheath, while, on the same day, the Columbia Road flower market, in the East End, is a wonderful place to spend time comparing flora while chomping on a bagel from a local café.

The more mainstream shopper might do well to steer clear of frenetic Oxford Street. Regent Street is a more alluring thoroughfare with its mid-priced fashion stores and hallowed names. If you're after a destination with a real touch of class, then nearby Jermyn Street is the place for bespoke men's clothing, but if your taste is for more outré threads, then Notting Hill or Camden are good bets. Back in the centre of town, Covent Garden is packed with speciality stores, quirky alleyways, and – if you choose the wrong time to go – an awful lot of people!

Escape can always be found in the relative quiet of a good bookshop, and London is full of them. Still in Covent Garden, Stanford's is the city's number one travel bookshop, while not far away in Charing Cross Road, the legendary Foyles has thrown over its fusty image with a stylish makeover. But for the marriage of real elegance with a good read, head to Daunt Books in Marylebone High Street, which is set in an Edwardian building with long oak galleries and skylights; the bustle of London's streets will seem a million miles away.

To tip or not to tip

Generally speaking, tips are proffered in taxis, hotels, hairdressers and, if someone serves you at your table, in bars. There's no set procedure in restaurants: always check whether a service charge has been added to your bill (this can range from 10 to 15 per cent). Sometimes, the establishment leaves the amount open, and it's up to you to leave a tip for the waiter if you've been happy with the service. Beware of those restaurants that try their luck by adding service to the bill but who then also leave the slip open.

Where to **eat**

Stéphanie Guillaume/Fotolia.com

Starred restaurants

Within this selection, we have highlighted a number of restaurants for their particularly good cooking. When awarding one, two or three Michelin Stars there are a number of factors we consider: the quality and compatibility of the ingredients, the technical skill and flair that goes into their preparation, the clarity and combination of flavours, the value for money and, above all, the taste. Equally important is the ability to produce excellent cooking not once but time and time again. Our inspectors make as many visits as necessary, so that you can be sure of the quality and consistency.

A two or three star restaurant has to offer something very special in its cuisine; a real element of creativity, originality or personality that sets it apart from the rest. Three stars – our highest award – are given to the very best.

Cuisines in any style and of any nationality are eligible for a star. The decoration, service and comfort have no bearing on the award.

For every restaurant awarded a star we include six specialities that are typical of their cooking style.

These specific dishes may not always be available.

Let us know what you think, not just about the stars but about all the restaurants in this guide.

The awarding of a star is based solely on the quality of the cuisine.

N: highlights those establishments newly promoted to one, two or three stars.

☸ ☸ ☸

Exceptional cuisine, worth a special journey.
One always eats here extremely well, sometimes superbly. Distinctive dishes are precisely executed, using superlative ingredients.

Alain Ducasse at		Gordon Ramsay	ҲxxX 255
The Dorchester	ҲxҲxX 38		

☸ ☸

Excellent cooking, worth a detour.
Skillfully and carefully crafted dishes of outstanding quality.

L'Atelier de Joël Robuchon	Ҳ 105	Ledbury	ҲxX 276
Le Gavroche	ҲxxX 60	Marcus Wareing at	
Hélène Darroze at		The Berkeley	ҲxxX 124
The Connaught	ҲxxX 66	Square	ҲxxX 93
Hibiscus	ҲxX 67		

☸

A very good restaurant in its category.
A place offering cuisine prepared to a consistently high standard.

Amaya	ҲxX 118	North Road N	ҲX 216
Apsleys	ҲxxX 119	Petersham Nurseries Café	Ҳ 373
Arbutus	Ҳ 41	Pétrus	ҲxX 128
L'Autre Pied	ҲX 138	Pied à Terre	ҲxX 170
Benares	ҲxX 48	Pollen Street Social N	ҲX 81
Chez Bruce	ҲX 379	Quilon	ҲxX 129
Club Gascon	ҲX 204	Rasoi	ҲX 262
Dinner by Heston		Rhodes Twenty Four	ҲxX 220
Blumenthal N	ҲxX 248	Rhodes W1 (Restaurant)	ҲxxX 150
Galvin at Windows	ҲxxX 59	River Café	ҲX 368
Galvin La Chapelle	ҲxX 334	St John (Clerkenwell)	Ҳ 222
Gauthier - Soho	ҲxX 61	Semplice	ҲX 88
The Glasshouse	ҲX 369	Seven Park Place	ҲxX 89
Greenhouse	ҲxX 63	Sketch (The Lecture	
Hakkasan Hanway Place	ҲX 166	Room and Library)	ҲxxX 91
Hakkasan Mayfair N	ҲX 64	Tamarind	ҲxX 94
Harwood Arms	🍴 362	Texture	ҲX 153
Kai	ҲxX 70	La Trompette	ҲxX 357
Kitchen W8	ҲX 274	Umu	ҲxX 97
Locanda Locatelli	ҲxX 146	Viajante	ҲX 327
Maze	ҲX 73	Wild Honey	ҲX 99
Murano	ҲxX 76	Yauatcha	ҲX 101
Nobu	ҲX 77	Zafferano	ҲxX 133
Nobu Berkeley St	ҲX 78		

Bib Gourmand

Restaurants offering good quality cooking for less than £28 (price of a 3 course meal excluding drinks)

Al Duca	✗	39	Great Queen Street	✗	164
Anchor and Hope	🍴	192	Hereford Road	✗	180
Azou **N**	✗	365	Iberica	✗✗	144
Barrafina **N**	✗	44	José **N**	✗	208
Bar Trattoria Semplice	✗	45	Kateh **N**	✗	180
Benja Bangkok Table	✗	47	Koya **N**	✗	71
Bocca di Lupo	✗	51	Mango and Silk	✗	360
Bradley's	✗✗	301	Market	✗	292
Brawn **N**	✗	326	Medcalf	✗	212
Brown Dog	🍴	347	Morito	✗	214
Cafe Spice Namaste	✗✗	338	Opera Tavern **N**	✗✗	112
Canton Arms	🍴	337	Polpo	✗	82
Chapters	✗✗	326	St John Bread and Wine **N**	✗	336
Charlotte's Bistro	✗✗	354	Salt Yard	✗	171
Comptoir Gascon	✗	203	Simply Thai	✗	377
da Polpo **N**	✗	107	Sushi-Say **N**	✗	304
Dehesa	✗	56	Terroirs	✗	113
Drapers Arms	🍴	317	Triphal **N**	✗	375
500	✗	290	Trishna **N**	✗	154
Fox and Grapes **N**	🍴	380	Trullo	✗	313
Galvin Café a Vin	✗	333	28°-50°	✗	224
Giaconda Dining Room	✗	164	Zucca	✗	229
Goldfish City	✗	206			

American

Automat	✗	42
Spuntino	✗	92

Argentinian

Casa Malevo	✗	179

Asian

Champor-Champor	✗	200
Cicada	✗	201
E and O	✗✗	272
Eight over Eight	✗✗	249
Goldfish	✗	296
Goldfish City	✗⊛	206
Great Eastern Dining Room	✗✗	316
Singapore Garden	✗✗	302
Spice Market	✗✗	90
XO	✗✗	292

Asian influences

Galoupet	✗✗	253
Kopapa	✗	165

Beef specialities

Goodman	✗✗	62
Goodman City	✗✗	206
Hawksmoor (Spitalfields)	✗	335
Hawksmoor (Seven Dials)	✗	109
Kew Grill	✗✗	370
Maze Grill	✗✗	72
Redhook	✗✗	219

British

Anchor and Hope	🍴⊛	192
Anglesea Arms	🍴	365
Bedford and Strand	✗	106
Bennett	✗✗	349
Bentley's (Grill)	✗✗✗	49
Bluebird	✗✗	240
Bolingbroke	🍴	350
Builders Arms	🍴	241
Bull and Last	🍴	294
Bumpkin (North Kensington)	✗	270
Bumpkin (South Kensington)	✗	242
Butlers Wharf Chop House	✗	197
Cadogan Arms	🍴	242
Canton Arms	🍴⊛	337
Cat and Mutton	🍴	313
Chelsea Ram	🍴	246
Chiswell Street Dining Rooms	✗✗	201
Corrigan's Mayfair	✗✗✗	55
Dean Street Townhouse Restaurant	✗✗	55
Dinner by Heston Blumenthal	✗✗✗ ✿	248
Drapers Arms	🍴⊛	317
Engineer	🍴	299
Fox and Grapes	🍴⊛	380
Gilbert Scott	✗✗	301
Great Queen Street	✗⊛	164
Green	🍴	207
Harwood Arms	🍴❀	362
Hereford Road	✗⊛	180
Hix (Soho)	✗	65
Hix Oyster and Chop House	✗	208
Inn the Park	✗	69
Magdalen	✗✗	211
Manson	✗✗	361
Market	✗⊛	292
Medcalf	✗⊛	212
The National Dining Rooms	✗	75
Owl and Pussycat	🍴	335
Paradise by way of Kensal Green	🍴	298
Paternoster Chop House	✗	217
Peasant	🍴	218
Prince Arthur	🍴	314
Prince of Wales	🍴	371
Queens Pub and Dining Room	🍴	294
Quo Vadis	✗✗	84
Ransome's Dock	✗	352
Restaurant at St Paul's Cathedral	✗	219
Rhodes Twenty Four	✗✗✗ ✿	220
Rivington Grill (Greenwich)	✗	331
Rivington Grill (Shoreditch)	✗	321
Roast	✗✗	221

Rules ✗✗ 112
St John (Clerkenwell) ✗❀ 222
St John (Soho) ✗ 86
St John Bread and Wine ✗🍴 336
Sands End 🍴 364
Savoy Grill ✗✗✗ 113
Shepherd's ✗✗✗ 131
Tate Modern (Restaurant) ✗ 224
Victoria 🍴 360
Well 🍴 227
Wells 🍴 297

Chinese

Baozi Inn ✗ 44
Barshu ✗ 45
Ba Shan ✗ 46
Beijing Dumpling ✗ 46
China Tang ✗✗✗✗ 54
Good Earth ✗✗ 254
Hakkasan Hanway Place ✗✗❀ 166
Hakkasan Mayfair ✗✗❀ 64
Haozhan ✗✗ 65
Imperial China ✗✗✗ 69
Kai ✗✗✗❀ 70
Mao Tai ✗✗ 363
Min Jiang ✗✗✗ 277
Mr Chow ✗✗ 258
Pearl Liang ✗✗ 181
Phoenix Palace ✗✗ 148
Plum Valley ✗✗ 80
Red N Hot ✗✗ 295
Royal China ✗✗ 152
Seventeen ✗✗ 278
Yauatcha ✗✗❀ 101

Eastern European

Baltic ✗✗ 193

French

L'Absinthe ✗ 299
Alain Ducasse at
The Dorchester ✗✗✗✗✗ ❀❀❀ 38
Almeida ✗✗ 316
Angelus ✗✗ 178
L'Atelier de Joël Robuchon ✗ ❀❀ 105
Aubaine (South Kensington) ✗ 236
Aubaine (Mayfair) ✗ 42
L'Aventure ✗✗ 139
Bar Battu ✗ 193
Bar Boulud ✗✗ 238

Bellamy's ✗✗ 47
Bibendum ✗✗✗ 238
Bistro Aix ✗ 293
Bistro K ✗✗ 239
Bistrot Bruno Loubet ✗ 195
Bleeding Heart ✗✗ 162
Le Boudin Blanc ✗ 51
Boundary ✗✗✗ 320
Brula ✗✗ 378
Cassis ✗✗ 244
Cellar Gascon ✗ 199
Le Cercle ✗✗ 243
Chabrot ✗ 245
Chelsea Brasserie ✗✗ 245
Chez Bruce ✗✗❀ 379
Cigalon ✗✗ 202
Clos Maggiore ✗✗ 107
Club Gascon ✗✗❀ 204
La Cocotte ✗ 296
Le Colombier ✗✗ 247
Comptoir Gascon ✗🍴 203
Coq d'Argent ✗✗✗ 205
Les Deux Salons ✗✗ 108
French Kitchen ✗ 163
Galvin at Windows ✗✗✗✗❀ 59
Galvin Bistrot de Luxe ✗✗ 142
Galvin Café a Vin ✗🍴 333
Galvin La Chapelle ✗✗✗❀ 334
Gauthier - Soho ✗✗✗❀ 61
Le Gavroche ✗✗✗✗ ❀❀ 60
Gordon Ramsay ✗✗✗✗ ❀❀❀ 255
Hélène Darroze
at The Connaught ✗✗✗✗ ❀❀ 66
Henry Root ✗ 250
Koffmann's ✗✗✗ 123
Lobster Pot ✗ 332
Luc's Brasserie ✗✗ 210
Marcus Wareing
at The Berkeley ✗✗✗✗ ❀❀ 124
Mon Plaisir ✗✗ 167
Morgan M ✗✗ 310
My dining room 🍴 363
1901 ✗✗✗ 215
Notting Hill Brasserie ✗✗ 277
Pearl ✗✗✗ 169
Le Pont de la Tour ✗✗✗ 218
Racine ✗✗ 261
Rétro Bistrot ✗✗ 376
Rhodes W1 (Restaurant) ✗✗✗❀ 150
Roussillon ✗✗✗ 130

Modern European

Where to **eat** ▶ Cuisine Type

23

Restaurants with outside dining

Paternoster Chop House	✗	217
St John's Tavern	▯	290
Petersham Nurseries Café	✗✿	373
Sands End	▯	364
Phoenix	▯	260
Santini	✗✗✗	131
Plateau	✗✗	329
Toto's	✗✗✗	264
Le Pont de la Tour	✗✗✗	218
La Trompette	✗✗✗✿	357
Princess Victoria	▯	374
Victoria	▯	360
Quadrato	✗✗✗	329
Wapping Food	✗	338
Queens Pub and Dining Room	▯	294
Waterway	▯	183
Ransome's Dock	✗	352
Well	▯	227
Ritz Restaurant	✗✗✗✗	85
Wells	▯	297
River Café	✗✗✿	368
Wright Brothers Soho	✗	100
Rose and Crown	✗✗	298
York and Albany	✗✗	293

Open late

Time of last orders in brackets

Arbutus (23.30)	✗✿	41
L'Atelier de Joël Robuchon (00.00)	✗✿✿	105
Automat (23.45)	✗	42
Bentley's (Grill) (23.45)	✗✗✗	49
Bentley's (Oyster Bar) (00.00)	✗	49
Boisdale (23.15)	✗✗	120
Bombay Brasserie (23.30)	✗✗✗	240
Cambio de Tercio (23.30)	✗✗	243
Le Caprice (00.00)	✗✗	52
Casa Batavia (23.15)	✗✗	270
Cecconi's (23.30)	✗✗✗	53
China Tang (00.00)	✗✗✗✗	54
Chutney Mary (23.30)	✗✗✗	246
Cinnamon Kitchen (23.15)	✗✗	202
Daphne's (23.15)	✗✗	247
da Polpo (23.15)	✗☺	107
Dean Street Townhouse Restaurant (23.30)	✗✗	55
Le Deuxième (00.00)	✗✗	108
Eighty-Six (23.45)	✗✗	249
Eleven Park Walk (00.00)	✗✗✗	250
Fakhreldine (23.15)	✗✗	57
Forge (00.00)	✗✗	109
Hakkasan Hanway Place (23.30)	✗✗✿	166
Hakkasan Mayfair (00.00)	✗✗✿	64
Haozhan (02.00)	✗✗	65
Imperial China (00.00)	✗✗✗	69
The Ivy (23.30)	✗✗✗	110
J. Sheekey (00.00)	✗✗	110
J. Sheekey Oyster Bar (00.00)	✗	111
Levant (23.30)	✗✗	145
Malabar (23.30)	✗✗	275
Mao Tai (23.30)	✗✗	363
Mon Plaisir (23.15)	✗✗	167
Moro (23.45)	✗	214
Mr Chow (23.45)	✗✗	258
Nobu Berkeley St (23.30)	✗✗✿	78
Noura Brasserie (23.30)	✗✗	125
Opera Tavern (23.30)	✗✗☻	112
Ozer (23.30)	✗✗	147
Paramount (23.30)	✗	168
Phoenix Palace (23.15)	✗✗	148
Plum Valley (00.00)	✗✗	80
Poissonnerie de l'Avenue (23.30)	✗✗	261
Red Fort (23.30)	✗✗✗	85
St John (Clerkenwell) (23.45)	✗✿	222
St John (Soho) (02.00)	✗	86
Singapore Garden (23.15)	✗✗	302
Sketch (The Gallery) (00.30)	✗✗	90
Spice Market (23.30)	✗✗	90
Spuntino (00.00)	✗	92
Sumosan (23.30)	✗✗	92
Theo Randall (23.15)	✗✗✗	96
Toto's (23.30)	✗✗✗	264
The Wolseley (23.45)	✗✗✗	98
Yauatcha (23.30)	✗✗✿	101
Zafferano (23.30)	✗✗✗✿	133

Where to **eat** ▶ Open on Sunday

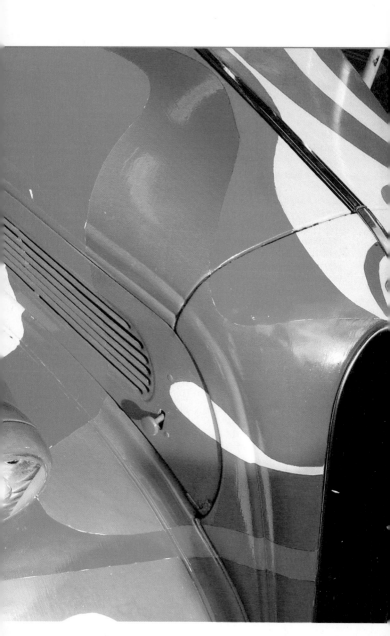

Central London

K. Blackwell / MICHELIN

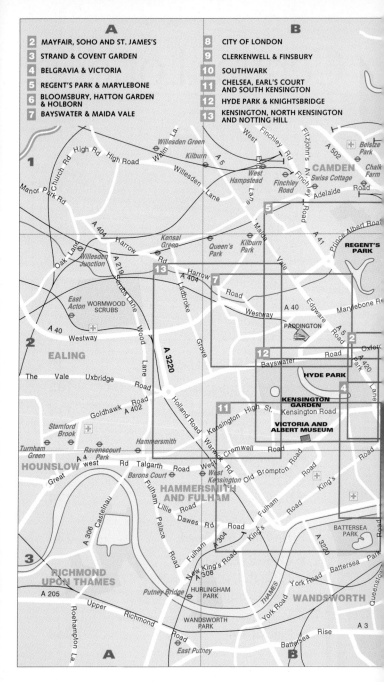

A

2	MAYFAIR, SOHO AND ST. JAMES'S
3	STRAND & COVENT GARDEN
4	BELGRAVIA & VICTORIA
5	REGENT'S PARK & MARYLEBONE
6	BLOOMSBURY, HATTON GARDEN & HOLBORN
7	BAYSWATER & MAIDA VALE

B

8	CITY OF LONDON
9	CLERKENWELL & FINSBURY
10	SOUTHWARK
11	CHELSEA, EARL'S COURT AND SOUTH KENSINGTON
12	HYDE PARK & KNIGHTSBRIDGE
13	KENSINGTON, NORTH KENSINGTON AND NOTTING HILL

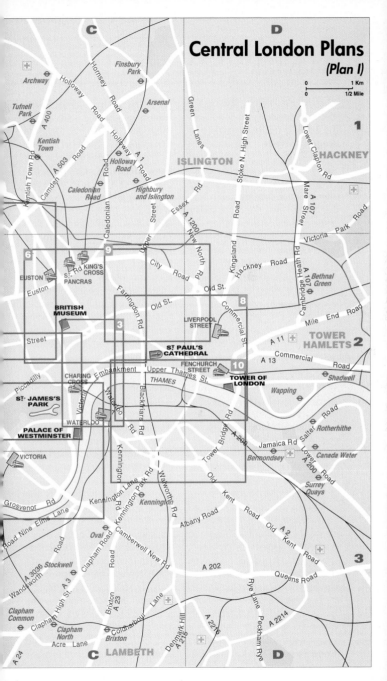

Central London Plans
(Plan I)

0   1 Km
0   1/2 Mile

HACKNEY

ISLINGTON

Archway

Tufnell Park

Kentish Town

Finsbury Park

Arsenal

Holloway Road

Hornsey Road

Holloway A1 Road

Holloway Road

Caledonian Road

Highbury and Islington

Kentish Town Rd

Camden A 503 Road

Caledonian Road

Upper Street

Essex Rd

Green Lanes

Stoke N. High Street

Lower Clapton Rd

Mare Street

A 107

Victoria Park Road

A 107 Road

Bethnal Green

Cambridge Heath Rd

Kingsland Road

Hackney Road

Mile End Road

TOWER HAMLETS

A 11

A 13 Commercial Road

Shadwell

Wapping

Rotherhithe

Jamaica Rd

Bermondsey

Salter Road

Canada Water

Lower Road

A 200

Surrey Quays

6

EUSTON

Euston Street

9

KING'S CROSS ST. PANCRAS

BRITISH MUSEUM

City Road

Farringdon Rd

Old St.

Old St.

3

St PAUL'S CATHEDRAL

New North Rd

8

LIVERPOOL STREET

Commercial St.

FENCHURCH STREET

10

TOWER OF LONDON

Upper Thames St.

THAMES

Blackfriars Rd

Waterloo Rd

Tower Bridge Rd A 200

Old Kent Road

Piccadilly

CHARING CROSS

Embankment

Victoria

Waterloo

St JAMES'S PARK

PALACE OF WESTMINSTER

VICTORIA

Grosvenor Rd

Kennington Lane

Kennington Park Rd

Kennington

Walworth Rd

Albany Road

Old Kent Road

A 2

Old Kent Road

Queens Road

Road Nine Elms Lane

Oval

Camberwell New Rd

Clapham Road

A 3036 Stockwell

Wandsworth Road

A 3 Clapham High St.

Brixton A 23

Coldharbour Lane

Brixton

Denmark Hill

A 215

A 202

A 2216

Rye Lane

Peckham Rye

A 2214

Clapham Common

Clapham North

Acre Lane

LAMBETH

33

Mayfair · Soho · St James's

There's one elegant dividing line between Mayfair and Soho - the broad and imposing sweep of **Regent Street** - but mindsets and price tags keep them a world apart. It's usual to think of easterly Soho as the wild and sleazy half of these ill-matched twins, with Mayfair to the west the more sedate and sophisticated of the two. Sometimes, though, the natural order of things runs awry: why was rock's legendary wild man Jimi Hendrix, the embodiment of Soho decadence, living in the rarefied air of Mayfair's smart 23 Brook Street? And what induced Vivienne Westwood, punk queen and fashionista to the edgy, to settle her sewing machine in the uber-smart Conduit Street?

Mayfair has been synonymous with elegance for three and a half centuries, ever since the Berkeley and Grosvenor families bought up the local fields and turned them into posh real estate. The area is named after the annual May fair introduced in 1686, but suffice it to say that a raucous street celebration would be frowned upon big time by twenty-first century inhabitants. The grand residential boulevards can seem frosty and imposing, and even induce feelings of inadequacy to the humble passer-by but should he become the proud owner of a glistening gold card, then hey ho, doors will open wide. Claridge's is an art deco wonder, while **New Bond Street** is London's number one thoroughfare for the most chi-chi names in retailing. **Savile Row** may sound a little 'passé' these days, but it's still the place to go for the sharpest cut in town, before sashaying over to compact **Cork Street** to indulge in the purchase of a piece of art at one of its superb galleries. Science and music can also be found here, and at a relatively cheap price: the Faraday Museum in **Albemarle Street** has had a sparkling refurbishment, and the Handel House Museum in Brook Street boasts an impressive two-for-one offer: you can visit the beautifully presented home of the German composer and view his musical scores… before looking at pictures of Hendrix, his 'future' next door neighbour.

Soho challenges the City as London's most famous square mile. It may not have the money of its brash easterly rival, but it sure has the buzz. It's always been fast and loose, since the days when hunters charged through with their cries of 'So-ho!' Its narrow jumbled streets throng with humanity, from the tourist to the tipsy, the libertine to the louche. A lot of the fun is centred round the streets just south of **Soho Square,** where area legends like The Coach & Horses ('Norman's Bar'), Ronnie Scott's and Bar Italia cluster in close proximity. There's 80s favourite, the Groucho Club, too, though some of its lustre may have waned since a corporate takeover. The tightest t-shirts in town are found in **Old Compton Street,** where the pink pound jangles the registers in a

C. Barrely / MICHELIN

swathe of gay-friendly bars and restaurants. To get a feel of the 'real' Soho, where old engraved signs enliven the shop fronts and the market stall cries echo back to the 1700s, a jaunt along **Berwick Street** is always in vogue, taking in a pint at the eternally popular Blue Posts, an unchanging street corner stalwart that still announces 'Watney's Ales' on its stencilled windows.

Not a lot of Watney's ale was ever drunk in **St James's**; not a lot of ale of any kind for that matter. Champagne and port is more the

style here, in the hushed and reverential gentlemen's clubs where discretion is the key, and change is measured in centuries rather than years. The sheer class of the area is typified by **Pall Mall's** Reform Club, where Phileas Fogg wagered that he could zip round the world in eighty days, and the adjacent **St James's Square,** which was the most fashionable address in London in the late seventeenth century, when dukes and earls aplenty got their satin shoes under the silver bedecked tables.

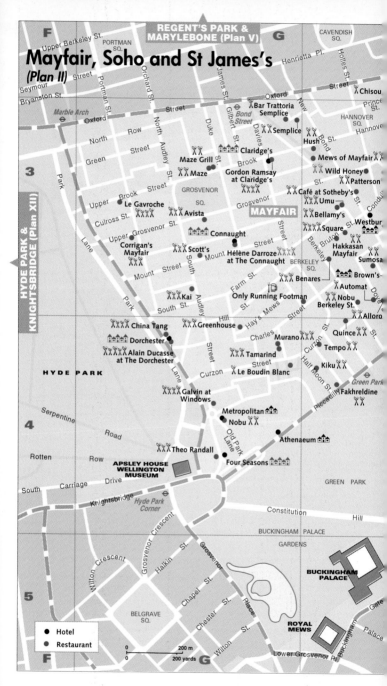

Mayfair, Soho and St James's
(Plan II)

CAVENDISH SQ.

Upper Berkeley St.
PORTMAN SQ.

Henrietta Pl.

Holles St.

Seymour Street

Upper Berkeley St.

Bryanston St.

Oxford Street

Chisou

Prince

HANNOVER SQ.

Hannove

Marble Arch

Oxford Street

North Row

Green Street

North Audley St.

Orchard St.

Duke St.

Gilbert St.

Davies St.

New Bond St.

Bar Trattoria Semplice

Semplice

Hush

Bond St.

HYDE PARK & KNIGHTSBRIDGE (Plan XII)

Brook Street

Maze Grill

Maze

Claridge's

Gordon Ramsay at Claridge's

Mews of Mayfair

Wild Honey

Patterson

Le Gavroche

Avista

GROSVENOR SQ.

Grosvenor Street

Café at Sotheby's

Umu

MAYFAIR

Bellamy's

Westbur

Upper Brook Street

Upper Grosvenor St.

Culross St.

Corrigan's Mayfair

Scott's

Connaught

Mount Street

Hélène Darroze at The Connaught

Square

Hakkasan Mayfair

Brown's

Sumosa

Berkeley Street

Conduit

BERKELEY SQ.

Bruton St.

Farm St.

Benares

Kai

South St.

Audley St.

Greenhouse

Hay's Mews

Only Running Footman

Automat

Nobu Berkeley St.

Alloro

HYDE PARK

China Tang

Dorchester

Alain Ducasse at The Dorchester

Charles St.

Tamarind

Curzon Street

Le Boudin Blanc

Murano

Quince

Tempo

Kiku

Curzon St.

Half Moon St.

Galvin at Windows

Green Park

Fakhreldine

Piccadilly

Park Lane

Metropolitan

Nobu

Old Park Lane

Athenaeum

Serpentine Road

Rotten Row

Theo Randall

APSLEY HOUSE
WELLINGTON MUSEUM

Four Seasons

South Carriage Drive

Knightsbridge

Hyde Park Corner

Constitution Hill

GREEN PARK

BUCKINGHAM PALACE GARDENS

BUCKINGHAM PALACE

Wilton Crescent

Grosvenor Crescent

Halkin St.

Grosvenor Pl.

Chapel St.

Chester St.

Wilton Pl.

ROYAL MEWS

Buckingham Palace Gate

Lower Grosvenor Pl.

BELGRAVE SQ.

● Hotel
● Restaurant

0   200 m
0   200 yards

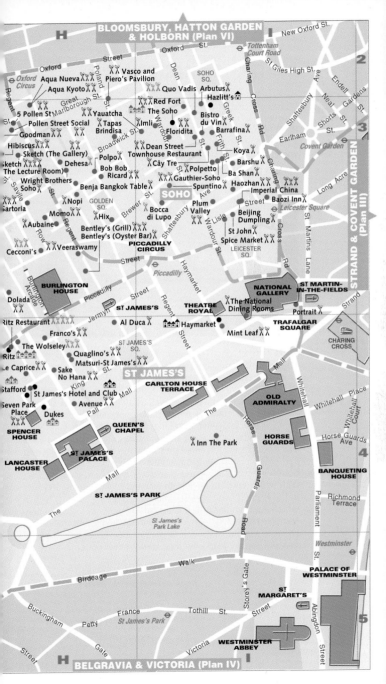

New Oxford St.
Tottenham
Court Road

Oxford   Street   Oxford   St.
Oxford
Circus

Aqua Nueva
Aqua Kyoto

Vasco and
Piero's Pavilion

SOHO
SQ.

Charing

St Giles High St.

Endell

Poland   St.

Great

Marlborough   St.

Quo Vadis   Arbutus
Hazlitt's

5 Pollen St
Pollen Street Social
Goodman

Yauatcha
Tapas
Brindisa
Imli

Red Fort
The Soho

Bistro
du Vin

Shaftesbury   Ave

Neal   St.

Shorts   St.

Hibiscus
Sketch (The Gallery)
Sketch
(The Lecture Room)
Wright Brothers
Soho

Dehesa

Polpo
Bob Bob
Ricard

Benja Bangkok Table

Floridita

Dean Street
Townhouse Restaurant

Cây Tre

Gauthier-Soho

Koya

Barrafina

Barshu

Ba Shan

Earlham

Covent Garden

STRAND & COVENT GARDEN (Plan III)

Long   Acre

Greek   St.

Frith   St.

Dean   St.

Wardour   St.

Sartoria
Aubaine
Cecconi's

Nopi
Momo

Veeraswamy

GOLDEN
SQ.

Hix

Brewer   St.

Bocca
di Lupo

SOHO

Polpetto

Haozhan

Imperial China

Baozi Inn

Spuntino

Plum
Valley

Leicester Square

Beijing
Dumpling

St John
Spice Market

St Martins   Lane

LEICESTER
SQ.

Shaftesbury   Ave

Wardour   St.

Lisle   St.

Charing   Cross   Rd

Bentley's (Grill)
Bentley's (Oyster Bar)

PICCADILLY
CIRCUS

Regent   St.

Haymarket

Piccadilly

Street

Piccadilly

BURLINGTON
HOUSE

Burlington   Arcade

Dolada

Ritz Restaurant

Franco's

The Wolseley

Ritz

Le Caprice

Stafford

Seven Park
Place

Dukes

Jermyn   Street

ST JAMES'S

Al Duca

Quaglino's

Matsuri-St James's

Sake
No Hana

St James's Hotel and Club

Avenue

SPENCER
HOUSE

LANCASTER
HOUSE

ST JAMES'S
SQ.

King   St.

Pall   Mall

QUEEN'S
CHAPEL

ST JAMES'S
PALACE

The   Mall

THEATRE
ROYAL

The National
Dining Rooms

Haymarket

Mint Leaf

NATIONAL
GALLERY

Portrait

ST MARTIN-
IN-THE-FIELDS

TRAFALGAR
SQUARE

Strand

CHARING
CROSS

CARLTON HOUSE
TERRACE

The   Mall

Horse   Guards   Road

Inn The Park

OLD
ADMIRALTY

HORSE
GUARDS

Whitehall

Whitehall   Place

Horse Guards
Ave

Whitehall
Court

ST JAMES'S PARK

St James's
Park Lake

BANQUETING
HOUSE

Parliament   St.

Richmond
Terrace

Westminster   St.

Birdcage   Walk

Buckingham   Gate

Petty   France
St James's Park

Tothill   St.

Storey's Gate

Victoria   Street

Westminster

St   Margaret   St

ST
MARGARET'S

PALACE OF
WESTMINSTER

Abingdon   Street

WESTMINSTER
ABBEY

Alain Ducasse
at The Dorchester ✿ ✿ ✿

French ✗✗✗✗✗

Park Ln.
✉ W1K 1QA
☎ (020) 7629 8866
www.alainducasse-dorchester.com

Menu £50/78

⊖ **Hyde Park Corner**
Closed Easter, 13 August-4 September,
1-10 January, 26-31 December,
dinner 25 December,
Saturday lunch, Sunday and Monday

A/C

VISA
M/C
AE

Alain Ducasse

Coco Chanel once said that "luxury must be comfortable, otherwise it is not luxury". The London outpost of über-chef Alain Ducasse's global empire is, without doubt, a sumptuous and extravagant affair. Patrick Jouin's design uses tans and creams, leather and wood, as well as 30,000 green silk buttons to reflect the colours of the park opposite. The tables are immaculately laid and the striking, semi-private Table Lumière is surrounded by a curtain of 4,500 fibre optics. Waiting staff are a sincere and eager lot, although sometimes impenetrable accents can make communication a little wearisome. The choice is between a set tasting menu, a seasonal menu and the à la carte, with which you can have both fish and meat courses. 16 chefs in the kitchen use the best available prime ingredients, half of which are from the British Isles, half brought over from France, to create supremely refined and sophisticated dishes that reflect Ducasse's lighter approach to gastronomy. An experience here may not come cheap - but then luxury never does.

First Course

- Sauté of lobster, truffled chicken quenelles and homemade pasta.
- Warm Scottish crab, delicate royale and coral jus.

Main Course

- Fillet of beef Rossini with 'sacristain' potatoes.
- Roast loin of Limousin farmhouse veal with 'blanquette' of vegetables.

Dessert

- 'Baba like in Monte-Carlo'.
- Exotic fruits contemporary vacherin.

Al Duca 😊

H4

4-5 Duke of York St.
✉ SW1Y 6LA
✆ (020) 7839 3090
www.alduca-restaurant.co.uk

⊖ **Piccadilly Circus**
Closed Easter, 25 December,
Sunday and bank holidays

Menu £28

A/C

😮

VISA

M©

AE

Al Duca has become as much a part of the fabric of St James's as many of the shirt makers who have made neighbouring Jermyn Street home over the years. It is also one of the those restaurants that manage the trick of appearing quiet one minute and full to the rafters the next without anyone noticing and this ensures that the atmosphere is never less than spirited. The serving team are a young, confident bunch and the manager knows who his regulars are. The menu is priced per course; there is plenty of choice and the cooking is crisp and confident, with plenty of well-priced bottles to match. The rib-eye with porcini mushrooms is a highlight. Prices are also pretty keen, especially for a restaurant in this neck of the woods.

Alloro

H3

19-20 Dover St
✉ W1S 4LU
✆ (020) 7495 4768
www.atozrestaurants.com/alloro

⊖ **Green Park**
Closed 25 December, Saturday lunch
and Sunday – booking essential

Menu £35/39

A/C

🍽

VISA

M©

AE

Alloro celebrated its 10th anniversary in 2010 and this comparative longevity owes much to its sensible prices, confident service and easy-to-eat Italian food. The current chef has been here for nearly half the restaurant's life; he comes from Piedmont and manages to sneak in a few specialties from his home region. The menu offers an appealing choice and nicely balanced selection, from a crisp chicory salad with bottarga to slow-cooked lamb shoulder, with all breads and pastas being made in-house. It's priced per number of courses taken; having all four represents the best value. Noise drifts in from the adjacent, boisterous baretto and so ensures that the atmosphere in the comfortable and urbane restaurant is always lively.

Aqua Kyoto

H3

Japanese 🍴🍴

240 Regent St.
(entrance on Argyll St.) ✉ W1F 7EB
✆ (020) 7478 0540
www.aqua-london.com

⊖ Oxford Circus
Closed 25 December
and 1 January

Carte £45/65 s

A/C
🛋
🎭
☼
VISA
MC
AE

Aqua London occupies all 17,000 square foot of the 5th floor of the former Dickins & Jones department store and boasts, along with a big bar and terrific terraces, two large restaurants. Aqua Kyoto is the more boisterous of the two, although getting to the table can be a drawn out affair, as you first give your name at the Argyll Street entrance, do so again when you get out of the lift, and only then are you handed over to the restaurant reception. However, Aqua Kyoto offers a fun night out, more so if you've come in a group – not just so you can compete with the noise, but also because the contemporary Japanese food is designed for sharing. Highlights include the eel teriyaki and the noodle dishes. Service means well but lacks direction.

Aqua Nueva

H3

Spanish 🍴🍴🍴

240 Regent St. (entrance on Argyll St.)
✉ W1B 3BR
✆ (020) 7478 0540
www.aqua-london.com

⊖ Oxford Circus
Closed 25 December and
1 January

Carte £45/74

A/C
🛋
🎭
☼
VISA
MC
AE

To reach the relative tranquillity of this Spanish restaurant, one first has to fight through the crowds enjoying a drink and a sense of exclusivity in Aqua Spirit, another part of this huge operation. Aqua Nueva feels more sophisticated than Aqua Kyoto with which its shares the 5th floor. It comes divided into two; the main room is more elegant and comfortable, but the tapas bar area, with its ceiling feature of 15,000 wooden beads, has more buzz and character and fills up first. The food comes in a stylised fashion that delivers the classic combinations of Spanish cuisine in original ways, although some subtle balances can get lost in the interpretation. The tapas, however, is more traditional and often features regional specialities.

Arbutus ✿

63-64 Frith St.
✉ W1D 3JW
℘ (020) 7734 4545
www.arbutusrestaurant.co.uk

⊖ **Tottenham Court Road**
Closed 25-26 December and 1 January
– booking advisable

Menu £17 (lunch) – Carte £27/38

A/C
✿
iОi
🎭
☼
VISA
MC
AE

Arbutus

When a restaurant makes it look as easy as this, you know that an enormous amount of work and experience have actually gone into it. Arbutus has also proved an enormous success because all its components dovetail together just so: the decoration is relaxed and contemporary but seems to work in harmony with the food; service is prompt and efficient but also bubbly and affable; the cooking is intelligent and honest and the prices are realistic and accessible. Despite the apparent simplicity of the food on the plate, this is highly accomplished cooking which demonstrates an inherent understanding of ingredients, textures and flavours. Dishes are dictated by the seasonal availability of their component parts and the skilled use of cheaper cuts like tripe, tongue and trotters rather than luxury ingredients highlights the kitchen's level of ability and also keeps prices down-to-earth. Factor in a wine list that makes experimenting with some serious wines an affordable practice and you have a restaurant that deserves its success.

First Course

- Squid and mackerel 'burger', razor clams and sea purslane.
- Gratin of ox tripe 'Spanish style'.

Main Course

- Saddle of rabbit, shoulder cottage pie.
- Sea bream, grilled fennel, mussels, chorizo and monks beard.

Dessert

- Cold chocolate fondant, salted caramel ice cream.
- Clafoutis of William pears with vanilla ice cream.

Aubaine

French ✗

4 Heddon St.
✉ W1B 4BS
☎ (020) 7440 2510
www.aubaine.co.uk

⊖ Oxford Circus
Closed dinner Sunday and bank holidays

Carte £22/52

This is the newer sister to the Brompton Road original, although they've had to tweak it slightly: they tried a food counter but that didn't work and there is no boulangerie here as the area is less residential. Being surrounded by so many offices and shops in the vicinity means they do a brisk trade throughout the day and particularly during lunch; its corner position also affords it a two-sided outdoor terrace and there aren't many of those in Mayfair. The look is of a farmhouse as imagined by a townie; avoid the basement room as it's dull by comparison. With a selection of salads, grilled fish, steaks and a burger, the menus wouldn't look out of place in a bistro. For dessert, you choose from the presented patisserie selection.

Automat

American ✗

33 Dover St.
✉ W1S 4NF
☎ (020) 7499 3033
www.automat-london.com

⊖ Green Park
Closed 25 December and 1 January

Carte £24/49

An antidote to Mayfair's inherent formality and overwhelming sense of Englishness can be found in the form of this American brasserie. Open from breakfast until late, it offers an appealingly accessible menu full of recognisable words that could have come straight out of NYC: crab cakes for starters, cheesecakes for dessert, with burgers, 'mac and cheese' or Nebraskan corn-fed beef in between. There are pasta dishes and more ambitious main courses too but it's best to stick to the classics, with a side order of fries. They'll try to palm you off with a table in the first section but don't have it – ask to sit in the mid-section, decked out in the style of a railway carriage, or in the rear with the open kitchen, which is the fun part.

Avenue

Modern European ✗✗

7-9 St James's St.
✉ SW1A 1EE
✆ (020) 7321 2111
www.avenue-restaurant.co.uk

⊖ **Green Park**
Closed 25-26 December,
Saturday lunch and Sunday

Menu £24 (lunch) – Carte £25/55

A/C
😃😃
VISA
MC
AE

Judging by the number of suited business types standing around the long bar this is clearly a good place to close deals. Its brash and boisterous atmosphere puts it in sharp contrast to the Gentlemen's Clubs that still populate St James's and the unsullied sheer whiteness of the room keeps everyone alert. The number of larger tables also makes it less suited to those hoping for a little intimacy. The cooking is crisp and fresh, from an all-encompassing menu that keeps its influences within Europe but also has a growing British element. There's everything from smoked salmon, fishcakes and blade of beef to burgers, bream and – to celebrate the deal – oysters and caviar. Service comes with an urgency which isn't always called for.

Avista

G3

Italian ✗✗✗

Millennium Mayfair Hotel,
39 Grosvenor Sq ✉ W1K 2HP
✆ (020) 7596 3399
www.avistarestaurant.com

⊖ **Bond Street**
Closed Saturday lunch
and Sunday

Menu £26 (lunch) – Carte £30/66

A/C
⊡
😃😃
VISA
MC
AE
①

Avista occupies the generous space within the Millennium Hotel that was previously farmed out to Brian Turner. Not only did they soften the room but they also added a separate street entrance which helps in establishing the restaurant's identity, despite the best efforts of the intrusively anodyne music. Veneto born Chef Michele Granziera, a Zafferano alumnus, has created a menu that traverses Italy and marries the rustic with the more refined. There are dishes designed for sharing as well as pre-starter 'snacks' if you really can't wait. The homemade pastas are a particular highlight, while the kitchen's creativity is given full rein on the 'Surprise' seven course menu which is available at dinner.

MAYFAIR, SOHO & ST JAMES'S ▶ PLAN II

Baozi Inn

13

Chinese ✗

25 Newport Court
✉ WC2H 7JS
✆ (020) 7287 6877

⊖ Leicester Square
Closed 24-25 December

Carte approx. £14

☼ Further proof that Chinatown is shaking off its tired, touristy image comes in the shape of Baozi Inn. Granted, there's nothing particularly noteworthy about the predictable surroundings of red lanterns and chunky tables but the friendly staff are welcoming and eager to please and the food is generously sized. It's also hard to blow your budget, which is especially significant as they only take cash. The eponymous baozi, or steamed filled buns, are a good way to start, although one is certainly enough; dishes have a fiery Sichuan slant and you'll feel the force in the noodle soup. The peanut and rolled tofu skin salad makes a perfect, calming side dish. Only Chinese beer is served but that's the ideal accompaniment anyway.

Barrafina ☺

13

Spanish ✗

54 Frith St.
✉ W1D 3SL
✆ (020) 7813 8016
www.barrafina.co.uk

⊖ Tottenham Court Road
Closed 24 December and 1 January
– (bookings not accepted)

Carte £17/26

A/C
☼
VISA
MC
AE
⊙

London has been a bit iffy about restaurants that don't take reservations but Barrafina is the likely candidate to buck that trend. This is the younger sibling to the Hart brothers' Fino restaurant and its success is down to its mix of satisfyingly unfussy and authentic tapas and a buzzy atmosphere. Seafood is a speciality and the fish displays an exhilarating freshness; the Jabugo ham is also well worth trying. Four dishes per person is about par and the choice varies from razor clams a la plancha and tuna tartar to grilled chorizo and lamb sweetbreads with capers. It all centres around a counter, with seating for 20, so be prepared to talk to your neighbour - another thing that's never caught on in the capital. Be sure to try one of the sherries.

Barshu

28 Frith St.
⊠ W1D 5LF
✆ (020) 7287 8822
www.bar-shu.co.uk

⊖ Leicester Square
Closed 24-25 December –
booking advisable

Carte £19/47

Those who like their food with a kick won't be disappointed by Bar Shu as it features the fiery flavours of China's Sichuan Province. The menu, which looks more like a brochure, features a photo of each dish along with a chilli rating – a useful aid, as the staff can be a little reluctant to engage with customers. But it's not all mouth-numbingly hot and some of the dishes do display a more subtle balance of flavours. The legendary chillies and pepper are imported directly from China and, with the chef coming from the province too, authenticity is assured, particularly with the 'Five colour appetiser platter', which includes duck tongues and pig intestines. Lots of carved wood and lanterns decorate the place; larger groups should head downstairs.

MAYFAIR, SOHO & ST JAMES'S ▶ PLAN II

Bar Trattoria Semplice ☺

22 Woodstock St.
⊠ W1C 2AR
✆ (020) 7491 8638
www.bartrattoriasemplice.com

⊖ Bond Street

Menu £17 (lunch) – Carte £22/37

Bar Trattoria Semplice was opened in 2008 by the same expert team behind Semplice which is just yards away. This is a simpler, more accessible but by no means inferior little sister. The tone is set by the old Berkel meat slicer by the entrance and the cheeses and cured meats above the bar. Oak-topped tables, creams and burgundies and a photo of a Tuscan dawn add to the relaxed feel of the room. The kitchen goes back to basics, with its emphasis on flavour and value. There's a giveaway set lunch menu and each month specialities from a different region of Italy, such as Piedmont or Lazio, feature. Desserts come from the trolley just like trattorie of old; wines are available in 500ml carafes and the bar has an easy, all-day menu.

Ba Shan

I3

24 Romilly St.
✉ W1D 5AH
✆ (020) 7287 3266

⊖ Leicester Square
Closed 24-25 December – booking
advisable

Carte £17/30

A/C
📺
☀
VISA
MC
AE

Ba Shan is the third enterprise from the team who brought you Bar Shu and Baozi Inn. While this cosy place still has some Sichuan leanings, it mainly focuses on traditional styles from Northern areas and Henan province. Somewhat confusingly, there are two menus: one 'snack', the other 'home-style' - but just pick from both. Dry-wok dishes are plentiful and the guotie dumplings are their own take on a classic. Shaanxi flatbread 'sandwiches' or pork Chaoshou are a good way to start; noodles and vegetables come dressed with a provocative amount of chilli. Decoratively, it treads a fine line between cute and kitsch. There are three or four tables in each of the five rooms and service copes well with the constant influx of customers.

Beijing Dumpling

I3

23 Lisle St.
✉ WC2H 7BA
✆ (020) 7287 6888

⊖ Leicester Square
Closed 24-25 December

Carte £15/25

A/C
☀
VISA
MC
AE

Flashing neon or hanging roast ducks in the window appear to be the popular Chinatown method of attracting passers-by; this little restaurant catches their attention by showing its chefs hard at work preparing dumplings. It's also a lot less frenzied than many of its more excitable neighbours and is a cut above the norm with its food. It serves freshly prepared dumplings of both Beijing and Shanghai styles and, although the range is not quite as comprehensive as the restaurant's name would suggest, they are still the highlight, especially varieties of the famed Siu Lung Bao. The rest of the menu has a wide base but its worth exploring the specials which include the occasional Taiwanese offering like spicy chicken.

Bellamy's

H3

18 Bruton Pl.   ⊖ Bond Street
✉ W1J 6LY   Closed Saturday lunch,
℘ (020) 7491 2727   Sunday and bank holidays
www.bellamysrestaurant.co.uk

Menu £29 – Carte £38/54

A/C

VISA

MC

AE

If Audrey Tautou ever opened a shop it would probably look a little like Bellamy's: it's sweet, petite and pretty. The counter doubles as the oyster bar but turn left and you'll find yourself in a roomy, ersatz French brasserie, complete with assorted Gallic posters and accented waiters. The menu covers all bases, from foie gras and caviar to duck rillettes and entrecôtes and the kitchen keeps to the classic techniques and combinations. The good value little set menu offers some financial sanctuary from the more robust prices on the à la carte, although the cover charge is an unwelcome anachronism. The lunchtime crowd are mostly male, suited and serious but dinner is more relaxed, while the mews location adds to the feeling of exclusivity.

Benja Bangkok Table ☺

H3

17 Beak St.   ⊖ Oxford Circus
✉ W1F 9RW
℘ (020) 7287 0555
www.benja-bankoktable.com

Menu £10/15 – Carte £18/22

A/C

☼

VISA

MC

AE

①

A recent makeover left this Thai restaurant on the edge of Soho with a new name and a simpler look – and it is all the better for it. Styled on a typical Bangkok eatery, the interior is bright and well-lit and offers intimate – or, depending on your view, slightly cramped – surroundings, which are spread over three floors. The food offers true tastes of Thailand and the menu is suitably wide-ranging, from their signature Pad Thai to crisp salads, assorted snacks, punchy soups and nicely balanced curries. Those looking for the best value for money should head straight for the set menus, which are named after Bangkok streets familiar to every backpacker. Staff have that endearing charm and easy confidence so typical of Thailand.

Benares ✿

Indian XXX

H3

12a Berkeley Square House
✉ W1J 6BS
📞 (020) 7629 8886
www.benaresrestaurant.com

⊖ **Green Park**
Closed 25- 26 December
and 1 January

Menu £30 (lunch) – Carte £55/95

A/C

VISA

MC

AE

D

Benares

When Benares was re-launched a couple of years ago after an extended hiatus caused by a kitchen fire, it seemed that not a great deal had changed in its appearance although, apparently, much work did take place behind the scenes. One terrific addition, however, was the Chef's Table with its floor to ceiling windows looking directly into the kitchen; the Sommelier's Table doesn't quite have the same cachet. Another difference came in the subtle evolution of Atul Kochhar's cooking. His dishes appear a little simpler on the plate; the main ingredient takes centre stage, with the Indian spices adding interesting and complementary flavours but without being the dominant force. Those who want to experience as much of the cooking as they can are able to do so thanks to the Grazing menu, although those who don't care for too much modernity with their Indian food will find enough recognisable dishes to satisfy them. Much thought has also gone into the wine list and in choosing the right pairings for the food.

First Course

- Fennel lamb chop, mustard chicken tikka and king prawn platter.
- Goan spiced mackerel, gooseberry chutney and pickled pear slivers.

Main Course

- Roasted fillet of roe deer, venison biryani and sesame peanut sauce.
- Kafir lime marinated tandoori prawns, lemon rice and prawn pickle.

Dessert

- Lime mousse, lemon thyme jelly and basil sorbet.
- Caramel chocolate fondant, ivoire foam and allspice ice cream.

Bentley's (Grill)

H3

11-15 Swallow St.
✉ W1B 4DG
☎ (020) 7734 4756
www.bentleys.org

⊖ Piccadilly Circus
Closed 25-26 December
and 1 January

Carte £47/60

A/C
⌁
🕐
☼
VISA
MC
AE

The beloved institution called Bentley's continues to enjoy its new lease of life. The green neon sign is still outside but these days the upstairs dining room has a contemporary feel with leather chairs, fabric covered walls and paintings of boats and fish for those who haven't twigged that seafood is the main draw here. One thing that will probably never change is the clubby feel and the preponderance of suited male customers. Much of the produce comes from St Ives and Looe in Cornwall and the freshness is palpable. Fish on the bone dissected at the table remains something of a speciality. Dover and Lemon soles feature strongly, as do oysters and soups, whilst the breads and beef remind you that owner Richard Corrigan is Irish.

Bentley's (Oyster Bar)

Seafood 𝕏

H3

11-15 Swallow St.
✉ W1B 4DG
☎ (020) 7734 4756
www.bentleys.org

⊖ Piccadilly Circus
Closed 25 December
and 1 January

Menu £25 (lunch) – Carte £35/50

☂
A/C
🕐
☼
VISA
MC
AE

There's something about Swallow Street that always seems to get the taste buds going. Bentley's small reception area acts for both the upstairs restaurant and the ground floor Oyster Bar so be patient; dining on the ground floor means you'll be ushered through the curtain into a dimly lit bar, with marbled-topped tables, banquette seating and places laid up at the counter. Oysters are naturally one of the main features, and the fish pie is a popular choice, but there are usually lots of daily specials and these often represent the most appealing option. The restaurant's illustrious past is almost tangible and the atmosphere is chummy and clubby, helped along with noise from the bar on the other side and the evening pianist.

Bistro du Vin

13

Modern European ✗

36 Dean St
✉ W1D 4PS
✆ (020) 7432 4800
www.bistroduvin.co.uk

⊖ Tottenham Court Road
Closed 25 December

Carte £25/48

A/C

VISA

MC

AE

The paint had hardly dried on their first London bistro in Clerkenwell when the owners behind the Hotel du Vin group opened their second branch. This one's slightly bigger but otherwise follows roughly the same formula, by offering an appealing selection of brasserie classics and a decent selection of well-priced wines. The zinc-topped bar is the focal point, the back section surprisingly roomy, and there's a 'salon' ideal for a pre-prandial; the 'wine room' is great for small parties. The Josper grill takes centre stage and steaks from the British Isles are well-hung and flavoursome; the contents of the charcuterie and cheese room are also worth exploring. The 'Enomatic' wine dispenser allows the chance to try some fine wines.

Bob Bob Ricard

H3

Traditional ✗✗

1 Upper James St
✉ W1F 9DF
✆ (020) 3145 1000
www.bobbobricard.com

⊖ Oxford Circus
Closed 25-26 December,
1 January, Sunday and Monday

Menu £24 (lunch) – Carte £29/70

A/C

VISA

MC

AE

"Taste is the enemy of creativeness" said Pablo Picasso. The creatively decorated Bob Bob Ricard was set up to compete with the traditional grand cafés and diners by serving anything to anyone at anytime. Your table could be getting stuck into beef Wellington while your neighbours are spooning an evening bowl of cornflakes – and no one raises an eyebrow. If your doctor has prescribed a diet of caviar and jelly then this place is ideal. Each table even has a button to press if you want more champagne. Don't get palmed off with a table by the entrance: to get the full, flamboyant effect of all the smoked glass and marble you need to be in the body of the restaurant. But spare a thought for the waiters in those bubblegum-pink waistcoats.

Bocca di Lupo 🐺

Italian ✗

12 Archer St
✉ WID 7BB
✆ (020) 7734 2223
www.boccadilupo.com

⊖ Piccadilly Circus
Closed 24 December-
4 January and Sunday dinner –
booking essential

Carte £24/35

A/C ⌁ 🎭 VISA Ⓜ AE

Deservedly busy from the day it opened, Bocca di Lupo is one of the best things to have arrived in Soho since the espresso bar. But be sure to sit at the marble counter in front of the chefs rather than at one of the faux-distressed tables at the back – not only is the atmosphere here more fun but the food is often better as it hasn't hung around the waiters' station waiting to be delivered. Each item has its region of origin within Italy noted on the menu and is available in a large or smaller size. The flavours don't hang back and over-ordering in all the excitement is very hard to resist. Highlights include the veal and pork agnolotti, the poussin in bread, and tripe; leave room for dessert or visit their Gelato shop opposite.

Le Boudin Blanc

French ✗

5 Trebeck St.
✉ W1J 7LT
✆ (020) 7499 3292
www.boudinblanc.co.uk

⊖ Green Park
Closed 24-26 December

Menu £15 (lunch and early dinner) – Carte £28/49

⛱ ⌁ 🎭 ☀ VISA Ⓜ AE

Le Boudin Blanc fits perfectly into Shepherd Market: it's lively, atmospheric and doesn't take itself quite so seriously as some of the establishments who share its Mayfair postcode. It's essentially two houses knocked together and they've certainly managed to squeeze in plenty of tables over the two floors. Try to sit by the window on the ground floor as you'll be out of the path of the young French staff who run around at quite a pace. The menu provides a comforting read of French classics and country cooking from all regions. The snails are popular, as is the boudin blanc. The lunch prix fixe is a steal; there are daily specials on the board and the wine list ranges from quaffing wines of the Languedoc to premier crus from Bordeaux.

Cafe at Sotheby's

H3

34-35 New Bond St.
✉ W1A 2AA
✆ (020) 7293 5077
www.sothebys.com

⊖ **Bond Street**
Closed 5-31 August, Saturday,
Sunday and bank hoildays –
booking essential – (lunch only)

Carte £26/32 s

VISA
MC
AE
DC

It's usually the seasons that inform the menu of most restaurants but here at Sotheby's they change the style of the dishes according to the art being sold. For instance, experience has shown that modern and Impressionist artists attract a diet-conscious crowd who like their salads, while the Old Masters appeal to those who favour a more substantial, well-lubricated lunch which ends with a proper pudding. The lobster sandwich is a perennial feature and the wine list is brief but appealingly eclectic. Occupying a cosy space just off the lobby of the auction house, this is a little gem of a restaurant which is smarter than the 'café' moniker would suggest. Service is well-judged and the many regulars are discreetly acknowledged.

Le Caprice

H4

Arlington House, Arlington St.
✉ SW1A 1RJ
✆ (020) 7629 2239
www.le-caprice.co.uk

⊖ **Green Park**
Closed 25-26 December

Carte £21/46

A/C
iO
AE
VISA
MC
AE
DC

Thanks to its cocktail bar, slick interior and self-assured clientele, Le Caprice has always felt like a restaurant with more than a touch of Manhattan about it, so the only surprise is that New Yorkers had to wait until 2009 for their own version of this St James's institution, which opened here back in 1981. The monochrome decoration and David Bailey photos are striking but the clever part is the menu, which offers everything from a burger or eggs Benedict to roast game or the ubiquitous fishcakes. The enthusiasm of the staff is directly related to your degree of celebrity or the frequency of your visits. It isn't cheap either but then, if the size of a restaurant bill is something that concerns you, you shouldn't be here in the first place.

Cây Tre

42-43 Dean St
✉ W1D 4PZ
☎ (020) 7317 9118
www.caytreesoho.co.uk

⊖ Tottenham Court Road
Booking advisable

Menu £14/21 – Carte £20/40

The West End could do with having plenty more Vietnamese restaurants, so hopefully others will follow the lead of Cây Tre. The bright and sleek surroundings of this Soho branch are smarter than the original in Hoxton and the bustling environment provides plenty of atmosphere. Staff know their menu and go about their business with determined efficiency. Dishes are made for sharing and influences cover all points from north to south. Standouts include Cha La lot (spicy ground pork wrapped in betel leaves) and the fragrant slow-cooked Mekong catfish, with its well-judged sweet and spicy sauce. Pho (noodle soup) is available in six different versions and represents good value; the set menu is a great starting point for neophytes.

Cecconi's

5a Burlington Gdns
✉ W1S 3EP
☎ (020) 7434 1500
www.cecconis.com

⊖ Green Park
Booking essential

Carte £30/44

It's obviously a winning formula because Cecconi's are now popping up in various appropriately fashionable cities around the world. One can certainly see the appeal as they do feel like a private members club and even have a roped off VIP area to induce envy amongst those who find themselves insufficiently famous. The bar is the place to sit if you want to give the impression you're a regular who's often in for a quick bite; and if you are one such regular then you'll be assured of good service. The all-day menu offers a good selection of cicchetti, or small Italian tapas; prosciutto is sliced to order; the salads are popular at lunch and the classic, no-nonsense main courses are clearly prepared with care.

China Tang

G4

Chinese XXXX

Park Ln
✉ W1A 2HJ
✆ (020) 7629 9988
www.thedorchester.com

⊖ Hyde Park Corner
Closed 25 December

Menu £15 (lunch) – Carte £40/70

A/C

⟨⟩

⊙

☼

VISA

MC

AE

①

Sir David Tang's atmospheric, art deco inspired Chinese restaurant at The Dorchester Hotel is always a blur of activity, with noise spilling out from the large tables in the centre; regulars head for the library side, from where one can take in the whole room. In contrast to the sleek and decorative surroundings, the kitchen is a model of conservatism and rightly sticks to what it does best, namely classic Cantonese cooking. Peking duck and roasted meats are the highlights, but check out the chef's recommendations at the back of the menu too. The standard is good considering the numbers of customers and you can have dim sum in the striking bar for lunch or dinner. Apart from the set lunch menu, it isn't cheap – but it is fun.

Chisou

H2

Japanese X

4 Princes St.
✉ W1B 2LE
✆ (020) 7629 3931
www.chisourestaurant.com

⊖ Oxford Circus
Closed Christmas-New Year,
Sunday and bank holidays

Menu £14 (lunch) – Carte £18/43

A/C

⟨⟩

VISA

MC

AE

Chisou proves that limited space should be no obstacle to providing good service so you'll find plenty of staff are on hand to guide you through the Japanese food. While it may be intimate, they are generous with the table size and spacing. The kitchen is headed up by a Japanese speaking Sri Lankan; he's often seen manning the sushi counter and has the owner's permission to source ingredients entirely on quality rather than cost restrictions. Specialities, from a menu that covers all points, include Tuna yukke, Gyu tataki (seared beef) and Hourensou (spinach) salad. There are some good value set lunch menus and next door is the useful 'Go Chisou', where the growing local Japanese community go to get their Bento boxes.

Corrigan's Mayfair

British XXX

G3

28 Upper Grosvenor St.
✉ W1K 7EH
✆ (020) 7499 9943
www.corrigansmayfair.com

⊖ Marble Arch
Closed 25-26 December,
1 January and Saturday lunch

Menu £27 (lunch) – Carte £39/88

A/C
⊡
☼
VISA
MC
AE

Richard Corrigan's flagship restaurant feels as though it has been part of the London scene for years. It's comfortable, clubby yet quite glamorous and Martin Brudnizki's design includes some playful features, such as the feather-covered lamps that give a nod to the restaurant's forte, which is game. The menu is lengthy and the food largely a celebration of British and Irish cooking. It is also fiercely seasonal, which makes having the day's special always a worthwhile choice. This relatively straightforward style of cooking still requires care and precise timing but sometimes the kitchen takes its eye off the ball. Service is smooth and well organised but the anachronistic cover charge is an unwelcome sight.

Dean Street Townhouse Restaurant

British XX

I3

69-71 Dean St.
✉ W1D 3SE
✆ (020) 7434 1775
www.deanstreettownhouse.com

⊖ Tottenham Court Road
Booking essential

Menu £20 (lunch) – Carte £23/31

🍴
A/C
◷
☼
VISA
MC
AE
⊕

As this Georgian house was once home to the bacchic Gargoyle Club, it's fitting that its incarnation is attracting clusters of pleasure-seeking celebrities. The designers have cleverly made this restaurant seem as though it's been here for years. The first thing you notice is the beautiful, long zinc-topped bar, although eating at one of the nearby tables does mean you're in danger of having someone sitting on your food, as this area does get packed. If you want a quieter spot, ask for the 'parlour' which is decorated just as its name suggests. The appealingly British menu includes retro dishes like prawns and avocado, and mince with boiled potatoes; puddings are stout and satisfying. You can also come for afternoon or high tea.

Dehesa

Mediterranean ✗

25 Ganton St
✉ W1F 9BP
☎ (020) 7494 4170
www.dehesa.co.uk

⊖ Oxford Circus
Closed Sunday dinner

Carte £20/29

Dehesa does now take bookings, except for lunch on Saturday, so there's no longer a need to get here quite so early. It's a few streets away from its sister restaurant, Salt Yard, and repeats the format of offering delicious Spanish and Italian tapas. The menu is not an exact copy but the bestsellers all feature: the pork belly with cannellini beans; courgette flowers with Monte Enebro and honey; and the soft chocolate cake with Frangelico ice cream. They recommend 2-3 plates per person. Between 3pm and 5pm the kitchen takes a breather so the choice becomes ham on or off the bone, charcuterie and cheese. The drinks list is worthy of a visit in itself. Dehesa is a wooded area of Spain and home to Ibérico pigs who produce such great ham.

Dolada

H3

Italian ✗✗

13 Albemarle St.
✉ W1S 4HJ
☎ (020) 7409 1011
www.dolada.co

⊖ Green Park
Closed 24- December-4 January, Saturday
lunch, Sunday and bank holidays

Menu £30/35 – Carte £30/39

Basement restaurants can sometimes be somewhat lifeless places but Dolada has turned its subterranean location to its advantage by creating an intimate, almost clubby atmosphere. The immaculate room has been cleverly lit so that you don't even notice the lack of natural light. What's more, service is warm and chatty, with staff going the extra mile to help. They are more than willing to recommend certain dishes from the appealing menu and one of the most popular is invariably the deconstructed spaghetti carbonara, whose component parts sit separately in a bowl, waiting to be mixed. The Italian chef is a passionate fellow – he even found the wood for the chef's table himself – and his enthusiasm imbues all parts of the operation.

Fakhreldine

H4

Lebanese ✗✗

85 Piccadilly   ⊖ Green Park
✉ W1J 7NB
✆ (020) 7493 3424
www.fakhreldine.co.uk

Menu £14/33 – Carte approx. £31

This first-floor Lebanese restaurant, with views over Green Park, may be approaching its 30th birthday but, thanks to fairly frequent and dramatic redesigns, it keeps itself fresh and relevant. A striking copper-topped bar is the first thing one notices and this, along with the adjacent lounge, attracts a fairly youthful weekend crowd. Beech panelling, mirrors and glass combine to create an elegant restaurant where nattily-dressed waiters provide competent service. The menu keeps things classical, from falafel to baba ghanoush, kibbe to makanek. The day's specials are pinned to the front of the menu and are usually a good bet, although the four set menus at the back will provide a nicely balanced meal.

5 Pollen St

H3

Italian ✗✗

5 Pollen St   ⊖ Oxford Circus
✉ W1S 1NE   Closed Sunday – booking advisable
✆ (020) 7629 1555
www.5pollenst.com

Menu £36 (lunch) – Carte dinner £50/60

A new breed of hip and energetic Italian restaurants may have sprung up over London in recent years but 5 Pollen Street pitches its glamorous tent firmly in the traditional camp. It's more 'Harry's Bar' than 'Polpo' and aims itself squarely at a Mayfair crowd for whom value for money is a concept as unfamiliar as queuing. Even more eye-catching than the clientele is the striking Gary Hume artwork and wallpaper which have been used to great effect. Stefano Cavallini, the chef who put the Halkin hotel on the map a few years ago, leads the kitchen team and his menu covers all bases. There's a degree of richness and elaboration to the cooking but it's the pasta and well-timed fish dishes that stand out, along with the size of the final bill.

Floridita

I3

100 Wardour St.
✉ W1F 0TN
☎ (020) 7314 4000
www.floriditalondon.com

⊖ **Tottenham Court Road**
Closed Sunday, Monday and bank holidays
– (dinner only and lunch in December)

Menu £28 – Carte £24/56

A/C

VISA

It's Salsa all the way, from the spicy food to the live music and dancing. If you think the ground floor with its Mediterranean tapas is busy, try downstairs for size. Here you'll find yourself in a huge nightclub-style space boasting an impressive cocktail list and a variety of Latin American dishes, from Cuban classics like ropa vieja to a whole-roast suckling pig and a large selection of assorted cuts of Argentinean beef aged for 28 days. It's not cheap but then again everything is done very well and everyone is here for a Big Night Out. The bands are flown in from Cuba, the music starts at 7.30pm and the party atmosphere never lets up. Those whose pace is more Cohiba than Mojito can nip next door to La Casa del Habano.

Franco's

H4

61 Jermyn St
✉ SW1Y 6LX
☎ (020) 7499 2211
www.francoslondon.com

⊖ **Green Park**
Closed Sunday and bank holidays
– booking essential

Menu £26 (lunch) – Carte £35/55

A/C

VISA

There can be few things more English than afternoon tea or the sound of Alan Bennett reading from The Wind in the Willows and, surprisingly enough, both can be enjoyed here at Franco's, one of London's oldest Italian restaurants that was relaunched in the mid-noughties. Open from breakfast onwards, it attracts a largely well-groomed clientele as befits its Jermyn Street address and boasts a clubby feel. Indeed, if you're not a regular visitor, you may find yourself with time to admire the service being enjoyed by other tables. The chef hails from Northern Italy but his menu covers all parts. There is a popular grill section, along with classics like Beef Rossini – ideal accompaniment for one of those big Tuscan reds on the wine list.

Galvin at Windows ❀

French 🍴🍴🍴🍴

G4

22 Park Ln (28th floor)
✉ W1K 1BE
📞 (020) 7208 4021
www.galvinatwindows.com

Menu £29/65

⊖ **Hyde Park Corner**
Closed Saturday lunch,
Sunday dinner
and bank holiday Mondays

A/C
VISA
MC
AE
◐

Galvin at Windows

There have never been any doubts about the magnificence of
the views from this restaurant on the 28th floor of the Hilton
Hotel, nor about the capabilities of the well-drilled serving
brigade who are attentive without being over-solicitous; but
now many of the customers come for the quality of the cooking,
which displays similarly lofty ambitions. André Garrett and
his team have great confidence in their own abilities and so
know when to allow the ingredients to speak for themselves,
whether that's a tender fillet of Scottish beef with foie gras or
a braised fillet of halibut with crab and lemon oil. Flavours
are adeptly balanced and complementary, while presentation,
notwithstanding some crowd-pleasing use of gold leaf, is
measured and appetising. The menus are nicely balanced in
content but also vary in price so that eating here does not need
to end in bankruptcy. The best tables for lunch are those on
the near side looking down over Buckingham Palace; the far
side gazing north over twinkling lights is the better option for
dinner.

First Course
- Cured salmon,
  Cornish crab,
  avocado cream and
  fennel.
- Ballottine of organic
  pork, crispy trotter,
  pickled apple and
  mustard.

Main Course
- Rack, shoulder and
  lamb's kidney with
  anchovy, capers and
  aubergine.
- Braised turbot,
  cucumber, oyster,
  linguini, wasabi and
  oyster velouté.

Dessert
- Apple tarte Tatin,
  vanilla ice cream and
  caramel sauce.
- Soufflé of banana,
  chocolate and
  caramelised peanut.

Le Gavroche ✿✿

French 𝗫𝗫𝗫𝗫

G3

43 Upper Brook St
✉ W1K 7QR
✆ (020) 7408 0881
www.le-gavroche.co.uk

⊖ Marble Arch
Closed Christmas-New Year, Saturday
lunch, Sunday and bank holidays
– booking essential

Menu £52 (lunch) – Carte £60/128

A/C
✿
VISA
MC
AE
D

Le Gavroche

Along with Volvos, Radio 4 and Mahler, dining at Le Gavroche is something you appreciate more the older you get. That's not to say it's stuffy or old-fashioned, rather that it's reassuring in its timelessness and doesn't pander to passing fads; it's not about being seen, it's about treating oneself. The basement room still has its clubby, masculine feel and there are enough long-standing members of staff to ensure that a regular will always be recognised; the manager spent a decade working his way up to the top job and the Austrian twins and the sommelier have all been here for more than ten years. The menu of unapologetically extravagant French dishes is a paean to indulgence – just reading it will harden your arteries. Many of the customers come here for specific dishes, be it the grouse, soufflé Suissesse or the omelette Rothschild; consistency comes courtesy of a kitchen team of 20, overseen by Michel Roux and his head chef Rachel Humphrey. The ice cream trolley is a great feature and the wine list offers one of the best selections of French wines in London.

First Course	*Main Course*	*Dessert*
• Soufflé Suissesse.	• Râble de lapin et galette au parmesan.	• Palet au chocolat amer et praliné croustillant.
• Coeur d'artichaut 'Lucullus'.	• Homard rôti à l'escargot et sauce béarnaise.	• Nougat glacé à l'amaretto et cerises.

Gauthier - Soho ✿

13

21 Romilly St
✉ W1D 5AF
📞 (020) 7494 3111
www.gauthiersoho.co.uk

⊖ **Leicester Square**
Closed Saturday lunch, Sunday and
bank holidays

Menu £25/35

A/C
VISA
MC
AE

Gauthier Soho

Having to ring a bell to gain admittance is not unknown in Soho but this charming, creaky 18C house is probably unique in that it delivers on its promise. It's spread over three floors, each of which offers subtle differences in personality: the ground floor is the more intimate; the first floor is brighter and better suited for lunch and the top floor is used for private parties. A narrow house like this also throws up certain operational challenges – for starters, waiters need to have calves like cyclists to cope with going up and down stairs to and from the basement kitchen – but they cope admirably and service at the table is positively serene. Alex Gauthier is a chef who not only shuns the media spotlight but also avoids any culinary excesses on the plate. This is a man who will talk at length, and in animated terms, simply about the quality of lamb his supplier has found and this attitude towards the sourcing of great ingredients has always underpinned his cooking. Each dish focuses on natural, balanced and harmonious flavours.

First Course

- Warm lobster salad with lemon balm and peach.
- Terrine of foie gras with truffle and young leeks.

Main Course

- Cuts of roe deer with truffle and celeriac.
- Glazed monkfish tail, clams, mussels sautéed in broad beans and fish jus.

Dessert

- Orange blossom soufflé with warm madeleines.
- Strawberry iles flottantes with vanilla custard and crunchy caramel.

Goodman

Beef specialities ✗✗

26 Maddox St
✉ W1S 1QH
☎ (020) 7499 3776
www.goodmanrestaurants.com

⊖ Oxford Circus
Closed Sunday and bank holidays
– booking essential

Menu £20 (lunch) – Carte £42/54

A/C
VISA
MC
AE

Goodman is a Russian-owned New York steakhouse in Mayfair, which sounds like a sketch from the UN's Christmas party. Wood and leather give it an authentic feel and it has captured that macho swagger that often seems to accompany the eating of red meat. Tables are usually full of guffawing men, with their jackets thrown over the back of their chairs and their sleeves rolled up. The American and Irish beef is mostly grain-fed and either dry or wet aged in-house – Australian beef is an option at lunch. It is cooked in a Josper oven using a blend of three types of charcoal and offered with a choice of four sauces. While the steaks, especially the rib-eye, are certainly worth coming for, side dishes tend to be more variable in quality.

Gordon Ramsay at Claridge's

Modern European ✗✗✗✗

Brook St.
✉ W1K 4HR
☎ (020) 7499 0099
www.gordonramsay.com/claridges

⊖ Bond Street
Booking essential

Menu £30/70

A/C
🕸
☼
VISA
MC
AE
①

As befits a restaurant within the sumptuous surroundings of Claridge's hotel, all is elegance and grandeur here. Sit in the main room as that is where the action is, although the Davies Room and The Salon on the raised level are better suited to the romantically inclined. The service is ceremonial and structured and the more confident members of the team really roll out the red carpet for their guests. It is clear that many come here for a celebration and this is reflected in the impressive selection of champagne on offer. The menu is faithful to the Gordon Ramsay formula of largely classical combinations with just a few embellishments to keep it fresh, although the cooking doesn't quite sparkle as it once did.

Greenhouse ✿

Innovative XXX

G4

27a Hay's Mews
✉ W1J 5NY
✆ (020) 7499 3331
www.greenhouserestaurant.co.uk

⊖ **Hyde Park Corner**
Closed Saturday lunch,
Sunday and bank holidays

Menu £29/75

A/C
⟷
🎗
VISA
MC
AE
①

The Greenhouse

The Greenhouse looks as fresh and contemporary as ever, thanks to regular reinvestment; and its terrific location in a charming mews adds to the somewhat clubby and exclusive feel. Antonin Bonnet trained under celebrated French chef Michel Bras and spent time as personal chef to Marlon Abela, whose restaurant this is. He is the kind of chef who is always looking at new techniques and approaches to cooking and his style leans towards artfully constructed dishes, where the main ingredient is subtly enhanced with contrasting textures and creative combinations. France provides the main influence but he is not afraid of using, for example, the occasional Moroccan spice or Asian twist. The restaurant has clear ambitions and this goes a long way in accounting for the number of loyal and supportive guests, although the kitchen can sometimes overreach itself in trying to be original. The wine list is one of the most comprehensive you'll come across and service is undertaken in a structured and formal manner.

First Course

- Calves sweetbreads with black garlic and glazed cabbage.
- Cider marinated mackerel with horseradish snow and pickled black radish.

Main Course

- Roasted Anjou pigeon breast, pomegranate and a giblet and pancetta jus.
- Sea bass with chard, sea buckthorn and beef vinaigrette.

Dessert

- "Snix" - chocolate, salted caramel and peanuts.
- Moissac cherries and vanilla soup with Sicilian pistachio parfait.

63

Hakkasan Mayfair ঞ

H3

Chinese ✗✗

17 Bruton St
✉ W1J 6QB
✆ (020) 7907 1888
www.hakkasan.com

⊖ **Green Park**
Closed 25 December –
booking essential

Carte £50/100 s

A/C
⏲
☀
VISA
MC
AE

Hakkasan Mayfair

This is less a copy, more a sister to the original Hakkasan; a sister who's just as fun and glamorous but simply lives in a far nicer part of town. As with many of the best addresses, it doesn't draw attention to itself – you could easily walk past the entrance without knowing, and that adds to the appeal. The biggest difference is that this Hakkasan has a funky, more casual ground floor to go with the downstairs dining room; but it's still worth booking for the lower level, as a walk down the stairs will heighten the sense of occasion and add a little mystery. The menu of Cantonese treats is an appealing tome; dim sum must surely be the only way to go at lunch, while the signature dishes, such as silver cod with champagne and honey, and Jasmine tea smoked chicken, can be saved for dinner. Desserts are unashamedly tailored towards European tastes but there's a fine range of speciality teas, as well as an impressive selection of cocktails. The staff, dressed in black – what else? – know their menu backwards, so are more than willing to help those seeking guidance.

First Course

- Salt and pepper squid.
- Dim sum platter.

Main Course

- Stir-fried rib-eye of beef with black pepper and Merlot.
- Alaskan royal king crab in black bean sauce.

Dessert

- Chocolate soufflé with vanilla ice cream and raspberry sauce.
- Grand Marnier chocolate crémeaux.

Haozhan

Chinese ✖✖

I3

8 Gerrard St
✉ W1D 5PJ
☎ (020) 7434 3838
www.haozhan.co.uk

⊖ **Leicester Square**
Closed 24-26 December

Carte £21/41

A/C
⏱
☼
VISA
MC
AE
◑

A plethora of Chinatown restaurants vie for your attention by offering special deals or just brightening their neon. Haozhan adopts the more worthy policy of serving food that's a cut above the norm. Inside the somewhat garish looking menu is not the usual vast list but rather an interesting collection of dishes that owe more to a fusion style, with mostly Cantonese but other Asian influences too; head straight for the specialities, such as jasmine ribs or wasabi prawns. You'll find there's a freshness to the ingredients that also marks this restaurant out – for example, try the Tom Yum prawns in their pancake cones and leave room for the egg custard buns. Appropriately enough, the name Haozhan translates as "a good place to eat".

Hix

British ✖

H3

66-70 Brewer St.
✉ W1F 9UP
☎ (020) 7292 3518
www.hixsoho.co.uk

⊖ **Piccadilly Circus**
Closed 25-26 December

Menu £23 (lunch) – Carte £29/61

A/C
⌨
☼
VISA
MC
AE
◑

Leaded, frosted windows similar to The Ivy hint at exclusivity within, as does the huge wooden door and the discreet name plaque. Once entry has been secured, one finds oneself in an enormous space with specially commissioned artwork from Damien Hirst, Sue Webster and Sarah Lucas, reflecting Mark Hix's close relationship with London's artists. Meanwhile, his menu reflects his passion for British recipes and ingredients, which translates as plenty of game in season, unusual cuts of meat, rediscovered classics and proper puddings. Portions aren't over-generous and side dishes are required which makes the bill rise quickly – and sometimes a dish doesn't quite deliver the promise of the menu. But it's a fun, inclusive place.

Hélène Darroze
at The Connaught ❀ ❀

French XXXX

G3

Carlos Pl.
✉ W1K 2AL
☎ (020) 3147 7200
www.the-connaught.co.uk

⊖ Bond Street
Closed 2 weeks August, 2-9 January,
Sunday and Monday –
booking essential

Menu £35/80

VISA
MC
AE
DC

The Connaught

London's diverse and vibrant dining scene has had quite an influence on Hélène Darroze and although she insists it is France and her native region of Landes that informs her cooking, she also uses interesting flavours of a more international persuasion. In essence, the dishes appear relatively simple on the plate, even though their descriptions on the menu can be quite florid. She is keen to champion the high quality produce they use, much more of which now comes from within the UK. Bayonne ham sliced on their gleaming Berkel machine heralds the start of one's meal and delightful mignardises round things off. Dishes can be surprisingly robust and the presentation is often exquisite. Service is courteous and professional, and the staff also manage to inject personality into the proceedings. Meanwhile, the room itself is warm and elegant, thanks to India Mahdavi's clever softening of all that mahogany wall panelling. A small private dining room has been added adjacent to the wine cellar, two floors below.

First Course

- Line-caught calamari, ravioli with confit tomatoes.
- Duck foie gras from Les Landes confit in spiced sangria wine.

Main Course

- Black pork from Pays Basque, larded with black truffle.
- Blue lobster in paella jus with saffron pistil, chicken wing and Iberico lomo.

Dessert

- Manjari chocolate mousse and cumin ice cream.
- Comice pear, speculoos wafers, blackcurrant sorbet, pear and marscapone cream.

Hibiscus ✿ ✿

H3

29 Maddox St
✉ W1S 2PA
✆ (020) 7629 2999
www.hibiscusrestaurant.co.uk

⊖ Oxford Circus
Closed 23 December-3 January,
Monday lunch,
Sunday and bank holidays

Menu £34/80

A/C

VISA

M©

AE

Hibiscus

Now that his restaurant is firmly established on the circuit of pre-eminent Mayfair restaurants, chef-owner Claude Bosi can breathe a sigh of relief, content in the knowledge that his move from the pastoral surrounds of Ludlow to the metropolitan hotbed of competitiveness has been vindicated. But that's not to say he feels he's cracked it, because his cooking continues to develop and evolve. The breads and all the little extras such as the canapés and petit fours are executed with as much care as the main courses and there is an impressive selection of menus available, including a vegetarian option. The kitchen team are a well-drilled outfit; they may use the occasional Asian note to bring out the flavour of a particular ingredient but they also have a very solid classical base. The restaurant itself, with its oak panelling and splashes of colour courtesy of the large floral display in the centre of the room, has a somewhat sombre feel so the atmosphere is usually generated by the diners.

First Course

- Ravioli of spring onion and lime, broad bean and mint purée.
- Terrine of foie gras, compote of green mango and aloe vera.

Main Course

- Smoked and roasted chicken, onion fondue and liquorice.
- Roast John Dory, fricasse of potato, asparagus and broad beans, rhubarb and maple syrup.

Dessert

- Chocolate tart with basil ice cream.
- Cream tart of white asparagus, white chocolate, goat's cheese ice cream.

Hush

H3

Modern European ✕✕

8 Lancashire Ct., Brook St.
✉ W1S 1EY
✆ (020) 7659 1500
www.hush.co.uk

⊖ Bond Street
Closed Easter, 25-26 December,
1 January and Sunday –
booking essential

Carte £27/44

Hush celebrated its 10th anniversary in 2010 by doing what all restaurants should do – it listened to its customers. They, for example, liked the slick upstairs dining room but preferred the more accessible, brasserie-style menu from the ground floor room. The result was that this same menu is now served throughout the building. One can see the appeal: it offers straightforward classics, from burgers to risotto and salads to sausages as well as all-day favourites like eggs Benedict. Upstairs also has a stylish destination bar but the best seats are on the delightful courtyard terrace. Add in several private dining rooms and you have a hostess who is more air-traffic controller and staff who spend time rushing hither and thither.

Imli

I3

Indian ✕

167-169 Wardour St
✉ W1F 8WR
✆ (020) 7287 4243
www.imli.co.uk

⊖ Tottenham Court Road
Closed 25-26 December
and 1 January

Menu £20 (dinner) – Carte £16/20

'Relatively timely food' may not sound quite as snappy as 'fast food' but Imli proves that, if you don't want to linger long over a meal, there are alternatives to multinationals. It may be an Indian restaurant but 'tapas' is the shorthand for dishes that are diminutive and involve sharing. The menu is short, well-priced and to the point; three dishes per person should suffice, although the hungry should go for the 'Taste of Imli'. The cooking is a combination of street food and some regional, particularly Northern Indian, influences; vegetarians will find themselves with plenty of choice. Where Imli has borrowed from the 'experts' is in its use of bright lighting and vivid colours to encourage a rapid turnover.

Imperial China

Chinese 🍴🍴🍴

13

White Bear Yard, 25a Lisle Street
✉ WC2H 7BA
☏ (020) 7734 3388
www.imperial-china.co.uk

⊖ Leicester Square
Closed 24-25 December –
booking advisable

Menu £19 – Carte £30/50

A/C
⊡
🕐
☀
VISA
MC
AE

Heave open the heavy smoked-glass double doors, cross the bamboo bridge and you'll be transported to a calm oasis that seems a world away from the bustle outside. Sharp, well-organised service and comfortable surroundings are not the only things that set this restaurant apart: the Cantonese cooking exudes freshness and vitality, whether that's the steamed dumplings or the XO minced pork with fine beans. Indeed, they pride themselves on seafood and their 'lobster feasts' are very popular - the personable staff are also more than happy to offer recommendations. There are eight private rooms of various sizes available upstairs and these are often in full swing. The owners also run Beijing Dumpling a few doors down.

Inn the Park

British 🍴

14

St James's Park
✉ SW1A 2BJ
☏ (020) 7451 9999
www.innthepark.com

⊖ Charing Cross
Closed 26 December
and 1 January

Carte £25/39

⪋
📶
☀
VISA
MC

When the sun has a little spring warmth and the season's first asparagus has appeared, few restaurants can compete with Oliver Peyton's place in the park. Its eco-friendly credentials are such that it resembles a camouflaged bunker; approach from the east and you won't see it. The entrance can be a little confusing: to avoid the self-service section, head for the 'waiter service' reception. The terrace is terrific and quickly fills in summer. The menu makes much of its Britishness and uses many small suppliers. The kitchen does have a somewhat heavy hand that lessens the impact and service can also lack a little humour but, despite these shortcomings, the restaurant is worthy without being pious and the setting is glorious.

Kai ✿

G3

Chinese XXX

65 South Audley St.
✉ W1K 2QU
✆ (020) 7493 8988
www.kaimayfair.co.uk

⊖ Hyde Park Corner
Closed 25-26 December
and 1 January – booking essential

Menu £27 (lunch) – Carte £36/84

Kai

Displays of perfect, polished red apples – to represent the Chinese flag – along with oil paintings and antique mirrors add to the air of opulence, while the music is incongruously clubby. But what underpins the operation is chef Alex Chow's skilled kitchen. His extensive menu comes with a plethora of little anecdotes and stories which, although too long to read in company, do at least highlight the restaurant's overriding enthusiasm. Dishes come packed with clean flavours and equal care goes into preparing the classics as goes into the more innovative choices. Regulars, of which there are many, ensure that certain dishes can never be removed from the menu; these include the wasabi prawns, the Peking duck – which comes from Scotland – and the excellent pumpkin cream dessert. Prices can vary quite wildly, from the very costly Imperial Delicacies to the more reasonably priced poultry dishes. The restaurant is spread over two floors; the ground floor is where the action is. This being Mayfair means that the wine list is a serious tome.

First Course	*Main Course*	*Dessert*
• Honey roasted Duke of Berkshire char siew pork.	• Sea bass with chickpeas, shallots and ginger.	• Rice dumplings with honey ice ceam.
• Softshell crab with julienne of green mango.	• Lamb with Sichuan peppercorns.	• Caramel and almond cannelloni.

Kiku

H4

Japanese 🍴🍴

17 Half Moon St.
✉ W1J 7BE
☎ (020) 7499 4208
www.kikurestaurant.co.uk

⊖ **Green Park**
Closed 25-26 December, 1 January,
Sunday and lunch on bank holidays

Menu £20/50 – Carte £25/56

AC
VISA
MC
AE
DC

Kiku is a traditional Japanese restaurant, which makes it something of a rarity these days. The menus are numerous and varied, offering sushi to assorted kaiseki, a selection of soba noodle dishes, salads and casseroles; the lunch time menus are very popular locally. Apart from the kaiseki set menus, the prices are not unreasonable when one considers the Mayfair location, the crisp and understated décor and the endearingly charming staff, who can swiftly soothe the most cantankerous of diner, and who are also on hand to offer sensible advice. The best place to sit is in the raised section at the back with its own sushi counter; here it's never quite so busy and you get to really appreciate the skills of the chefs.

Koya 😋

I3

Japanese 🍴

49 Frith St
✉ W1D 4SG
☎ (020) 7434 4463
www.koya.co.uk

⊖ **Tottenham Court Road**
Closed Christmas –
(bookings not accepted)

Carte £14/18

AC
☀
VISA
MC
AE

Authenticity is the key to Koya's success: the Japanese wheat is kneaded by foot, while the dashi base stock is freshly made every day. Do your bit by slurping unselfconsciously to get the full benefit of these delicious noodles with their wonderful chewiness or 'koshi'. They come in three styles: hot in a hot broth, cold with a hot broth or cold with a cold dipping sauce, and arrive on a bamboo mat and with a sprinkling of nori (seaweed). Be sure to order some small plates too, such as the onsen tamago, a delicate poached egg, or crisp tempura. A small selection of sake, shochu, beer and wine is also available. The decoration is modest, service is sweet and if you aren't here before the noren curtain is put out then be prepared to queue.

Matsuri – St James's

Japanese ✗✗

15 Bury St.
✉ SW1Y 6AL
✆ (020) 7839 1101
www.matsuri-restaurant.com

⊖ **Green Park**
Closed 25 December
and 1 January

Menu £35 (dinner) – Carte £28/39

A/C
⟨⟩
🎭
☀
VISA
MC
AE
①

Matsuri is now as much of a St James's stalwart as some of the galleries and gentlemen's outfitters that surround it. This original branch remains very traditional in feel and its longevity can be put down to its reliable food and sweet-natured service. You're escorted downstairs to one of the teppan-yaki tables, or alternatively you can sit at the sushi counter, where you'll find yourself presented with a plethora of menus. The food is largely traditional, which makes a nice change from the current fad of 'reinterpreting' Japanese cuisine, and the Scottish beef is the star of the theatrical teppan-yaki. Dinner doesn't come cheap but, thanks to the assorted set menus, lunch represents decent value.

Maze Grill

Beef specialities ✗✗

10-13 Grosvenor Sq.
✉ W1K 6JP
✆ (020) 7495 2211
www.gordonramsay.com

⊖ **Bond Street**

Menu £24 (lunch and early dinner) – Carte £27/52

A/C
☀
VISA
MC
AE
①

Use the Grosvenor Square entrance as it offers a little more charm than if one wanders in from the adjacent Marriott Hotel, for which this restaurant also acts as the breakfast room. But then again, this is less about glamour, more about just enjoying good quality beef. The assorted cuts, from Casterbridge grain-fed and Hereford grass-fed through to Creekstone prime USDA corn-fed and Wagyu, are brought to your table in their raw state for you to hear about their differing personalities. Your preferred steak is then given a blast in the super-hot broiler before being served on a wooden board. The sides and sauces are numerous, varied and individually priced so your wallet can also end up feeling a little tender.

Maze 🕸

G3

10-13 Grosvenor Sq   ⊖ Bond Street
✉ W1K 6JP
✆ (020) 7107 0000
www.gordonramsay.com

Menu £25 (lunch) – Carte £29/46

A/C
VISA
M/C
AE
D

Gordon Ramsay Holdings

MAYFAIR, SOHO & ST JAMES'S ▶ PLAN II

Such is the well-tuned nature of this Gordon Ramsay operation that a couple of quick changes of head chef in 2010 and 2011 made very little difference and the restaurant wisely adopted the adage, 'if it ain't broke, don't fix it'. Maze remains the most original of the restaurants in the Ramsay stable and boasts the most buoyant atmosphere, thanks largely to the glamour of the David Rockwell designed room – this is a restaurant where diners like to dress up and make an occasion of it. It has also always benefited from its close proximity to the US Embassy, which ensures that it gets busy from around 5.30pm. The kitchen produces diminutive constructions that pack a punch but are also balanced and satisfying. While there's a degree of originality and boldness, it also understands the importance of textural contrast and has a fundamental grasp of what goes with what. Four dishes per person should suffice, although around half of all customers have the tasting menu, which better demonstrates the kitchen's ability.

First Course	*Main Course*	*Dessert*
• Jasmine and miso cured salmon, ponzu dressing.	• Devon duck breast, beetroot and preserved lemon.	• Pistachio parfait, cherry sorbet.
• Pressed terrine of rabbit and foie gras, mandarin, apricot, fennel and macadamia salad.	• Sichuan spiced Suffolk pork belly with edamame beans, pickled black radish and spring greens.	• Peanut butter and raspberry jam sandwich with tonka bean cream and dehydrated raspberries.

73

Mews of Mayfair

H3

10-11 Lancashire Ct, Brook St (1st floor)
✉ W1S 1EY
☎ (020) 7518 9388
www.mewsofmayfair.com

⊖ Bond Street
Closed 25-26 December,
Sunday dinner and bank holidays

Carte £29/38

Mews manages that trick of being cool and bright in summer and warm and inviting in winter. The relative serenity of the pretty restaurant is in sharp contrast to the crowds in the narrow lane and busy cocktail bar below, while the private dining room on the next floor up is a very pleasant space. The menu is very appealing and sufficiently sensitive to the changing seasons, so expect venison in winter, spring lamb and summer fruit. Simpler dishes are also pepped up, so burgers come with an optional foie gras topping and fish and chips arrive with a wasabi tartare. Flavours are sometimes compromised by an over-eagerness to make dishes look pretty but prices are generally sensible and the atmosphere thoroughly civilised.

Mint Leaf

I4

Suffolk Pl.
✉ SW1Y 4HX
☎ (020) 7930 9020
www.mintleafrestaurant.com

⊖ Piccadilly Circus
Closed 25 December, 1 January,
lunch Saturday and Sunday

Menu £18 (lunch and early dinner) – Carte £38/60

Indian restaurants come in a variety of guises these days: Mint Leaf is from the contemporary, slick and designery school. This vast subterranean space with its moody lighting can seat over 250 but it comes divided into seven different areas so you're never rattling around. There is even an enormous bar running the length of the room for those wanting to make a night of it. The menu is also quite a lengthy affair, with many choices available in small or larger sizes. The best bet is to share a few dishes such as the soft shell crab or jumbo prawns, and then have your own curry – the kitchen's strength. The serving team are a mixed bunch: some will explain dishes enthusiastically; others seem keener upselling drinks.

Momo

Moroccan ✗✗

25 Heddon St.
✉ W1B 4BH
℘ (020) 7434 4040
www.momoresto.com

⊖ Oxford Circus
Closed Sunday lunch

Menu £19/49 – Carte £35/40

Lanterns, rugs, trinkets and music all contribute to the authentic Moroccan atmosphere that makes Momo such a fun night out. That being said, it's even more fun if you come with friends as tables of two can get somewhat overawed. The menu is divided into three: a somewhat expensive set menu, traditional dishes and Momo specialities. The traditional section is the best as here you'll find the classics from pastilla to tagines; the Momo specialities are more contemporary in their make-up. Whatever you order, you'll end up with a pile of couscous and enough good food to last the week. The wine list lacks affordable bottles but there's a great bar downstairs. If it weren't for the absence of cigarette smoke, you could be in Marrakech.

The National Dining Rooms

British ✗

Sainsbury Wing, The National Gallery,
Trafalgar Sq ✉ WC2N 5DN
℘ (020) 7747 2525
www.peytonandbyrne.co.uk

⊖ Charing Cross
Closed 24-26 December –
(lunch only)

Carte £27/37

There's usually a queue but don't panic – it's either those wanting the bakery section or others realising they should have booked. Oliver Peyton's restaurant on the first floor of the National Gallery's Sainsbury Wing is a bright, open affair, enriched by Paula Rego's complex mural 'Crivelli's Garden'. Ask for a table by the window, not just for the views of Trafalgar Square but also because the other half of the room is darker and under the eaves of the early Renaissance on the floor above. The menu champions British cooking and produce; fish and cheeses are the highlight – pies and puds will write-off the afternoon. The set menu represents decent value and is popular with the customers, who resemble a bridge club up from Winchester for the day.

Murano ❀

G4

20 Queen St
✉ W1J 5PP
✆ (020) 7495 1127
www.angela-hartnett.com

⊖ **Green Park**
Closed Christmas and Sunday

Menu £30/65

A/C
VISA
MC
AE

Murano

Angela Hartnett became her own boss in 2010, when she bought this restaurant from Gordon Ramsay. The Murano style is most evident in the glassware and the swirls on the wall and, less obviously, in the ceiling light 'sculpture'. The room is a long and narrow one – ask for a table by the front window as they're slightly more packed in towards the back – while the creams and greens combine to create a luminous feel that becomes quite intimate when they lower the lights in the evening. Angela established her reputation through a fairly unique style of cooking that combines classical techniques with Italian influences. Stars of the show include the dried meats and the expertly rendered risottos and pasta dishes, which predominantly feature as starters. Many ingredients come from within the British Isles and from wherever they are best, such as Cornish lamb or Scottish beef. Combinations are well-judged and flavours clear. Lunch represents very decent value and there's also a very appealing vegetarian menu.

First Course

- Pumpkin tortellini with sage emulsion.
- Red mullet, courgette flower, cuttlefish and red pepper vinaigrette.

Main Course

- Canon of lamb with courgettes and black olives.
- Monkfish meunière, razor clams, tomato, lardo and almond purée.

Dessert

- Apricot soufflé with biscotti.
- Coffee crémeaux, mascarpone ice cream and sponge.

Nobu ✿

Japanese ✕✕

G4

19 Old Park Ln
✉ W1Y 1LB
✆ (020) 7447 4747
www.noburestaurants.com

⊖ Hyde Park Corner
Closed 25-26 December –
booking essential

Menu £60/95 – Carte £37/68

Nobu

Nobu restaurants now number over twenty and are spread around the world, but this one was the first to open in Europe, back in 1997, and came not long after the original in Manhattan. The two London branches can be considered the pick of the bunch and much of the credit is down to the long-standing executive chef, Mark Edwards. He has also been responsible for introducing the Osusume menu, which is exclusive to London and is aimed at offering neophytes the opportunity to discover what makes the food – Japanese with South American influences – quite so interesting. The reason is that the flavours are unique, the combinations wholly complementary and the ingredients top-notch – it's little wonder the dishes have been plagiarised across the city. The enthusiasm of the staff is undimmed and while the restaurant is perhaps less obviously glitzy than its younger sibling, that does mean that the fashionable crowd here are a little less excitable. Those who don't have the time to visit can now simply pick up a lunch or pre-theatre bento box.

First Course

- Yellowtail jalapeño.
- Lobster tempura with creamy wasabi.

Main Course

- Black cod with miso.
- Anticucho Peruvian style spicy rib-eye steak.

Dessert

- Chocolate bento box with green tea ice cream.
- Spiced warm rice pudding.

Nobu Berkeley St ❀

J a p a n e s e ✕✕

15 Berkeley St.
✉ W1J 8DY
☎ (020) 7290 9222
www.noburestaurants.com/berkeley

⊖ **Green Park**
Closed 25-26 December,
Saturday and Sunday lunch and
bank holiday Mondays –
booking essential

Menu £32/90

A/C
i⊘
VISA
MC
AE

Nobu

As a general rule, if there are paparazzi outside a restaurant, then the talent inside is unlikely to be in the kitchen. But there are exceptions and Nobu Berkeley St is one of them. This is a restaurant that still does things properly, despite serving around 900 people each day. There are 45 chefs in the kitchen, 60% of whom are Japanese, and considerable care is taken with the food. Nobu tacos are a good way of getting things started and staff are well-informed if you need help. Greatest hits like yellowtail sashimi, black cod with miso and shrimp tempura remain on the menu but each Nobu has some unique element and at Nobu Berkeley St it is the wood oven. The cabbage steak with truffles and lamb anti cucho miso are top sellers, and the chocolate tart is catching the chocolate bento box in popularity. Lunch sees regular or deluxe bento boxes with organic juices. Anyone whose fame does not extend beyond their own home needs to book well in advance to get their desired time; although, if you're prepared to wait in the busy bar, it may be worth just pitching up.

First Course

- King crab claw tempura with butter ponzu.
- Chinese cabbage steak, Matsuhisa dressing.

Main Course

- Black cod with miso.
- Secreto Iberian pork with spicy ponzu.

Dessert

- Chocolate tart with sake kasu ice cream and chocolate sauce.
- Oatmeal crunch with Yuzu cream, served with dulce de leche ice cream.

Nopi

H3

21-22 Warwick St. ⊖ Piccadilly Circus
✉ W1B 5NE
☎ (020) 7494 9584
www.nopi-restaurant.com

Carte £32/40

A/C
☼
VISA
MC
AE

After relishing his delis and devouring his cookbooks, fans of Yotam Ottolenghi are now flocking to his first 'proper' restaurant. It's an enthusiastically run and luminous affair and is spread over two floors, all whitewashed walls, tiles, marble and brass. The communally minded can ask to share one of the two large tables downstairs which face the open kitchen and are surrounded by the chefs' supplies. Flavours take in the Mediterranean, the Middle East and various parts of Asia, and the menu is subdivided under the headings of Veg, Fish or Meat; one of each per person should suffice. The veggie dishes are best, such as burrata with coriander seeds, but the fish creations like grilled mackerel with a pea and mint salad are also refreshing.

Only Running Footman

GH3

5 Charles St ⊖ Green Park.
✉ W1J 5DF
☎ (020) 7499 2988
www.therunningfootmanmayfair.com

Carte £21/37

⟳
☼
VISA
MC
AE

Apparently the owners added 'only' to the title when they found out that theirs was the only pub in the land called 'The Running Footman'. Spread over several levels, it offers cookery demonstrations and private dinners along with its two floors of dining. Downstairs is where the action usually is, with its menu offering pub classics from steak sandwiches to fishcakes, but you can't book here and it's always packed. Upstairs is where you'll find a surprisingly formal dining room and here they do take reservations. Its menu is far more ambitious and European in its influence but the best dishes are still the simpler ones, with desserts a strength. You can't help feeling that you would be having a lot more fun below stairs, though.

Patterson's

Modern European ✗✗

H3

4 Mill St
✉ W1S 2AX
✆ (020) 7499 1308
www.pattersonsrestaurant.com

⊖ Oxford Street
Closed 25-26 December
and Sunday

Menu £25/47 – Carte £47/55

A family moving from a small fishing village in the Scottish borders to the middle of Mayfair may sound like one of those dependable fish-out-of-water comedies, but that is exactly what the Pattersons did back in 2003, and theirs remains one of the few family-run restaurants in this part of town. Father and son in the kitchen still get much of the seafood from their erstwhile home and even supply a number of other restaurants. Their fairly extensive menus feature a lot of Scottish produce in general and it's the seafood that's best; the cooking influences come largely from within Europe. It's a deceptively large place, fresh and uncluttered in its decoration, but can still provide a fairly intimate setting.

Plum Valley

Chinese ✗✗

I3

20 Gerrard St.
✉ W1D 6JQ
✆ (020) 7494 4366

⊖ Leicester Square
Closed 24-25 December

Menu £38 – Carte £23/44

Is Chinatown finally casting off its tourist-trap reputation? Plum Valley is the latest venture with genuine aspirations to open in Gerrard Street and its contemporary styling gives the street a much-needed boost. The striking black façade makes it easy to notice, while flattering lighting and layered walls give the interior a dash of sophistication. The chef is from Chiu Chow, a region near Guangdong, and his menu is largely based on Cantonese cooking, with occasional forays into Vietnam and Thailand as well as the odd nod towards contemporary presentation. Dim sum is his kitchen's main strength which fits nicely with the all-day opening of the restaurant. If only those doing the service could muster the same levels of enthusiasm.

Pollen Street Social ✿

H3

8-10 Pollen St
✉ W1S 1NQ
✆ (020) 7290 7606
www.pollenstreetsocial.com

⊖ Oxford Circus
Closed Sunday and bank holidays
– booking essential

Menu £25 (lunch) – Carte £38/55

A/C
⊟
VISA
MC
AE

Pollen Street Social

MAYFAIR, SOHO & ST JAMES'S ▶ PLAN II

Having spent over a decade with Gordon Ramsay, Jason Atherton branched out on his own in 2011 and opened Pollen Street Social. The word 'social' is more than merely a means of perking up the restaurant's name: the idea was to create a sufficiently relaxed environment that was equally welcoming to those just wanting to pop in for a quick bite as it was to anyone making an occasion of it. This flexibility is reflected not only in the restaurant's layout but also in the menu: you can eat what you want, where you want. Starters can be reduced in size to form part of a tasting menu, you can grab a snack in the bar or settle down for the full à la carte experience in the handsome dining room, with its dessert bar and glass-fronted kitchen. Atherton's cooking is an extension of the style he displayed at Maze and reveals his talents as a creative chef. His food is exciting, innovative, delicate in looks but assured in flavour; it is also imaginative and, with starters like the 'full English breakfast', at times playful.

First Course
- 'Full English breakfast'.
- BBQ mackerel, cucumber chutney, frozen ajo blanco and scallop.

Main Course
- Roasted Dingley Dell pork, beetroot, hops, seeds and grains.
- Roasted halibut, Catalan paella, sprouting broccoli, pork ham fat and mussel stock.

Dessert
- Peanut butter parfait, cherry jam and creamed rice puffs.
- Rice pudding with hay ice cream and lime jelly.

81

Polpetto

I3

Italian 🍴

46 Dean St. (1st floor)
✉ W1D 5BG
☎ (020) 7734 1969
www.polpetto.co.uk

⊖ Leicester Square
Closed 24 December-2 January,
Sunday and bank holidays

Carte £18/20

VISA
Ⓜ️©
AE

The baby sister, or baby octopus, to Polpo is smaller and simpler and is located, somewhat incongruously, upstairs at The French House, a pub inexorably linked to Soho's literary and artistic communities. You can't book for dinner and there's nowhere to wait – they just take your mobile number and text you. It's just one small but thoughtfully designed room, with exposed brick, a tin ceiling, zinc tables and some red banquettes; the paper mat doubles as the menu. Choose a couple of cicheti, some bread, one vegetable, a meat and a fish dish and you'll have more than enough; pigeon saltimbocca or the soft shell crab are good. The small dishes are keenly priced; it's all great fun and is ideal for a quick bite before the theatre.

Polpo

H3

Italian 🍴

41 Beak St.
✉ W1F 9SB
☎ (0207) 7344 479
www.polpo.co.uk

⊖ Oxford Circus
Closed 25 December-1 January, Sunday
dinner and bank holidays – (bookings not
accepted at dinner)

Carte £15/25

A/C
🛋️
VISA
Ⓜ️©
AE
Ⓓ

Opening a Venetian bacaro in an 18C townhouse where Canaletto once lodged does seem providential and Polpo has indeed been packing them in since day one. The stripped-down faux-industrial look is more New York's SoHo than London's Soho, as is the no-reservation policy which means you'll probably have to wait. But the fun atmosphere and the appealing prices of the small plates will assuage any impatience you feel in waiting your turn. Order a couple of cicheti, like arancini or prosciutto, a plate of fritto misto, ham and pea risotto or Cotechino sausage along with a vegetable dish per person and you should leave satisfied; if you do over-order, it's not going to break the bank. Venetian wines, available by the carafe, complete the picture.

Portrait

I3

National Portrait Gallery,　　　　　　⊖ **Charing Cross**
(3rd floor), St Martin's Pl.　⊠ WC2H 0HE　　Closed 24-26 December –
✆ (020) 7312 2490　　　　　　　　booking essential –
www.searcys.co.uk　　(lunch only and dinner Thursday-Saturday)

Menu £25 – Carte £32/40

Portrait is on the third floor of the Ondaatje wing of the National Portrait Gallery and is run by the Searcy's catering company. You needn't ask for a window seat because the views, of recognisable rooftops and Nelson standing proudly in Trafalgar Square, are just as good from any of the tables. Although open for breakfast and tea, this is principally a lunchtime operation, with dinner limited to Thursdays and Fridays - the nights of the gallery's extended opening hours. The à laCarte menu keeps things relatively light and the influences mostly from Europe; there is a good value set menu at weekends. This is a useful spot, not only for gallery visitors but also for those attending matinee performances at the numerous theatres nearby.

Quaglino's

H4

16 Bury St　　　　　　　　　　⊖ **Green Park**
⊠ SW1Y 6AJ　　　　　Closed Sunday – booking essential
✆ (020) 7930 6767
www.quaglinos.co.uk

Menu £25 (lunch) – Carte £43/59

It's easy to forget the impact the iconic Quaglino's had when Sir Terence Conran reopened it back in the early '90s. It was big, bold and boisterous and getting a table could prove quite a challenge. But the smart crowd moved on and today much of that sparkle and glamour has gone. This is a restaurant that needs to be near capacity for there to be an atmosphere and, fortunately, current owners D&D are aware that the place needs reinvigorating and are pulling it up by the scruff of its neck. The menu may no longer look quite so original but there is still enough there to appeal to most, from the fruits de mer to the coq au vin. London needs glamorous restaurants like Quaglino's so let's hope it rediscovers its pizzazz.

Quince

H4

Turkish XX

Stratton St
✉ W1J 8LT
☎ (020) 7915 3892
www.quincelondon.com

⊖ **Green Park**
Closed Saturday
and Sunday lunch

Menu £24 (lunch) – Carte £37/53

A/C

VISA

MC

AE

As a hotel known mostly for attracting youthful celebrity guests, it's perhaps appropriate that The Mayfair turned to a celebrity TV chef to run its restaurant. Bulgarian born Silvena Rowe has brought along her inimitable Eastern Mediterranean cooking and her personality is evident throughout, from the personal references on the menu – "a homage to my grandfather Mehmed" – to the Ottoman-influenced style of the room. The menu kicks off with a selection of small plates – 'mezze' by any other name – although these can quickly crank up the bill. The best bet is to head straight for the main courses, whether they're grilled, like the sea bass with fennel tzatziki or roasted in the stone oven, as with the slow-cooked shoulder of lamb.

Quo Vadis

I3

British XXX

26-29 Dean St.
✉ W1D 3LL
☎ (020) 7437 9585
www.quovadis.co.uk

⊖ **Tottenham Court Road**
Closed Christmas, Sunday
and bank holidays

Menu £20 (lunch) – Carte £31/46

A/C

VISA

MC

AE

As Quo Vadis is so inescapably linked to Soho's history one feels the Hart brothers are not so much the owners, more the current custodians. Its neon signs and stained glass windows have long been familiar Dean Street landmarks and the timeless, quite masculine interior tells of sophistication and self-assurance. A smart bar with its own small menu now occupies the first section of the room and this has relieved some of the pressure on the dining room. Service is quite formally structured, although staff do need the occasional prompt. The menu is an appealing roll-call of British classics; grilled meats such as Longhorn beef and Middlewhite pork are popular but the kitchen's strength lies more in the handling of shellfish and seafood.

Red Fort

Indian ☓☓☓

77 Dean St.
✉ W1D 3SH
✆ (020) 7437 2525
www.redfort.co.uk

⊖ Tottenham Court Road
Closed 25 December, lunch Saturday,
Sunday and bank holidays – booking
advisable at dinner

Menu £20/35 – Carte £35/41

Red Fort has been in Soho since 1983, although anyone who hasn't visited for a while will be surprised to see how up-to-date it now is in the looks department. It's still quite a sizeable place but neatly broken up; the far end even boasts a little waterfall. Service isn't quite so memorable and staff could do with being a little more willing to engage with their customers but the menu does impress. It is not overlong and comes divided between starters, grills and main courses. Much of the produce comes from within the UK, such as Herdwick lamb, and there are also more unusual ingredients like rabbit used. Cooking is nicely balanced but the final bill can be a little high, especially when one has added breads, rice and vegetables.

Ritz Restaurant

Traditional ☓☓☓☓☓

150 Piccadilly
✉ W1J 9BR
✆ (020) 7493 8181
www.theritzlondon.com

⊖ Green Park

Menu £39/48 s – Carte £71/94 s

Dining at The Ritz is not just a mightily grand occasion but also provides a lesson in how things used to be done. The room is certainly unmatched in the sheer lavishness of its Louis XVI decoration; the table settings positively gleam thanks to all that polishing and there are probably more ranks to the serving team than in a ship's company. Little wonder they insist on jackets and ties. There's a plethora of menus: Ritz Classics could be saddle of Kentish lamb or roast sirloin; Ritz Traditions might include smoked salmon carved at your table or Dover sole filleted in front of you. For the full experience, have the six-course Sonata Menu, go at a weekend for a dinner dance and don't tell your bank manager.

St John

I3

1 Leicester St.
✉ WC2H 7BL
✆ (020) 3301 8069
www.stjohnhotellondon.com

⊖ **Leicester Square**
Booking advisable

Carte £28/46

A/C
⊙
☀
VISA
MC
AE
OO

After many delays, St John Hotel finally opened its doors in the spring of 2011. The ground floor restaurant is the heart of the operation and shares the same features as the Clerkenwell original: terse menu descriptions; fiercely seasonal, no-nonsense "nose to tail" British-inspired cooking; equally unadorned, municipal-white surroundings and bright, knowledgeable staff. For decades this was Manzi's and, in a nice touch, they've not only kept the signs outside proclaiming "Langouste, Huîtres and Moules" but also ensure that they feature on the menu when in season. As it has bedrooms, it's open early for breakfast and stays serving until 2am, although it takes some daring to be walking these particular streets at that time of night.

Sake No Hana

H4

23 St James's St
✉ SW1A 1HA
✆ (020) 7925 8988
www.sakenohana.com

⊖ **Green Park**
Closed Saturday lunch and Sunday

Carte £38/50

A/C
VISA
MC
AE

As with most restaurants, things look a little different now than they did when the place opened. At Sake No Hana the idea of not offering wine along with the shochu and sake lasted about six months. The menu is also now shorter and less adventurous. It is dominated by sashimi and sushi, after which one is expected to order a grilled dish and perhaps one of their 'special plates'- which could be fried tofu with bonito flakes – then end with some miso soup. Service can be hit and miss and whilst all that cedar wood goes some way towards hiding the ugliness of this stangely iconic '60s building, one does get the impression that this isn't yet the finished article, as the overall experience can be a little lacklustre and quite expensive.

Sartoria

Italian XXX

20 Savile Row
✉ W1S 3PR
☎ (020) 7534 7000
www.sartoriabar.com

⊖ Green Park
Closed 25 December, Saturday lunch,
Sunday and bank holidays

Menu £25 – Carte £30/53

AC
⊡
😇
VISA
M©
AE

If you're going to have any restaurant occupying a prime site in Savile Row then it might as well be Italian as they know one or two things about tailoring themselves. Sartoria is an elegant, smartly dressed restaurant that always seems to exude a certain poise and self-assurance, along with a little charm. There are subtle allusions to tailoring in the decoration and the sofa-style seating in the middle of the room is very appealing. The à laCarte menu is an extensive number and prices can quickly add up, but the cooking, which covers all parts of the country, is undertaken with care and it's apparent that the ingredients are top-notch. Service is also not lacking in confidence and is overseen by assorted suited managers.

MAYFAIR, SOHO & ST JAMES'S ▶ PLAN II

Scott's

Seafood XXX

20 Mount St
✉ W1K 2HE
☎ (020) 7495 7309
www.scotts-restaurant.com

⊖ Bond Street
Closed 25-26 December

Carte £36/56

AC
⊡
☼
VISA
M©
AE
①

Scott's is one of those rare restaurants which is both fashionable and also has a palpable sense of history. As soon as you're through the door, you'll find the aroma and the bustle an enticing draw. Purportedly Ian Fleming's favourite restaurant, it still appeals to those whose faces we recognise and everyone looks as though they've dressed up for the occasion. The wood panelling is juxtaposed with modern art and the bar forms a striking centrepiece. The menu offers an enticing and varied choice, from caviar to razor clams, oysters to spider crabs and sea bass and turbot. The fish is cooked with skill and innate understanding. If only the taciturn staff could crack the occasional smile and add some personality to their efficiency.

Semplice ✿

G3

9-10 Blenheim St
✉ W1S 1LJ
☎ (020) 7495 1509
www.ristorantesemplice.com

Menu £30 (lunch) – Carte £40/51

⊖ Bond Street
Closed 2 weeks Christmas,
Easter, Saturday lunch,
Sunday and bank holidays –
booking essential at dinner

A/C
📷
🎱
VISA
MC
AE

Semplice

The young owners' enthusiasm for their restaurant and their determination to uphold its reputation is palpable. As such, the chef-owner is intent on instilling in his brigade the importance of using good produce and the respect one should show it. Along with many ingredients imported directly from small, specialist suppliers in Italy, fresh fish arrives each day from Cornwall. The kitchen remains loyal to its North Italian roots and the main ingredient of each dish is allowed to shine. The Fassone carpaccio and the Milanese risotto with bone marrow are two choices that keep the many regulars particularly content, but those who are more trusting leave the decisions about what they'll eat to the kitchen. The gold waves on the walls, leather and lacquered ebony panels add a hint of luxury to the room, which takes on a more intimate feel in the evening. The lunch set menu allows newcomers the chance to experience Semplice without breaking the bank. Bar Trattoria Semplice is the simpler sibling a few yards away.

First Course

- Fassone beef carpaccio.
- Steamed diver-caught scallops with foie gras, baby spinach and winter black truffle from Norcia.

Main Course

- Milk-fed Piedmontese veal with courgettes, sweet potato sauce.
- Milanese risotto with saffron and bone marrow.

Dessert

- Coffee tiramisu with tiramisu ice cream.
- Warm pumpkin cake, Amedei white chocolate mousse, seasonal fruit, lavender sauce.

Seven Park Place ❀

H4

7-8 Park Pl
✉ SW1A 1LS
✆ (020) 7316 1614
www.stjameshotelandclub.com

⊖ **Green Park**
Closed Sunday and Monday
– booking essential

Menu £30/55

A/C
⌖
VISA
MC
AE
DC

St James's Hotel & Club

The problem facing the owners of the St James's Hotel when
they converted it from a private club, was in operating within
the limited amount of space available. Accordingly, this small
restaurant is somewhat concealed at the end of a bar, through
which one has to navigate. It's divided between two very
contrasting rooms: the plush back room is the place to sit, as
it holds just three large tables in its gilded setting; the outer
room is not quite so intimate. The restaurant does, however,
have a grown-up feel to it and the professional serving team
make everyone feel suitably relaxed. The hotel has also got
the right chef, cooking the right food. William Drabble made
his name at Michael's Nook in Grasmere and Aubergine in
Chelsea and his food has always displayed a sense of clarity,
offering clean, unadulterated flavours. It is French at its base
but the ingredients are decidedly British and mostly from more
northerly parts, so expect lamb from the Lune Valley, game
from Cumbria and shellfish from the west coast of Scotland.

First Course

- Lobster tail with
  asparagus, pea
  shoots and truffle
  dressing.
- Wild duck ham and
  rillette, New Forest
  mushrooms and
  celeriac.

Main Course

- Saddle of lamb with
  peas, lettuce and
  onions.
- Poached fillet of brill
  with celeriac, apples,
  mussels and chives.

Dessert

- Piña colada bavarois
  with poached
  pineapple.
- Caramel parfait with
  slow cooked apples.

MAYFAIR, SOHO & ST JAMES'S ▶ PLAN II

89

Sketch (The Gallery)

H3

International 🍴🍴

9 Conduit St
✉ W1S 2XG
☎ (020) 7659 4500
www.sketch.uk.com

⊖ Oxford Street
Closed 25-26 December, Sunday and bank
holidays – booking essential – (dinner only)

Carte £35/63

🅰🅲
🍴
VISA
ⓂⒸ
🅰🅴

Fund managers and footballers' wives flock to this lively, fun space, which transforms itself during the day into a gallery showing mostly video art; during dinner, lifestyle aphorisms are projected onto its white walls. The cocktail list is an essential element, while the food menu is international in its scope but in tune with the culinary zeitgeist in its constrained use of oil and dairy. Dishes come with plenty of flavour and colour and, as the staff are young, good-looking and fully conversant in the concept of up-selling, one needs to stand firm and politely decline their offer of a side dish because the main courses don't need them. It's loud, busy and it doesn't come cheap – but then exclusivity never does.

Spice Market

I3

Asian 🍴🍴

10 Wardour St
✉ W1D 6QF
☎ (020) 7758 1000
www.spicemarketlondon.co.uk

⊖ Leicester Square

Menu £18/24 – Carte £29/51

🅰🅲
🛋
🍴
☀
VISA
ⓂⒸ
🅰🅴
Ⓓ

Leicester Square might not be as hip as Manhattan's Meatpacking district but this offshoot of Jean-Georges Vongerichten's New York original may just start to change things around here. This London branch certainly learnt about service from its American cousin because staff are all very confident, keen and clued-up. The restaurant is spread over two floors, linked by a spiral staircase, with eye-catching screens of gold mesh, walls of spices and ceilings of upturned woks. The kitchen traverses various Asian countries for influences and dishes are designed for sharing; ingredients are good and curries are a highlight. 'Street food' is how they describe their cooking, although the street in question is clearly a well-to-do one.

Sketch
(The Lecture Room & Library) ✿

French 🍴🍴🍴🍴

H3

9 Conduit St (1st floor) ✉ W1S 2XG
✆ (020) 7659 4500
www.sketch.uk.com

⊖ Oxford Street
Closed last 2 weeks August,
Saturday lunch, Sunday and Monday –
booking essential

Menu £35 (lunch) – Carte £70/129

A/C
🍇
VISA
MC
AE

Sketch

Sketch was always designed as an ever-changing restaurant concept and, sure enough, there have been a few adjustments to proceedings in the Lecture Room and Library. The main difference is in the presentation of the food, most specifically with the main courses. In the past they came sub-divided into various equally sized components which arrived in a number of assorted vessels; now one plate dominates and is complemented by the other dishes that surround it. The quality of the ingredients, however, remains irreproachable and the room is as stunning as ever, with the odd quirky decorative touch adding to the general theatre of things. The wine list continues to dazzle, both in the array of French growths but also in the prices that sit alongside them. Another not quite so welcome change is that the serving team can sometimes cross the line from being confident into making guests feel lucky to have got a table. However, what remains constant is the sense of glamour, energy and vitality one experiences here.

First Course

- Scallop, morel and braised veal sweetbreads 'osso buco'.
- 'Perfume of the earth'.

Main Course

- Quercy lamb saddle, rack and sweetbreads.
- Skate and red mullet, smoked haddock, enoki and champagne, aioli tartlet.

Dessert

- Pierre Gagnaire's 'grand dessert'.
- Dark Manjari chocolate soufflé, blackberry parfait, goat's milk jelly, pistachio cream, chocolate sauce.

Spuntino

I3

61 Rupert St.
✉ W1D 7PW
www.spuntino.co.uk

⊖ Piccadilly Circus
Closed 25 December-2 January and dinner
24 December – (bookings not accepted)

Carte £12/22

A/C
⊙
☼
VISA
MC
AE

Despite its Italian name – meaning 'snack'– Spuntino draws its influences from Downtown New York and is so convincing you feel you could be on Clinton Street. It has the so-discreet-you-walk-straight-past-it entrance, a no-reservations policy (not even a phone number) and an interior that more than hints at a former industrial life – this was once a dairy. Just grab, or wait for, space at the counter and, from the brown paper menu, go for the more American dishes such as Mac 'n' Cheese, soft-shell crab, farmhouse cheddar grits or 'sliders', which are mini burgers. The peanut butter and jelly sandwiches for dessert will be always on your mind. The staff, who look like they could also fix your car, really add to the fun.

Sumosan

H3

26 Albemarle St.
✉ W1S 4HY
℘ (020) 7495 5999
www.sumosan.com

⊖ Green Park
Closed lunch Saturday-
Sunday and bank holidays

Carte £29/74

A/C
⊙
VISA
MC
AE
◐

Sumosan isn't the only restaurant serving this kind of contemporary Japanese food in London, or indeed in Mayfair, but what it does do is offer a greater degree of sophistication. The lighting is seductive, the booths discreet and the design chic; it still appeals to a young and prosperous crowd but one that is a little less shouty. Deciding what and how much to order is a little confusing, and assistance from the staff isn't always forthcoming, but the kitchen is sufficiently flexible to allow for ordering as you go along. Its understanding of flavour combinations is showcased in dishes like duck with lingonberry sauce and turbot with wasabi risotto. Those who prefer things more traditional should head straight for the sushi bar.

Square ✿ ✿

French 🗙🗙🗙🗙

H3

6-10 Bruton St.
✉ W1J 6PU
☎ (020) 7495 7100
www.squarerestaurant.com

⊖ **Green Park**
Closed 25 December, 1 January and
lunch Saturday,
Sunday and bank holidays

Menu £35/80

A/C
⊙
88
VISA
MO
AE

The Square

Philip Howard is one of the capital's more personable chefs
and has been responsible for the development of a number of
talented young chefs now cementing their own reputations in
London. Despite being involved in Kitchen W8 in Kensington,
he never took his hand off the tiller here at The Square. His
food continues to be true to his classical roots yet he manages
to bring in subtle modern influences without them jarring. The
menu changes completely with the seasons but varies more in
summer when certain ingredients are only available for short
periods, although the regulars will never allow the removal of
the two signature dishes of langoustine and lasagne of crab. The
cheese board is now much improved and offers a selection of
around 40 British and continental cheeses; it's worth asking as
they don't 'sell' it as much as they could. They're also working
on the service in an attempt to lighten it somewhat, especially
for weekend visitors, who are inclined to interact with the
serving team more than corporate weekday diners.

First Course

- Langoustine with
  parmesan gnocchi
  and truffle.
- Terrine of chicken,
  foie gras and girolles
  with grilled spring
  onions and hazelnut
  oil.

Main Course

- Loin of lamb,
  crushed broad
  beans, broccoli and
  mint.
- Fillet of turbot with
  Jersey Royal, pea and
  mint ravioli.

Dessert

- Brillat-Savarin
  cheesecake with
  pink grapefruit and
  champagne.
- Warm chocolate
  fondant with 100s
  and 1000s milk ice
  cream.

Tamarind ⁂

Indian 🍴🍴🍴

20 Queen St.
✉ W1J 5PR
☎ (020) 7629 3561
www.tamarindrestaurant.com

⊖ Green Park
Closed 25-26 December, 1 January
and Saturday lunch

Menu £20/56 – Carte £45/68

A/C ☼ VISA MC AE OD

Tamarind

The earnest Alfred Prasad and his reinvigorated kitchen take familiar dishes and raise them to exceptional heights. The delicate and fragrant curries show particular care but also worthy of special mention are the tandoor chefs who produce, in considerable heat, specialities ranging from the delightfully light breads to kebabs of tender lamb. Spicing is subtle and brings out the natural flavours of the ingredients, whether that's the simmered chicken in the Adraki Murgh or the plump tiger prawns in the Kadhai Jhinga. Vegetable dishes are prepared with equal care and provide interesting counterpoints to the main dishes. The restaurant has always made the best of its basement location, albeit one that's in the heart of Mayfair. The smoked mirrors, gilded columns and copper-coloured chargers give the room a sophisticated veneer. Service is more polished and assured than in previous years and all these factors, plus the slight reduction in the prices of certain dishes, have made Tamarind as popular as ever.

First Course

- Grilled scallops, roasted peppers and tomato chutney.
- Aloo tikki potato cakes and tamarind chutney.

Main Course

- Fillet of sea bass, mango and curry leaf sauce.
- Hyderabadi slow-cooked lamb shank.

Dessert

- Tandoor grilled pineapple, rose petal ice cream.
- Carrot fudge with melon seeds and raisins with vanilla ice cream.

Tapas Brindisa

H3

Spanish ✗

46 Broadwick St.
✉ W1F 7AF
☎ (020) 7534 1690
www.brindisa.com

⊖ Oxford Circus
Closed 25 December –
(bookings not accepted)

Carte £18/44

☀
VISA
MC
AE

There were quite a few changes here in 2011. The bar moved to the front and a change of name from 'Tierra' to 'Tapas Brindisa' was made, to emphasise the true nature of this operation as well as to attempt to replicate the success of their Borough Market site. The taking of bookings was also scrapped as, in true tapas style, they wanted people to simply stroll in, have a drink and get something to eat. The menu is now easier to read, with specialities marked out in bold, such as Basque salt cod with spicy tomato sauce. The owners' expertise in importing Spanish produce is evident; although it's amazing how quickly the bill mounts up. However, service is obliging and there's no 'push' to move you off, despite the clamour in the bar.

Tempo

H4

Italian ✗✗

54 Curzon St.
✉ W1J 8PG
☎ (020) 7629 2742
www.tempomayfair.co.uk

⊖ Green Park
Closed 25-27 December,
Saturday lunch,
Sunday and bank holidays

Menu £23 (lunch) – Carte £29/52

A/C
VISA
MC
AE

Henry Togna, the affable and well-connected hotelier, took over a failing Italian restaurant, revamped it from top-to-toe and reopened it as Tempo in the summer of 2010. He adds a comforting presence to proceedings but is also wise enough to surround himself with an experienced team. The ground floor is cosy and neat, while the upstairs salon, where the small bar is located, is clubbier and a tad funkier. The main menu is an unobjectionable document and includes the popular cicchetti, or small plates. The cooking is executed with care and stays true to the principles of an Italian kitchen; a good selection of breads kick things off and the tagliolini with Cornish crab and the lemon tart have quickly become favourites.

Theo Randall

G4

 I t a l i a n

1 Hamilton Pl, Park Ln.
✉ W1J 7QY
✆ (020) 7318 8747
www.theorandall.com

⊖ Hyde Park Corner
Closed 25-26 December, 1 January,
Saturday lunch,
Sunday and bank holidays

Menu £29 (lunch) – Carte £50/74

It may have taken a little longer to settle down than most pundits expected but now this large, contemporary restaurant on the ground floor of the InterContintental Hotel seems to have found its niche, and increased TV exposure for its eponymous chef has had a knock-on effect on business. Theo Randall's years at the River Café inform his cooking and, even now, a familiar dish like flourless chocolate cake can seem peculiarly out of context. The menu changes daily and loosely follows the formula of cooking dishes from the north of Italy in winter and more southerly ones in the summer; the wood oven also plays a major role. As this is also a hotel dining room catering for all tastes, the wine list has something for everyone.

Vasco and Piero's Pavilion

H2/3

I t a l i a n

15 Poland St
✉ W1F 8QE
✆ (020) 7437 8774
www.vascosfood.com

⊖ Oxford Circus
Closed Saturday lunch, Sunday and bank
holidays – booking essential at lunch

Menu £20 (lunch and early dinner) – Carte £30/38

This Soho institution celebrated its fortieth anniversary in 2011; if you ask them for the secret of their success the reply will be, "we just do what we believe in". That means a menu that changes twice a day, ingredients and influences from Umbria and simple but effective cooking, with homemade pasta a highlight. Service can sometimes lack a little enthusiasm but it does get the job done – it is not as if they don't care, more that their customers are often regulars who know the score, so why over-egg the pudding? The owners' confidence in their operation and their honest endeavours add to the grown-up feel. The restaurant, which was originally located in Oxford Street, remains fresh and bright.

Umu ✿

14-16 Bruton Pl.
✉ W1J 6LX
☎ (020) 7499 8881
www.umurestaurant.com

⊖ **Bond Street**
Closed Saturday lunch,
Sunday and bank holidays

Menu £26 (lunch) – Carte £35/151

A/C
88
VISA
MC
AE

Umu

The latest head chef arrived here in 2010, from Kyoto via Switzerland and New York, and his first task was to find ingredients to match the quality he had become used to back in Japan; so far, it is the Scottish langoustines that have bowled him over. The table in the former wine cave, ideal for couples in the early throws of romantic entanglement but perhaps too much of a squeeze for parties of four, remains a popular spot. The hostess greets arrivals with enough enthusiasm to compensate for the somewhat po-faced persona of the waiting staff, from whom advice sometimes has to be coaxed. The menu consists of three pages of parchment – if you want the full experience head to one of the seasonally changing, multi-course kaiseki menus, although these have been adapted somewhat for western tastes. The perfect accompaniment, especially for the sashimi, is sake; not only is the list impressive in its depth and range but the charming female sommelier also offers thoughtful advice.

First Course	*Main Course*	*Dessert*
• Tuna tartare salad, Japanese pickles.	• Wild Scottish lobster, seven pepper shichimi.	• 'Charamisu' Japanese tiramisu with macha tea and sake.
• Tiger prawn tempura with seasonal vegetables.	• Lamb loin with Japanese laver bread, demi-glace soy, chive oil and sanshyo seeds.	• Chocolate fondant with white miso ice cream.

Veeraswamy

H3

Indian ✕✕

Victory House, 99 Regent St
(entrance on Swallow St.) ✉ W1B 4RS
✆ (020) 7734 1401
www.realindianfood.com

⊖ Piccadilly Circus

Menu £21 (lunch and early dinner) – Carte £37/51

A/C

⬦

☻

☼

VISA

⓶Ⓒ

ᴀᴇ

⓪

The manager here knows not to come between a regular and their favourite table: some were first brought here by their grandparents and are now, in turn, introducing their own grandchildren to London's oldest surviving Indian restaurant, which dates from 1926. You'd be excused for thinking it might be a tad old-fashioned but Veeraswamy is anything but: it is awash with vibrant colours and always full of bustle. The Hyderabad lamb biryani may have been on the original menu but there are plenty of other dishes with a more contemporary edge. The meaty Madagascar prawns are a good way of kicking things off; slow-cooked lamb dishes are also done very well. There's a tasting menu available and desserts, prepared with a flourish, shouldn't be ignored.

The Wolseley

H4

Modern European ✕✕✕

160 Piccadilly
✉ W1J 9EB
✆ (020) 7499 6996
www.thewolseley.com

⊖ Green Park
Closed 25 December, dinner 24 and
31 December and August bank holiday
– booking essential

Carte £24/48

A/C

◉

☼

VISA

⓶Ⓒ

ᴀᴇ

⓪

Opened back in 2003, The Wolseley did not take long to earn iconic status, thanks to its stylish décor, celebrity following and smooth service. Its owners, Chris Corbin and Jeremy King, created a restaurant in the style of a grand European café, all pillars, arches and marble. Open from breakfast until late, the flexible menu offers everything from Austrian and French classics to British staples, so the daily special could be coq au vin or Lancashire hotpot. Pastries come from the Viennoiserie and lunch merges into afternoon tea. So, one table could be tucking into Beluga caviar or a dozen oysters while their neighbours enjoy a salt beef sandwich or eggs Benedict. The large clock reminds you that there are probably others waiting for your table.

Wild Honey ✿

Michelin

H3

12 St George St.
✉ W1S 2FB
✆ (020) 7758 9160
www.wildhoneyrestaurant.co.uk

⊖ Oxford Circus
Closed 25-26 December
and 1 January

Menu £19 (weekday lunch) – Carte £29/39

A/C
▦
☼
VISA
MC
AE

MAYFAIR, SOHO & ST JAMES'S ▶ PLAN II

Wild Honey is all about relaxed and comfortable dining; the highly skilled cooking is a model of resourcefulness and the prices – when one considers the postcode and the quality of the food – are laudable. The kitchen proves that good – but not necessarily expensive – ingredients mean good food. The menus are hugely appealing and the seasonal ingredients are used at their peak; plates are never overcrowded and each component serves a purpose – there is nothing ostentatious here. The bouillabaisse and the wild honey ice cream are constants and the wine list is as magnanimous in its pricing as the menu, with all bottles available by the carafe. Like a talented sportsman, a lot of hard work and experience goes into making all this seem so easy. The fixed menu is a steal and there's now a short 'sweet and savoury' menu on offer for those who want an afternoon bite. Service is personable and unobtrusive and the atmosphere is far more animated than one would expect in a wood-panelled room that was once a private members club.

First Course	Main Course	Dessert
• Belly pork with snails and onion purée. • Line-caught Cornish mackerel, alphonso mango and sweet spice.	• Short rib of Wagyu beef and a bone marrow gratin. • Bouillabaisse 'traditional Marseille style'.	• Vanilla cheesecake scented with rosewater. • Meringue of Gariguette strawberries, 'pavlova'.

Wright Brothers Soho

Seafood ✗

H3

13 Kingly St.
✉ W1B 5PW
✆ (020) 7434 3611
www.thewrightbrothers.co.uk

⊖ Oxford Circus
Closed 25-27 December
and bank holidays

Carte £24/35

Bigger than the original Wright Brothers in Borough Market, this branch is spread over three levels but the best seats are on the lower floor and certainly at the counter if you want to watch the expert oyster shucking. Oysters are the first choice of many as they grow their own in Cornwall; the plates of fruits de mer are also popular and designed for sharing. The menu is divided between cold and hot starters and 'house staples' which include everything from prawn cocktail to fish pie. The specials board also has plenty on offer, from sardines on toast to a perfectly judged whole sea bream. Desserts are something of an afterthought – it's all about fishy things here. There's an all-day menu and the restaurant opens out into Kingly Court.

The sun is out – let's eat alfresco! Look for 🌤.

Yauatcha ✿

13

Chinese 🍴🍴

15 Broadwick St
✉ W1F 0DL
✆ (020) 7494 8888
www.yauatcha.com

⊖ Tottenham Court Road
Closed 24-25 December and lunch 26
December and 1 January

Carte £30/50

A/C
🕙
☼
VISA
MC
AE

Yauatcha

China and Britain: two countries inexorably linked through tea.
If you want to see what this looks like in practice, then go along
one afternoon to Yauatcha and witness a British institution
given an Asian twist. The cakes, tarts and pastries are good
too, although for that we have to thank a French pastry chef
- and that's a whole different story. There is nowhere quite
like Yauatcha: a dim sum restaurant that's so successful, where
the food is so good and the surroundings so slick and stylish,
that customers find it hard to be in and out in the allocated
1hr 45minutes. The trick is to spend time eating and chatting,
rather than ordering so crack on with that bit. Around three
dim sum per person followed by some sharing of noodles or a
stir-fry should do the trick and, while you wait for it to arrive,
have one of their terrific cocktails. Stand-out dishes are the
scallop shui mai, prawn cheung fun, the baked venison puff
and the Kung Po chicken; but don't ignore dessert, especially
the roasted pineapple with praline parfait.

First Course
- Scallop shui mai.
- Wild mushroom
  dumpling.

Main Course
- Jasmine tea smoked
  ribs.
- Dover sole with
  shiitake and soya.

Dessert
- Milk chocolate
  praline cake with
  kalamansi sorbet.
- Coconut charlotte.

101

Strand · Covent Garden

It's fitting that Manet's world famous painting 'Bar at the Folies Bergère' should hang in the **Strand** within a champagne cork's throw of theatreland and Covent Garden. This is the area perhaps more than any other which draws in the ticket-buying tourist, eager to grab a good deal on one of the many shows on offer, or eat and drink at fabled shrines like J.Sheekey or Rules. It's here the names already up in lights shine down on their potential usurpers: celeb wannabes heading for The Ivy, West Street's perennially fashionable restaurant. It's here, too, that Nell Gwyn set up home under the patronage of Charles II, while Oscar Wilde revelled in his success by taking rooms at the Savoy.

The hub of the whole area is the piazza at **Covent Garden,** created by Inigo Jones four hundred years ago. It was given a brash new lease of life in the 1980s after its famed fruit and veg market was pulled up by the roots and re-sown in Battersea. Council bigwigs realised then that 'what we have we hold', and any further redevelopment of the area is banned. Where everyone heads is the impressive covered market, within which a colourful jumble of arts and crafts shops gels with al fresco cafés and classical performers proffering Paganini with your cappuccino. Outside, under the portico of St Paul's church, every type of street performer does a turn for the tourist trade. The best shops in Covent Garden, though, are a few streets north of the market melee, emanating out like bicycle spokes from Seven Dials.

For those after a more highbrow experience, one of London's best attractions is a hop, skip and *grand jeté* from the market. Around the corner in **Bow Street** is the city's famed home for opera and ballet, where fire – as well as show-stopping performances – has been known to bring the house down. The **Royal Opera House** is now in its third incarnation, and it gets more impressive with each rebuild. The handsome, glass-roofed Floral Hall is a must-see, while an interval drink at the Amphitheatre Café Bar, overlooking the piazza, is de rigeur for show goers. At the other end of the Strand the **London Coliseum** offers more opera, this time all performed in English. Down by Waterloo Bridge, art lovers are strongly advised to stop at **Somerset House** and take in one of London's most sublime collections of art at the Courtauld Gallery. This is where you can get up close and personal to Manet's barmaid, as well as an astonishing array of Impressionist masters and twentieth century greats. The icing on the cake is the compact and accessible eighteenth century building that houses the collection: real icing on a real cake can be found in a super little hidden-away café downstairs.

Of a different order altogether is the huge **National Gallery** at

Trafalgar Square which houses more than two thousand Western European pieces (it started off with 38). A visit to the modern Sainsbury Wing is rewarded with some unmissable works from the Renaissance. It can get just as crowded in the capital's largest Gallery as in the square outside, so a good idea is to wander down **Villiers Street** next to Charing Cross station and breathe the Thames air along the Victoria Embankment. Behind you is the grand Savoy Hotel, which reopened in 2010 after major refurbishment;

for a better view of it, you can head even further away from the crowds on a boat trip from the **Embankment,** complete with on-board entertainment. And if the glory of travel in the capital, albeit on the water, has whetted your appetite for more, then pop into the impressively renovated Transport Museum in Covent Garden piazza, where gloriously preserved tubes, buses and trains from the past put you in a positive frame of mind for the real live working version you'll very probably be tackling later in the day.

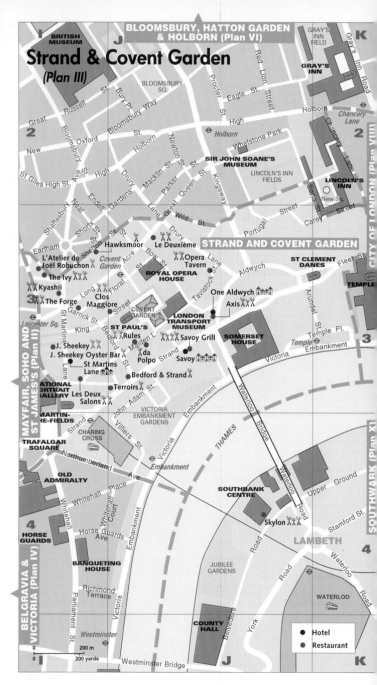

Strand & Covent Garden
(Plan III)

BLOOMSBURY, HATTON GARDEN & HOLBORN (Plan VI)

BRITISH MUSEUM

GRAY'S INN FIELD

GRAY'S INN

BLOOMSBURY SQ.

SIR JOHN SOANE'S MUSEUM

LINCOLN'S INN FIELDS

LINCOLN'S INN

CITY OF LONDON (Plan VIII)

STRAND AND COVENT GARDEN

Hawksmoor

Le Deuxième

Opera Tavern

ST CLEMENT DANES

L'Atelier de Joël Robuchon

Covent Garden

ROYAL OPERA HOUSE

The Ivy

Kyashii

The Forge

Clos Maggiore

COVENT GARDEN

LONDON TRANSPORT MUSEUM

One Aldwych

Axis

TEMPLE

ST PAUL'S

SOMERSET HOUSE

Rules

J. Sheekey

J. Sheekey Oyster Bar

St Martins Lane

da Polpo

Savoy Grill

Savoy

NATIONAL PORTRAIT GALLERY

Bedford & Strand

MARTIN-THE-FIELDS

Les Deux Salons

Terroirs

VICTORIA EMBANKMENT GARDENS

TRAFALGAR SQUARE

CHARING CROSS

OLD ADMIRALTY

THAMES

HORSE GUARDS

SOUTHBANK CENTRE

BANQUETING HOUSE

Skylon

LAMBETH

SOUTHWARK (Plan XI)

JUBILEE GARDENS

WATERLOO

COUNTY HALL

Westminster

Westminster Bridge

BELGRAVIA & VICTORIA (Plan IV)

MAYFAIR, SOHO AND ST JAMES'S (Plan II)

0   200 m
0   200 yards

● Hotel
● Restaurant

L'Atelier de Joël Robuchon ✿✿

13

13-15 West St.
✉ WC2H 9NE
☎ (020) 7010 8600
www.joelrobuchon.co.uk

⊖ **Leicester Square**
Closed 25-26 December,1 January,
Sunday and bank holiday Mondays

Menu £29/125 – Carte £45/83

A/C
🕐
🎭
VISA
MC
AE

L'Atelier de Joel Robuchon

STRAND & COVENT GARDEN ▶ PLAN III

London's L'Atelier de Joël Robuchon differs from his other 'branches' dotted around the world's culinary hotspots by being two restaurants under one roof: on the ground floor is L'Atelier itself, with an open kitchen and large counter; upstairs is the monochrome La Cuisine, a slightly more structured, sleek and more brightly-lit affair with table seating. Apart from a few wood-fired dishes upstairs, the menus are largely similar. The cooking is artistic, creative and occasionally playful; it is technically very accomplished and highly labour intensive – there are over thirty chefs in the building – but it is never overworked and each dish is perfectly balanced, its flavours true and its taste exquisite. French is the predominant influence, supported by other Mediterranean flavours, and ordering a number of smaller dishes is the best way to fully appreciate Robuchon's craft and vision, although your final bill can be pretty lofty. Service is expertly timed and confident and sitting at the counter will give you some insight into this most polished of operations.

First Course

- Chicken broth with foie gras ravioli and zesty whipped cream.
- Crispy langoustine fritters with basil pistou.

Main Course

- Free-range quail stuffed with foie gras and truffled mashed potatoes.
- Black cod caramelised with Asian spices, carrot mousseline and baby spinach.

Dessert

- Warm yuzu soufflé with vanilla infused raspberry sorbet.
- Passion fruit and banana cream with rum granité and coconut foam.

Axis

Modern European XXX

J3

1 Aldwych
✉ WC2B 4RH
✆ (020) 7300 0300
www.onealdwych.com

⊖ Temple
▶ **Plan II**
Closed Sunday and Monday

Menu £20 (lunch and early dinner) – Carte £34/39

[A/C]
⟨⟩
😮
VISA
MC
AE
⓪

Expectation is everything and the spiral marble staircase leading down to this restaurant always adds a little excitement. The room, which must have one of the highest ceilings in London, is neatly laid out and service is well-organised, if perhaps a little too formal for its own good. One wise decision was the moving of the bar to downstairs; this means there is always a little noise, even when the restaurant has a lull just after the theatre-goers have left. They have made the menu a little lighter by adding salads and a seafood section. More European influences now also sit alongside the British dishes, so you can have smoked salmon, salt beef and a treacle sponge or scallops with chorizo, beef bourguignon and a crème brûlée.

Bedford & Strand

British X

J3

1a Bedford St
✉ WC2E 9HH
✆ (020) 7836 3033
www.bedford-strand.com

⊖ Charing Cross
Closed 24 December-2 January,
Sunday and bank holidays –
booking essential

Menu £18 (dinner) – Carte £26/35

VISA
MC
AE

Maybe it's the basement location or the discreet entrance, but Bedford & Strand has an almost secretive, clubby feel. The bar dominates proceedings although in a good way – you'll hear the laughter as you come down the stairs – and the character of the place makes you quickly forget about its subterranean location. Wine is given equal billing with the food; the list is sensibly laid out and there's plenty by the glass and carafe. The food menu complements it well and is appealingly to the point; highlights are the British classics like shepherd's pie, potted crab and treacle tart. The young staff make up in eagerness what they lack in direction and the atmosphere is pleasantly unhurried, despite its proximity to scores of theatres.

Clos Maggiore

French ✗✗

J3

33 King St   ⊖ **Leicester Square**
✉ WC2E 8JD   Closed 25 December and 1 January
℘ (020) 7379 9696
www.closmaggiore.com

Menu £20 (lunch and early dinner) – Carte £32/36

Despite its touristy location, Clos Maggiore has an air of old-fashioned sophistication, with its richly decorated look and poised, attentive staff. Do ask for a table in the little rear conservatory, whose roof opens in summer, as it's an enchanting spot. The kitchen's repertoire is largely French but uses mostly British ingredients. Dishes come with a delicacy to their presentation but not at the expense of flavour; vegetarians are well looked after and desserts are done especially well. The restaurant's greatest attraction, however, is the price of its lunch and pre-theatre menus – with an even greater choice at weekends – making this one of the hottest tickets in town. They also take very late bookings for post-theatre debriefing.

da Polpo ⊛

Italian ✗

J3

6 Maiden Ln.   ⊖ **Leicester Square**
✉ WC2E 7NA   Closed dinner 24 December-1 January
℘ (020) 7836 8448   – (bookings not accepted at dinner)
www.dapolpo.co.uk

Carte £15/25

After sewing up Soho with their first three restaurants, this clever little group then turned its attention to neighbouring Covent Garden to open this Venetian bacaro. Behind the delicately embroidered linen screens is another shrewdly designed spot, with a tin ceiling imported from New York and church pews contrasting with the ersatz industrial look. It covers two floors – the ground floor is best. Over-ordering is easy, as the small plates are surprisingly filling, with delights such as the wonderfully fresh flavours of pizzette of white anchovy vying with fennel and almond salad, fritto misto competing with spaghettini and meatballs. A no-bookings policy after 5.30pm means that there will be queues but turnover is naturally quick.

Le Deuxième

Modern European ✗✗

J3

65a Long Acre
✉ WC2E 9JH
☎ (020) 7379 0033
www.ledeuxieme.com

⊖ Covent Garden
Closed 24-25 December

Menu £17 (lunch) – Carte £29/38

🅰🅲
🕐
🎭
☀
VISA
Ⓜ🅒
🅰🅴

Don't think that because it's busy in the early evening before curtain-up in all the local theatres that's it's going to quieten down when all the early-diners have gone – it seemingly stays busy most of the evening, most nights. This certainly gives the room plenty of energy but it also means that this is the sort of place where, if you get the attention of the waiter or waitress, you'll want to be ready with your order so as not to waste the opportunity. The menu offers an extensive range of dishes, whose influences come largely from within Europe. In amongst the pastas and the salads are some fairly classic French dishes and this is where the kitchen's experience lies. Side dishes, though, can quickly bump up the bill.

Les Deux Salons

French ✗✗

I3

40-42 William IV St
✉ WC2N 4DD
☎ (020) 7420 2050
www.lesdeuxsalons.co.uk

⊖ Charing Cross
Closed 25-26 December
and 1 January

Menu £16 (lunch) – Carte £28/40

🅰🅲
🎋
🎱
🎭
☀
VISA
Ⓜ🅒
🅰🅴

After the success of Arbutus and Wild Honey, Will Smith and Anthony Demetre turned their attention towards France and came up with Les Deux Salons – a Parisian brasserie so authentic in its look you half expect to see Sartre sitting in the corner. Of the two salons, the ground floor is the more atmospheric and visually impressive, with its smoked mirrors, globe lights, zinc-topped bar and striking mosaic floor. The menu makes for an appealing read; you'll find French classics like bouillabaisse, assorted meats grilled on the Josper and even the occasional interloper from this side of the Channel, like cottage pie; desserts are full-on Gallic and all the better for it. It's been busy since opening its doors; service is swift, but not pushy.

108

Forge

Modern European ✕✕

I3

14 Garrick St
✉ WC2E 9BJ
✆ (020) 7379 1432
www.theforgerestaurant.co.uk

⊖ Leicester Square
Closed 2 days Easter
and 24-26 December

Menu £17/30 – Carte £29/38

A/C

For those who can't decide what they want to eat or at what time, there is The Forge. Open all day, every day, with last orders at midnight, it offers an exhaustive choice of dishes to satisfy both the late-riser and the early-reveller. Omelettes and oysters vie with snails and salads; there's a pasta section and main courses range from whole Dover sole to liver and bacon; so whether it's tournedos Rossini or a hamburger you're after, you'll probably find what you want. Waiters weave between tables and make up in confidence what they sometimes lack in direction. The décor mixes the old with the new and, while the front of the restaurant is more intimate, the back is more fun. There is a good value pre and post theatre menu.

Hawksmoor

Beef specialities ✕

I3

11 Langley St
✉ WC2H 9GJ
✆ (020) 7856 2154
www.thehawksmoor.com

⊖ Covent Garden
Closed 2-4 January ,
24-30 December and Sunday dinner

Menu £23 (lunch and early dinner) – Carte £36/55

A/C

Impressive renovation work from those clever Hawksmoor people has turned this former brewery cellar into a very atmospheric restaurant whose primary function is the serving and eating of red meat – a suitably apt activity as an 18C owner of the brewery used to host a steak club. You'll get a friendly greeting at the bottom of the stairs and can either eat in the bar or in the large and bustling dining room with its ersatz industrial look. Steaks from Longhorn cattle lovingly reared in North Yorkshire and dry-aged for at least 35 days are the stars of the show. A blackboard shows availability and meat is priced per 100g. But beware as side orders and competitive over-ordering on the size of the cut can push up the final bill.

The Ivy

International XXX

13

1-5 West St
✉ WC2H 9NQ
✆ (020) 7836 4751
www.the-ivy.co.uk

⊖ Leicester Square
Closed 25-26 December

Carte £38/50

[A/C]

The members-only Ivy Club may have siphoned off the top tier of regulars but The Ivy restaurant continues to attract new blood. It's still the sort of place where everyone looks up from their food to see who's just arrived but nowadays that's just as likely to be a reality TV contestant as a theatrical knight. Getting a table remains a challenge; try calling on the day – if they offer the bar, accept, because you may get bumped up into the main room. But the great thing about The Ivy is that it's impossible not to find the menu appealing: perfectly gratinated shepherd's pie, plump fishcakes, eggs Benedict, nursery puddings – they're all here and all done well. Staff earn their crust by frequently but discreetly re-laying the tables.

J. Sheekey

Seafood XX

13

28-34 St Martin's Ct.
✉ WC2 4AL
✆ (020) 7240 2565
www.j-sheekey.co.uk

⊖ Leicester Square
Closed 25-26 December –
booking essential

Menu £28 (weekends) – Carte £30/72

Named after the restaurant's first chef who cooked for its then owner Lord Salisbury, J. Sheekey proves that longevity and tradition need not mean old and crusty. It is as fashionable now as it was in 1896 and remains one of the first choices for the theatrical world and those whose business is show. The wood panelling and silver on the tables add to the timeless British feel and service is as charming and efficient as ever. Fish and seafood are handled deftly: the Arbroath smokie and potted shrimps are permanent fixtures and the fish pie and lemon sole are rightly renowned. Avoiding pre and post-theatre times will shorten the odds of your getting a table and ask for 'dining room 4' which is the largest of the five rooms.

J. Sheekey Oyster Bar

13

33-34 St Martin's Ct.
✉ WC2 4AL
✆ (020) 7240 2565
www.j-sheeky.co.uk

⊖ **Leicester Square**
Closed 25-26 December

Carte £24/57

And you can't even see the join. When the opportunity arose for J. Sheekey to expand next door, the obvious decision would have been to extend the restaurant which has, after all, been working well since 1896. Instead, they decided to create this terrific oyster bar – and for that we should all be grateful. There are four or five tables but you're much better off sitting at the bar as you can chat with the chaps behind it and, if you're on the far side, watch the chefs in action. The tablemat doubles as a menu, which offers the same high quality seafood as next door but at slightly lower prices. Along with favourites like oysters and the individual fish pie, come dishes designed for sharing such as the fruits de mer.

Kyashii

13

4a Upper St Martin's Lane
✉ WC2H 9NY
✆ (020) 7836 5211
www.kyashii.co.uk

⊖ **Leicester Square**
Closed 25 December

Carte £25/43

Another restaurant satisfying the demand for contemporary Japanese food and glossy surroundings is Kyashii, housed in premises formerly occupied by The Kingly Club. The ground floor is an eye-catching mix of cream leather, mirrors and fish tanks, contrasting nicely with a long dark marble sushi bar; and if you think the music's too loud then you're too old to be here. Cooking is well-executed and the kitchen adds just enough originality to give the food personality. Kushiyaki skewers and single bowl Teishoku lunches are specialities. Shaker, whose name presumably refers to their impressive selection of cocktails rather than the religious sect known for their furniture, is the name of the achingly trendy bar upstairs.

Opera Tavern 🐶

J3

23 Catherine St.
✉ WC2B 5JS
☎ (020) 7836 3680
www.operatavern.co.uk

⊖ Covent Garden
Closed 24 December-2 January
and dinner Sunday and bank holidays

Carte £22/39

A/C
⠿
🕪
VISA
M©
AE

That many of its more touristy areas now boast some decent restaurants is testament to London's maturing dining scene. Opera Tavern comes from the people who brought you Salt Yard and Dehesa, so they know what they're doing, but this time they're doing it in a converted old boozer dating from 1879, albeit one that's had a complete makeover. If you haven't booked a table in the upstairs dining room then try your luck on the lively ground floor; order 2 or 3 dishes per person and be prepared to share – stand-outs are the Ibérico ham, chorizo with piquillo pepper and crispy squid. The wine list also swings between Spain and Italy and includes some rare and ancient grape varieties. The staff are all reassuringly confident and clued up.

Rules

J3

35 Maiden Ln
✉ WC2E 7LB
☎ (020) 7836 5314
www.rules.co.uk

⊖ Leicester Square
Closed Christmas – booking essential

Carte £34/47

A/C
⟨⊡⟩
😊
☀
VISA
M©
AE

Some restaurants don't even last 1798 days; Rules opened in 1798, at a time when the French were still revolting, and has been a bastion of Britishness ever since. Virtually every inch of wall is covered with a cartoon or painting and everyone from Charles Dickens to Buster Keaton has passed through its doors. The first floor is now a bar; time it right and you'll spot some modern-day theatrical luminaries who use it as a Green Room. The hardest decision is whether to choose the game, which comes from their own estate in the Pennines, or one of their celebrated homemade pies. Be sure to leave room for their proper puddings, which come with lashings of custard - no wonder John Bull was such a stout fellow. It makes you proud.

Savoy Grill

British 🍴🍴🍴🍴

J3

Strand   ⊖ Charing Cross
✉ WC2R 0EU
📞 (020) 7592 1600
www.gordonramsay.com/thesavoygrill

Carte £30/56

[A/C]
[icon]
[icon]
[icon]
[VISA]
[MC]
[AE]
[DC]

The Savoy Grill prepared for the future by going back to its roots. Archives were explored, designers briefed and much money spent, with the result that The Savoy Grill has returned to the traditions that made it famous. As befits the name, it is the charcoal grilling of meats that takes centre stage. Beef from the Lake District and Essex is dry-aged for a minimum of 35 days and offered in an impressive selection of cuts. There's also a daily trolley – it could be beef Wellington one day, leg of lamb the next – and an enticing section entitled 'Roasts, Braises and Pies'. The shiny art deco inspired interior evokes the 1930s, photos of past guests adorn the walls and even the table layout and numbering remains true to the original.

Terroirs 😊

French 🍴

J3

5 William IV St   ⊖ Charing Cross
✉ WC2N 4DW   Closed 25-26 December, 1 January,
📞 (020) 7036 0660   Sunday and bank holidays
www.terroirswinebar.com

Carte £19/31

[icon]
[VISA]
[MC]
[AE]

The ground floor is as busy and as fun as ever but now you can also eat 'Downstairs at Terroirs', where the menu is slightly more substantial and there's a greater variety of cooking methods used; there are also dishes for two such as the roast Landaise chicken. Tables down here are a little bigger which makes sharing easier and, despite being two floors down, it is more atmospheric. If you recognise the banquette seating it's because it comes from Mirabelle. Meanwhile, both levels share the same respect for flavoursome and satisfying French cooking, with added Italian and Spanish influences. The wine list is interesting, varied and well-priced. Service remains a mixed bag and can be of the headless chicken variety.

Belgravia · Victoria

The well-worn cliché 'an area of contrasts' certainly applies to these ill-matched neighbours. To the west, Belgravia equates to fashionable status and elegant, residential calm; to the east, Victoria is a chaotic jumble of backpackers, milling commuters and cheap-and-not-always-so-cheerful hotels. At first sight, you might think there's little to no common ground, but the umbilical cord that unites them is, strange to say, diplomacy and politics. Belgravia's embassies are dotted all around the environs of **Belgrave Square,** while at the furthest end of bustling Victoria Street stands **Parliament Square.**

Belgravia – named after 'beautiful grove' in French - was developed during the nineteenth century by Richard Grosvenor, the second Marquess of Westminster, who employed top architect Thomas Cubitt to come up with something rather fetching for the upper echelons of society. The grandeur of the classical designs has survived for the best part of two centuries, evident in the broad streets and elegant squares, where the rich rub shoulders with the uber-rich beneath the stylish balconies of a consulate or outside a high-end antiques emporium. You can still sample an atmosphere of the village it once was, as long as your idea of a village includes exclusive designer boutiques and even more exclusive mews cottages.

By any stretch of the imagination you'd have trouble thinking of **Victoria** as a village. Its local railway station is one of London's major hubs and its bus station brings in visitors from not only all corners of Britain, but Europe too. Its main 'church', concealed behind office blocks, could hardly be described as humble, either: **Westminster Cathedral** is a grand concoction based on Istanbul's Hagia Sophia, with a view from the top of the bell tower which is breathtaking. From there you can pick out other hidden charms of the area: the dramatic headquarters of Channel 4 TV, the revolving sign famously leading into New Scotland Yard, and the neat little Christchurch Gardens, burial site of Colonel Blood, last man to try and steal the Crown Jewels. Slightly easier for the eye to locate are the grand designs of **Westminster Abbey,** crowning glory and resting place of most of England's kings and queens, and the neo-gothic pile of the **Houses of Parliament.** Victoria may be an eclectic mix of people and architectural styles, but its handy position as a kind of epicentre of the Westminster Village makes it a great place for political chit-chat. And the place to go for that is The Speaker, a pub in Great Peter Street, named after the Commons' centuries-old peacekeeper and 'referee'. It's a backstreet gem, where it's not unknown for a big cheese from the House to be filmed over a pint.

visitlondon.com

Winston Churchill is someone who would have been quite at home holding forth at The Speaker, and half a mile away in King Charles Street, based within the **Cabinet War Rooms** – the secret underground HQ of the war effort - is the Churchill Museum, stuffed full of all things Churchillian. However, if your passion is more the easel and the brush, then head down to the river where another great institution of the area, **Tate Britain,** gazes out over the Thames. Standing where the grizzly Millbank Penitentiary once festered, it offers, after the National Gallery, the best collection of historical art in London. There's loads of space for the likes of Turner and Constable, while Hogarth, Gainsborough and Blake are well represented, too. Artists from the modern era are also here, with Freud and Hockney on show, and there are regular installations showcasing upwardly mobile British talent. All of which may give you the taste for a trip east along the river to Tate Modern. This can be done every twenty minutes courtesy of the Tate-to-Tate boat service, which handily stops enroute at the London Eye, and, even more handily, sports eye-catching Damien Hirst décor and a cool, shiny bar.

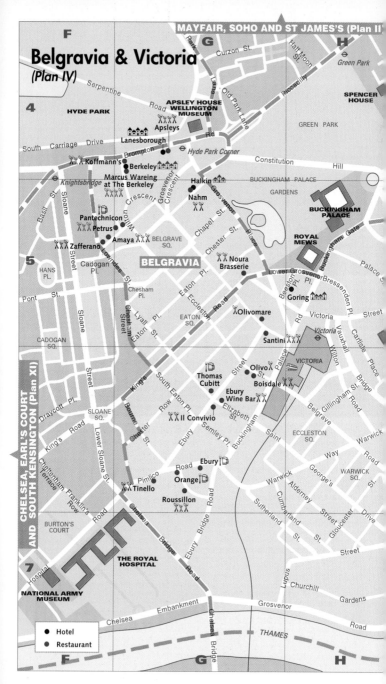

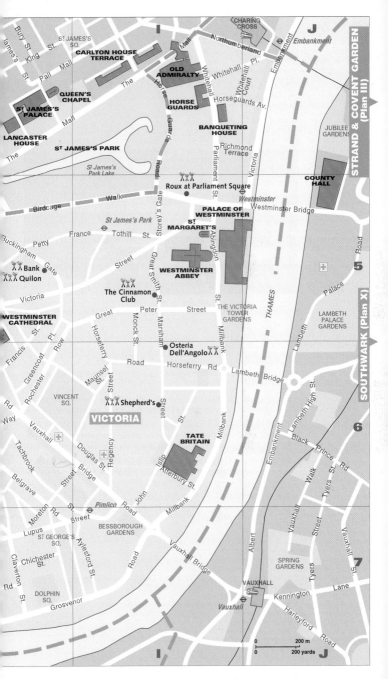

Amaya ✿

F5

Halkin Arcade, 19 Motcomb St
✉ SW1X 8JT
☎ (020) 7823 1166
www.realindianfood.com

⊖ Knightsbridge
Closed 25 December

Menu £29/42 – Carte £36/70

A/C

VISA
MC
AE

Amaya

Since its opening back in 2004, Amaya has built up a tremendous following thanks to the quality and consistency of its food. The tandoor, the tawa griddle and the sigri charcoal grill are all used to great effect and the spicing enhances the natural flavours of the ingredients. Dishes arrive as and when they are ready; to best experience the variety and range of the menu, order a number of small plates to share and then finish with a curry or biryani – or else plump for the Gourmet or Tasting menus where the selection has already been made for you. Seafood plays a large part, with rock oysters, grouper and prawns competing with the ever-popular tandoori monkfish. The delicate and flavoursome lamb chops are another dish that almost everyone seems to order and one shouldn't ignore the imaginative vegetable dishes. The interior is suitably bright and colourful, with the raised section nearest the open kitchen offering the best seats. Service can be a touch muted at times; a possible consequence of the sheer volume of business.

First Course
- Tarragon and turmeric chicken tikka.
- Griddled fillet of lemon sole with coconut and herb crust.

Main Course
- Duck grilled wtih tamarind glaze.
- Masala lobster in the shell.

Dessert
- Mango brûlée.
- Lime tart.

Apsleys ✿

Hyde Park Corner ⊖ Hyde Park Corner
✉ SW1X 7TA
✆ (020) 7333 7254
www.apsleysrestaurant.com

Menu £35 (lunch) – Carte £59/81

The Lanesborough

BELGRAVIA & VICTORIA ▶ PLAN IV

Heinz Beck is a German-born chef responsible for some pretty exceptional Italian cooking in his restaurant La Pergola in Rome. Apsleys is very much his creation and he is actively involved in the operation, although he does have a head chef who is extremely committed and passionate about his craft. The sourcing of the finest ingredients is the starting point; vegetables are imported from Italy but meat and fish are from much nearer to home. Proving that not all Italian food has to be of the rustic, thrown-together variety, the cooking displays a deft, light touch and there are subtle hints of innovation, such as in one of the signature dishes, carbonara fagottelli. Designed by the ubiquitous Adam Tihany, the room is elegant and undeniably opulent, but its grandeur never intimidates, thanks largely to the assured serving team who are adept at putting their guests at ease. They are also well-versed in the menu and offer fuller explanations, which is just as well as the menu descriptions are understated to say the least.

First Course
- Fish crudo.
- Skate with caper vinaigrette and cherry tomatoes.

Main Course
- Carbonara fagottelli.
- Suckling pig.

Dessert
- Chocolate soufflé with vanilla and raspberry.
- Coffee surprise.

Bank

Modern European ✕✕

45 Buckingham Gate
✉ SW1E 6BS
✆ (020) 7630 6644
www.bankrestaurants.com

⊖ St James's Park
Closed Sunday and bank holidays
– booking essential at lunch

Menu £38 – Carte £35/80

Unlike certain financial institutions, this bank seems to know what it's doing. It occupies a generous space within the Crowne Plaza Hotel but, as it has its own street entrance, feels very much like a stand-alone restaurant. It's bright and breezy inside, with the long Zander bar running down the length of one wall and the conservatory overlooking a pleasant little courtyard garden. The menu is an international affair, with the kitchen travelling to all parts, but it's clearly laid out. Steaks are a popular choice; there are plenty of pasta dishes and whether you like your fish in a pie or cooked with Thai herbs, there's something for you. The biggest surprise is the thoroughly cheerful and unexpectedly enthusiastic service.

Boisdale

Scottish ✕✕

15 Eccleston St
✉ SW1W 9LX
✆ (020) 7730 6922
www.boisdale.co.uk

⊖ Victoria
Closed 1 week Christmas,
Saturday lunch and Sunday

Carte £29/77

Acres of tartan, whiskies galore, haggis, mash and neeps - Boisdale couldn't be more Scottish if it sang 'Scots Wha Hae' and did the Highland Fling. Owner Ranald Macdonald bought various parts of the building at different times, hence the charmingly higgledy-piggledy layout. The original Auld Restaurant is the more characterful; the Macdonald Bar has more buzz and nightly live jazz and a large cigar selection add to the masculine feel. The menu features plenty of Scottish produce, from Orkney herring to Shetland scallops, but the stand-outs are the four varieties of smoked salmon, followed by the 28-day aged Aberdeenshire cuts of beef. Ignore the lacklustre tomato and watercress garnish and just savour the quality of the meat.

The Cinnamon Club

I5

30-32 Great Smith St
✉ SW1P 3BU
☏ (020) 7222 2555
www.cinnamonclub.com

⊖ St James's Park
Closed 26 December,
1 January and Sunday

Menu £22 (lunch) – Carte £40/75

A/C ⬚ 🎭 VISA Ⓜ️Ⓒ AE Ⓞ

The Grade II listed former Westminster library may seem an unlikely setting for an Indian restaurant but it works surprisingly well. The shelves of books are still there on the mezzanine level of the large main room where the action is, although the smaller front room has better air-conditioning. There are two bars - the one downstairs is the livelier. A variety of menus are on offer and prices can get quite steep but the cooking clearly displays ambition and innovation. Many of the ingredients may be more European, like Herdwick lamb or Anjou pigeon, but the cooking techniques, colours and spices are resolutely Indian. Staff are on the ball, as you'd expect from somewhere serving over 200 people twice a day.

Il Convivio

G6

143 Ebury St
✉ SW1W 9QN
☏ (020) 7730 4099
www.ilconvivio.co.uk

⊖ **Sloane Square**
Closed Christmas-New Year
and Sunday

Carte £32/51

A/C ⬚ VISA Ⓜ️Ⓒ AE

If only passing by, you'll find yourself being drawn in by the appealing façade of this handsome Georgian townhouse – and there's usually an eager welcome to boot, whether you're a regular or first-timer. Inside is equally pleasant, with Dante's poetry embossed on the wall to remind you you're in an Italian restaurant and a retractable roof at the back, under which sit the best tables. All pasta is made on the top floor of the house; the squid ink spaghetti with lobster is a menu staple. Dishes are artfully presented but not so showy as to compromise the flavours. Artisanal cheeses are carefully selected and looked after, while service is confident and able. Using the private dining room allows you to imagine being the owner of the house.

Ebury

G6

Modern European 🍴🍺

11 Pimlico Rd
✉ SW1W 8NA
☎ (020) 7730 6784
www.theebury.co.uk

⊖ Sloane Square.

Carte £30/39

A/C
☀
VISA
MC

Grab a passing waiter to get yourself seated otherwise they'll assume you've just come for a drink at the bar and will ignore you. Once you've got your feet under one of the low-slung tables, however, you'll find everything moves up a gear. This is a rather smart affair and provides an object lesson in how to draw in punters. That means a varied menu, from burger to black bream, assorted salads that show some thought, three vegetarian dishes and main courses that display a degree of originality. Add to that a conscientious kitchen, a wine list that offers plenty by the glass and carafe, and weekend brunch that goes on until 4pm and it's little wonder the place is always so busy. The waiters come with French accents and self-confidence.

Ebury Wine Bar

G6

Modern European 🍴🍴

139 Ebury St.
✉ SW1W 9QU
☎ (020) 7730 5447
www.eburyrestaurant.co.uk

⊖ Victoria
Closed 22 December-2 January

Menu £22 (lunch and early dinner) – Carte £31/39

A/C
☀
VISA
MC
AE

There are probably many reasons why Ebury Wine Bar has been going strong for over 50 years but likeability and adaptability must surely be two. It has an endearing honesty that is largely down to the eagerness of the longstanding staff, and changing habits have meant that the focus is now more on the food than the wine; even the bar offers a decent snack menu. Go through to the dining room, with its trompe l'oiel, and you'll find a kitchen that brings imaginative international influences to some dishes but is equally happy doing the classics such as lamb cutlets or liver and bacon. The set menu includes a glass of champagne; there are separate dairy and gluten free menus and the wine list is thoughtfully compiled and keenly priced.

Koffmann's

G4

Wilton Pl. ⊖ Knightsbridge
✉ SW1X 7RL
☎ (020) 7235 1010
www.the-berkeley.co.uk

Menu £26 (lunch) – Carte £51/73

[A/C]
🚗
☀
VISA
MC
AE

Retirement isn't for everyone and, it appears, it wasn't for Pierre Koffmann. After years of rumour and following the success of his 'pop-up' restaurant in Selfridges, one of London's most fêted chefs came back to the stove and returned to his previous address; although this time he's on the other side of the building. Those with fond memories of his classic dishes will enjoy getting reacquainted with the scallops with squid ink or the braised pig's trotter. This time around his food stays truer to his Gascon roots, although the gutsy flavours can sometimes be compromised in the dish's final execution. The dining room's off-white colour and textured walls add to the light, fresh feel; the further in you go, the better the table.

Nahm

G5

5 Halkin St ⊖ Hyde Park Corner
✉ SW1X 7DJ Closed lunch Saturday and Sunday
☎ (020) 7333 1234 – booking advisable
www.halkin.como.bz

Menu £25/60 – Carte £45/60

[A/C]
⟨⟩
VISA
MC
AE
①

An appealing mix of copper tones, wood and candlelight, along with an understated hint of Asian design, allows the restaurant to blend effortlessly into the slick and stylish surroundings of the boutique Halkin hotel in which it is located. The cuisine served here is based on Royal Thai traditions and the flavours and combinations of ingredients are authentic. However, the cooking has lost some of its essential vitality, which is one of the fundamental elements of Thai cuisine, and dishes can sometimes be let down by careless execution. Perhaps it was the opening of another Nahm, this time in Bangkok itself, that lead to the slight drop in the standard here at the original outpost.

Marcus Wareing at The Berkeley ✿ ✿

French XXXX

G4

Wilton Pl. ✉ SW1X 7RL
✆ (020) 7235 1200
www.marcus-wareing.com

Menu £38/98

⊖ **Knightsbridge**
Closed 1 January,
Saturday lunch and Sunday

A/C

VISA
MC
AE

Marcus Wareing at The Berkeley

Thanks to Koffmann's on its north side, The Berkeley is book-ended by two good restaurants. On his side of the hotel, Marcus Wareing delivers a formal dining experience involving confident and expertly constructed dishes, in surroundings that are quite sombre yet undoubtedly comfortable. He remains a chef who appreciates the importance of using the best quality produce and, as such, will treat a carrot with as much respect as he does a lobster. His 'Prestige' and 'Gourmand' menus allow the diner to sample the full diversity of his cooking, which is mostly French in its influences and techniques but is not afraid of a little originality here and there. Indeed, Marcus' Head Chef, James Knappett, has brought a slightly bolder and more daring approach to some of the dishes. Desserts are a strength of the kitchen and, if you are one of those who likes to see how it's all done, then consider the Chef's Table, which is one of the best in town. Service is structured and deliberate but now comes with a little more personality than seen in previous years.

First Course

- Layered foie gras with prune and Armagnac purée.
- Langoustine, black pudding, clementine, leeks.

Main Course

- Best end of lamb with pickled cucumber and pink peppercorn yoghurt.
- Cornish sea bass, cauliflower, almonds, polonaise.

Dessert

- Chocolate moelleux, salted caramel centre and banana ice cream.
- Iced lime mousse, sweet and sour pineapple, soft baked meringue.

Noura Brasserie

G5

Lebanese ✗✗

16 Hobart Pl.
✉ SW1W 0HH
✆ (020) 7235 9444
www.noura.co.uk

⊖ Victoria

Menu £18/45 – Carte £24/40

[A/C]
[clock]
[sun]
VISA
MC
AE
[DC]

The Belgravia branch was the first of the Lebanese Noura restaurants to appear on these shores and such is its appeal that it's an all-day operation. You're greeted by the enticing sight of sweet, sticky pastries and it's here at the bar where you can grab a quick bite. The majority go through to the large, lustrous restaurant where there's seating for over 100; the vast kitchen occupies the whole of the basement. Everything is prepared from scratch so the food is fresh and zingy and hummus comes with authentic oomph. Platters and mezzes are the way to go but be sure to finish with the pastries or the homemade ice creams, the flavours of which could include rosewater or clotted cream. Staff have a certain seen-it-all insouciance.

Olivo

G6

Italian ✗

21 Eccleston St
✉ SW1W 9LX
✆ (020) 7730 2505
www.olivorestaurant.com

⊖ Victoria
Closed lunch Saturday-Sunday
and bank holidays

Menu £28 (lunch) – Carte dinner £25/32

[A/C]
VISA
MC
AE

Despite the constant banging of the front door, the somewhat monosyllabic waitress and the permanently aloof manager, Olivo is one of those places that's always bursting with bonhomie. The restaurant is simply kitted out in blues and yellows and its infectious atmosphere is most evident at lunch. It celebrates all things Sardinian, so start with a glass of Vernaccia and carta di musica bread and finish with a glass of Mirto after you've had the sebada cheese fritters for dessert. Lunch is set-priced and dinner à la carte; both are nicely balanced and appealing affairs, with the 'spaghetti alla bottarga' being an unquestionable highlight. The wine list is concise but decent value and bottles can be bought at nearby Olivino.

Olivomare

Seafood ✗

10 Lower Belgrave St
✉ SW1W 0LJ
℘ (020) 7730 9022
www.olivorestaurants.com

⊖ **Victoria**
Closed bank holidays

Carte £29/38

Olivomare is a restaurant that makes you want to live by the sea and, looking at the produce in their shop next door, that sea would be the Tyrrhenian. The room's piscatorial decoration – a sort of Philippe Starck gone fishin' – works well, especially when it's so cleverly lit. The menu changes every fortnight and has a Sardinian base to it. The kitchen buys the freshest fish, treats it with respect and uses traditional recipes. The fritto misto is excellent; razor clams and octopus have quite a following and the spaghetti with bottarga or half a lobster are favourites too. Be sure to end with gelato, which is also available in the shop, Olivino. Service would be better if they took their blinkers off and looked around more.

Orange

Modern European 🍴🍺

37 Pimlico Rd
✉ SW1W 8NE
℘ (020) 7881 9844
www.theorange.co.uk

⊖ **Sloane Square.**

Carte £24/41

The Belgravia-Victoria-Pimlico quarter is clearly working for the team behind The Thomas Cubitt and Pantechnicon Rooms because their latest pub, The Orange, is within shouting distance of their other two and appears to be equally busy. There are a couple of differences: this pub has bedrooms, nicely decorated and named after the local streets, and the food is a little more down-to-earth and family-friendly. Pizza in the bar from their wood-fired oven is always a popular choice; there's Film Night on Mondays and, unusually, the first floor restaurant is noisier than the bar. The building's stucco-fronted façade may be quite grand but the colonial feel inside and the particularly friendly service create a pleasantly laid-back atmosphere.

Osteria Dell' Angolo

Italian XX

47 Marsham St.
✉ SW1P 3DR
✆ (020) 3268 1077
www.osteriadellangolo.co.uk

⊖ St. James's Park
Closed Easter, 20 August-2 September,
24 December-3 January, Saturday
lunch, Sunday and bank holidays

Menu £21 (lunch) – Carte £32/39

In over 30 years in London, Claudio Pulze has opened more than 50 restaurants so you could say he knows what he's doing. One of his most recent ventures is this Italian restaurant opposite the Home Office which is altogether smarter than the name suggests. It's bright and sunny inside, with a front bar; larger groups should ask for tables 14 or 15. The enthusiastic team is run by an effusive manager who recognises all his regulars. There is a subtle Tuscan element to the cooking but the kitchen is also prone to adding a little playfulness or doing a little reinterpreting of the classics. Pastas and breads, made downstairs, are very good. The wine list is well-priced and includes a decent choice by the glass.

Pantechnicon

Gastropub

10 Motcomb St
✉ SW1X 8LA
✆ (020) 7730 6074
www.thepantechnicon.com

⊖ Knightsbridge
Closed 25 December-1 January

Carte £32/46

The name 'Pantechnicon' either refers to a large removal wagon or the antique repository which once sat on Motcomb Street until it was destroyed by fire in the 1870s. It's no clearer inside, as you'll find both sepia photos of assorted removal vehicles as well as a painting depicting the fire. But one thing is certain: this is the antithesis of a spit 'n' sawdust pub. The ground floor is first-come-first-served and is always lively but upstairs is an altogether more gracious affair, designed for those who like a little formality with their pheasant. The cooking is traditional but with a twist. Oysters are a perennial; there's a decent salad selection and they set their stall by the traceability of their mature Scottish steaks.

Pétrus ✿

Modern European XXX

1 Kinnerton St
✉ SW1X 8EA
✆ (020) 7592 1609
www.gordonramsay.com/petrus

⊖ Knightsbridge
Closed 25 December and Sunday

Menu £30/60

A/C

VISA
M/C
AE

Gordon Ramsay Holdings

Following his divorce from Marcus Wareing, Gordon Ramsay came away with custody of the name Pétrus and he used the appellation for this smart Belgravia restaurant, opened in 2010, in challengingly close proximity to the premises of his former protégé. It's attractively decorated in understated tones of silver, oyster and – to add warmth and as a nod to the name – claret. Tables are immaculately dressed and service is under the watchful eye of an experienced team who never let things get too reverential. Downstairs is the 'show' kitchen with its horseshoe shaped chef's table, for those whose enjoyment of a meal is sharpened by watching a large brigade of chefs – in this case around 14 – beavering away in front of them. Sceptical diners should initially try lunch, when they'll find a set menu that won't break the bank. There are also vegetarian and chef's menus alongside the appealing à la carte of French-based dishes. In a break with tradition and in a nod to Thomas Keller, the cheese trolley is replaced by a single cheese offered as a 'savoury pudding'.

First Course

- Langoustine tails with confit chicken leg, baby artichokes and buttered leeks.
- Roasted quail breast with crispy quail's egg, parmesan polenta and Swiss chard.

Main Course

- Best end of lamb with spring vegetables and a thyme jus.
- Fillet of lemon sole with clams, courgettes and champagne velouté.

Dessert

- Chocolate sphere with milk ice cream and honeycomb.
- Star anise crème brûlée with caramelised pear and liquorice.

Quilon ✿

Quilon

H5

41 Buckingham Gate
✉ SW1E 6AF
✆ (020) 7821 1899
www.quilon.co.uk

⊖ St James's Park
Closed 25 December and
Saturday lunch

Menu £24/41 – Carte dinner £45/60

A/C
☀
VISA
MC
AE
①

BELGRAVIA & VICTORIA ▶ PLAN IV

The flower-filled window boxes and the mellow lighting draw you in while an effusive welcome reassures you that you've made the right choice. Chef Sriram Aylur and his brigade are a committed and enthusiastic lot who understand the importance of consistency in their cooking. Their menu is influenced by India's southwest coast and changes with the seasons. Much of the produce is from the UK but spices are imported from India and ground in the kitchen. Fish is naturally a strength, whether in a broth, a curry or roasted in a plantain leaf, and, as in Kerala, there are plenty of vegetarian dishes. The kitchen's light touch is evident while the spicing is assured and balanced and rice and breads are prepared with equal care. It is also clear that the serving team enjoy a good relationship with the kitchen – which is not something that happens in all restaurants – so one can happily mix and match starters or even have a smaller sized main courses if one requires a little flexibility. The room is quite large but one never feels at sea.

First Course

- Crab cakes with curry leaves, ginger and green chillies.
- Lotus stem and soya bean chop.

Main Course

- Seared fillet of monkfish in a shrimp, scallop and mustard sauce.
- Malabar lamb biryani.

Dessert

- Rice pudding with rose ice cream.
- Bibinca and dodhol.

Roussillon

G6

French XXX

16 St Barnabas St
✉ SW1W 8PE
✆ (020) 7730 5550
www.roussillon.co.uk

⊖ **Sloane Square**
Closed 25 December, Saturday lunch
and Sunday, restricted opening on
Bank Holidays

Menu £35/65

A/C
88
VISA
MC
AE

Circumstances force even the most dependable of restaurants to change. In 2010, Roussillon faced the upheaval caused by the departure of their longstanding chef, and inevitably it will take a while for it to find its feet once again. However, this comfortable and grown up restaurant has always attracted a loyal local following who appreciate that their 'hidden jewel' keeps itself below the fashion radar. The cooking is currently a little less French in its influence than it once was and therefore somewhat at odds with the restaurant's name. However, as we went to print, news came that a talented chef will be moving here from Wales. He will hopefully breathe new life into this discreet and well run restaurant.

Roux at Parliament Square

I5

French XXX

RICS, Parliament Sq.
✉ SW1P 3AD
✆ (020) 7334 3737
www.rouxatparliamentsquare.co.uk

⊖ **Westminster**
Closed 23 December-3 January,
Saturday,
Sunday and bank holidays

Menu £25 (lunch) – Carte £39/55

A/C
⌂
VISA
MC
AE
①

In this part of Westminster, chartered surveyors and Members of Parliament have never been faced with a plethora of restaurants from which to choose, but the opening of Roux at Parliament Square has helped fill the void. Knowing that the Roux is Michel, of Le Gavroche fame, means that the cooking was never going to be anything other than intricate and visually impressive – but while the base is French, the kitchen does have a lighter than expected touch and flavours are contemporary. The decoration is cool and comfortable, with plenty of natural light flooding through the Georgian windows. Service comes from a well-trained team but is not without personality and there is a particularly attractive private dining room in the library.

Santini

Italian XXX

29 Ebury St
✉ SW1W 0NZ
☎ (020) 7730 4094
www.santini-restaurant.com

⊖ **Victoria**
Closed Easter, 24-26 December,
1 January and lunch
Saturday-Sunday

Menu £25 (lunch) – Carte £32/54

Like many of its bronzed customers, Santini really comes into its own in the summer: the white walls and marble flooring are crisp and cooling and the terrace must be one of the largest around. Family-owned since 1984, it has never been the cheapest Italian around but then this was never the sort of place that pretended to be accessible to all and the service is decidedly old-school; the type that intimidated you when you were young. But the food, with its mild Venetian accent, is very good. Homemade pastas are excellent and the zabaglione is a gloriously rich concoction. Further evidence of the restaurant's self-belief is in the number of times its name appears in dishes, so you can follow insalata Santini with branzino Santini.

Shepherd's

British XXX

Marsham Ct., Marsham St.
✉ SW1P 4LA
☎ (020) 7834 9552
www.langansrestaurants.co.uk

⊖ **Pimlico**
Closed Saturday, Sunday
and bank holidays
– booking essential

Carte £22/26

Looking at the number of shiny pates and pin-striped suits that pile into Shepherd's for lunch you'd be forgiven for thinking that 'Blair's Babes' never left much of a legacy. This is a classic, old-school blokey institution that could show some of those new restaurants a thing or two. For starters, it runs on wheels and gives the punters what they want. The atmosphere is animated throughout, but the booths are the best places to sit. The menu is a combination of classic dishes and brasserie favourites but your best bet is to head for those bits of the menu that read like a UKIP manifesto – the fiercely British specialities, like the daily roast or the Dover Sole, followed by an indulgent dessert like a sponge pudding.

Thomas Cubitt

G6

44 Elizabeth St
✉ SW1W 9PA
✆ (020) 7730 6060
www.thethomascubitt.co.uk

⊖ **Sloane Square.**
Closed Christmas and New Year –
booking essential

Carte £29/49

The Thomas Cubitt is a pub of two halves: on the ground floor it's perennially busy and you can't book which means that if you haven't arrived by 7pm then you're too late to get a table. However, you can reserve a table upstairs, in a dining room that's a model of civility and tranquillity. Here, service comes courtesy of a young team where the girls are chatty and the men unafraid of corduroy. Downstairs you get fish and chips; here you get pan-fried fillet of brill with oyster beignet and truffled chips. The cooking is certainly skilled, quite elaborate in its construction and prettily presented. So, take your pick: upstairs can get a little pricey but is ideal for entertaining the in-laws; if out with friends then crowd in downstairs.

Tinello

G6

87 Pimlico Rd
✉ SW1W 8PH
✆ (020) 7730 3663
www.tinello.co.uk

⊖ **Sloane Square**
Closed Sunday and bank hoildays
– booking essential at dinner

Carte £38/44

Italian restaurants have always thrived in this neighbourhood but it's no bad thing for a newcomer to shake things up and that's exactly what Tinello is doing. It is run by two Italian brothers, Max and Federico, who previously worked as sommelier and head chef respectively at Locanda Locatelli. The majority of the menu leans on their native Tuscany for inspiration and this is especially evident in the tempting antipasti or 'small eats' section. Pasta is exemplary and main courses ooze confidence. Service is undertaken with a refreshing earnestness and the sleek restaurant is spread over two floors; the ground floor is more fun, but if you are downstairs you do get to see the kitchen in action through the glass windows.

Zafferano ✿

F5

15 Lowndes St
✉ SW1X 9EY
✆ (020) 7235 5800
www.zafferanorestaurant.co.uk

⊖ **Knightsbridge**
Booking essential

Menu £26/45 – Carte £36/52

A/C
🖧
88
🕜
☼
VISA
MC
AE

Zafferano

Such is the enduring nature of Zafferano's popularity that it is always busy, almost from the moment they unlock the front door each day. We all like a bit of bustle and bonhomie in a restaurant and this place doesn't disappoint, although the waiters do have a propensity to charge around as though their pants are on fire. If you favour less frenzy then ask to sit in the smaller end room. The deli may not have worked but the bar has proved a big success - regulars sometimes just pop in there for a plate of pasta. In fact, a plate of pasta should be ordered wherever you're sitting as it is a real strength of the kitchen, which operates under the expert guidance of Andy Needham - who proves that Yorkshire doesn't just produce great cricketers. His menu provides an object lesson in how to satisfy your customers: dishes are reassuringly recognisable yet also seasonal and are supplemented with a few daily specials. The assured cooking ensures that natural flavours are to the fore. The wine list also continues to grow, with the recent addition of more choice from southern parts.

First Course

- Octopus salad with potatoes and olives.
- Bresaola della Valtellina with rocket and goat's cheese.

Main Course

- Rib of beef with bone marrow.
- Shellfish and squid with tomato and sweet chilli.

Dessert

- Tiramisu.
- Hazelnut parfait with fresh mango and passion fruit.

Regent's Park · Marylebone

The neighbourhood north of chaotic Oxford Street is actually a rather refined place where shoppers like to venture for the smart boutiques, and where idlers like to saunter for the graceful parkland acres full of rose gardens and quiet corners. In fact, Marylebone and Regent's Park go rather well together, a moneyed village with a wonderful park for its back garden.

Marylebone may now exude a fashionable status, but its history tells a very different tale. Thousands used to come here to watch executions at Tyburn gallows, a six hundred year spectacle that stopped in the late eighteenth century. Tyburn stream was covered over, and the area's modern name came into being as a contraction of St Mary by the Bourne, the parish church. Nowadays the people who flock here come to gaze at less ghoulish sights, though some of the inhabitants of the eternally popular Madame Tussauds deserved no better fate than the gallows. South across the busy Marylebone Road, the preponderance of swish restaurants and snazzy specialist shops announces your arrival at **Marylebone High Street.** There are patisseries, chocolatiers, cheese shops and butchers at every turn, nestling alongside smart places to eat and drink. At St Marylebone Church, each Saturday heralds a posh market called Cabbages & Frocks, where artisan food meets designer clothing in a charming garden. Further down, the century old Daunt Books has been described as London's most beautiful bookshop: it has long oak galleries beneath graceful conservatory skylights. Close by, the quaintly winding Marylebone Lane boasts some truly unique shops like tiny emporium The Button Queen, which sells original Art Deco, Victorian and Edwardian buttons. In complete contrast, just down the road from here is the mighty **Wigmore Hall,** an art nouveau gem with great acoustics and an unerringly top-notch classical agenda that can be appreciated at rock-bottom prices. Meanwhile, art lovers can indulge an eclectic fix at the **Wallace Collection** in **Manchester Square,** where paintings by the likes of Titian and Velazquez rub shoulders with Sevres porcelain and grand Louis XIV furniture.

Regent's Park – an idyllic Georgian oasis stretching off into London's northern suburbs - celebrates its two hundredth birthday in 2011. Before architect John Nash and his sponsor The Prince Regent gave it its much-loved geometric makeover, it had been farming land, and prior to that, one of Henry VIII's hunting grounds. His spirit lives on, in the sense that various activities are catered for, from tennis courts to a running track. And there are animals too, albeit not roaming free, at **London Zoo,** in the park's northerly section. Most people,

C. Eymenier / MICHELIN

though, come here to while away an hour or two around the boating lake or amble the Inner Circle which contains **Queen Mary's Gardens** and their enchanting bowers of fragrant roses. Others come for a summer sojourn to the Open Air Theatre where taking in a performance of 'A Midsummer Night's Dream' is very much *de rigueur*. The Regent's Canal provides another fascinating element to the park. You can follow its peaceful waters along a splendid walk from the **Little Venice** houseboats in the west, past the golden dome of the **London Central Mosque,** and on into the north-west confines of Regent's Park as it snakes through

London Zoo, before it heads off towards Camden Lock. On the other side of Prince Albert Road, across from the zoo, the scenic glory takes on another dimension with a climb up Primrose Hill. Named after the grassy promontory that sets it apart from its surrounds, to visitors this is a hill with one of the best panoramas in the whole of London; to locals (ie, actors, pop stars, media darlings and the city set) it's an ultra fashionable place to live with pretty Victorian terraces and accordingly sky-high prices. Either way you look at it (or from it), it's a great place to be on a sunny day with the breeze in your hair.

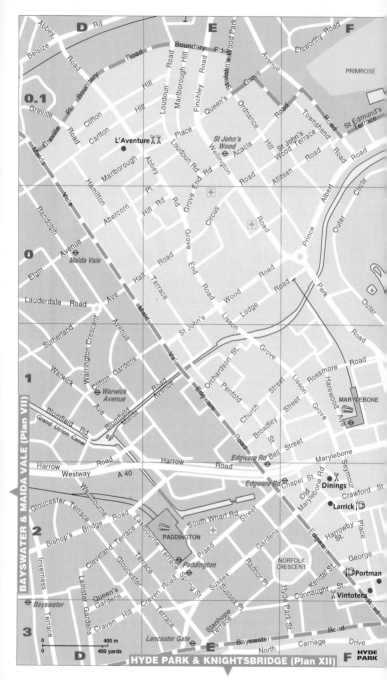

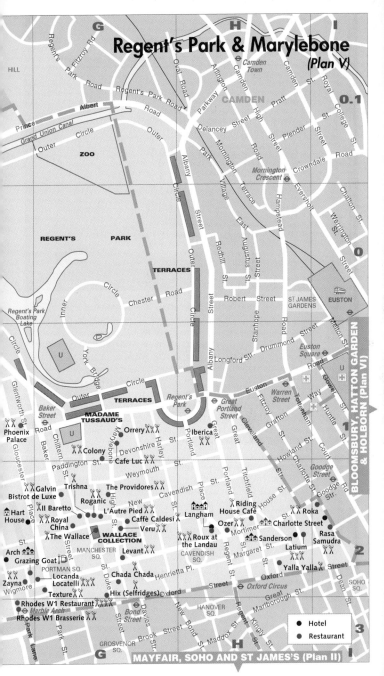

Regent's Park & Marylebone
(Plan V)

G   **H**   **I**

HILL

Prince   Albert   Road

Grand Union Canal

Outer   Circle

ZOO

REGENT'S   **PARK**

Regent's Park Road

Regent's Park Road

Fitzroy Rd

Oval Road

Arlington Road

Camden Town

Camden High Street

Camden Road

Royal College St

Chalton St.

Pratt Street

CAMDEN   **O.1**

Delancey Street

Parkway

Mornington Street

Plender Street

Crowndale Road

Mornington Crescent

Albany Street

Park Village East

Augustus St.

Redhill St.

Mornington Terrace

Hampstead Road

Eversholt Street

Wellington St.

Arlington Road

O

TERRACES

Outer   Circle

Robert   Street

ST JAMES GARDENS

Stanhope St.

Chester Road

Regent's Park Boating Lake

Inner   Circle

U

Circle

York Bridge

Outer   Circle

TERRACES

Baker Street

MADAME TUSSAUD'S

Chiltern St.

Baker   St.

Glentworth St.

Gloucester   Pl.

U

Regent's Park

Longford St.

Drummond Street

Albany Street

Robert Street

Stanhope Street

EUSTON

Melton St.

Euston Square

Euston Road

Gower Street

Tottenham Court Road

Hampstead Road

U

BLOOMSBURY, HATTON GARDEN & HOLBORN (Plan VI)

1

✗ **Phoenix Palace**
✗✗ **Orrery** ✗✗✗
✗✗ **Colony**
✗✗ **Cafe Luc**

Devonshire St.

Paddington St.

Weymouth St.

Marylebone High St.

Harley St.

Portland Place

Great Portland Street

Great Portland Street

Iberica ✗

Warren Street

Fitzroy Street

Grafton Way

Cleveland Street

Howland St.

Charlotte Street

Huntley St.

Gower St.

Goodge Street

Goodge Str.

Galvin ✗✗ **Bistrot de Luxe**
✗ **Trishna**
✗✗ **Il Baretto**
Roganic ✗✗
✗✗ **Royal China**
✗ **The Wallace**

The Providores ✗✗
L'Autre Pied ✗✗
Caffè Caldesi ✗
Veru ✗

New Cavendish St.

Langham

Portland Place

Titchfield St.

Mortimer St.

Margaret St.

Riding House Café ✗
Ozer ✗
✗✗ **Roux at the Landau**

Charlotte Street ✗
Sanderson ✗✗

Roka ✗ ✗

Latium ✗✗
Rasa Samudra ✗✗

2

Hart House
✗✗ **Arch**
● **Grazing Goat**

Manchester St.

MANCHESTER SQ.

WALLACE COLLECTION

Levant ✗✗

CAVENDISH SQ.

Duke St.

Henrietta Pl.

Regent St.

Yalla Yalla ✗ Street

SOHO SQ.

Zayna ✗✗
Locanda Locatelli ●
Texture ✗✗ ✗✗✗

Chada Chada ✗

Hix (Selfridges) ✗

Wigmore St.

PORTMAN SQ.

Portman St.

Oxford   Street   **Oxford Circus**

HANOVER SQ.

Great Marlborough St.

Kingly St.

3

Rhodes W1 Restaurant ✗✗✗
Marble Arch
Rhodes W1 Brasserie ✗✗

Park Lane

Bond Street

Davies St.

New Bond Street

Brook Street

Maddox St.

GROSVENOR SQ.

H

●	Hotel
●	Restaurant

MAYFAIR, SOHO AND ST JAMES'S (Plan II)

L'Autre Pied ✿

Modern European ✗✗

G2

5-7 Blandford St. ✉ W1U 3DB
✆ (020) 7486 9696
www.lautrepied.co.uk

⊖ Bond Street
▶ Plan V
Closed 23 December-5
January and Sunday dinner

**Menu £23 (lunch and early dinner) –
Carte £39/47**

A/C
VISA
MC
AE

L'Autre Pied

Shane Osborn's departure from the kitchens of Pied à Terre resulted in promotion for Marcus Eaves, who'd made a name for himself here at L'Autre Pied, its baby sister. His place, in turn, was taken by young Irishman Andy McFadden, another Pied à Terre 'old boy', who was working in the Netherlands when he got the call from owner David Moore, inviting him to take over the reins of this now well-established Marylebone Village restaurant. His menu reads particularly well and dishes are made up of appealingly complementary ingredients, such as lemon sole with Jersey Royals and cucumber velouté or Best End of lamb with artichokes and aubergine purée. Flavours are well-defined and dishes often display pleasingly contrasting textures; the kitchen also adds just enough touches of originality to keep things interesting but doesn't try to be too clever. The restaurant is a lively spot in the evening, with the best tables by the window – try to avoid the middle section as it's a bit of a thoroughfare.

First Course

- Cauliflower risotto, scallops and almonds with lemongrass sauce.
- Chicken oysters, Grapes, Morteau sausage, tomato and verjus dressing.

Main Course

- Pan-fried cod with carrot and star anise purée and tarragon sauce.
- Pressed belly of suckling pig, tender stem broccoli, bergamot lemon purée and pink grapefruit sauce.

Dessert

- Ginger mousse, vanilla poached apricots and honey ice cream.
- Stawberry and macadamia nut crumble, strawberry sorbet and basil ice cream.

L'Aventure

DO/1

French 𝗫𝗫

3 Blenheim Terr
✉ NW8 0EH
✆ (020) 7624 6232

⊖ St John's Wood
▶ Plan V
Closed first week January, Saturday lunch,
Sunday and bank holidays

Menu £21/39

Tailor-made for anyone with a sound grasp of French wishing to impress a date - the menu is written entirely in French so politely decline the waiter's offer of a quick translation and wait for the admiring looks. What's more, if it's a warm day, you'll be sitting in the enchanting front terrace where the shrubs are covered in twinkly lights. This is a charming neighbourhood restaurant with a cosy and warm interior, owned and run by the delightful Catherine who'll make you feel you're being unfaithful if you don't return. The set menu is good value at lunch but pricier at dinner when the well-heeled locals come out. Expect the French bourgeois classics, from artichoke salad to rack of lamb and an ile flottante to finish.

Il Baretto

G2

Italian 𝗫

43 Blandford St.
✉ W1U 7HF
✆ (020) 7486 7340
www.ilbaretto.co.uk

⊖ Baker Street
Closed 25-26 December and lunch 1
January

Carte £40/53

Arjun Waney, the man behind Roka, Zuma and La Petite Maison, here gives Italy a go. The site had been Italian for a while and came complete with the wood-fired oven which is undoubtedly the star of the show. The ground floor wine bar doubles as a reception/holding area for the main basement room which comes with reclaimed-brick walls and terracotta tiled flooring; the open kitchens somehow compensate for the lack of windows. Look for dishes marked in red on the extensive menu, such as the succulent lamb cutlets or the whole sea bass as they are cooked in the wood-fired oven or on the robata grill. Unless you're sticking to pizza, the final bill can be more than expected. Staff are in black and display varying degrees of commitment.

Cafe Luc

Modern European 💥💥

50 Marylebone High St
✉ W1U 5HN
✆ (020) 7258 9878
www.cafeluc.com

⊖ Regent's Park
Closed 25 December

Menu £16 (lunch) – Carte £29/41

A/C
😊😊
☼
VISA
MC
AE

London has always liked a good brasserie and now Marylebone High Street has one of its own to go with all its other restaurants and cafés. The surprisingly spacious Cafe Luc opened mid 2010 and appears to take its cue from The Wolseley in its 'grand European café' look. It's enthusiastically run and the dark leather banquettes, bar and clusters of lights give it a comfortable yet reassuringly authentic feel. It's also family-owned, and the family in question founded the Le Pain Quotidien international chain so they should know what they're doing. The menu has something for everyone and offers a host of brasserie and continental classics, although sometimes it feels as though the cooking is a little overwhelmed by the surroundings.

Caffé Caldesi

Italian 💥

118 Marylebone Ln. (1st floor)
✉ W1U 2QF
✆ (020) 7487 0754
www.caldesi.com

⊖ Bond Street

Menu £20 (lunch) – Carte £28/44

A/C
☼
VISA
MC
AE

This former pub is the hub of the Caldesi family business, which takes in restaurants, cookbooks and cookery schools, and it fits perfectly into the fabric of local Marylebone life. Upstairs is simply but warmly decorated and is enthusiastically run by a young team of Italians – the owners maintain they have staff from all of Italy's 20 regions. The atmosphere is never less than cheery, thanks in no small part to the seasonal menu, which offers up classics from across Italy that have one thing in common – they are generously proportioned and really deliver on flavour; the pasta dishes are particularly satisfying. On the ground floor you'll find a less structured operation with a slightly abridged but more accessibly priced menu.

Chada Chada

G2

16-17 Picton Pl.
✉ W1U 1BP
✆ (020) 7935 8212
www.chadathai.com

⊖ Bond Street
Closed 25 December and lunch
Sunday-Monday

Carte £14/38

A/C
VISA
MC
AE

Chada Chada exudes a sense of authenticity that eludes the plethora of chain restaurants surrounding James Street. The menu offers a comprehensive tour around all parts of Thailand – for the main course you choose your primary ingredient, such as prawn or duck, and then decide on the best accompaniments. The kitchen does the familiar well, which makes sense as it has a regular following who know what they like. It also doesn't hang around in sending forth the dishes, which not only come in generous proportions but are also well-priced for W1; the only problem is accommodating all of the dishes on the small tables. There's another branch in Battersea which, surprisingly, is somewhat smarter than its West End cousin.

Colony

G1

8 Paddington St
✉ W1U 5QH
✆ (020) 7935 3353
www.colonybarandgrill.com

⊖ Baker Street

Menu £17 (lunch) – Carte dinner £23/33

A/C
⊡
☼
VISA
MC
AE

First impressions would suggest that Colony, with its chilled music and extensive cocktail list, is more of a lounge bar than a place to eat. But look closely and you'll see people are doing more than just snacking. This was originally set up by Atul Kochhar, of Benares fame, and although he is no longer involved, the food bears the hallmarks of his contemporary style of Indian cooking, albeit in smaller sizes and without quite reaching the same heights. Flavours from others countries such as the Caribbean or East Africa also get a look-in and some dishes pack quite a punch. Four of the tasting plates should be more enough for two; the grill and the tandoor are used extensively and it's definitely worth coming for a lunchtime thali.

141

Dinings

F2

22 Harcourt St.
✉ W1H 4HH
✆ (020) 7723 0666
www.dinings.co.uk

⊖ Marylebone
Closed Christmas, Saturday lunch
and Sunday – booking essential

Carte £34/51

VISA
MC
AE
DC

The smiling chefs greet you from behind the sushi counter which acts as a prompt to the girls in the basement to rush upstairs and escort you back down below. The idea behind Dinings is to resemble an after-work Japanese izakaya, or pub, and this they achieve. Staff outnumber guests and their service is endearingly sweet, while comfort levels are modest – chairs are built for purpose rather than comfort. The atmosphere is chummy and music loud. The young owner has come from Nobu-land and the food calls itself 'Japanese tapas'; shorthand for small plates of diligently prepared dishes, similar in style to his alma mater in its mix of traditional and modern but without the lofty price tag. Puddings are more your classic French variety.

Galvin Bistrot de Luxe

G2

66 Baker St.
✉ W1U 7DJ
✆ (020) 7935 4007
www.galvinrestaurants.com

⊖ Baker Street
Closed 25-26 December, 1 January and
dinner 24 December

Menu £20 (lunch and early dinner) – Carte £35/41

VISA
MC
AE

Despite the enormous success of Galvin La Chapelle in The City, brothers Chris and Jeff Galvin have never taken their eyes off the ball here at their eponymous 'bistrot de luxe' in Baker Street. Regulars still flock here for the clubby, relaxed atmosphere and the traditional French food, which may look simple on the plate but is carefully constructed behind the scenes. The emphasis is very much on flavour; the kitchen's understanding and appreciation of ingredients, and the classic combinations in which they are used, really comes through. The menu has enough variety to satisfy those happy to indulge but those with one eye on the cost should come for lunch or before 7pm if they want to take advantage of a good value fixed menu.

Grazing Goat

Traditional 🍽️🍺

6 New Quebec St
✉ W1H 7RQ
☎ (020) 7724 7243
www.thegrazinggoat.co.uk

⊖ Marble Arch.
Booking essential at dinner

Carte £30/45

The Portman Estate, owners of some serious real estate in these parts and keen to raise the profile of its investment, encouraged an experienced pub operator more at home in Chelsea and Belgravia to venture a little further north and take over the old Bricklayers Arms. Renamed in homage to a past Lady Portman (who grazed goats in a field where the pub now stands as she was allergic to cows' milk), it is now a smart city facsimile of a country pub. It's first-come-first-served in the bar but you can book in the upstairs dining room. Pub classics are the order of the day, such as pies or Castle of Mey steaks; Suffolk chicken is cooked on the rotisserie. The eight bedrooms are nicely furnished, with their bathrooms resembling Nordic saunas.

REGENT'S PARK & MARYLEBONE ▶ PLAN V

Hix (Selfridges)

Modern European 🍴

Mezzanine Fl, Selfridges, 400 Oxford St
✉ W1A 1AB
☎ (020) 7499 5400
www.hixatselfridges.co.uk

⊖ Bond St
Closed 25 December
and Sunday dinner

Menu £23 (lunch) – Carte £25/113

It comes as no surprise to learn that this outpost of Mark Hix's expanding group, found on the mezzanine floor of Selfridges overlooking the designer handbags, is an altogether daintier affair than his muscular Chop House in Clerkenwell. It mirrors the opening hours of the store so breakfast kicks things off at 9.30am and the champagne bar offers refuelling opportunities throughout the day. Lunch comes with the buzz generated by the promise of some post-prandial shopping, although the affordable wine list could make this a risky proposition. The cooking is a little lighter and more European than his other restaurants and there are also more salads; but it does share their philosophy of serving unadorned food using home-grown ingredients.

Iberica

Spanish ✕✕

195 Great Portland St
✉ W1W 5PS
☏ (020) 7636 8650
www.ibericalondon.co.uk

⊖ **Great Portland St**
Closed 1 January, Sunday dinner
and bank holidays –
booking advisable at dinner

Carte £20/36

[A/C] ⌨ [VISA] [MC] [AE] [①]

If you want an idea of how seriously this large operation, dedicated to Spanish 'food and culture', takes the sourcing of its ingredients, then wander into the deli and try resisting the Iberico hams with their ruby meat and creamy fat. It's even easier to get carried away by the appealing menu in the ground floor bar, although portion sizes are larger than one expects and prices can vary quite considerably. Flavours are punchy and satisfying and highlights include the squid and octopus dishes, along with the slow-cooked cockerel rice. Those after a fuller experience should consider pre-ordering the Segovian lamb or the suckling pig and if you want a more intimate and slightly more structured meal then book on the mezzanine floor.

Larrik

Traditional 🍺

32 Crawford Pl
✉ W1H 5NN
☏ (020) 7723 0066
www.thelarrik.com

⊖ **Edgware Road.**
Closed 25 December

Menu £13 (dinner) – Carte £25/37

☼ [VISA] [MC] [AE] [①]

Its airy feel and capable service mean that The Larrik has always been popular with larger groups and now, thanks to the obvious ambition of the owner, it's attracting plenty more customers for the quality of its food; so it's no surprise to find the place packed by 1pm on a daily basis. Try to sit at the front where it's brighter and more fun. Freshly made and substantial salads, a luxurious chicken liver parfait, plump salmon and haddock fishcakes with hollandaise and rewardingly rich desserts like chocolate brownies confirm a kitchen that's well grounded in the basics and aware of what people want from a pub. Add regularly changing real ales and you have a pub that's set to be part of the local landscape for some time to come.

Latium

Italian ❌❌❌

21 Berners St.
✉ W1T 3LP
✆ (020) 7323 9123
www.latiumrestaurant.com

⊖ Oxford Circus
Closed 25-26 December, 1 January,
Saturday lunch, Sunday
and bank holidays

Menu £23/36

AC

VISA

MC

AE

The last revamp made it brighter and more contemporary but such is the loyalty of its followers that a simple lick of paint would have been enough. There's now a window into the kitchen for those who like to know where their food comes from, and a chef's table for those who want to watch them at it. Tables by the entrance are given away first but it's worth asking to be seated further in; you'll almost certainly be accommodated as staff are a friendly and considerate bunch. The chef-owner is from Lazio, hence the name, so expect cooking that is free from over-elaboration. Recipes from across Italy also feature and many use British ingredients. The good value lunch menu changes weekly and homemade ravioli is the speciality.

Levant

Lebanese ❌❌

Jason Ct., 76 Wigmore St.
✉ W1U 2SJ
✆ (020) 7224 1111
www.levant.co.uk

⊖ Bond Street
Closed 25-26 December –
(dinner only and lunch Saturday-Sunday)

Menu £22/28 – Carte £30/45

AC

⊙

☼

VISA

MC

AE

The enticing scent of joss sticks and hookah pipes, pumping Arabic beats and belly dancing mean that Levant is guaranteed to provide a more exotic dining experience than most restaurants. Its basement location, lanterns and low-slung bar add further to the mystique and, as with anywhere offering a hint of spice, diners adopt the principle of safety in numbers and come in larger groups. With all these elements, it is almost a surprise to discover that equal care and enthusiasm has gone into the food. The kitchen uses good ingredients to create satisfying Lebanese dishes ideal for sharing. Avoid the more expensive set menus and head for the à laCarte, with its appealing selection of falafel, pastries, char-grills and slow-roasted specialities.

Locanda Locatelli ❀

G2

8 Seymour St.
✉ W1H 7JZ
✆ (020) 7935 9088
www.locandalocatelli.com

⊖ Marble Arch

Carte £32/62

A/C

∰

☀

VISA

MC

AE

①

Locanda Locatelli

When your clientele is made up of lots of buffed and shiny people then it is important that you're looking pretty good yourself. So every year the cherry wood is given a fresh coat of varnish and the tan leather seating gets a good clean and this keeps the room looking dapper and slick. Despite the vicissitudes of fashion, Locanda Locatelli has remained an ever popular choice for the cognoscenti, thanks largely to the excellence of the cooking. The large serving team in their black shirts and white ties may look like they've just come from a Sicilian wedding, but they get the job done with alacrity and efficiency. The menu offers around ten dishes per section so there is enough choice for everyone, even those with food allergies. Pasta is a perennial highlight, especially the risotto and gnocchi, and desserts, which always include the toothsome tiramisu and tart of the day, are expertly rendered with flair and care. Thinly sliced calf's head makes an interesting start, while unfussy presentation allows the quality of fish to really shine.

First Course
- Pan-fried scallops with celeriac purée and saffron vinaigrette.
- Ox tongue with green sauce.

Main Course
- Homemade pasta ribbons with broad beans and rocket.
- Pan-fried red mullet, Parma ham, warm fennel salad, black olives and tomato.

Dessert
- Tasting of Amedei chocolate.
- Cannoli Siciliani with blood orange and pistachio ice cream.

Orrery

Modern European XXX

55 Marylebone High St
✉ W1U 5RB
☎ (020) 7616 8000
www.orrery-restaurant.co.uk

⊖ Regent's Park
Booking essential

Menu £25 (lunch) – Carte £37/48

Enthusiastic post-prandial shopping can be a perilously expensive pastime – the danger is doubled here as Orrery is perched temptingly above a Conran shop. These are actually converted stables from the 19C but, such is the elegance and style of the building, you'd never know. What is sure is the long, narrow restaurant looks its best when the daylight floods in; on warm days make time to have a drink on the terrific rooftop terrace. To complement these charming surroundings you'll be offered a bewildering array of menus, all of which feature quite elaborate, modern European cooking. Dishes are strong on presentation and there is the occasional twist but it's usually done with some meaning rather than merely straining for effect.

Ozer

Turkish XX

5 Langham Pl., Regent St.
✉ W1B 3DG
☎ (020) 7323 0505
www.ozer.co.uk

⊖ Oxford Circus

Menu £21/24

Huseyin Ozer may have built the successful Sofra chain but Ozer is clearly where his heart lies. His passion and pride in Turkish and Ottoman cuisine is clear for all to see – anyone who prints on their menu an offer to replace any dish not enjoyed must feel confident about his kitchen. The hot and cold meze is the main attraction here, especially the platters which represent good value. The crusty bread and hummus is almost a meal in itself and the borek, kofte and the skewered and chargrilled meats are all done well. There's an occasional modern twist and any overeating can be justified by considering just how healthy this cuisine is. The large front bar gets as packed as ever and the restaurant itself has just as many devotees.

Phoenix Palace

Chinese

F1

5 Glentworth St.
✉ NW1 5PG
☎ (020) 7486 3515
www.phoenixpalace.co.uk

⊖ Baker Street
Closed 25 December –
booking advisable at dinner

Menu £28 (dinner) – Carte approx. £24

You have to admire the ambition of the owners of Phoenix Palace, because despite the fact that their place can already seat over 100 people, they are still hoping to open an extension. To take it all in, sit in the raised section where you'll find polished wood, pretty lanterns and larger groups of families or friends creating what is clearly a contented atmosphere. Try to ignore the sheer number of different dishes on the vast menu, especially those involving kangaroo and ostrich. This is Cantonese cooking and the rotisserie meats are a specialty – some of which do need to be pre-ordered. Crab with chilli sauce served with a crispy Peking bun is a favourite, while the extensive dim sum during the day draws in plenty of Hong Kong businesspeople.

Portman

Modern European

F2

51 Upper Berkeley St
✉ W1H 7QW
☎ (020) 7723 8996
www.theportmanmarylebone.com

⊖ Marble Arch.

Carte £22/31

When it went by the name of The Masons Arms this pub was widely known for its gruesome history. It was here that the condemned, on their way to Tyburn Tree gallows, would take their last drink, which purportedly led to the phrase "one for the road". Reincarnated as The Portman, the pub these days boasts a less disreputable clientele who are more attracted by the quality of the cooking. Food is served all day and you can choose to eat in the busy ground floor bar or in the unexpectedly formal upstairs dining room, all thick-pile carpet and starched tablecloths. Fortunately, the style of food remains thoroughly down-to-earth and satisfying and is accompanied by a well-organised wine list and an interesting selection of cocktails.

The Providores

Innovative ✗✗

G2

109 Marylebone High St.
✉ W1U 4RX
✆ (020) 7935 6175
www.theprovidores.co.uk

⊖ Bond Street
Closed 24 December-4 January

Menu £46 – Carte £34/49

A/C
☼
VISA
MC
AE

'Marylebone Village' offers so many restaurants and cafés that it's becoming a destination in itself. Included in the roll call is this fusion restaurant within a former Edwardian pub. The warmth of the staff and the general buzz hit you immediately in the ground floor Tapa Room, where tables and tapas are shared. Upstairs is a slightly more sedate room but the staff are equally charming. Here all dishes come in starter size to "minimise food envy" and allow for sharing; three courses plus a dessert should suffice. There is no doubting the quality of the ingredients, although sometimes there's a flavour or two too many on the plate. The wine list champions New Zealand. Bookings are needed upstairs; downstairs, it's first-come-first-served.

Rhodes W1 Brasserie

Modern European ✗✗

F3

Cumberland Hotel,
Great Cumberland Pl. ✉ W1H
✆ (020) 7616 5930
www.rhodesw1.com

⊖ Marble Arch

Menu £21 (lunch) – Carte £24/43

A/C
☼
VISA
MC
AE

They've got their work cut out filling a space as big as this, because it does need to be close to capacity to get the atmosphere going. That said, the serving team do keep themselves busy and genuinely look after their customers. It's actually better to approach it from the lobby of the hotel than its separate street entrance which leads you through the equally large bar. The menu content differs little between lunch and dinner except for the Express lunch for those on the run: you get a starter, main course and dessert all on one plate. Gary Rhodes's signature dishes like salmon fishcakes are all in evidence, but so are other more European influences, so expect risotto, Greek salads, osso bucco, crab bisque and the like.

Rhodes W1 (Restaurant) ✿

French XXXX

F3

Cumberland Hotel,
Great Cumberland Pl. ✉ W1H 7DL
✆ (020) 7616 5930
www.rhodesw1.com

⊖ **Marble Arch**
Closed 2 weeks January, 2 weeks
August, Saturday lunch,
Sunday, Monday and bank holidays
– booking advisable

Menu £26/50

Rhodes W1

There are just twelve tables and when you book one it's yours
for however long you want it – this isn't the sort of restaurant
where they try to re-lay your table while you're ordering coffee.
Kelly Hoppen's design is about texture and warmth, with
crystal chandeliers hanging seductively over each table. The
atmosphere is unexpectedly relaxed too, thanks largely to the
staff who are a confident lot, know what they are talking about
and are ready with a smile. Gary Rhodes may be best known
as a champion of British traditions and recipes but here more
of the influences come from across the Channel. Whether the
cooking techniques are French or the ingredients from more
southerly parts, what does remain steadfastly Rhodesesque
is the uncluttered and crisp presentation, the complementary
flavour combinations and the ease of eating. The food is also
quite masculine and some of the starters in particular are
appealingly robust. The set menu is purely for the trusting and
the brave as you are not told beforehand of its contents.

First Course

- Fillet of mackerel,
  honey and sesame
  caramel and sea
  purslane.
- Pressed rabbit and
  carrot terrine, pickled
  prune, radish and
  sage mayonnaise.

Main Course

- Pigeon with foie
  gras, chicory and
  pickled blackberries.
- Slow cooked skate
  wing, crisp pork
  belly, brown shrimps,
  sweetcorn, beurre
  noisette jus.

Dessert

- Prune and Armagnac
  soufflé, vanilla bean
  ice cream.
- Mandarin 'Arctic roll',
  blood orange and
  mandarin sorbet.

Riding House Café

H2

Modern European ✗

43-51 Great Titchfield St
✉ W1W 7PQ
☎ (020) 7927 0840
www.ridinghousecafe.co.uk

⊖ Oxford Circus
Closed 25-26 December

Carte £24/42

A/C
⊡
☼
VISA
MC
AE

For their third project, the owners of The Garrison and Village East ventured uptown, albeit to an area hitherto untroubled by the presence of decent restaurants. It's less a café, more an all-day Manhattan-style brasserie and cocktail bar, with some charming touches of quirky design. You turn left for the restaurant but it's more fun in the main section where you can't book – either at a counter facing the kitchen or on a large refectory table where you rub shoulders with strangers. It's the same menu throughout, starting with breakfast and followed by a choice of 'small plates' along with more straightforward main courses like steak or burgers. It's easy to over-order so stick with the small plates which have a bit more zing to them.

Roganic

G2

Innovative ✗✗

19 Blandford St
✉ W1U 3DH
☎ (020) 7486 0380
www.roganic.co.uk

⊖ Baker Street
Closed Sunday and Monday –
booking advisable

Menu £29/80

A/C
VISA
MC
AE

Despite being busy pushing the boundaries of modern cooking at L'Enclume in the Lake District, chef Simon Rogan has always wanted to make an impact on the London dining scene. In late 2011 he realised his dream when he created this "extended pop-up restaurant" by taking on the remaining two years of the lease from the old Michael Moore restaurant. From a choice of 3, 6 or 10 course tasting menus come dishes of invention and originality, although portion sizes are a little on the diminutive size. There are a few signature dishes from L'Enclume, such as Cumbrian hogget, but the majority of dishes are new; all use plenty of top quality ingredients from their own small farm. Service is young and enthusiastic.

Roux at the Landau

H2

French XXX

1c Portland Pl., Regent St.
✉ W1B 1JA
☏ (020) 7965 0165
www.thelandau.com

⊖ Oxford Circus
▶ **Plan V**
Closed Saturday lunch and Sunday

Menu £48 (lunch and early dinner) – Carte £37/67

A/C
⟨⟩
VISA
MC
AE
①

It does have its own street entrance but it's best to enter this grand, oval-shaped restaurant from the hotel, as you don't often get the chance to walk through a 'wine corridor'. The hotel brought in the considerable experience of the Roux organisation – which means Albert and Michel Jr – to add vigour and ambition to the operation. Classical, French-influenced cooking is the order of the day but one can detect the emergence of a lighter style of cuisine with the odd twist. The restaurant is also sensible enough to keep its more traditionally minded regulars happy by ensuring that their favourites, like grilled Dover Sole, remain constants. The daily special from the trolley goes down well with the busy lunchtime corporates.

Royal China

G2

Chinese XX

24-26 Baker St
✉ W1U 7AB
☏ (020) 7487 4688
www.royalchinagroup.co.uk

⊖ Baker Street

Menu £30 – Carte £31/42

A/C
☼
VISA
MC
AE

It could be just as at home in Hong Kong's Wanchai or Central districts but, as it is, Royal China sits very comfortably in Baker Street. The large kitchen is staffed exclusively by Chinese chefs, including the early rising dim sum chef, who is responsible for the specialities served between midday and 5pm each day. The Cantonese dishes are strong on aroma and colour and, while the restaurant does not sell a great deal of seafood due to a lack of tank space, the lobster dishes remain one of the more popular choices. However, it is the barbecued meats, assorted soups, stir-fries and the choice of over 40 different types of dim sum that draw the large groups and ensure that this branch of the Royal China group remains as bustling as ever.

Texture ⍟

G2

34 Portman St.
✉ W1H 7BY
☎ (020) 7224 0028
www.texture-restaurant.co.uk

⊖ Marble Arch
Closed Christmas-New Year,
2 weeks August, Sunday
and Monday

Menu £24 (lunch) – Carte £50/64

A/C
⟨⟩
❀
VISA
MC
AE

Texture

REGENT'S PARK & MARYLEBONE ▶ PLAN V

Chef-owner Agnar Sverrisson and his business partner Xavier Rousset, who trained as a sommelier, have steadily gone about creating an exceedingly good restaurant. The Champagne bar at the front has become a destination in itself and is separated from the restaurant by a large cabinet so you never feel too detached from it. The high ceilings add a little grandeur and the service is very pleasant, with staff all ready with a smile. Agnar's cooking is a little less showy than when Texture opened in 2007 and is all the better for that; you feel he's now cooking the food he wants to cook rather than the food he thought he should be cooking. Iceland is his country of birth so it is no surprise to find lamb, cod (whose crisp skin is served with drinks), langoustine and skyr, the dairy product that nourished the Vikings. There's considerable technical skill and depth to the cooking but dishes still appear light and refreshing and, since the use of cream and butter is largely restricted to the desserts, you even feel they're doing you good.

First Course

- Organic Scottish salmon, horseradish and cucumber.
- Chargrilled Anjou quail, sweetcorn, shallot, bacon popcorn and red wine essence.

Main Course

- Icelandic salted cod, barley risotto and prawns.
- Pyrenean lamb shoulder, with wild Icelandic herbs and mustard.

Dessert

- Skyr ice cream, strawberry and muesli.
- Almonds, anise, vanilla cake, cardamom ice cream and pear.

153

Trishna 🐾

15-17 Blandford St.   ⊖ Baker Street
✉ W1U 3DG   Closed 25-28 December and 1-3 January
✆ (020) 7935 5624
www.trishnalondon.com

Menu £18 (lunch) – Carte £24/37

[A/C]
Trishna has added much to Marylebone's already interesting
foodie quarter, despite its dodgy acoustics and service that can
sometimes be a little slow off the mark. Those familiar with the
Mumbai original will find the cooking here a little more subtle
as less butter and garlic are used. The emphasis is firmly on fish
and seafood; dishes even come with wine pairing suggestions.
[VISA]
They have substituted the Indian species for domestic varieties
[MC]
and dishes are for sharing – this is the sort of food which
makes you want to roll up your sleeves. Stand-outs include the
[AE]
gloriously rich Cornish brown crab and the crisp Isle of Wight
plaice with pea and mint. Avoid the à la carte and head for the
more reasonably priced 8 course tasting menu.

Verru

69 Marylebone Ln   ⊖ Bond Street
✉ W1U 2PH
✆ (020) 7935 0858
www.verru.co.uk

Menu £17 (lunch) – Carte £35/42

The great thing about this part of town is that you can still
come across tiny, tucked away restaurants doing something a
[VISA]
little different. This is a warm, genially run and smartly dressed
little place but it's not just the look that's appealing on a
[MC]
winter's night: Verru's chef-owner is Estonian and accordingly
his cooking not only displays a Baltic boldness of flavour but
[AE]
also uses influences from the more northerly parts of Europe.
[①]
Despite the occasional tendency to gild the lily, the kitchen
produces dishes that have an appealing frankness to them but
they are also underpinned by some sound classical techniques
– and you certainly won't leave hungry. Sit at the front for more
atmosphere; at the back for greater intimacy.

Vinoteca

Modern European ✗

15 Seymour Pl.
✉ W1H 5BD
✆ (020) 7724 7288
www.vinoteca.co.uk

⊖ Marble Arch
Closed 25-26 December, 1 January and
Sunday dinner – booking advisable

Carte £24/30

A/C
⅋
VISA
MC
AE

They've transferred the winning formula from their Clerkenwell original, so expect a great selection of wines, gutsy and wholesome cooking, young and enthusiastic staff and almost certainly a wait for a table. One side of the room is given over to shelves of wine; not only is the selection immeasurably appealing but the staff display both a knowledge and, more importantly, enormous enthusiasm when giving advice. The daily changing menu takes its cue from the sunnier parts of Europe and includes thoughtfully compiled salads and good charcuterie. There are also some firmly British dishes too, like mutton and oyster pie, and each one comes with its own wine pairing recommendation. It's great fun, basic in comfort and always very busy.

The Wallace

French ✗

Hertford House, Manchester Sq
✉ W1U 3BN
✆ (020) 7563 9505
www.thewallacerestaurant.com

⊖ Bond Street
Closed 24-26 December –
(lunch only and dinner
Friday-Saturday)

Carte £30/39

☼
VISA
MC

Away from the bustle of Marylebone High Street sits Hertford House and the Wallace Collection of 18C and 19C paintings. Go past the Canalettos on the ground floor and through the French doors and you'll find yourself in a huge glass-roofed courtyard. The restaurant takes up most of the space, although there's also an all-day café. The menu is largely French in influence and cooking is done ably enough. There's a popular fruits de mer section and terrines are the speciality, ranging from foie gras to pork rillettes. Mains are never too heavy and cheeses are kept in good order. There may occasionally be larger parties in but the size of this atrium means there's room for everyone. Staff make up in alacrity what they lack in personality.

Yalla Yalla

H2

Lebanese ✗

12 Winsley St.
✉ W1W 8HQ
✆ (020) 7637 4748
www.yalla-yalla.co.uk

⊖ Oxford Circus
Closed 27-29 August and Sunday

Carte £18/22

A/C

VISA

MC

D

Close to the clamour of Oxford Street is this fun, good value restaurant whose Beirut street food is much tastier than anything you'll find along the Edgware Road. The name means "Hurry up!" which is a message no doubt endorsed by those waiting for a table as bookings are only taken for larger parties. The crowds come for the broad selection of mezze, which ranges from fattoush and sawda djej (chicken livers) to soujoc (spicy sausages). For the main course, succulent charcoal-grilled lamb dishes stand out, while desserts come from the enticing pastry corner. They also do a brisk takeaway trade in flatbreads, pastries and wraps. Wines from the Bekaa Valley are available alongside the juices and teas. The tiny, original branch is in Soho.

Zayna

F2

Indian ✗✗

25 New Quebec St.
✉ W1H 7SF
✆ (020) 7723 2229
www.zaynarestaurant.co.uk

⊖ Marble Arch

Menu £15 (lunch) – Carte £30/39

A/C

☼

VISA

MC

AE

When a restaurant is named after the owner's daughter you know there's going to be a lot of love around. Zayna reflects the personality of Riz Dar who spent his formative years around Kashmir and Punjab and whose first job was in his father's restaurant in Pakistan. It's no surprise then to find a menu of North Indian and Pakistani delicacies. It comes divided according to cooking method, from the pan, grill, tawa or oven; but look out for the refined street food using offal. He is passionate about produce: spices are roasted and ground in house and only halal meat and free-range chicken are used. Dishes come packed with flavour, although the final bill can quickly mount up. The ground floor is the more elegant of the two rooms.

Bloomsbury · Hatton Garden · Holborn

A real sense of history pervades this central chunk of London. From the great collection of antiquities in the British Museum to the barristers who swarm around the Royal Courts of Justice and Lincoln's Inn; from the haunts of Charles Dickens to the oldest Catholic church in Britain, the streets here are dotted with rich reminders of the past. Hatton Garden's fame as the city's diamond and jewellery centre goes back to Elizabethan times while, of a more recent vintage, Bloomsbury was home to the notorious Group (or Set) who, championed by Virginia Woolf, took on the world of art and literature in the 1920s.

A full-on encounter with **Holborn** is, initially, a shock to the system. Coming up from the tube, you'll find this is where main traffic arteries collide and a rugby scrum regularly ensues. Fear not, though; the relative calm of London's largest square, part-flanked by two quirky and intriguing museums, is just round the corner. The square is **Lincoln's Inn Fields,** which boasts a canopy of characterful oak trees and a set of tennis courts. On its north side is **Sir John Soane's Museum,** a gloriously eccentric place with twenty thousand exhibits where the walls open out like cabinets to reveal paintings by Turner and Canaletto. On its south side, the Hunterian Museum, refitted a few years ago, is a fascinating repository of medical bits and pieces. Visitors with a

Damien Hirst take on life will revel in the likes of animal digestive systems in formaldehyde, or perhaps the sight of half of mathematician Charles Babbage's brain. Others not so fascinated by the gory might flee to the haunting silence of **St Etheldreda's church** in Ely Place, the only surviving example of thirteenth-century Gothic architecture in London. It survived the Great Fire of 1666, and Latin is still the language of choice.

Contemplation of a different kind takes centre stage in the adjacent **Hatton Garden.** This involves eager-eyed couples gazing at the glittering displays of rings and jewellery that have been lighting up the shop fronts here for many generations, ever since the leafy lane and its smart garden environs took the fancy of Sir Christopher Hatton, a favourite of Elizabeth I. After gawping at the baubles, there's liquid refreshment on hand at one of London's most atmospheric old pubs, the tiny Ye Old Mitre hidden down a narrow passageway. The preserved trunk of a cherry tree stands in the front bar, and, by all accounts, Elizabeth I danced the maypole round it (a legend that always seems more believable after the second pint).

Bloomsbury has intellectual connotations, and not just because of the writers and artists who frequented its townhouses in the twenties. This is where the University of London has its headquarters, and it's also home

C. Eymenier / MICHELIN

to the **British Museum,** the vast treasure trove of international artefacts that attracts visitors in even vaster numbers. As if the exhibits themselves weren't lure enough, there's also the fantastic glass-roofed Great Court, opened to much fanfare at the start of the Millennium, which lays claim to being the largest covered public square in Europe. To the north of here by the Euston Road is the **British Library,** a rather stark red brick building that holds over 150 million items and is one of the greatest centres of knowledge in the world. Meanwhile,

Dickens fans should make for the north east corner of Bloomsbury for the great man's museum in **Doughty Street:** this is one of many London houses in which he lived, but it's the only one still standing. He lived here for three years, and it proved a fruitful base, resulting in Nicholas Nickleby and Oliver Twist. The museum holds manuscripts, letters and Dickens' writing desk. If your appetite for the written word has been truly whetted, then a good tip is to head back west half a mile to immerse yourself in the bookshops of Great Russell Street.

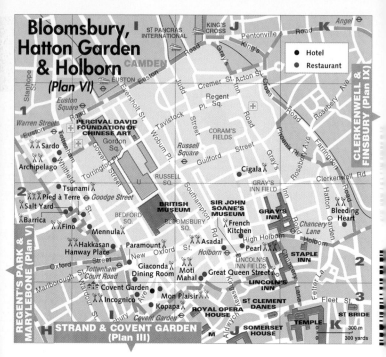

● Hotel
● Restaurant

Archipelago

H1

Innovative ✗✗

110 Whitfield St.
✉ W1T 5ED
✆ (020) 7383 3346
www.archipelago-restaurant.co.uk

⊖ **Goodge Street**
Closed 24-27 December, Saturday
lunch, Sunday and bank holidays

Carte £28/38

VISA
MC
AE
①

Bored with beef? Tired of chicken? How about zebra? Or crocodile? Not only is the gloriously oddball Archipelago unlike any other restaurant in London but tales of your meal can also be used to frighten small children. 'Exploring the exotic' is their slogan although 'eating the exotic' would be more exact: the menu reads like an inventory at an omnivore's safari park and the place itself is like an eccentric Oriental bazaar that's running out of space. Several dishes are given an Asian twist and side dishes include the 'love-bug salad' made with locusts and crickets. For dessert, try the chocolate covered scorpion; they now use smaller ones as they are, apparently, 'tastier'. It's all great fun and certainly memorable.

Asadal

227 High Holborn
✉ WC1V 7DA
✆ (020) 7430 9006
www.asadal.co.uk

⊖ Holborn
Closed 25-26 December, 1 January
and Sunday lunch

Menu £14/20 – Carte £17/31

A/C
⟐
VISA
MC
AE

If it was any nearer Holborn Tube station you'd need an Oyster card to get in. But head down the stairs and you'll soon be oblivious to what's going on at street level, thanks to a comfortable room which is divided up and kitted out with lots of wood. Those unfamiliar with Korean food will find that, by and large, the menu explains itself, since many of the dishes have had their photo taken. One thing to note is that the more there are in your party the better, as sharing is the key. Kimchi provides the perfect starter; there's plenty of seafood but the stars of the show are the hotpots, the delicate dumplings and the barbecues where meats are cooked on the hot-plate on the table. The young staff cope well with the early evening rush.

Barrica

62 Goodge St
✉ W1T 4NE
✆ (020) 7436 9448
www.barrica.co.uk

⊖ Goodge Street
Closed 25-26 December, 1 January, Sunday
and bank holidays – booking essential

Carte £18/20

A/C
VISA
MC
AE

If the zeitgeist is epitomised by informality and sharing then it's little wonder that tapas bars are sprouting up all over the place. Barrica opened in close proximity to a couple of well-established competitors but manages to hold its own. You'll have to fight through the after-work group at the front to get to the tables and noise levels can overawe at times, but the food is good and the atmosphere fun. The menu is sensibly laid out and supplemented by daily specials. Highlights include braised veal cheeks, duck rillettes and marinated sardines. Cured meats hang above the bar and the cosy room is warm and intimate. If you haven't got a booking, you may get a counter seat or else you can try the Spanish way of eating standing up.

Bleeding Heart

K2

Bleeding Heart Yard (off Greville St.)
✉ EC1N 8SJ
✆ (020) 7242 8238
www.bleedingheart.co.uk

⊖ Farringdon
Closed Christmas-New Year,
Saturday and Sunday –
booking essential

Menu £25 (lunch) s – Carte £28/43 s

Dickensian tales of murder and intrigue still haunt the wonderfully evocative Bleeding Heart Yard, while contented bankers and modern day industrialists sit in its candlelit and atmospheric restaurant, feasting on classic French cuisine. Weekly changing set menus sit alongside the fairly pricey à la carte, which comes written in French and English, and well-drilled French staff exhibit a fair degree of personality. The kitchen can sometimes overcomplicate dishes so you're better off going for the more traditional choices with their relative simplicity. The wine list is a splendid affair and the owners have their own estate in New Zealand. If you want something altogether less formal then cross the yard for the Bistro.

Cigala

J1

54 Lamb's Conduit St.
✉ WC1N 3LW
✆ (020) 7405 1717
www.cigala.co.uk

⊖ Russell Square
Booking essential

Menu £18 (lunch) – Carte £24/32

Cigala and Lamb's Conduit are a perfect fit; grab an outside table in summer and watch the world go by on this part-pedestrianised street. However, it is inside where you'll find the infectious vibe. The menu is cleverly divided, one side being tapas and/or starters, and main courses on the other, so you can choose to have lots of dishes, order a bigger dish – or go for an even bigger one like the paella for two which takes half an hour to prepare. The tapas are particularly good, especially the salt cod fritters, Padrón peppers and the morcilla blood sausage. The exclusively Spanish wine list has some little gems on it and the prices are commendably down to earth. The young Spanish girls serving display varying degrees of enthusiasm.

Fino

Spanish ✗✗

33 Charlotte St. (entrance on Rathbone St.)   ⊖ Goodge Street
✉ W1T 1RR   Closed Saturday lunch,
☎ (020) 7813 8010   Sunday and bank holidays
www.finorestaurant.com

Menu £18 (lunch) – Carte £21/49

VISA
MC
AE

Fino's basement location and discreet entrance engender in its clientele that warm, satisfyingly smug feeling of being 'in the know'. While it is more formally structured than most restaurants that serve tapas, the atmosphere is always lively and the crowd, particularly at night, is pleasingly mixed. Start with a sherry and some coquetas while you scour the sensibly laid out menu. The young staff all know what's on offer and the more effort you put in with them the more they'll be inclined to offer guidance. Then order a bottle of Albariño and dig in; seafood is a delight, especially the squid from the plancha. Dishes are easy to share and, as in life, the more people in your party the greater will be your enjoyment.

French Kitchen

French ✗

95-97 High Holborn   ⊖ Holborn
✉ WC1V 6LF   Closed 25 December
☎ (020) 7242 4580
www.french-kitchen.co.uk

Carte £20/32

When it first opened this was part of the Villandry group but in 2011 it changed its name and set out on its own. It aims to attract customers from early morning to late evening, offering everything from a breakfast menu to assorted charcuterie, from children's menus and pizzas to comforting French classics – and all at a fair price, where service is not automatically added. There's a good selection of wine by the glass and carafe, including a decent house wine from Languedoc. The place is too big to be considered a bistrot and its somewhat austere layout means that the noise bounces around, but it does have an appealingly rustic and honest feel. Service is friendly, if at times a little overconfident.

Giaconda Dining Room 🙂

I2

9 Denmark St.
✉ WC2H 8LS
☎ (020) 7240 3334
www.giacondadining.com

⊖ **Tottenham Court Road**
Closed 3 weeks August, 2 weeks Easter,
2 weeks Christmas-New Year, Saturday
lunch, Sunday, Monday and bank holidays
– booking essential

Carte £22/30

AC
VISA
MC
AE

In the shadow of Centre Point lies a frayed little area that's 'not quite Soho'. Here you'll find Denmark Street - London's own historic Tin Pan Alley – which is home to the Giaconda Dining Room. Aussies Paul and Tracey Merrony have a small but perfectly formed little place; spartanly decorated, busy from day one and great fun. Paul describes his cooking as "Frenchy, with day trips to Italy", which translates on the plate as confident, gutsy, no-nonsense and immeasurably satisfying. Tripe; steak tartare; pork sausage stew; risotto; a deconstructed pig's trotter and a daily changing fish or grilled special - there's something for everyone and, with most wine bottles in the £20s, it's all done at a credit-crunch busting price.

Great Queen Street 🙂

J2

32 Great Queen St
✉ WC2B 5AA
☎ (020) 7242 0622

⊖ **Holborn**
Closed Christmas-New Year
and bank holidays – booking essential

Carte £25/30

VISA
MC

This is one of those restaurants that is perfect on a cold winter's night, with its candlelight, burgundy coloured walls, busy atmosphere and, most importantly, its heartwarming food. Its popularity does mean that service can sometimes need a prompt but there is no doubting the staff's enthusiasm for the food they serve. The menu descriptions are unapologetically concise but then dishes come equally unembellished. There's little difference between what constitutes a starter or main course and there's always a daily special or two. Highlights are the shared dishes such as the roast chicken crown or the shoulder of lamb, but offal is also done very well. Wine is served in tumblers and the list is thoughtfully put together.

Incognico

Modern European ✗✗

117 Shaftesbury Ave.
✉ WC2H 8AD
✆ (020) 7836 8866
www.incognico.com

⊖ Tottenham Court Road
Closed Sunday and bank holidays

Menu £25 (lunch) – Carte £29/38

Incognico, somewhat ironically, deserves to be better known, and not just as a well-placed pre-theatre spot. It is a comfortable and smartly dressed restaurant, the dark wood lending a masculine, clubby feel. It is also enthusiastically run, although service can sometimes be a little too formal and solicitous for its own good. As soon as you sit you're assailed somewhat with a plethora of menus – there's a menu of the day, a specials menu and the somewhat expensive à la carte. The kitchen looks towards both France and Italy for inspiration; the former has greater influence but the Italian dishes are executed with greater aplomb. Dishes come pleasingly understated in presentation and flavours are nicely balanced.

Kopapa

Asian influences ✗

32-34 Monmouth St
✉ WC2H 9HA
✆ (020) 7240 6076
www.kopapa.co.uk

⊖ Covent Garden
Closed 25 December –
booking advisable

Menu £25 (lunch and early dinner) – Carte £24/34

Too often 'fusion' cooking demands the addition of the prefix 'con', but, like many of his fellow Kiwis, Peter Gordon is a chef with a greater understanding of this sort of culinary promiscuity. Kopapa, a Maori word for a gathering, is his just-drop-in-anytime place; it's ideal for Covent Garden and is staffed by many of his enthusiastic countrymen. Ok, it may be cramped and austerely kitted out, but this isn't about long, lingering lunches, more about grabbing a table and getting stuck in. There's a wide choice, from breakfast items to quick bites and platters, but the highlights are found in the tapas section. You may not recognise all the ingredients listed, but you'll know that your taste buds have been given a workout.

Hakkasan Hanway Place ✿

Chinese ✕✕

8 Hanway Pl.
✉ W1T 1HD
✆ (020) 7927 7000
www.hakkasan.com

⊖ Tottenham Court Road
Closed 24-25 December

Carte £40/89

A/C
I◎I
☼
VISA
MC
AE

Hakkasan

The original, subterranean Hakkasan remains as cool and seductive as ever and, despite the opening of another branch in Mayfair, its popularity shows no sign of slowing. Despite the size and general bustle, it is actually possible to have quite an intimate experience here, thanks to the clever lighting and good acoustics. However, service can be a little hit and miss and depends largely on who your waiter is and their levels of enthusiasm. Lunchtime dim sum is a real highlight, although they sometimes appear curiously reluctant to offer you that particular menu. There are 20 chefs in the kitchen, many of whom are, like the head chef, from Singapore. The extensive menu is laid out clearly and logically, although there can be a marked difference in price between similar sounding dishes. Cantonese remains the starting point but the kitchen adds its own signature of inventiveness to give the dishes zip and the flavours depth. One thing the waiting staff do get right is telling you when you've unwittingly but understandably succumbed to over-ordering.

First Course

- Peking duck with Royal Beluga caviar.
- Sweetcorn soup with corn-fed chicken and blue swimmer crab.

Main Course

- Roasted silver cod.
- Spicy double-cooked Duke of Berkshire pork with pressed beancurd and Chinese cabbage.

Dessert

- Jivara hazelnut bomb.
- Yuzu posset.

Mennula

12

Italian ✗

10 Charlotte St.
✉ W1T 2LT
✆ (020) 7363 2833
www.mennula.com

⊖ **Goodge Street**
Closed 1 week Christmas, Saturday lunch
and bank holidays

Menu £20 (lunch and early dinner) – Carte approx. £30

A/C
⊡
☼
VISA
MC
AE
①

Those who still mourn the passing of Passione, which occupied this space for quite some time, will be pleased to find in its place another Italian restaurant, this time with a Sicilian accent. The enthusiastically run Mennula shows that there's more to this region than cannoli and cassata by offering a varied selection of specialities, from arancini to spaghetti with sardines, and pasta cake. The name means 'almond' and they make several appearances, whether served smoked with your drinks or to accompany the lamb. The set lunch and early evening menus are attractively priced. The place is quite compact, which means that one larger table can dominate the room, but it's bright and crisply decorated; try to snare one of the three booths.

Mon Plaisir

13

French ✗✗

19-21 Monmouth St.
✉ WC2H 9DD
✆ (020) 7836 7243
www.monplaisir.co.uk

⊖ **Covent Garden**
Closed Christmas-New Year,
Sunday and bank holidays

Menu £19 (lunch and early dinner) – Carte £30/41

iⓄ
🎭
VISA
MC
AE

Mon Plaisir couldn't be more French if it wore a beret and whistled La Marseillaise; but because this institution has been around since the 1940s, and under the current ownership since the '70s, it can also give one an unexpected but palpable sense of old London. It's divided into four rooms, all of which have slightly different personalities but share the Gallic theme; even the bar was reportedly salvaged from a Lyonnais brothel. Service may lack some of the exuberance of the past but that's just down to the relative lack of experience of the current serving team. All the authentically tasting classics are on offer, from snails to terrines, duck to coq; the set menu represents good value while the à la carte can be a little pricey.

Moti Mahal

J2

45 Great Queen St.
✉ WC2B 5AA
✆ (020) 7240 9329
www.motimahal-uk.com

⊖ Holborn
Closed Christmas, Sunday and lunch
Saturday and bank holidays

Carte £37/46

AC
🛋
VISA
MC
AE
①

To get the most out of your visit to Moti Mahal, order dishes from the menu which follows the path of the Grand Trunk Road, built in the 16C and stretching the 2500km from Bengal to the North West of India and the Pakistan border. This journey also takes little detours along the way to include specialities cooked on a clamp grill and there is no distinction between starters and main courses – just order a selection to share with your table. There is also a 'classics' menu for those who insist on only ordering dishes with recognisable names. The flavoursome cooking is done with care and service is conscientious and endearing. The restaurant is split between a bright and busy ground floor and a more intimate basement level.

Paramount

I2

Centre Point (31st floor)
101-103 New Oxford St. ✉ WC1A 1DD
✆ (020) 7420 2900
www.paramount.uk.net

⊖ Tottenham Court Road
Closed 25-26 December
and Sunday dinner

Menu £24 (lunch and early dinner) – Carte £30/46

≼
AC
🛋

VISA
MC
AE

Restaurants with great views usually hope you'll spend so much time gawping out of the window that you won't notice the quality of the cooking. But Paramount, on the 32nd floor of the iconic Grade II listed Centre Point building, is owned by experienced restaurateur Pierre Condou and he has invested in a decent kitchen team. Getting to the restaurant can be a little laborious as you first get buzzed in on the ground floor, go to reception, get in a lift and then repeat the name-giving at another reception. But this is a fun place with keen staff and sweeping views across London; there's also a champagne bar one floor up. The ambition of the kitchen is shown by the presence of a tasting menu; cooking is surprisingly elaborate and the ingredients are good.

Pearl

J2

French XXX

252 High Holborn
✉ WC1V 7EN
☎ (020) 7829 7000
www.pearl-restaurant.com

⊖ Holborn
Closed 2 weeks August,
Sunday and bank holidays

Menu £30/60

A/C
⊡
🎧
VISA
MC
AE
①

A room as grand as this has to be busy otherwise the tables feel a little cast adrift. This former banking hall is within what was once Pearl Assurance's HQ; its high ceiling, chandeliers and columns certainly add some grandeur to proceedings but they clearly didn't make life easy when it came to adding the lighting. Waiting staff come dressed in black and are an enthusiastic, well-drilled bunch who do a good job ensuring that the surroundings don't become the main event. Chef Jun Tanaka, who pulls in plenty of the customers himself thanks to his television appearances, offers a menu high in originality but grounded in a classical French base. The wine list is a particularly impressive tome in both its depth and variety.

Rasa Samudra

I2

Indian XX

5 Charlotte St.
✉ W1T 1RE
☎ (020) 7637 0222
www.rasarestaurants.com

⊖ Goodge Street
Closed 25 December-1 January,
lunch Sunday and bank holidays

Menu £23/30 – Carte £22/32

VISA
MC
AE

It still shines like a beacon on Charlotte Street, thanks to its shocking pink hue, and it is forever busy regardless of what time you arrive for dinner. The front room fills first but the back rooms are slightly more intimate. Service can be somewhat disorganised but the staff are so well meaning and eager to please that no one gets particularly grouchy about it. The menu specialises in the food of India's southwest region of Kerala so expect fish, creamy coconut dishes and plenty for vegetarians. The Meen curry, made with roasted coconut and tamarind, is a highlight. The homemade chutneys and pre-meal snacks are also worth ordering – and don't ignore the madhuram or desserts, which will certainly fill you up if you weren't already.

Pied à Terre ✿

Innovative 💥💥💥

12

34 Charlotte St
✉ W1T 2NH
☎ (020) 7636 1178
www.pied-a-terre.co.uk

⊖ **Goodge Street**
Closed last week December, first week
January, Saturday lunch and Sunday

Menu £30/75

A/C
🛋
🍇
VISA
MC
AE

Pied a Terre

There are chapters and episodes in the life of every restaurant,
especially those that have been going strong for over twenty
years. In 2011 Pied à Terre underwent a change when Shane
Osborn, who had run the kitchen since 1999, sailed off into the
sunset with his family. Owner David Moore – who, like Arsène
Wenger, has always preferred to develop talent from within
his organisation rather than going out into the marketplace to
buy it – promoted Marcus Eaves to the top job. Marcus had
been head chef at their sister property, L'Autre Pied, since 2007
but also worked under Shane, so there are clear similarities in
the style of cooking and some of Shane's dishes have been
retained. The menu remains an appealing read and the cooking
is elaborate in its makeup, using ingredients of unimpeachable
quality. Although at the moment flavours can sometimes be a
little too concentrated for one another and newer dishes can
display a lack of conviction, this is still a talented kitchen. Time
will tell whether we have seen another seamless transition
from one chef to the next.

First Course

- Terrine of foie gras
  and smoked eel
  with wasabi vinaigrette.
- Brined scallops with
  a salad of celeriac,
  almonds, truffle
  and lemon, minus 8
  vinegar.

Main Course

- Poached lobster
  with confit pineapple
  and pata negra.
- Best End of lamb,
  honey-glazed turnip,
  garlic and Morteau
  sausage.

Dessert

- Millefeuille 'Peach
  Melba'.
- Bitter sweet
  chocolate tart,
  stout ice cream and
  macadamia nut
  cream.

Roka

I2

Japanese ✗✗

37 Charlotte St
✉ W1T 1RR
✆ (020) 7580 6464
www.rokarestaurant.com

⊖ Goodge Street
Closed 24-26 December

Carte £35/65

A/C
☼
VISA
MC
AE
①

Roka has one of those appealingly perceptible pulses that only really busy, well-run restaurants enjoy. It attracts a handsome crowd although they don't just come to glory in their mutual attractiveness but to share food that's original, easy to eat and just as pretty as they are. The kitchen takes the flavours, delicacy and strong presentation standards of Japanese food and adds its own contemporary touches. The menu can appear bewildering but just skip the set menus and order an assortment from the various headings; ensure you have one of the specialities from the on-view Robata grill. Sometimes too many dishes can arrive at once but the serving team are a friendly and capable bunch and they'll ease up on the delivery if you ask.

Salt Yard 🐶

H2

Mediterranean ✗

54 Goodge St.
✉ W1T 4NA
✆ (020) 7637 0657
www.saltyard.co.uk

⊖ Goodge Street
Closed 24 December-4 January,
Saturday lunch and Sunday

Carte approx. £20

A/C
🍇
VISA
MC
AE

The ground floor is the more boisterous and you'll feel like you're in the middle of a fun party; downstairs is better if you don't know your dining companion that well, although it too is full of life. This is all about tapas, although not just about Spanish tapas. One side of the menu has bar snacks, charcuterie and cheese but after ordering some olives or boquerones, turn over and you'll find three headings: Fish, Meat and Vegetable – one plate of each per person should do it. Unusual dishes, like braised gurnard with smoked Jersey Royals, sit alongside more traditional pairings like duck breast with parsnip purée. Prices are excellent; sharing is encouraged and service, young and sincere. Spain and Italy dominate the wine list.

Sardo

H1

Italian ✗✗

45 Grafton Way
✉ W1T 5DQ
☎ (020) 7387 2521
www.sardo-restaurant.com

⊖ **Warren Street**
Closed Christmas,
Saturday lunch and Sunday

Carte £26/34

A|C
VISA
MC
AE
D

Sardo always looks warm and inviting, especially as it stands on one of Bloomsbury's somewhat less hospitable streets. Inside is simplicity itself, with plain white walls and a minimum amount of decorative embellishment but the atmosphere is one of general bonhomie, thanks to a plethora of regulars and the young, friendly service. The highlights of the menu are dishes whose roots lie in Sardinia such as the rich bottarga; the salsiccia is also very robust, but desserts such as panna cotta also reveal the kitchen's lightness of touch. There's plenty of homemade pasta, three or four daily seasonal specials and tasty baskets of bread for which you will be charged. The first two pages of the wine list also celebrate the Italian island.

Tsunami

H2

Japanese ✗

93 Charlotte St.
✉ W1T 4PY
☎ (020) 7637 0050
www.tsunamirestaurant.co.uk

⊖ **Goodge Street**
Closed Saturday lunch and Sunday

Carte £30/38 s

A|C
VISA
MC
AE
D

You'll never find anyone from Clapham in Nobu or Roka because they always insist they have their own cheaper version in Tsunami. Now we all have the opportunity of seeing what they mean, thanks to their second branch here in the West End. Appropriately enough, it is at the less showy end of Charlotte Street but is prettily decorated with lacquered walls and a floral motif, with colour changing lights and lounge music. Staff have good intentions but do tend to go missing at crucial moments. The contemporary Japanese food is carefully prepared and the menu covers all points and includes plenty of originality. Seafood, whether grilled, as tempura or as sashimi salad, is a highlight and much can be shared without breaking the bank.

Bayswater · Maida Vale

There may not appear to be an obvious link between Maida Vale and Italy, but the name of this smart area to the west of central London is derived from a battle fought over two hundred years ago in Southern Italy, and the most appealing visitor attraction in the neighbourhood is the charming canalside **Little Venice.** To stroll around here on a summer's day brings to mind promenading in a more distant European clime; it's hard to believe that the ear-shattering roar of the Westway is just a short walk away. South of this iconic elevated roadway – a snaking route out from Maryle-bone to the western suburbs – is Bayswater, a busy area of impo-sing nineteenth century buildings that's the epicentre of London's Middle Eastern community.

During its Victorian heyday, **Bayswater** was a grand and gla-morous address for affluent and elegant types who wanted a giant green space (Hyde Park) on their doorstep. The whole area had been laid out in the mid 1800s, when grand squares and cream stuccoed terraces started to fill the acres between Brunel's curvy Paddington station and the park. But during the twentieth century Bayswater's cachet nose-dived, stigmatised as 'the wrong side of the park' by the arrivistes of Knightsbridge and Kensington. Today it's still a backpacker's pa-radise: home to a bewildering number of shabby tourist hotels, bedsits and B&Bs, converted from the grand houses. But this tells only a fraction of the modern story, because the area is under-going a massive facelift that will transform it forever. The hub of this makeover is the **Paddington Basin,** a gigantic reclamation of the old Grand Union Canal basin in the shadow of the rail terminus. From a ramshackle wasteground, it's now a shimmering zone of metal, steel and glass, a phantas-magoria of blue chip HQs, homes, shops and leisure facilities. Even the barges have been turned into permanently moored 'retail op-portunities'. Tree-lined towpaths along the perimeter complete the picture of a totally modern waterscape.

Lovers of the old Bayswater can still relish what made it famous in the first place: radiating out from **Lancaster Gate,** away from Hyde Park, is a web of streets with hand-some squares and tucked-away mews, and it still retains pockets of close-knit communities, such as Porchester Square, west of Pad-dington station. Meanwhile, the 'cathedral' of the area, Whiteleys shopping centre in **Queensway**, remains a pivotal landmark, as it has been for more than a century. Just beyond Whiteleys heading away from central London, **West-bourne Grove** is still reassuringly expensive, or at least the bit that heads determinedly towards Not-ting Hill. But the wind of change has rustled other parts of the

S. Ollivier / MICHELIN

neighbourhood: Connaught Street has evolved into a villagey quarter of boutiques, galleries and restaurants, while, further west, Craven Hill Gardens is the height of chic, courtesy of The Hempel, a boutique hotel.

Little Venice pretty much acts as a dividing line between Bayswater and Maida Vale. Technically, it's the point where the Paddington arm of the Grand Union Canal meets the **Regent's Canal,** but the name, coined by poet Robert Browning who lived close by, has come to encompass the whole area just to the north of the soaring Westway. Narrow boat moorings vie for attention alongside

the cafés and pubs that mercifully lack the frantic high street buzz so typical of their kind away from the water's edge. The permanently moored boats were here a long time before those upstarts at Paddington Basin. This is where you can find old-time favourites including a floating art gallery and a puppet theatre barge, and all overseen by the Warwick Castle pub, a stalwart of the area that's a minute's walk from the canal. Suitably refreshed, a wander round the residential streets of Maida Vale is very pleasant, dominated by the impressive Edwardian blocks of flats that conjure up a distinctive well-to-do scene.

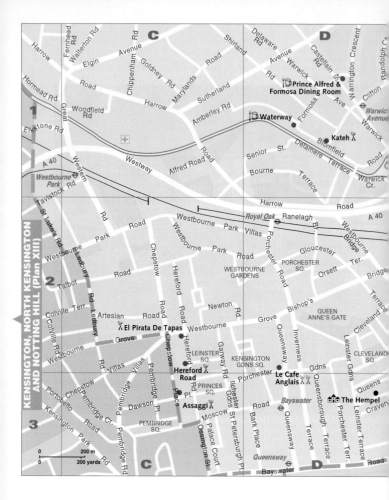

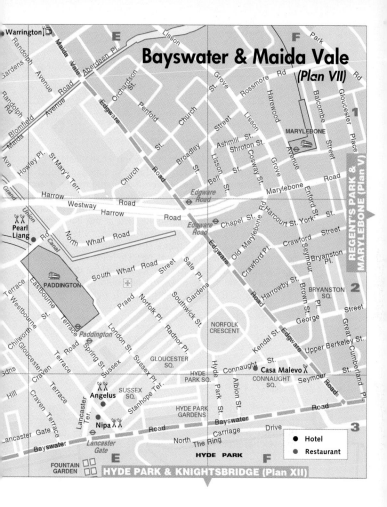

Bayswater & Maida Vale
(Plan VII)

Warrington

MARYLEBONE

REGENT'S PARK & MARYLEBONE (Plan V)

Pearl Liang

PADDINGTON

Paddington

Casa Malevo

NORFOLK CRESCENT

BRYANSTON SQ.

GLOUCESTER SQ.

HYDE PARK SQ.

SUSSEX SQ.

Angelus

HYDE PARK GARDENS

Nipa

CONNAUGHT SQ.

Lancaster Gate

HYDE PARK

FOUNTAIN GARDEN

- ● Hotel
- ● Restaurant

HYDE PARK & KNIGHTSBRIDGE (Plan XII)

Angelus

French 🍴🍴

4 Bathurst St.
✉ W2 2SD
℘ (020) 7402 0083
www.angelusrestaurant.co.uk

⊖ Lancaster Gate
Closed 24 December-2 January

Menu £32 (lunch) – Carte £39/54

A/C
⟨⟩
☼
VISA
M©
A≣

This 19C former pub, with its Murano chandeliers and art nouveau mirrors, has a warm and inclusive feel, and much of the credit for that goes to its very hospitable owner, Thierry Tomasin, who knows all his regulars and has put together an equally committed team. Along with the front restaurant, there is a surprisingly large sitting area at the back. Thierry has resisted the temptation to put in more tables, although with the downstairs area and a chef's table in the kitchen he probably has enough. The cooking style is French with British ingredients and he has a 'proper' kitchen which does the right things at the right time of year: who could resist braised ox cheek on a cold winter's night? Equal thought has gone into the wine list.

Assaggi

Italian 🍴

39 Chepstow Pl,
(above Chesterfield pub)
✉ W2 4TS
℘ (020) 7792 5501

⊖ Bayswater
Closed 2 weeks Christmas,
Sunday and bank holidays –
booking essential

Carte £37/50

A/C
VISA
M©

Assaggi has always been about simplicity, from the pared-down surroundings of this room above a pub to the handwritten bill at the end. The cooking has also always been about honest flavours and quality produce but a little inconsistency in delivery means that sometimes dishes don't always shine as they can. This is a pity because Assaggi has always been a spirited and inclusive restaurant and showed everyone that good food need not be accompanied by great ceremony. What hasn't changed is the warm and effusive service and the great atmosphere; its many regulars, who are kissed on the way in and the way out, treat the place like their local trattoria. However, for most of us, the prices represent a special night out.

Le Café Anglais

Modern European XX

8 Porchester Gdns
✉ W2 4BD
☎ (020) 7221 1415
www.lecafeanglais.co.uk

⊖ Bayswater
Closed 25-26 December
and 1 January

Menu £24 (weekday lunch) – Carte £25/52

A/C
☼
VISA
MC
AE

The terminal blandness of Queensway received a boost when Rowley Leigh, formerly of Kensington Place, opened this vast brasserie within Whiteley's, the Grade II listed shopping centre. His place shares the same conviviality and culinary accessibility as 'KP' but on a bigger scale and with better acoustics. The art deco styling, leather banquettes and big windows may reflect Whiteley's 1911 roots but it's still best to take the lift up from the side entrance. The menu offers a huge range of brasserie classics, from rabbit rillettes and the wonderful parmesan custard to the daily specials and meats turning slowly on the rotisserie. The wine list is resolutely Old World. You can always just pop in and sit at the oyster bar.

Casa Malevo

F2

Argentinian X

23 Connaught St
✉ W2 2AY
☎ (020) 7402 1988
www.casamalevo.com

⊖ Marble Arch
Closed Sunday dinner

Menu £17 (lunch) – Carte £26/36

A/C
⟨⟩
VISA
MC
AE

Carnivores are in clover these days due to the high number of places specialising in the cooking of red meat. Adding to the choice is this local Argentinian restaurant, with its bare brick walls and intimate lighting. Kick off by sharing the 'picada de campo': a board of grilled peppers, focaccia, pork cheek terrine and chicken matambre; then select from the grill, a piece of beef imported from Argentina – rib-eye, sirloin or fillet. The accompaniments may not quite come up to the mark but when you've got a steak and a bottle of Malbec from their exclusively Argentinian wine list, what else do you need? Those who have brought their own defibrillator can share the 'parrillada' containing rib-eye, fillet, chicken, lamb, chorizo and morcilla.

Hereford Road 😋

British 🍴

C2

3 Hereford Rd.
✉ W2 4AB
✆ (020) 7727 1144
www.herefordroad.org

⊖ Bayswater
Closed 24 December-3 January and 27-29
August – booking essential

Menu £16 (weekday lunch) – Carte £22/27

A/C
☼
VISA
M©
AE

Hereford Road is, first and foremost, a local restaurant. Lunch is a relaxed affair, with the room brightened by the large domed skylight, while dinner is the livelier feast, where everyone gives the impression that they walked here. Owner-chef Tom Pemberton is often the first person you see as the open kitchen is by the entrance – this was once a butcher's shop. He is an acolyte of St John and his cooking shares the same principles but not the same prices. So expect seasonal, British ingredients in very tasty dishes devoid of frippery. Offal is handled with aplomb and dishes designed for two, such as the shoulder of lamb or the whole oxtail, are so good you won't actually want to share them. Staff are enthusiastic and articulate.

Kateh 😋

Persian 🍴

D1

5 Warwick Pl
✉ W9 2PX
✆ (020) 7289 3393
www.kateh.net

⊖ Warwick Avenue
Booking essential –
(dinner only and lunch Friday-Sunday)

Carte £17/30

⛱
A/C
☼
VISA
M©
AE

Booking is imperative if you want to join those locals who have already discovered what a little jewel they have here in the form of this buzzy, busy Persian restaurant. Kateh is a type of rice from the Gilan Province in Iran; the fishermen there cook it to a sticky consistency and mix it with their daily catch. It features as a traditional accompaniment here, along with herbs and fruits. The baby calamari is delicious, the stews are very satisfying and the grilling is expertly done over charcoal. Warm sesame-coated flatbreads are moreish and be sure to finish with an authentic dessert like 'kolouche' (date and walnut pastries) along with tea made with cardamom. There's a delightful decked terrace at the back.

Nipa

E3

Thai ✗✗

Lancaster Terr
✉ W2 2TY
☎ (020) 7551 6039
www.niparestaurant.co.uk

⊖ Lancaster Gate
Closed Christmas-NewYear,
Saturday lunch and Sunday

Menu £29 – Carte £23/32

A/C
VISA
MC
AE
D

You'll find Nipa to be a little oasis of calm and hospitality, once you've made it up to the first floor of the Royal Lancaster and sidestepped the businessmen on their laptops in the adjacent lounge. Its teak panelling and ornaments are all imported from Thailand and they've done a convincing job of replicating the original Nipa in Bangkok's Landmark Hotel – if anything, it's even a little smarter. The menu is comprehensive, with a mix of the recognisable blended with more regional specialities. Dishes are marked 1-3 in chillies for their respective heat, come in decent sizes and the harmonious blend of flavours and textures successfully delivers what the aromas promise. Set menus are at the back and provide a convenient all-round experience.

Pearl Liang

E2

Chinese ✗✗

8 Sheldon Sq., Paddington Central
✉ W2 6EZ
☎ (020) 7289 7000
www.pearlliang.co.uk

⊖ Paddington
Closed 24 and 25 December

Menu £25 – Carte £24/42

A/C

☀
VISA
MC
AE

Chain restaurants tend to dominate corporate developments like 'Paddington Central' therefore thanks should be extended to Pearl Liang for flying the flag of independence. The weighty menu dedicates each page to a different main ingredient, be it poultry, fish, prawns or duck. There is the occasional interloper from other Asian cuisines but it's best to stick to the Chinese specialities. Prices allow for enthusiastic ordering and the prawn and pork dishes score highly, especially the king prawn with chilli. It's a big place whose large tables are more likely to be occupied by business types than families but the fast and furious service gives it an authentic edge. The surrounding offices make use of the takeaway lunch menu.

El Pirata De Tapas

C2

Spanish ✗

115 Westbourne Grove
✉ W2 4UP
☎ (020) 7727 5000
www.elpiratadetapas.co.uk

⊖ Bayswater
Closed 24-26 December,
2-3 September and 1 January

Menu £10/25 – Carte £16/18

A/C
☼
VISA
MC
AE

Spanish restaurants and tapas-style eating satisfy our appetite for a shared, less structured dining experience and El Pirata is no exception. It's spread over two floors, although you wouldn't want to be the first table downstairs, and is decorated in a contemporary yet warm style. The staff give helpful advice on a menu that is quite lengthy but helpfully divided up into sections, from charcuterie to fish, croquettes to vegetarian, meat to paellas; there are also a couple of appealing and balanced set menus and the pricing structure is far from piratical. The kitchen shows respect for traditional flavours but is not afraid of trying new things or adding a note of playfulness to some dishes. A good place to come with friends.

Prince Alfred
& Formosa Dining Room

D1

Modern European 🍺

5A Formosa St
✉ W9 1EE
☎ (020) 7286 3287
www.theprincealfred.com

⊖ Warwick Avenue

Menu £16 (lunch) – Carte £25/39

A/C
☼
VISA
MC
AE

Original plate glass, panels and snugs make The Prince Alfred a wonderful example of a classic Victorian pub. Unfortunately, the eating is done in the Formosa Dining Room extension on the side but at least it's a lively room with capable cooking. There's a rustic theme running through the menu, with a strong British accent, so traditionalists will enjoy the fish pie, potted trout, steak and ale pie and calves liver but there are also risottos, parfaits and terrines for those whose tastes are more continental. The open kitchen is not averse to sprucing up some classics, for example your burger arrives adorned with foie gras and truffles. Prices are realistic, even with a charge made for bread, and the friendly team cope well under pressure.

Warrington

D1

Modern European 🍴🍺

93 Warrington Cres   ⊖ Maida Vale
✉ W9 1EH
☏ (020) 7592 7960
www.gordonramsay.com

Menu £22 (lunch and early dinner) – Carte £27/36

A/C

VISA

MC

AE

The British pub appears to be steadily breaking up into two rival camps: there's the traditional pub, where you can stand at the bar with a sausage roll in one hand and a pint in the other; and the modern one, where you're given a table and someone serves you pork belly and a glass of Pinot Noir. The joy of The Warrington is that both types are available under one roof. The wood-panelled ground floor with its friezes and mosaic is full of atmosphere and the menu here includes fish pie and bangers. Upstairs is altogether smarter and the mood a little more subdued. Here the menu is much more sophisticated, as you'd expect from a Gordon Ramsay restaurant, although it's still commendably British and could include braised duck or pan-fried bream.

Waterway

D1

Modern European 🍴🍺

54 Formosa St   ⊖ Warwick Avenue.
✉ W9 2JU
☏ (020) 7266 3557
www.thewaterway.co.uk

Carte £26/36

A/C

VISA

MC

AE

A canalside setting offering refreshment to passing narrowboaters; a large terrace besieged by drinkers; and live music on a Thursday night – it sounds like a pub and even has the necessary warmth and bustle, but inside it's all surprisingly smart. There's a bar occupying one side and a restaurant the other, with no sign anywhere of any spit or sawdust. The menu and cooking are both comparable to the most urbane of urban gastropub: the muscular flavours of black pudding with chorizo and hen's egg are in contrast to its delicate presentation, while fillet of bream with prawn mash reveals the kitchen's lighter touch. Things tail off somewhat with desserts but prices are realistic. Service is youthful, bubbly and capable.

City of London · Clerkenwell Finsbury · Southwark

Say what you like about London, **The City** is the place where it all started. The Romans developed this small area – this square mile – nearly two thousand years ago, and today it stands as the economic heartbeat of not only the capital, but the country as a whole. Each morning it's besieged with an army of bankers, lawyers and traders, and each evening it's abandoned to an eerie ghost-like fate. Of course, this mass exodus is offset by the two perennial crowd-pullers, **St Paul's** and the **Tower of London**, but these are both on the periphery of the area, away from the frenetic commercial zone within. The casual visitor tends to steer clear of the City, but for those willing to mix it with the daytime swarm of office workers, there are many historical nuggets hidden away, waiting to be mined. You can find here, amongst the skyscrapers, a tempting array of Roman ruins, medieval landmarks and brooding churches designed by Wren and Hawksmoor. One of the best ways of encapsulating everything that's happened here down the centuries is to visit the Museum of London, on London Wall, which tells the story of the city from the very start, and the very start means 300,000 BC.

For those seeking the hip corners of this part of London, the best advice is to head slightly northwest, using the brutalist space of the **Barbican Arts Centre** as your marker. You're now entering **Clerkenwell**. Sliding north/south through here is the bustling and buzzy **St John Street,** home to some of the funkiest eating establishments and gastropubs in London, their proximity to **Smithfield** meat market giving a clue as to much of the provenance. Clerkenwell's revivalist vibe has seen the steady reclamation of old factory space: during the Industrial Revolution, the area boomed with the introduction of breweries, print works and the manufacture of clocks and watches. After World War II decline set in, but these days city professionals and loft-dwellers are drawn to the area's zeitgeist-leading galleries and clubs, not to mention the wonderful floor-to-ceiling delicatessens. Clerkenwell is home to The Eagle, one of the city's pioneering gastropubs and still a local favourite, brimming over with newspaper journalists (it's near The Guardian offices). It even has its own art gallery upstairs. Meanwhile, the nearby **Exmouth Market** teems with trendy bars and restaurants, popular with those on their way to the perennially excellent dance concerts at Sadler's Wells Theatre.

The area was once a religious centre, frequented by monks and nuns; its name derives from the parish clerks who performed Biblical mystery plays around the Clerk's Well set in a nunnery wall. This can be found in **Farringdon Lane** complete with an exhibition explaining all. Close by in St John's

C. Eymenier / MICHELIN

Lane is the 16C gatehouse which is home to the Museum of the Order of St John (famous today for its ambulance services), and chock full of fascinating objects related to the Order's medieval history.

Not too long ago, a trip over London Bridge to **Southwark** was for locals only, its trademark grimness ensuring it was well off the tourist map. These days, visitors treat it as a place of pilgrimage as three of London's modern success stories reside here. **Tate Modern** has become the city's most visited attraction, a huge former power station that generates a blistering

show of modern art from 1900 to the present day, its massive turbine hall a must-see feature in itself. Practically next door but a million miles away architecturally is Shakespeare's **Globe,** a wonderful evocation of medieval showtime. Half a mile east is the best food market in London: **Borough Market.** Foodies can't resist the organic feel-good nature of the place, with its mind-boggling number of stalls selling produce ranging from every kind of fruit and veg to rare-breed meats, oils, preserves, chocolates and breads. And that's just for hors-d'œuvres...

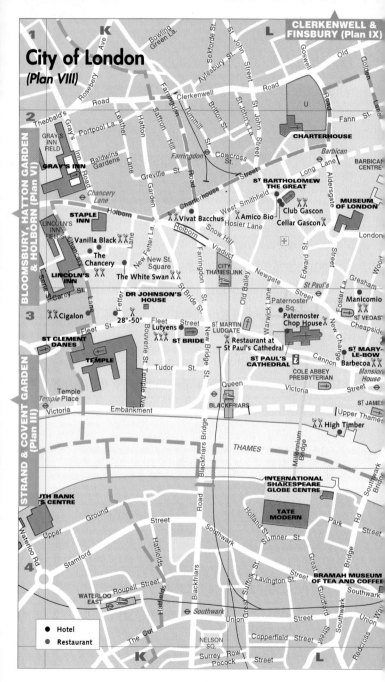

City of London
(Plan VIII)

BLOOMSBURY, HATTON GARDEN & HOLBORN (Plan VI)

STRAND & COVENT GARDEN (Plan III)

Bowling Green La.
Sekfords St.
St John Street
Goswell
Old
Golden La.
Fann St.

Rosebery Ave
Gray's Inn Road
Clerkenwell Road
Farringdon Road
St John's Rd.
Aylesbury St.
Britton St.

Theobald's Road
Portpool La.
Leather La.
Hatton
Saffron Hill
Tunmill St.
Cowcross St.
Charterhouse

CHARTERHOUSE

GRAY'S INN FIELD

GRAY'S INN

Baldwins Gardens
Greville St.
Garden
Hatton Garden

Chancery Lane

STAPLE INN

Holborn

Long Lane
Aldersgate
BARBICAN CENTRE

MUSEUM OF LONDON

St BARTHOLOMEW THE GREAT

⚔ Vivat Bacchus
West Smithfield
Snow Hill
Hosier Lane
⚔ Amico Bio Club Gascon
Cellar Gascon ⚔

London Wood

LINCOLN'S INN FIELDS

⚔ Vanilla Black

New Fetter La.
New St. Square

The Chancery

Holborn Viaduct

CITY THAMESLINK

Newgate
Edward St.
Old Bailey
Warwick Lane
St Paul's

Gresham

Foster La.
⚔ Manicomio
St VEDAS

LINCOLN'S INN

⚔ The White Swan

New Bridge St.
Fleet
Paternoster Sq.
Paternoster Chop House ⚔

St Paul's
New Change
Cheapside

St Carey St.

DR JOHNSON'S HOUSE

Fetter St.

⚔ Cigalon

28°-50°
Fleet St.
Bouverie St.
Lutyens ⚔
St BRIDE ⚔

St MARTIN LUDGATE

Restaurant at St Paul's Cathedral ⚔

St PAUL'S CATHEDRAL

St MARY-LE-BOW
⚔ Barbecoa

ST CLEMENT DANES

TEMPLE

Temple Ave
Tudor St.

Cannon Street
COLE ABBEY PRESBYTERIAN
Mansion House

Temple Place
Victoria
Embankment

Queen
BLACKFRIARS

Victoria Street
St JAMES
Upper Thames
⚔ High Timber

THAMES

Blackfriars Bridge
Millennium Bridge

Southwark Bridge

UTH BANK 'S CENTRE

INTERNATIONAL SHAKESPEARE GLOBE CENTRE

TATE MODERN

Waterloo Rd
Upper Ground
Stamford Street
Hatfields
Blackfriars Road
Southwark Street
Holland St.
Sumner St.
Park Street

BRAMAH MUSEUM OF TEA AND COFFEE

WATERLOO EAST
Roupell Street
Southwark
Union Street
Great Suffolk Street
Lavington St.
Great Guildford Street
Southwark
Southwark St.
Redcross Way

NELSON SQ.
The Cut
Surrey Row
Pocock Street
Copperfield Street

● Hotel
● Restaurant

K   L

186

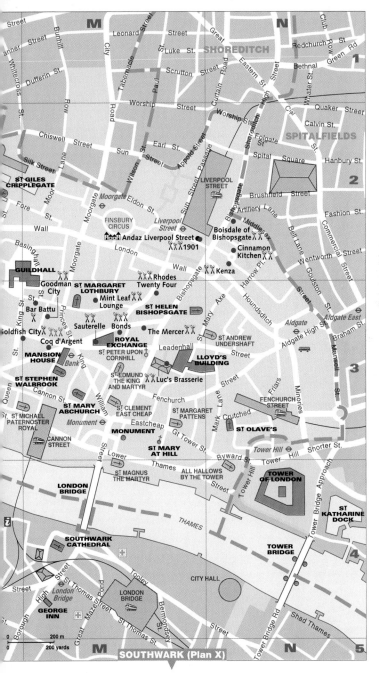

Street
Leonard Street
Street
Great
Club
Redchurch Row St.
SHOREDITCH
Bethnal Green Rd
Whitecross St
Tanner Street
Bunhill
City Road
St Luke St.
Scrutton Street
Eastern St.
Shoreditch High Street
Water St.
Quaker Street
Dufferin St.
Paul Street
Curtain Road
Worship Street
Calvin St.
Folgate St.
SPITALFIELDS
Worship Street
Shoreditch Station
Chiswell Street
Earl St.
Spital
Square
Hanbury St.
Silk Street
Row
Tabernacle Street
Sun Street
Wilson Street
Appold Street
Sun Street Passage
Bishopsgate
Brushfield Street
Fashion St.
ST GILES
CRIPPLEGATE
Moorgate
Eldon St.
LIVERPOOL
STREET
Artillery Lane
Middlesex St.
Bell Lane
Commercial Street
Fore St.
Moorgate
FINSBURY
CIRCUS
Liverpool
Street
Boisdale of
Bishopsgate
Cinnamon
Kitchen
Wentworth Street
Goulston Street
Wall
Moor St.
🏨 Andaz Liverpool Street
London
1901
Basinghall St.
Wall
Kenza
Harrow Pl.
Aldgate East
GUILDHALL
Moorgate
Rhodes
Twenty Four
Houndsditch
Braham St.
Goodman
City
ST MARGARET
LOTHBURY
Mint Leaf
Lounge
ST HELEN
BISHOPSGATE
St Mary Axe
Aldgate
Aldgate High St.
Mansell St.
Bar Battu
Princes St.
Bishopsgate
Goldfish City
Sauterelle
Bonds
The Mercer
ST ANDREW
UNDERSHAFT
Coq d'Argent
ROYAL
EXCHANGE
Leadenhall
Street
MANSION
HOUSE
King St.
Bank
ST PETER UPON
CORNHILL
LLOYD'S
BUILDING
Minories
ST STEPHEN
WALBROOK
ST EDMUND
THE KING
AND MARTYR
Luc's Brasserie
Fenchurch
FENCHURCH
STREET
Friars
ST MICHAEL
PATERNOSTER
ROYAL
Cannon St.
William St.
ST CLEMENT
EAST CHEAP
ST MARGARET
PATTENS
Mark Lane
Crutched
ST OLAVE'S
Queen
ST MARY
ABCHURCH
Monument
Eastcheap
MONUMENT
Gt Tower St.
CANNON
STREET
Lower
ST MARY
AT HILL
Byward St.
Tower Hill
Shorter St.
Thames
Street
LONDON
BRIDGE
ST MAGNUS
THE MARTYR
ALL HALLOWS
BY THE TOWER
Tower Hill
TOWER
OF LONDON
Tower Bridge Approach
ST
KATHARINE
DOCK
THAMES
TOWER
BRIDGE
Shad Thames
SOUTHWARK
CATHEDRAL
CITY HALL
London
Bridge
Tooley
LONDON
BRIDGE
High Street
St Thomas Street
GEORGE
INN
Borough
Great Maze Pond
St Thomas St.
Bermondsey
Street
Tower Bridge Rd
0   200 m
0   200 yards
SOUTHWARK (Plan X)

187

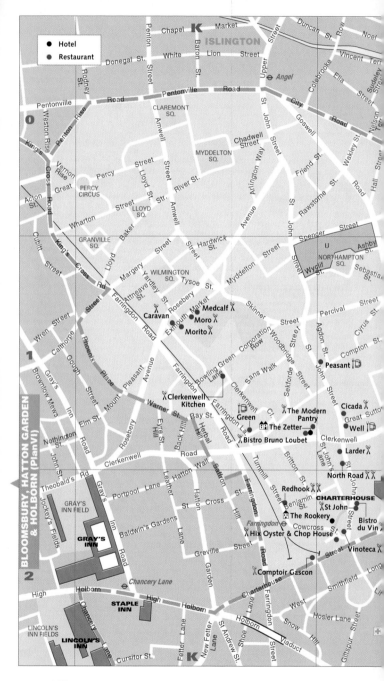

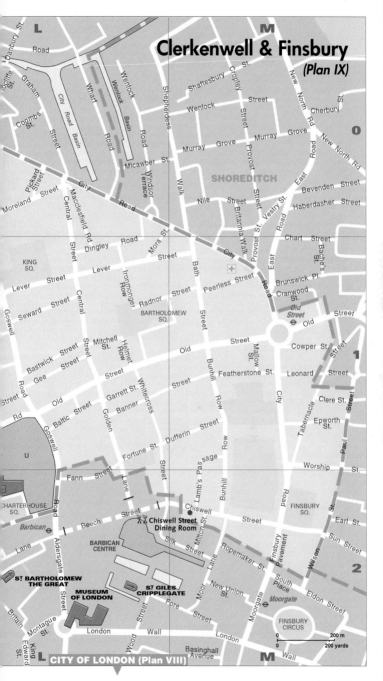

Clerkenwell & Finsbury
(Plan IX)

SHOREDITCH

KING
SQ.

BARTHOLOMEW
SQ.

Old
Street

CHARTERHOUSE
SQ.

Barbican

Chiswell Street
Dining Room

FINSBURY
SQ.

BARBICAN
CENTRE

St BARTHOLOMEW
THE GREAT

MUSEUM
OF LONDON

ST GILES
CRIPPLEGATE

FINSBURY
CIRCUS

Moorgate

0   200 m
0   200 yards

CITY OF LONDON (Plan VIII)

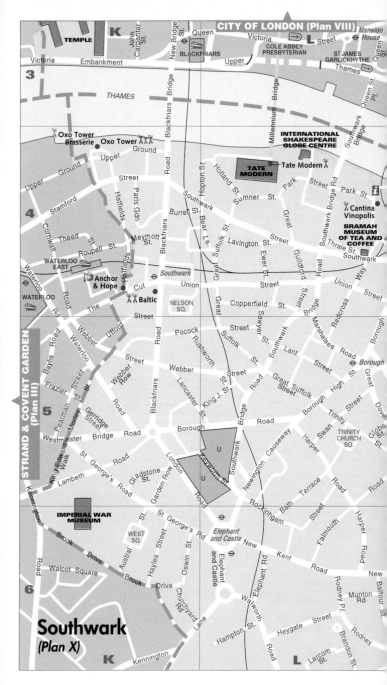

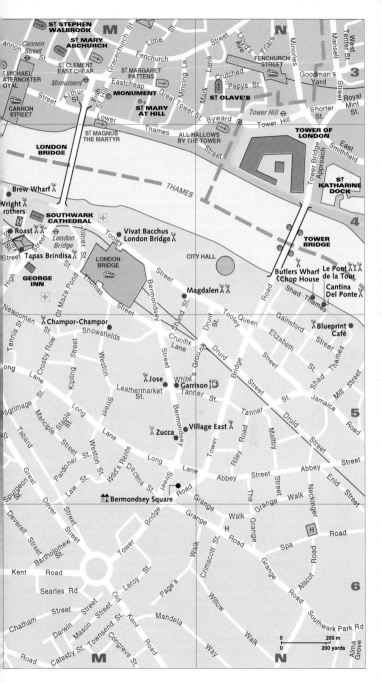

Amico Bio

Italian vegetarian ✗

L2

44 Cloth Fair
✉ EC1A 7JQ
✆ (0207) 6007 778
www.amicobio.co.uk

⊖ Barbican
Closed 25 December, Saturday lunch,
Sunday and bank holidays

Carte £21/26

A/C
VISA
M©
A≡

Opening a vegetarian restaurant just yards from Smithfield Market may seem like a grand ironic gag but a dish of the baked red peppers with capers and olives could turn the most committed of carnivores. This simple little Italian place is owned by an experienced chef and his cousin and all their organic produce comes from their family farm in Capua. The menu changes as the produce comes and goes so don't be surprised if a dish suddenly runs out. The cooking is light and fresh with combinations of flavours that remain true to the chef's upbringing in Campania. He's happy to engage with his customers so it's worth asking for his recommendations. Photos of the farm adorn the walls and prices are unimpeachably generous.

Anchor & Hope 😊

British 🍺

K4

36 The Cut
✉ SE1 8LP
✆ (020) 7928 9898

⊖ Southwark.
Closed Christmas-New Year, Sunday
dinner, Monday lunch and bank holidays
– (bookings not accepted)

Carte £23/32

☝
VISA
M©

The Anchor & Hope is still running at full steam and its popularity shows no sign of abating. It's not hard to see why: combine a menu that changes with each service and is a paragon of seasonality, with cooking that is gutsy, bold and wholesome, and you end up with immeasurably rewarding dishes like suckling kid chops with wild garlic, succulent roast pigeon with lentils or buttermilk pudding with poached rhubarb. The place has a contagiously congenial feel and the staff all pull in the same direction; you may spot a waiter trimming veg or a chef delivering dishes. The no-reservation policy remains, so either get here early or be prepared to wait – although you can now book for Sunday lunch, when everyone sits down at 2pm for a veritable feast.

Baltic

Eastern European ✗✗

74 Blackfriars Rd
✉ SE1 8HA
✆ (020) 7928 1111
www.balticrestaurant.co.uk

⊖ Southwark
Closed 24-25 December, 1 January and
bank holidays – booking advisable at
dinner

Menu £18 (weekday lunch) – Carte £27/37

VISA
MC
AE

Baltic celebrated ten years in 2011 and is as busy as ever, serving over 100 diners every night. The façade may have faded over time but the atmosphere inside is as contagious as ever, as the noise from the bar competes with the clatter from the large dining area at the back. Just kick back, order a vodka and get down to choosing from the menu. If you don't know your pierogi from your pelmeni, don't panic – most of the staff are Polish so help is at hand. Starters include soups such as botwinka and zurek; blinis come with all the toppings and meat dishes outnumber fish choices 2 to 1. Just be sure you're wearing your eating-boots because portions are big and dishes are packed with flavour. There's jazz on Sunday nights.

Bar Battu

French ✗

48 Gresham St
✉ EC2V 7AY
✆ (020) 7036 6100
www.barbattu.com

⊖ Bank
Closed 24 December-2 January,
Saturday, Sunday and bank holidays

Menu £20 – Carte £24/38

A/C
⅗
VISA
MC
AE

So named because this was previously a somewhat neglected and unloved site, Bar Battu captures the zeitgeist not only with its bare brick interior and lively atmosphere but also through its loyalty to small, artisanal producers and, in particular, with its appealing menu of small plates and rustic pan-European main courses. The best dishes tend to be the gutsiest, such as the snail and oxtail ragout, but the charcuterie is also well-sourced and the homemade ice creams well worth exploring. It is also a self-styled 'natural wine bar' and features a list of unfiltered wines made in small quantities from organically grown grapes. The wine list is thoughtfully put together and many of the wines are available by the glass, carafe and bottle.

Barbecoa

L3

20 New Change Passage
✉ EC4M 9AG
✆ (020) 3005 8555
www.barbecoa.com

⊖ St. Paul's
Booking essential

Carte £28/45

A/C
☼
VISA
MC
AE

There are many things that us Brits lead the world in, but barbecuing ain't one of them. Thankfully we have American chef Adam Perry Lane, in collaboration with our own Jamie Oliver, to show us how it should be done. For a start, they have a kitchen with all the right kit to ensure the prime meats are cooked to perfection, whether that's rib-eye or half a chicken. But to really see the standard to aim for when next entertaining in your garden, order the pulled pork shoulder with BBQ sauce and cornbread, and then roll up your sleeves. If you haven't quite got the appetite for crispy pig cheeks, then start with one of the interesting salads; by dessert you may be willing to share so go for Chocolate Nemesis, Jamie's homage to his alma mater.

Bistro du Vin

L2

40 St John St
✉ EC1M 4DL
✆ (020) 7490 9230
www.bistroduvinandbar.com

⊖ Farringdon

Carte £26/45

A/C
⟨▢⟩
⅜
☼
VISA
MC
AE
⓪

They've nailed the bistro aesthetic and oenologists will find much to savour, so there can be no arguing with the name. The first stand-alone restaurant from the people behind the Hotel du Vin group is a spirited affair, with a risk-free but appealing menu and a thoughtfully compiled wine list – they even have a hi-tech by-the-glass 'vending' machine dispenser that lets you try some fairly special wines. French and British dishes dominate the menu, with a few Italian specialities thrown in; the 'plat du jour' could be bouillabaisse, a roast or osso bucco. However, the stars of the show are the various cuts of beef which are dry-cured in-house and cooked on (and in) the Josper grill in the open kitchen.

Bistrot Bruno Loubet

K1

St John's Sq., 86-88 Clerkenwell Rd.
✉ EC1M 5RJ
✆ (020) 7324 4455
www.bistrotbrunoloubet.com

⊖ **Farringdon**
Closed 25-26 December –
booking advisable

Carte £30/40

The original Bistrot Bruno's heyday in Soho was around 1994, at a time when London house prices were struggling to recover, England were no-shows at the World Cup and Silvio Berlusconi was Italy's prime minister. So 2010 seemed as good a time as any for Bruno Loubet to return to the capital after his sojourn in Australia. He did surprise a few people by pitching up in Clerkenwell, at the trendy Zetter hotel, but it's a good fit for his satisfying and rustic cooking. There is actually more depth and sophistication to the food than the menu suggests and it's not exclusively French: a little Asian spicing or Moroccan flavour can find their way in too. The room is bright; the staff unhurried and the clientele self-assured.

Blueprint Café

N5

Design Museum, Shad Thames,
Butlers Wharf ✉ SE1 2YD
✆ (020) 7378 7031
www.blueprintcafe.co.uk

⊖ **London Bridge**
Closed Sunday dinner

Menu £20/22 – Carte £24/38

You'll find Blueprint Café at the less frenzied end of Shad Thames, sitting proudly in its elevated position above the Design Museum. Lunch is the more relaxed affair, when you can take advantage of the retractable windows and the views of the comings and goings on the river, thanks to the binoculars placed on each table. Long-standing chef Jeremy Lee, who despite doing more telly work these days is still often at the stove, has long been a champion of British produce and his simple, yet informed, technique is evident in dishes like beetroot salad with horseradish, hare and beef pie and steamed ginger pudding with custard. Do ensure you order vegetables as dishes arrive unadorned and as understated as the menu suggests.

Boisdale of Bishopsgate

N2

Swedeland Crt., 202 Bishopsgate
✉ EC2M 4NR
✆ (020) 7283 1763
www.boisdale.co.uk

⊖ Liverpool Street
Closed 25 December-2 January, Saturday,
Sunday and bank holidays

Carte £28/52

A/C
VISA
MC
AE

It's easy to miss and the ground floor is a popular spot for those who like some champagne and oysters on their way home; but follow the tartan carpet down to the relative calm of the cosy and characterful restaurant, complete with live music. That carpet was a clue as this is all about Scotland. Admittedly some of the Scottish accents are as unconvincing as Mel Gibson's but there is no denying that the food is the real thing. The large menu is made up of plenty of Scottish specialities and reminds us just how spectacular the produce is north of the border. Salmon, shellfish, beef and, of course, haggis are the perennial favourites but so are the daily specials of game, fish and assorted pies. You'll leave with an urge to hike somewhere.

Bonds

M3

5 Threadneedle St.
✉ EC2R 8AY
✆ (020) 7657 8088
www.theetoncollection.com

⊖ Bank
Closed Saturday,
Sunday and Bank Holidays

Menu £23 (lunch and early dinner) – Carte £37/51

A/C

VISA
MC
AE
①

Bonds repays the investment of its customers by providing plenty of interest, in both the menu choice and the surroundings. This former banking hall dates from the 1850s and its marble, pillars and panelling make it a grand old room in which to house a restaurant. The cooking is equally bold and the experienced kitchen produced well-versed dishes that are unfussy and keep their roots largely within Europe. Slow-cooking is a popular technique and is used with veal shin, rump of lamb and pork belly, while fish from Newhaven is handled deftly. Service is up to speed at lunch; dinner is less frenzied, when the lower lighting helps create a more intimate atmosphere. The cocktail list makes the adjacent bar worth visiting.

Brew Wharf

Traditional ✗

Brew Wharf Yard, Stoney St
✉ SE1 9AD
✆ (020) 7378 6601
www.brewwharf.com

⊖ London Bridge
Closed Sunday dinner
and bank holidays

Carte £23/35

Needless to say, anywhere with the word 'brew' in the title is not somewhere for a romantic evening. But if you're on a night out with a few friends then this has all the ingredients: a large screen showing sport in the bar, real ales from the restaurant's own microbrewery, bottled beers imported from everywhere from Cuba to Kenya, and the sort of food that's ideal with a pint. Don't bother messing around with starters; head straight for the main courses of steak and ale pie, liver and bacon, pork belly or confit of duck. Even the platters for two don't let up: one includes spring rolls, kebabs, fishcakes and chips. It's all well-organised; you can order a cask for your group and they hold their own beer festival in October.

Butlers Wharf Chop House

British ✗

36e Shad Thames, Butlers Wharf
✉ SE1 2YE
✆ (020) 7403 3403
www.chophouse.co.uk

⊖ London Bridge
Closed 1-2 January

Menu £27 (lunch) – Carte dinner £29/45

"Location, location, location" as every estate agent has said. A little summer sunshine and few restaurants in London can rival Butlers Wharf's delightful spot on the river. However, those terrace tables can't be booked – just join the queue at the bar. The menu reads like a roll-call of Britishness: expect potted shrimps, prawn cocktail, grilled lemon sole with Jersey Royals and the classic mixed grill. While the kitchen doesn't always quite deliver on the promise of the menu, dishes are generally satisfying. Seasonal offerings, such as the long list of strawberry dessert creations in June, are usually worth exploring. Levels of noise and general merriment are high and staff just about cope with the high numbers of customers.

Cantina Del Ponte

N4

Italian ✗

36c Shad Thames, Butlers Wharf
✉ SE1 2YE
☎ (020) 7403 5403
www.cantina.co.uk

⊖ London Bridge
Closed 25-27 December

Menu £18 (lunch) – Carte £20/28

A refurbishment a few years back revitalised this Italian stalwart. They kept the large mural on one wall and created a pleasantly relaxing, faux-rustic environment. The menu was also tweaked: it was out with the pizzas and in with a greater degree of authenticity. The focus is on appealing and flavoursome dishes and the set menu represents decent value. There's an appealing selection on offer, with the focus very much on recognisable standards and old favourites. However, flavours are well-defined and portions are bigger than expected. The wine list covers all of Italy and there's ample choice by the glass. The first tables to go on a summer's day are naturally those on the riverside terrace under the awning.

Cantina Vinopolis

L4

Mediterranean ✗

No.1 Bank End
✉ SE1 9BU
☎ (020) 7940 8333
www.cantinavinopolis.com

⊖ London Bridge
Closed bank holidays

Menu £30 – Carte £25/39

One of the advantages of a restaurant being beneath huge Victorian arches is that larger parties are in no danger of dominating the room: the rumble of passing trains and a vast vaulted brick ceiling ensure that any extra noise is easily absorbed. Cantina is the restaurant attached to the wine museum, Vinopolis, and its wine list is appropriately impressive in its range and reach. But this isn't just a restaurant for oenologists: due care is also given to the food, which comes with a healthy Mediterranean glow. The à laCarte can be a little pricey but the set menu, which is not too dissimilar and offers an adequate selection, represents better value. Salads are satisfying and the open kitchen also handles fish particularly well.

Caravan

K1

11-13 Exmouth Mkt ↔ **Farringdon**
✉ EC1R 4QD Closed Christmas-New Year
✆ (020) 7833 8115 and dinner Sunday –
www.caravanonexmouth.co.uk booking advisable

Carte £24/31

VISA

MC

AE

◑

A discernible Antipodean vibe pervades this casual eatery, from the laid-back, easy-going charm of the serving team to the kitchen's confident combining of unusual flavours; even in the excellent flat-whites served by the barista. There's an ersatz industrial feel to the room and a randomness to the decorative touches that belies the seriousness of the ambition. The 100% Arabica beans are roasted daily in the basement, the wine list features an unusual selection of producers and plenty of organic wines, and the owners' travels (hence the name) inform the innovative and inventive cooking. There's everything for everyone, from breakfast to small plates to share, or even main courses for two – this really is a caravan of love.

Cellar Gascon

L2

59 West Smithfield ↔ **Barbican**
✉ EC1A 9DS Closed 22 December-4 January,
✆ (020) 7600 7561 Saturday, Sunday and bank holidays
www.cellargascon.com – booking essential at lunch

Carte £14/19

A/C

🎍

VISA

MC

AE

Tucked into the side of Club Gascon is their narrow cellar, which began life as a wine bar with a few nibbles thrown in but now, with the whole 'small plates' thing being all the rage, the food enjoys more of a starring role. It's not unlike a smart tapas bar and the monthly changing menu has plenty of treats: pâtés, rillettes, farmhouse hams, cheeses and even some salads for the virtuous, but the Toulouse sausages and the Gascony pie of duck and mushrooms really stand out. The terrific value 'express' lunch, which includes a dish of the day, is hard to beat and understandably popular. The wine list is a shorter version of next door's and focuses on France's south west; they also hold monthly wine tasting evenings.

Champor-Champor

M5

62-64 Weston St.
✉ SE1 3QJ
☎ (020) 7403 4600
www.champor-champor.com

⊖ London Bridge
Closed 1 week Christmas, 1 week
Easter, Sunday and bank holidays –
(dinner only)

Carte £34/43

[A/C]
[⟨⟩]
[VISA]
[MC]
[AE]

It's no surprise that Champor-Champor celebrated its tenth birthday in 2010 as it has always managed to beguile diners with its quirky, colourful decoration, the warm service it extends to its regulars and its authentic cooking that delivers quite a punch. Booking is vital but then they do go to the trouble of putting little name cards on each table. Be sure to ask for the second room as it has more artefacts, better lighting and a very romantic mezzanine. The food is rooted in Malay traditions, with just a flick of modernity. Great homemade banana bread gets things going; main courses arrive in big bowls with rich and creamily spiced sauce or carefully judged broths, depending on the season; ice creams are also made in-house.

The Chancery

K2

9 Cursitor St
✉ EC4A 1LL
☎ (020) 7831 4000
www.thechancery.co.uk

⊖ Chancery Lane
Closed 24 December-4 January,
Saturday lunch and Sunday

Menu £35

[A/C]
[VISA]
[MC]
[AE]
[⦾]

Surrounded by the law courts, The Chancery, open only during the week, provides the perfect spot for that last meal of freedom or for celebrating an acquittal. It is the sister restaurant to The Clerkenwell Dining Room and the bright main room benefits from the large picture windows and understated decoration. This is room in which to reserve your table, rather than the basement which can lack something in atmosphere. Service is sufficiently fleet of foot and efficient to reassure those with an eye on the adjournment. The cooking comes suitably well-judged and is modern in style but underpinned by a solid understanding of the ingredients. The wine list has some well-chosen bottles under £25.

Chiswell Street Dining Rooms

British 🍴🍴

M2

56 Chiswell St   ⊖ Moorgate
✉ EC1Y 4SA
℘ (020) 7614 0177
www.chiswellstreetdining.com

Carte £30/52

A/C
☼
VISA
MC
AE

The Martin brothers used their successful Botanist restaurant as the model for their corner spot at the former Whitbread brewery. As it also acts as a hotel dining room for the Montcalm Hotel, it's open for breakfast, but the place really comes alive in the evening, thanks to its lively cocktail bar. There's a pleasing Britishness to the menu and the kitchen makes good use of nearby Billingsgate, with classics like whole Cornish lemon sole, and poached langoustines. Those who prefer more muscular cooking can head for the Hereford snail and smoked bacon pie or Aberdeen Angus rib-eye; and who cannot fail to smile when they see 'Knickerbocker Glory' on a menu? The smartly kitted-out staff cope very well with the constant buzzy atmosphere.

Cicada

Asian 🍴

L1

132-134 St John St.   ⊖ Farringdon
✉ EC1V 4JT   Closed 25 December, 1 January,
℘ (020) 7608 1550   Saturday lunch and Sunday
www.rickerrestaurants.com

Carte £24/34

🏮
💺
VISA
MC
AE
⓪

You'll need to book ahead to guarantee a table at this busy, noisy and infectiously entertaining Pan-Asian restaurant, which was the first in Will Ricker's London-wide chain. The semi-booth seating and open style kitchen add to the general drama and the bar is more than just an addendum to the restaurant. A pot of knives, forks and chopsticks on each table allow you to decide just how authentic you want the experience to be. The varied and lengthy menu changes often but perennial favourites like chilli salt squid are constants. The Chinese element is quite strong and dim sum forms a large part but there's also more Japanese influence than in the other branches, which comes in the form of sashimi, maki rolls and tempura.

Cigalon

French 🍴🍴

K3

115 Chancery Ln
✉ WC2A 1PP
☎ (020) 7242 8373
www.cigalon.co.uk

⊖ Chancery Lane
Closed 24 December-3 January,
Saturday, Sunday and bank holidays

Menu £25 (lunch) – Carte £26/31

A/C
🔲
VISA
MC
AE

A huge skylight bathes the room in light while the kitchen pays homage to the food of Provence – this is a restaurant that really comes into its own in the summer. A former auction house for law books, the space is stylishly laid out, with the booths in the centre being the prized seats – ask for No.9 if you want to watch the chefs in action. Along with the traditional dishes such as soupe au pistou, bouillabaisse, salade niçoise and pieds et paquets are popular grilled dishes such as venison, and there's even the occasional detour to Corsica. Equal thought went into the name: it refers to both a 1935 Marcel Pagnol film about a haughty chef and the local name for the summer cicada. There's also a busy bar downstairs in the cellar.

Cinnamon Kitchen

Indian 🍴🍴

N2

9 Devonshire Sq
✉ EC2M 4YL
☎ (020) 7626 5000
www.cinnamon-kitchen.com

⊖ Liverpool Street
Closed Saturday lunch,
Sunday and bank holidays

Menu £18/22 – Carte £31/56

🔖
A/C
🔲
🍽
VISA
MC
AE

Having successfully established Westminster's Cinnamon Club and made it a popular choice with those who run the country, the team behind it opened a second branch here in The City, to appeal to those who own, or thought they owned, the country. This is all about contemporary Indian dining: the cooking is creative and original, the surroundings light and unobtrusive and the service keen and sprightly. The menu bears little resemblance to the usual Indian fare and includes ingredients like quinoa, red deer and scallops. The arresting presentation doesn't come at the expense of the punchy flavours. The grill section is worth exploring and enthusiastic amateur cooks should position themselves at the Tandoor Bar to watch all the action.

Clerkenwell Kitchen

K1

27-31 Clerkenwell Cl
✉ EC1R 0AT
✆ (020) 7101 9959
www.theclerkenwellkitchen.co.uk

⊖ Farringdon
Closed Christmas-New Year, Saturday,
Sunday and bank holidays – booking
advisable – (lunch only)

Carte approx. £19

Time spent working in Dorset with Hugh Fearnley-Whittingstall has clearly influenced Emma, the owner of this busy, tucked away eatery: she sources her ingredients from small producers who use traditional methods and is committed to sustainability, recycling and the reduction of food miles. But this is more than just a worthy enterprise – the food is rather good too. Local office workers flock in for breakfast and takeaway sandwiches but it is well worth booking for the appealing daily changing lunch menu. Two of the six main courses will be vegetarian and offer, along with dishes like venison and pancetta pie, plenty of freshness and flavour. Even the juices are seasonal and the tarts, pies and cakes are all made daily.

Comptoir Gascon 😊

K2

61-63 Charterhouse St.
✉ EC1M 6HJ
✆ (020) 7608 0851
www.comptoirgascon.com

⊖ Farringdon
Closed 24 December-4 January,
Sunday and Monday – booking essential

Carte £24/36

This buzzy restaurant should be subsidised by the French Tourist Board as it does more to illustrate one component of Gascony's famed 'douceur de vivre' – sweetness of life – than any glossy brochure. The wines, breads, foie gras, duck and cheeses all celebrate SW France's reputation for earthy, proper man-food. The menu is divided into 'mer', 'vegetal' and 'terre'; be sure to order duck, whether as rillettes, confit or in a salade Landaise. After these big flavours, it'll come as a relief to see that the desserts, displayed in a cabinet, are delicate little things. The prices are also commendable; even the region's wine comes direct from the producers to avoid the extra mark-up. There's further booty on the surrounding shelves.

Club Gascon ⁂

L2

57 West Smithfield
✉ EC1A 9DS
✆ (020) 7796 0600
www.clubgascon.com

⊖ Barbican
Closed Christmas - New Year,
Saturday lunch, Sunday and bank
holidays – booking essential

Menu £29 (lunch) – Carte £50/69

A/C
♨
VISA
M©
AE

Club Gascon

The rich bounty of France's southwest region is celebrated in the bourgeoning empire of Pascal Aussignac and Vincent Labeyrie but their pre-eminent creation remains Club Gascon. The restaurant is now over a decade old but some subtle changes have prepared it for the next chapter. The colour-coordinated redesign has allowed the original marble to become more of a feature and the cooking has also developed. Traditional dishes such as cassoulet and the like are now available at their 'comptoir' nearby and this in turn allows the energetic Aussignac and his team to be a little more daring in the kitchen here. The southwest remains his greatest influence but these days he pushes a little at the boundaries. The size of the portions has also grown slightly, although the seasonal menu, with or without suggested wine pairings, is often the best way to go. Service always begins well but can sometimes wobble a little when the room reaches capacity, but it is very hard to leave Club Gascon without feeling a little better about life.

First Course

- Line-caught mackerel, pine, abalone and oyster sorbet.
- Goose foie gras, sherry, prune coulis, toasted hazelnuts.

Main Course

- Charolais beef variation, caviar and ox sauce.
- White haddock, peas and verbena pearls, oceanic lemon.

Dessert

- Turrón, sweet foie gras, Baileys, baby meringues and passion fruit.
- Papaya crisp, carrot cake, frosted sweet potato and verjuice.

Coq d'Argent

French XXX

1 Poultry ⊖ Bank
✉ EC2R 8EJ Closed 25-27 December, 1 January,
✆ (020) 7395 5000 Saturday lunch, Sunday dinner and bank
www.coqdargent.co.uk holidays – booking essential

Menu £32 (lunch) – Carte £36/45

Resembling the bow of a ship, Coq d'Argent stands in a commanding position on the top floor of a striking building, from where one can gaze imperiously over the Square Mile. The restaurant itself is slick and stylish; service is on the ball and the cooking is mostly French but with contemporary elements. The large chilled fish counter is appealing and there are plenty of luxurious ingredients on offer, including a caviar list, to entice anyone out celebrating a deal; those whose budgets have constraints will appreciate the better value lunch menu. But it is not just the food that attracts visitors up here: the bar, terrace and fantastic formal garden are great after-work spots or venues for private parties.

Garrison

Gastropub 🍺

99-101 Bermondsey St ⊖ London Bridge
✉ SE1 3XB Closed 25-27 December – booking
✆ (020) 7089 9355 essential at dinner
www.thegarrison.co.uk

Carte £23/30

'Sweet' is not an adjective that could apply to many of London's pubs but it does seem to fit The Garrison. The service has a certain natural charm and the place has a warm, relaxed vibe, while its mismatched style and somewhat vintage look work well. Open from 8am for smoothies and breakfast, it gets busier as the day goes on – and don't bother coming for dinner if you haven't booked. Booth numbers 4 and 5, opposite the open kitchen, are the most popular while number 2 at the back is the cosiest. The menu has a distinct Mediterranean flavour; salads dominate the starters and steaks and braised meats sit alongside pasta and fresh fish options. Puddings are more your classic pub variety. The owners' other place, Village East, is just down the street.

CITY OF LONDON, CLERKENWELL, FINSBURY & SOUTHWARK ▶ PLANS VIII-IX-X

Goldfish City 🏮

Asian ✗

46 Gresham St.
✉ EC2V 7AY
✆ (020) 7726 0308
www.goldfish-restaurant.co.uk

⊖ Bank
Closed Saturday, Sunday
and bank holidays – booking advisable

Carte £19/30

A/C
VISA
MC
AE

Having wowed the notoriously picky hordes of Hampstead with their first Goldfish, a second branch was opened here on the edge of The City in 2010. It's spread over three floors and the décor is soothing and discreet, with walls of Chinese symbols and fretwork alongside an aquarium of the eponymous fish. An appealing selection of attractively priced steamed dim sum pulls in the punters at lunch. The à laCarte menu is balanced and not overlong and mixes the classic with the more modern. Fish is clearly a strength of the kitchen and, whilst it is a little more expensive than the other choices, the steamed sea bass with soy sauce is a stand-out dish. Helpful and smartly dressed staff are on hand and make sensible recommendations.

Goodman City

Beef specialities ✗✗

11 Old Jewry
✉ EC2R 8DU
✆ (020) 7600 8220
www.goodmanrestaurants.com

⊖ Bank
Closed Saturday, Sunday
and bank holidays

Menu £21 (lunch) – Carte £48/68

A/C
↻
VISA
MC
AE

The Mayfair branch proved such a success that the opening of a second steakhouse was inevitable. For it, they chose the more appropriate setting of a semi-industrial looking space in The City, perfect for this incontestably macho style of food. Steaks are obviously the stars of the show: the corn-fed USDA beef is imported a tonne at a time and wet-matured for 60 days; the Scottish and Irish beef is grass-fed. Competitive eating from suited City types mean that steaks weighing an impressive 700g are the most popular; the meats are cut to order in the kitchen using a band saw. Commendably – and perhaps unusually for a steakhouse – equal care goes into the other dishes, whether that's calamari to start, or a sorbet at the end.

Green

British 🍴🍺

K1

29 Clerkenwell Gn   ⊖ **Farringdon.**
✉ EC1R 0DU   Closed 25-30 December
✆ (020) 7490 8010
www.thegreenec1.co.uk

Carte £24/34

29 Clerkenwell Green dates from 1580 and had become a tavern by 1720. It's therefore fitting that, after decades being used firstly as offices and then as a restaurant, The Green is now back to being known as a pub. Appetising and imaginative bar snacks like hog shank on toast are to be had in the ground floor bar, but the intimate upstairs is where the real eating goes on. Here you'll find an appealing menu of fresh, seasonal ingredients which might include Devon crab, Cornish mackerel, Wiltshire trout or Suffolk pork. The traditional fish pie is a favourite of many and the puds on the blackboard continue the British theme. Lunches get pretty busy with those wearing suits but dinner is more relaxed and the clientele in less of a hurry.

High Timber

Modern European 🍴🍴

L3

8 High Timber St.   ⊖ **Mansion House**
✉ EC4V 3PA   Closed 25 December-4 January, Saturday,
✆ (020) 7248 1777   Sunday and bank holidays
www.hightimber.com

Menu £19 (lunch) – Carte £25/55

Surprisingly few restaurants in London overlook the river, especially on the north side, so High Timber is already off to a good start. Add an impressive wine cellar with over 900 bins, including much from the owners' homeland of South Africa, and you've virtually guaranteed a good night out. Heavy wood tables and slate floors lend a slightly rustic look to what is the ground floor of a purpose-built office block; but the room has a fluid feel, as diners are encouraged to visit the cellar or indeed the cheese room to make their choice. The highlight of the concise, seasonal menu is the beef from the grill; they use 28-day matured Cumbrian beef, cut to order from the bone. Dishes have a muscular vigour and come served on slate or chopping boards.

Hix Oyster and Chop House

L2

British ✗

36-37 Greenhill Rents
✉ EC1M 6BN
℘ (0207) 1719 30
www.hixoysterandchophouse.co.uk

⊖ Farringdon
Closed 25-29 December

Menu £18 (lunch and early dinner) – Carte £26/50

Utilitarian surroundings, seasonal British ingredients, plenty of offal and prissy-free cooking: this may sound like a description of St John but is in fact the solo venture of Mark Hix, the chef who made The Ivy more than just a celebrity love-in. Smithfield Market seems an appropriate location for a restaurant that not only celebrates Britain's culinary heritage with old classics like rabbit brawn, nettle soup and beef and oyster pie but also reminds us of our own natural bounty, from sand eels and asparagus, whiting to laver bread. It's also called an Oyster and Chop House for a reason, with four types of oyster on offer as well as plenty of meat, including Aberdeen beef aged for 28 days and served on the bone.

José 😊

M5

Spanish ✗

104 Bermondsey St
✉ SE1 3UB
℘ (020) 7403 4902
www.josepizarro.com

⊖ London Bridge
Closed 25-26 December and Sunday dinner
– (bookings not accepted)

Carte approx. £25

Included on any list of 'things to be enjoyed while standing up' must surely be the eating of tapas. Here at this snug Bermondsey tapas bar they don't take bookings, but fear not – just turn up and you'll get in because they pack 'em in like boquerones and that adds to the charm. The eponymous José was formerly with Brindisa in Borough Market, so he knows what he's doing and is usually found at the counter carving the wonderful acorn-fed Iberico ham. Five plates per person should be more than enough but it's hard to stop ordering when you see what the person next to you has got. The food is dictated by the markets; you'll find the daily fishy dishes on the blackboard. There's a great list of sherries and all wines are available by the glass.

Kenza

L e b a n e s e ✕✕

10 Devonshire Sq.
✉ EC2M 4YP
✆ (020) 7929 5533
www.kenza-restaurant.com

⊖ Liverpool Street
Closed Saturday lunch, Sunday
and bank holidays

Carte £26/33

A/C
⊡
VISA
MC
AE

The newly regenerated Devonshire Square may not appear that mysterious but descend the stairs down into Kenza and you'll be transported into the exotic Levant. The name, Arabic for 'treasure', is well chosen and the floor tiles, lamps, carvings, colourful candles and satin cushions were all imported from Morocco. Moroccan and Lebanese cooking are the two main influences; the choices include samboussek pastries, kibbeh parcels, pureés and chargrills. There are also 'feast' menus for larger parties and the cooking is accurate and authentic; finish with theatrically poured mint tea and baklava. There's belly dancing, pumping music and large tables but the kitchen proves that a party atmosphere and good food are not mutually exclusive.

Larder

L1

M o d e r n   E u r o p e a n ✕

91-93 St John St.
✉ EC1M 4NU
✆ (020) 7608 1558
www.thelarderrestaurant.com

⊖ Farringdon
Closed 23 December-3 January,
Saturday lunch, Sunday
and bank holidays

Menu £15 (lunch) – Carte £26/37

A/C
⊡
VISA
MC
AE
①

An appropriate name as there is bounty galore. On one side is the bakery with plenty of artisanal breads and cakes. The restaurant, meanwhile, is one of those large, semi-industrial places with exposed brick and pipes and an open kitchen at the back. This kind of hard-edged space can push up the decibels but that's part of its appeal. Think modern European comfort food, from moules marinière to roast salmon with pumpkin ravioli, but alongside the halloumi you might find Lancashire cheese and next to the chicken breast with Puy lentils could be a Barnsley chop, so the Union flag is raised occasionally (the owners are from Liverpool). A side dish to accompany the main course is recommended and some thought has gone into them.

Luc's Brasserie

M3

French ✗✗

17-22 Leadenhall Mkt
✉ EC3V 1LR
✆ (020) 7621 0666
www.lucsbrasserie.com

⊖ Bank
Closed 23 December-3 January, Saturday,
Sunday and bank holidays –
booking essential at lunch – (lunch only
and dinner Tuesday-Thursday)

Menu £20 – Carte £27/42

VISA
MC
AE

Go into Leadenhall Market and look up – that's Luc's Brasserie, a restaurant which first appeared in the late 1890s and was reinvigorated and re-launched in 2006. The top floor is fairly sedate but the main room - from where you can admire the Victorian splendour of the market – is where the action is. The menu is an unapologetic paean to all things French, from snails to steak tartare, confit of duck to crème brûlée. The kitchen wisely sticks to conventional and classic recipes and it's easy to see why ties are quickly loosened. Staff do their bit by getting on with things but do so with a smile. As one would expect, the mood relaxes somewhat on the three nights they open for dinner, when a fixed price menu is also available.

Lutyens

K3

Modern European ✗✗✗

85 Fleet St.
✉ EC4Y 1AE
✆ (020) 7583 8385
www.lutyens-restaurant.com

⊖ St Paul's
Closed 1 week Christmas,
Saturday, Sunday and bank holidays

Menu £40 (dinner) – Carte £40/55

A/C
⟨⊡⟩
VISA
MC
AE

Having built one restaurant empire, Sir Terence Conran appears to have embarked on creating another. Lutyens opened in 2009 following the success of Boundary, and boasts that unmistakeable Conran look: timeless and effortless good looks mixed with functionality. He also found another building of note: the restaurant is within what was the HQ of Reuters and is named after its architect, Sir Edwin. The menu is an appealing Anglo-French affair, with an assortment of classics ranging from parfaits and fruits de mer to Dover sole and roast grouse, along with dishes from the rotisserie; sushi even makes an incongruous appearance. Service is clued-up but perhaps a little more formal than it needs to be. There's a busy bar on the Fleet Street side.

Magdalen

M4

152 Tooley St.
✉ SE1 2TU
✆ (020) 7403 1342
www.magdalenrestaurant.co.uk

⊖ **London Bridge**
Closed 24 December-5 January, 15-30
August, Saturday lunch,
Sunday and bank holidays

Menu £19 (lunch) – Carte £30/40

A/C

VISA

MC

AE

The Magdalen's kitchen is a clever one: super sourcing and direct contact with farmers take care of the ingredients; the cooking demonstrates a solid, unshowy technique and the influences are kept largely from within the British Isles. Shoulder of Middle White pork with fennel and lemon is a highlight and the rabbit leg with broad beans leaves you wondering why this meat isn't sold in every supermarket. French toast with apricots and vanilla ice cream provides a suitably comforting finale. The lunch menu is a steal, the wine list has been thoughtfully put together by someone who knows the menu well and staff are an eager, genial bunch. The restaurant is divided between two floors; it's unusually more fun on the ground floor.

Manicomio

L3

6 Gutter Ln.
✉ EC2V 8AS
✆ (020) 7726 5010
www.manicomio.co.uk

⊖ **St Paul's**
Closed 1 week Christmas,
Saturday, Sunday and bank holidays

Carte £31/54

A/C

VISA

MC

AE

This sibling to the King's Road branch opened in the summer of 2008 and is on the first floor of a Norman Foster designed building. On the ground floor is the deli/café while the bar is kept separately on the top floor, away from the restaurant which makes a nice change in this part of town. The owners' other business is importing Italian produce so they know their cipollas. There's also plenty of British meat, game and fish but prepared in an Italian way, with top notch Italian accompaniments. The cooking covers many regions, with daily specials; one or two side dishes are needed for the main course and these, together with the bread, may bump the bill up. The room has a bright, fresh feel; all the furniture is imported from Italy.

Medcalf 🏵

British 🍴

K1

40 Exmouth Mkt.
✉ EC1R 4QE
℘ (020) 7833 3533
www.medcalfbar.co.uk

⊖ Farringdon
Closed 31 December-3 January,
Sunday dinner and bank holidays –
booking essential

Carte £24/32

There is something very 'proper' about Medcalf: maybe it's the no-frills décor celebratiing the original butcher's shop that was here from 1912 (the lights are held up by meat hooks); maybe it's the loud and buzzy pub-like atmosphere, with the good range of draught beers, wines by the glass and assorted snacks; or maybe it's the fresh, appealing and very seasonal British cooking, with dishes like Barnsley chop or Calves liver, which has a satisfyingly robust, masculine feel to it. Whatever it is, it works as the restaurant gets very busy, very quickly. Those who think jellies and foams should only be found at children's playtime rather than on a dinner plate will find much to celebrate here at Medcalf.

The Mercer

Modern European 🍴🍴

M3

34 Threadneedle St
✉ EC2R 8AY
℘ (020) 7628 0001
www.themercer.co.uk

⊖ Bank
Closed 25 December, Saturday,
Sunday and bank holidays

Carte £28/37

The credit crunch means it's even less likely that a restaurant will ever be converted into a bank so, at the moment, the trend remains from bank to restaurant; here at The Mercer you can even see where the tellers used to sit. The high ceilings and windows let in plenty of light and the place has a pleasingly animated brasserie feel, with service that is slick and well paced. Open from breakfast, the kitchen concentrates on familiar flavours and comforting classics. While the cooking may not always live up to the promise of the menu, it is nonetheless satisfying. Scottish beef features in the Grill section and there are daily specials which could be corned beef hash or a fish pie. There's a huge choice of wines by the glass or carafe.

Mint Leaf Lounge

M3

Indian ✗✗

12 Angel Ct., Lothbury
✉ EC2R 7HB
✆ (020) 7600 0992
www.mintleaflounge.com

⊖ Bank
Closed 25-26 December, Saturday,
Sunday and bank holidays

Menu £18 (lunch and early dinner) – Carte £38/60

A/C
VISA
MC
AE

This was formerly NatWest's HQ and has been turned into a stylish and slick Indian restaurant. The bar is bigger and the dining area smaller than the original branch in St James's, but with the stock market the way it's been, you can't blame them for that. The menu cleverly allows for flexibility in that many of the dishes are available in both starter and main course size and the presentation on the plate is quite contemporary. The majority of influences come from the more southerly parts of India and dishes demonstrate genuine care in preparation. Fish, meat or vegetarian platters are available and there's a good value set lunch menu. Knowledgeable staff in ubiquitous black provide nicely paced service.

The Modern Pantry

K1

International ✗

47-48 St John's Sq.
✉ EC1V 4JJ
✆ (020) 7553 9210
www.themodernpantry.co.uk

⊖ Farringdon
Closed 25-26 December
and 29 August – booking advisable

Carte £35/39

A/C
VISA
MC
AE

This Georgian building has been everything from a foundry to a carpentry workshop but these days plays host to New Zealander Anna Hansen's fusion restaurant. The smart glass doors lead into a simple, crisp space; there's an upstairs too, split between two rooms, which offers a little more intimacy but lacks the buzz of downstairs. The kitchen's peregrinations are reflected in a menu that has few boundaries. You'll probably need to ask for an explanation of at least one ingredient but the staff are clued up, which is no mean feat since menus change daily as ingredients come in. Despite all that's happening on the plate, flavours are well-judged and complementary. Most dishes also come with thoughtfully suggested wine matches.

213

Morito 😊

K1

Spanish 🗙

32 Exmouth Mkt
✉ EC1R 4QE
📞 (020) 7278 7007

⊖ Farringdon
Closed Christmas-New Year,
Sunday and bank holidays

Carte approx. £21

VISA
MC

Morito may not seduce you with its looks but once you start eating you'll find it hard to tear yourself away. This authentic tapas bar comes courtesy of the owners of next door Moro and shares their passion for Moorish cuisine. It's modestly kitted out but endearingly so, with a two-tone formica counter and half a dozen small tables; just turn up and if they haven't got space they'll take your number and you can have a drink in Exmouth Market while you wait. Seven or eight dishes between two should be enough but at these prices you can never overspend. Highlights of the immensely appealing menu include jamon and chicken croquetas and succulent lamb chops with cumin and paprika, all served in authentic earthenware dishes.

Moro

K1

Mediterranean 🗙

34-36 Exmouth Mkt
✉ EC1R 4QE
📞 (020) 7833 8336
www.moro.co.uk

⊖ Farringdon
Closed Christmas-New Year
and Sunday – booking essential

Carte £29/36

A/C
🕐
VISA
MC
AE
◑

Despite being a feature of Exmouth Market for over a decade, Moro remains one of the busiest restaurants around, but anyone left frustrated by not getting a table should consider just pitching up and sitting at the zinc-topped bar: it's a great spot for tapas and some wonderful sherries, you'll get the full benefit of the wondrous aromas from the open kitchen and be able to watch the chefs in action. Moorish cooking is the draw which means Spain and the Muslim Mediterranean. The wood-burning oven and charcoal grill provide the smokiness and charring to improve and enhance the poultry, meat and sourdough bread. The cooking is colourful and invigorating and the menu changes fully every two weeks.

1901

French XXX

Liverpool St.
✉ EC2M 7QN
✆ (020) 7618 7000
www.andaz.com

⊖ Liverpool Street
Closed Saturday lunch,
Sunday and bank holidays

Menu £25 (lunch) – Carte £32/52

A/C
⟷
VISA
MC
AE
①

1901 is the redecorated, rebranded and relaunched version of what was previously called Aurora. It's one of several restaurants within the Andaz hotel and is very much their flagship. This is a hugely impressive room, which they've painted white to make the eye-catching cupola even more striking. A cocktail bar has been added, along with a cheese and wine room; the cheeses being of predominantly British provenance. The cooking is mostly French in preparation and technique but stoutly British in terms of the ingredients it uses. A refined and delicate touch is evident in dishes such as poached halibut with saffron potatoes and the smoked haddock boudin. There is an army of staff on hand who are well-practised but also friendly.

Oxo Tower

Modern European XXX

Oxo Tower Wharf (8th floor),
Barge House St ✉ SE1 9PH
✆ (020) 7803 3888
www.harveynichols.com

⊖ Southwark
Closed 25 December,
dinner 24 December
and lunch 26 December

Menu £35 (lunch) – Carte £39/52

≼
ⱨⱨ
A/C
⅓
☼
VISA
MC
AE
①

There can be few brighter restaurants than this one on the 8th floor of the Oxo Tower, thanks to its huge windows and enthusiastic application of white paint. The menu provides a fairly promising read, with dishes made up of ingredients from the luxury end of the spectrum, although the kitchen doesn't always quite deliver the goods. Meanwhile, service is a little more ceremonial than the brasserie next door and all this is reflected in the prices – the final bill can dazzle as much as the surroundings, so at least try to get a table by the window to make it memorable. Lunchtimes are largely invaded by city types from across the river, while at night the restaurant becomes a popular setting for those celebrating special occasions.

North Road ❀

Modern European ✕✕

L1

69-73 St John St   ⊖ Farringdon
✉ EC1M 4AN   Closed 23 December- 2 January,
✆ (020) 3217 0033   Saturday lunch and Sunday
www.nrrestaurant.com

Menu £20 (lunch) – Carte £32/41

A/C
◻
VISA
MC
AE

Michelin

Tired of cooking alone at his restaurant 'Fig' in Barnsbury, chef-owner Christoffer Hruskova made the move to a more conspicuous neighbourhood when he took over the premises previously occupied by The Clerkenwell Dining Rooms. Consequently, he is enjoying far greater exposure in these coolly designed and elegantly understated surroundings. His Danish roots and culinary training are most evident on the plate: dishes are prepared using little or no butter or cream, he makes expert use of sous-vide techniques but often keeps the actual cooking of ingredients to a minimum by serving many items either raw or smoked, sometimes in hay. He is also fully respectful of the seasons and his produce is largely sourced from small suppliers around the British Isles, including fish from Cornwall and Dorset, shellfish from Scotland, herbs from Kent and meat from Norfolk. The spacious dining room is equally devoid of unnecessary frills and frippery and its clean, fresh feel suits the style of cooking perfectly.

First Course

- Scallops with sea buckthorn, malt bread and wild herbs.
- Slow-cooked pork cheeks and onions, crispy onion broth and cress.

Main Course

- Whey poached turbot, asparagus and green strawberries.
- Herdwick mutton loin and shank in burnt hay with golden beetroot.

Dessert

- Yoghurt in textures and temperatures.
- Øllebrød and organic apple juice, rhubarb sorbet and thyme.

Oxo Tower Brasserie

K4

Oxo Tower Wharf (8th floor),
Barge House St ✉ SE1 9PH
📞 (020) 7803 3888
www.harveynichols.com

⊖ Southwark
Closed 25 December,
dinner 24 December
and lunch 26 December

Menu £27 (weekday lunch) – Carte £33/49

The light-filled, glass-encased brasserie on the eighth floor of the iconic Oxo Tower makes much of its riverside location but that's not to say that this is just a spot for a summer's day as the bold, zingy Mediterranean flavours ensure that the cooking is bright and sunny even when it's dull outside. They've moved the bar to the front so that everyone gets a better view these days. Even so, if you've never asked for a window table before, then now is the time to start. Better still, ask for the terrace and face east towards St Paul's for the best views. Staff do their bit by being a responsive bunch and the place really rocks in the evenings. It's much more fun than their restaurant and the prices are friendlier too.

Paternoster Chop House

L3

Warwick Ct., Paternoster Sq.
✉ EC4M 7DX
📞 (020) 7029 9400
www.paternosterchophouse.com

⊖ St Paul's
Closed 24 December-
1 January, Saturday,
Sunday dinner and bank holidays

Menu £27 – Carte £32/57

If you could make just one restaurant legally obliged to serve British food then it would probably be the one that lies in the shadow of St Paul's Cathedral, one of Britain's most symbolic landmarks. Fortunately, Paternoster Chop House negates the need of a bye-law by offering classics from all parts of these isles. The first thing you see on the neatly laid-out menu is the comfortingly patriotic sight of a 'Beer of the Day'. Their livestock comes from small farms, their fish from day boats in the southwest and all the old favourites are present and correct: native oysters, cottage pie, potted hough, liver and bacon, and apple crumble. The dining room is large and open; you might have to fight your way through the busy bar.

Peasant

L1

240 St John St
✉ EC1V 4PH
📞 (020) 7336 7726
www.thepeasant.co.uk

⊖ **Farringdon.**
Closed 25 December-1 January and bank
holidays except Good Friday –
booking essential

Carte £23/30

Come along too early in the evening and you'll find the bar four deep with city boys having a quick pint on the way home. However, things do quieten down later and, when they do, you'll notice what a characterful spot this is. Most of the eating gets done upstairs in the dining room with its dimmed chandeliers, open fire and circus-themed posters. The cooking has been simplified and returned to a core of British dishes accompanied by the occasional Mediterranean note. The result is that it is far more satisfying and the well-judged dishes – whether braised rib of beef with horseradish mash or roast pollock with shrimps – all largely deliver on flavour. You will need a side dish or two with your main course, which can push up the final bill.

Le Pont de la Tour

N4

36d Shad Thames, Butlers Wharf
✉ SE1 2YE
📞 (020) 7403 8403
www.lepontdelatour.co.uk

⊖ **London Bridge**

Menu £32/45

For over 20 years, Le Pont de la Tour has been the flagship restaurant of the Butlers Wharf development. Decoratively, it may not look quite as striking as it did in 1991 but there is no doubting the glory of its location, especially in summer when you can sit on the terrace and look out over the river and Tower Bridge. During the week the place is largely populated by noisier corporate types but at weekends the room takes on a more romantic air. The set price menu, which includes a few dishes which carry supplements, is not dissimilar to that found in a bistro moderne, but if you want even more rustic choices such as pork rillettes or coq au vin then sit in the livelier cocktail bar and grill, with its evening pianist.

Redhook

K2

Beef specialities 🍴🍴

89 Turnmill St
✉ EC1M 5QU
☏ (020) 7065 6800
www.redhooklondon.com

⊖ Farringdon
Closed Easter, 25 December, Saturday
lunch and Sunday – booking
advisable at dinner

Menu £18 (lunch) – Carte £24/41

A/C
⟨⟩
VISA
MC
AE

Brooklyn comes to Clerkenwell in the shape of Redhook, an appealingly designed American-style restaurant whose refreshingly unambiguous menu specialises in seafood and steaks. There's assorted fish and some pasta on the menu but most diners will be busy chowing down on the Canadian lobster or the assorted cuts of beef which come from Scotland, Ireland and the US; even that '70s symbol of culinary excess, 'surf & turf', makes a comeback here. The kitchen handles the ingredients with care and desserts are not as sweet as those served in the US. Staff contribute to the pleasant atmosphere; California dominates the wine list and the bare brick walls, booths and a faux industrial aesthetic add to the New York feel.

Restaurant at St Paul's Cathedral

L3

British 🍴

St Paul's Churchyard
✉ EC4M 8AD
☏ (020) 7248 2469
www.restaurantatstpauls.co.uk

⊖ St. Paul's
Closed 25 December –
booking advisable – (lunch only)

Menu £26

⟨⟩
☀
VISA
MC

Tucked away in a corner of the crypt of Sir Christopher Wren's 17C masterpiece is this earnest little restaurant, offering respite to tiring tourists and weary worshippers. The kitchen prepares everything from scratch and rightly promotes and celebrates all things British in both the food and the accompanying list of drinks – even the back of the menu is graced with a collection of interesting local food facts. Start by sharing some nibbles such as wild boar salami or potted shrimp; move on to corned beef hash or a shepherd's pie and finish with a comforting Bakewell tart or some Neal's Yard cheeses. Service is done on the run but the staff are a friendly bunch and if you stay put for long enough, they'll start serving afternoon tea.

Rhodes Twenty Four ❀

M3

Tower 42, (24th floor) 25 Old Broad St. ✉ EC2N 1HQ
☏ (020) 7877 7703
www.rhodes24.co.uk

⊖ **Liverpool Street**
Closed Christmas-New Year,
Saturday, Sunday and bank holidays

Carte £45/65

⤠

A/C

VISA

MC

AE

D

Rhodes Twenty Four

You will need to factor in a little extra time to allow for the security checks on the ground floor of Tower 42, and for catching the lift up to the 24th floor of what is still The City's tallest building. But once inside the restaurant, provided you've asked for a window table, you'll be rewarded with great views of the city skyline. The unmistakeable signature of Gary Rhodes is writ large on the menu: dishes of a pleasingly British persuasion and the reassuring sight of words like 'pudding', 'pie' and 'crumble'. This being The City, where the male form of the species appear to remain largely in the ascendancy, means that the menu also has a stoutness to it, so, even in summer you'll be able to start with the oxtail cottage pie with a red wine sauce and finish with a bread and butter pudding. What all dishes also have is a look of comparative simplicity, which often belies the depth of flavour and the skill that has gone into them. As with most restaurants, service gels better when it's busier, which usually means at lunch.

First Course

- Scallop raviolo with buttered samphire.
- Duck faggot on buttered potato, caramelised onion, duck gravy.

Main Course

- Steamed mutton and onion suet pudding with carrots.
- Pan-fried haddock, baby leeks and smoked bacon cockle chowder.

Dessert

- Warm chocolate pudding, passion fruit sorbet.
- A taste of plum - roast plum crumble, plum fool and plum ice cream.

Roast

British ✗✗

The Floral Hall, Borough Mkt.
✉ SE1 1TL
✆ (0845) 3473 00
www.roast-restaurant.com

⊖ London Bridge
Closed 25 December, 1 January
and Sunday dinner –
booking essential

Menu £28 (lunch and early dinner) – Carte £37/60

[A/C]
[☺☺]
[VISA]
[MC]
[AE]

It's in the one place where you don't look when you find yourself in the deliciously enticing surroundings of Borough Market – up. Jump into the lift and upstairs you'll be greeted and led into a vast room; the best seats are in the raised section beyond the bar. It's always busy here and the young team are a friendly bunch, although they can sometimes appear to be a man down. The food is all about being British and proud of it, reflecting the values of the market below and the importance of provenance. Start with the cocktail of the week, move on to Cornish herring or Arbroath smokie, followed by roast lamb or steak and onion pudding and finish with a Bakewell tart or rhubarb crumble. You'll leave whistling 'Land of Hope and Glory'.

Sauterelle

French ✗✗

The Royal Exchange
✉ EC3V 3LR
✆ (020) 7618 2483
www.sauterelle-restaurant.co.uk

⊖ Bank
Closed Saturday,
Sunday and bank holidays,

Menu £24 – Carte £35/53

[A/C]
[◌̇]
[VISA]
[MC]
[AE]
[⓪]

Sauterelle enjoys a hugely impressive setting on the mezzanine floor of The Royal Exchange and looks down over the Grand Café below which was the original trading floor. This City landmark was rebuilt in 1844, but its layout remains largely true to Sir Thomas Gresham's 1565 original. The striking ceiling and ornate arches add to the already comfortable feel of the restaurant. The menu is largely French, but more contemporary than classic which means the addition of the occasional Italian note. The kitchen certainly doesn't skimp on luxury ingredients: foie gras, turbot, Anjou pigeon and Pyrenean lamb make regular appearances and are appreciated by big spending customers for whom the credit crunch is but a distant memory.

St John ✤

L2

26 St John St
✉ EC1M 4AY
✆ (020) 3301 8069
www.stjohnrestaurant.com

⊖ Farringdon
Closed Christmas-New Year, Saturday
lunch, Sunday dinner and bank
holidays, – booking essential

Carte £26/44

A/C
🎵
⚙
VISA
MC
AE
D

St John

Despite opening a Soho outpost, there's been no drop in standards here. The walls, painted in a shade of detention centre white, add to the utilitarian feel of the room which was a smokehouse in the 19C. There's no standing on ceremony; indeed no ceremony at all, and that makes dining at St John such a joyful experience as the focus is entirely directed at the food. You can play it safe and go for some crab and then roast beef but this is the place to try new flavours, whether that's the cuttlefish or the ox tongue. Game is a real favourite and the only gravy will be the blood of the bird – this is natural, 'proper' food. Seasonality is at its core – the menu is rewritten for each service – and nothing sums up the philosophy more than the potatoes and greens: they are always on the menu but the varieties and types change regularly. The waiters wear chef's jackets and spend time in the kitchen so they know what they're talking about. There are dishes for two as well as magnums of wine for real trenchermen – and be sure to order a dozen warm madeleines to take home.

First Course

- Roast bone marrow and parsley salad with toasted bread and wet salt.
- Brown shrimp and white cabbage.

Main Course

- Braised rabbit, peas and bacon.
- Roast Middle White pork, chard and mustard.

Dessert

- Ginger loaf and butterscotch sauce with vanilla ice cream.
- Eccles cake and Lancashire cheese.

Skylon

Modern European XXX

1 Southbank Centre, Belvedere Rd
✉ SE1 8XX
☎ (020) 7654 7800
www.skylon-restaurant.co.uk

⊖ **Waterloo**
Closed 25 December
and Sunday dinner

Menu £29/45

The original Skylon was a steel structure built for the Festival of Britain in 1951 to promote better quality design. Its name now lives on as the restaurant within the Royal Festival Hall, which was built just yards from where this 'vertical feature' once stood. The South Bank is now a much appreciated area of London and the restaurant offers wonderful river views. It's a large space, with a busy central cocktail bar, a formally laid out restaurant on one side and a simpler grill-style operation on the other. The latter serves fishcakes, burgers, steaks and the like; the restaurant uses more expensive ingredients and puts a modern spin on classic combinations. Be sure to ask for a window table.

Tapas Brindisa

Spanish X

18-20 Southwark St., Borough Market
✉ SE1 1TJ
☎ (020) 7357 8880
www.brindisa.com

⊖ **London Bridge**

Carte £12/30

As in Spain, you have the option of standing or sitting for your tapas. The bar is a great place for a glass of Fino while you watch the acorn-fed Iberian charcuterie being sliced, and the list of hot and cold tapas is extensive, from cured fish and speciality cheeses to grilled chorizo and sautéed chicken livers. It all happens on the edge of Borough Market in what was once a potato warehouse; the owners spent years importing Spanish produce so they know what they're talking about. With its tightly packed tables and convivial atmosphere, it does get very busy and as they don't take reservations, be prepared to wait; if they are full then ask nicely and you can put your name down and then wander around the market.

Tate Modern (Restaurant)

L4

Tate Modern (7th floor), Bankside
✉ SE1 9TG
☎ (020) 7887 8888
www.tate.org.uk/modern/eatanddrink

⊖ Southwark
Closed 24-26 December –
(lunch only and dinner
Friday-Saturday)

Carte £28/34

Floor to ceiling windows on two sides and a large mural on a third allow light and colour to fill this large restaurant on the 7th floor of the Tate Modern and balance all that black. Even if you don't get a window table you'll still get a great view of St Paul's. There's seating for 145 but they stop taking reservations when they get to 100 to allow for the impulse diner. Lunch starts at 11.30 and ends at 3pm so there's every possibility of getting in but waiting at the bar is no hardship. The menu is an appealing mix of light, seasonal, fresh and zesty dishes, with a daily fish from Newlyn. The influences are mostly British, with the occasional Italian note. There's a good choice of wines by the glass and carafe as well as interesting soft drinks.

28°-50° 😊

K3

140 Fetter Ln
✉ EC4A 1BT
☎ (020) 7242 8877
www.2850.co.uk

⊖ Temple
Closed Saturday, Sunday
and bank holidays

Menu £22 (lunch) – Carte £26/30

Despite the lack of a displayed menu, an unprepossessing entrance and a long staircase down, you'll find this subterranean spot almost always heaving with customers. For their second project, the owners of Texture opted for this 'wine workshop and kitchen', named after the latitudes between which most wines are produced, and with a cellar effect enhanced by brick walls and oenological accessories. A bar menu of charcuterie, rillettes and cheese is there to accompany a choice of over 30 wines by the glass. Beyond is the simple restaurant with a concise menu of robust, mostly French dishes such as bouillabaisse, onglet of beef and baba au rhum, which shouldn't break the bank – unless you have an unquenchable thirst for 1989 Hermitage.

Vanilla Black

K2

17-18 Tooks Ct.
✉ EC4A 1LB
✆ (020) 7242 2622
www.vanillablack.co.uk

⊖ Chancery Lane
Closed 2 weeks Christmas-New Year,
Saturday lunch and Sunday

Menu £24/33

A/C

VISA

MC

AE

①

Those who think vegetarian food is all nut cutlets and knitted muesli should get along to Vanilla Black. Run by a Teesside couple who had a restaurant of the same name in York, they prove that vegetarian food can be varied, flavoursome and filling. The room is neat but quite stark and crisp in its decoration; sufficient warmth comes from the owner and her team of waiting staff. The set-priced menu represents fair value and the cooking displays sufficient originality and imagination. Certainly no one leaves hungry as the flavoursome dishes use liberal amounts of cheese and potato. This is a proper restaurant that could heal the wounds of any carnivore scarred in their youth by an unpleasant vegetarian experience.

Village East

M5

171-173 Bermondsey St.
✉ SE1 3UW
✆ (020) 7357 6082
www.villageeast.co.uk

⊖ London Bridge
Closed 25-27 December

Carte £27/38

A/C

VISA

MC

AE

Clever name - sounds a bit downtown Manhattan; but while Bermondsey may not be London's East Village, what Village East does is give this part of town a bit more 'neighbour' and a little less 'hood'. It's tricky to find so look for the glass façade and you'll find yourself in one of the bars, still wondering if you've come to the right place. Once, though, you've seen the open kitchen you know the dining area's not far away. Wood, brick, vents and large circular lamps give it that warehouse aesthetic. The menu is laid out a little confusingly but what you get is ample portions of familiar bistro-style food, as well as some interesting combinations. The separately priced side dishes are not really needed and can push the bill up.

Vinoteca

Modern European X

L2

7 St John St. ⊖ Farringdon
⊠ EC1M 4AA Closed Christmas-New Year, Sunday
✆ (020) 7253 8786 and bank holidays –
www.vinoteca.co.uk (bookings not accepted at dinner)

Carte £27/35

Vinoteca, a self-styled 'bar and wine shop', comes divided into two tiny rooms and is always so busy that you'll almost certainly have to wait for a table. But what makes this frenetic place so special is the young and very passionate team who run it so well. The wine list is thrilling: it is constantly evolving and covers all regions, including less familiar territories along with the organic and the biodynamic. In circumstances such as these, the food can often be an afterthought but here it isn't. Alongside the cheeses and the cured meats that are available all day are classic dishes like pear, chicory and Roquefort salad; potted shrimps; bavette steak and panna cotta; all fresh tasting, well-timed and enjoyable.

Vivat Bacchus

Traditional XX

K2

47 Farringdon St (basement) ⊖ Farringdon
⊠ EC4A 4LL Closed 25 December, 1 January,
✆ (020) 7353 2648 Saturday, Sunday and bank holidays
www.vivatbacchus.co.uk

Menu £18 – Carte £28/60

The wine list is just a teaser: they actually have 750 labels, 20,000 bottles and five cellars. Glory to the god of wine indeed. And few things complement wine better than red meat and cheese – the two other specialities here. The large premises are mostly taken up with the wine bar and deli, with an appealing selection of platters, cheeseboards and tapas. For a more intimate experience head to the basement for a menu of two halves: one modern European, the other specialising in meats. Côte de boeuf is for two brave people with similar appetites while the presence of Springbok and the huge number of South African wines, reveals the nationality of the owner. Customers are welcome to tour the cellars and the impressive cheese room.

CITY OF LONDON, CLERKENWELL, FINSBURY & SOUTHWARK ▶ PLANS VIII-IX-X

Vivat Bacchus London Bridge

Traditional ✗

4 Hays Ln
✉ SE1 2HB
✆ (0207) 2340 891
www.vivatbacchus.co.uk

⊖ London Bridge
Closed 23 December-2 January, Saturday
lunch, Sunday and bank holidays

Menu £17/18 – Carte £17/33

VISA
MC
AE

The owners have sensibly avoided the temptation to tamper with a winning formula and so their second branch closely follows the style of the original in The City. That means a packed wine bar on the ground floor where city types quaff wines with relish and feast on 'world platters' from assorted countries. This then leads down to a slightly industrial looking basement restaurant, with a fantastic cellar and cheese room. Buying 'en primeur', they have created an impressive list with a large South African section and such is their enthusiasm that staff almost drool over oenophiles. The food is appropriately robust and also contains South African specialities, including the excellent roast springbok. Be sure to sample the cheese.

Well

L1

British 🍺

180 St John St
✉ EC1V 4JY
✆ (020) 7251 9363
www.downthewell.com

⊖ Farringdon.
Closed 25-26 December

Carte £23/33

The Well is perhaps more of a locals pub than many others found around these parts. It's all quite small inside but, thanks to some huge sliding glass windows, has a surprisingly light and airy feel, and the wooden floorboards and exposed brick walls add to the atmosphere of a committed metropolitan pub. Monthly changing menus offer modern dishes ranging from potted shrimps to foie gras and chicken liver parfait or sea trout and samphire, as well as classic English puddings like Eton Mess and some particularly good cheeses. The downstairs bar with its seductive lighting and fish tank is only available for private hire; check out the picture of a parched desert and a well which follows the curve of the wall on your way down.

The White Swan

K2

108 Fetter Ln
✉ EC4A 1ES
☏ (020) 7242 9696
www.thewhiteswanlondon.com

⊖ Chancery Lane
Closed 25-26 December, Saturday,
Sunday and bank holidays

Menu £30 (lunch) – Carte £28/34

A/C
VISA
MC
AE

You'll find something akin to an assault course at the White Swan because to get to the first floor restaurant you have to fight your way through the drinkers in the ground floor bar and, at lunch time, this is more challenging than you think. Once upstairs, you'll find a small, neat room and service that is polite and friendly but also well-paced and professional. The mirrored ceiling and large windows add plenty of light, although the closeness of the tables can make private conversation tricky. However, the cooking is good enough to induce the odd contented silence. It is classical in its base but with the occasional contemporary tweak and dishes display a certain refinement. Pricing is also fair when one considers the location.

Wright Brothers

M4

11 Stoney St., Borough Market
✉ SE1 9AD
☏ (020) 7403 9554
www.wrightbrothers.co.uk

⊖ London Bridge
Closed bank holiday Mondays –
booking advisable

Carte £25/51

☀
VISA
MC
AE

If you want to take a breather from the hordes at Borough Market then nip into Wright Brothers, but do it early as it quickly fills. Their motto is 'not just oysters' but then they do excel in them – hardly surprising when you consider that this small place started as an oyster wholesaler. Grab a table and enjoy them raw or cooked, by candlelight, along with the perfect accompaniment – a glass of porter – or else share a bench or the counter and opt for a platter of fruits de mer and a bottle of chilled Muscadet. If the bivalve is not your thing, then there are daily specials such as skate knobs, as well as pies and, for dessert, either chocolate truffles or crème brûlée. An air of contentment reigns.

Zucca

M5

184 Bermondsey St
✉ SE1 3TQ
✆ (020) 7378 6809
www.zuccalondon.com

⊖ Borough
Closed 24 December-10 January, Easter,
Sunday dinner and Monday – booking
essential at dinner

Carte £18/25

A/C
⟐
⅋
VISA
MC
①

The suitably fresh faced young chef-owner seems to have got it all pretty spot-on: the simple but informed Italian cooking is driven by the ingredients, the prices are more than generous, the room is bright and crisp and the service, sweet and responsive. The antipasti forms the largest part of the weekly changing menu and the hard part – especially if you're sharing – is knowing when to stop ordering; but do always include the zucca fritti – the pumpkin speciality. The kitchen team are an unflustered group, largely because they don't fiddle with the food and know that less equals more. The freshly baked breads come with Planeta olive oil; there are usually two pasta dishes and the aromas that fill the room make it hard to leave.

Remember, stars
(✿✿✿...✿) are awarded
for cuisine only! Elements
such as service and décor
are not a factor.

Chelsea · Earl's Court · Hyde Park · Knightsbridge · South Kensington

Though its days of unbridled hedonism are long gone - and its 'alternative' tag is more closely aligned to property prices than counter-culture - there's still a hip feel to **Chelsea.** The place that put the Swinging into London has grown grey, distinguished and rather placid over the years, but tourists still throng to the **King's Road,** albeit to shop at the chain stores which have steadily muscled out SW3's chi-chi boutiques. It's not so easy now to imagine the heady mix of clans that used to sashay along here, from Sixties mods and models to Seventies punks, but for practically a quarter of a century, from the moment in 1955 when Mary Quant opened her trend-setting Bazaar, this was the pavement to parade down.

Chelsea's most cutting-edge destination these days is probably the gallery of modern art that bears the name of Margaret Thatcher's former favourite, Charles Saatchi. Which isn't the only irony, as Saatchi's outlandishly modish exhibits are housed in a one-time military barracks, the Duke of York's headquarters. Nearby, the traffic careers round **Sloane Square,** but it's almost possible to distance yourself from the fumes by sitting amongst the shady bowers in the centre of the square, or watching the world go by from a prime position in one of many cafés. Having said that, *the* place to get away from it all, and

yet still be within striking distance of the King's Road, is the delightful **Physic Garden,** down by the river. Famous for its healing herbs for over 300 years, it's England's second oldest botanic garden.

Mind you, if the size of a green space is more important to you than its medicinal qualities, then you need to head up to **Hyde Park,** the city's biggest. Expansive enough to accommodate trotting horses on Rotten Row, swimmers and rowers in the Serpentine, up-to-the-minute art exhibitions at the Serpentine Gallery, and ranting individualists at Speakers' Corner, the park has also held within its borders thousands of rock fans for concerts by the likes of the Rolling Stones, Simon and Garfunkel and Pink Floyd.

Just across from its southern border stands one of London's most imperious sights, The **Royal Albert Hall,** gateway to the cultural hotspot that is South Kensington. Given its wings after the 1851 Great Exhibition, the area round **Cromwell Road** invested heavily in culture and learning, in the shape of three world famous museums and three heavyweight colleges. But one of its most intriguing museums is little known to visitors, even though it's only a few metres east of the Albert Hall: the Sikorski is, by turns, a moving and spectacular showpiece for all things Polish.

No one would claim to be moved by the exhibits on show in nearby **Knightsbridge,** but there are certainly spectacular credit card transactions made here. The twin retail shrines of Harvey Nichols and Harrods are the proverbial honey-pots to the tourist bee, where a 'credit crunch' means you've accidentally trodden on your visa. Between them, in **Sloane Street,** the world's most famous retail names line up like an A-lister's who's who. At the western end of Knightsbridge is the rich person's Catholic church of choice, the Brompton Oratory, an unerringly lavish concoction in a baroque Italianate style. Behind it is the enchanting Ennismore Gardens Mews, a lovely thoroughfare that dovetails rather well with the Oratory.

Further west along Old Brompton Road is **Earl's Court,** an area of grand old houses turned into bedsits and spartan hotels. An oddly bewitching contrast sits side by side here, the old resting alongside the new. The old in this case is Brompton Cemetery, an enchanting wilderness of monuments wherein lie the likes of Samuel Cunard and Emmeline Pankhurst. At its southwest corner, incongruously, sits the new, insomuch as it's the home of a regular influx of newcomers from abroad, who are young, gifted and possessed of vast incomes: the players of Chelsea FC.

C. Eymenier/MICHELIN

CHELSEA · EARL'S COURT · HYDE PARK · KNIGHTSBRIDGE · SOUTH KENSINGTON ▶ Plans XI-XII

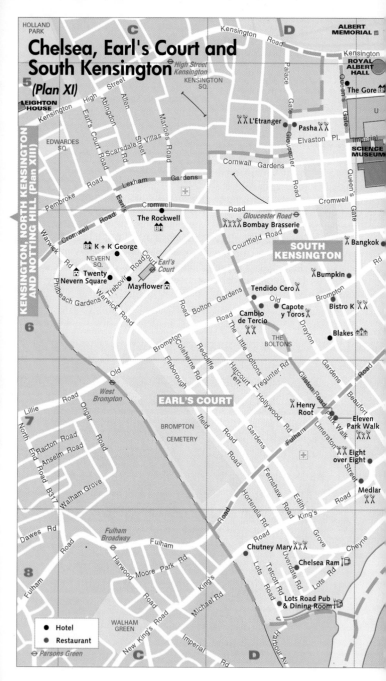

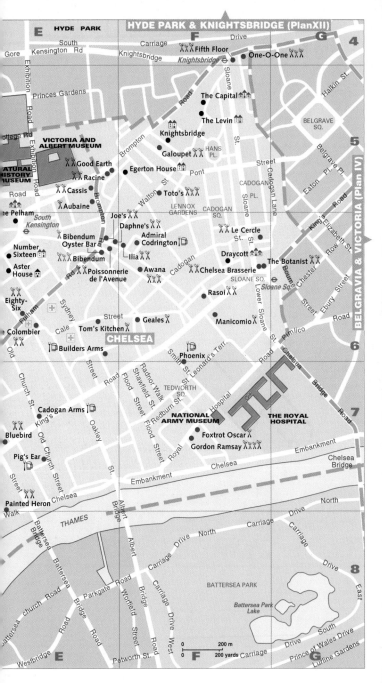

South
Kensington Rd
Gore   Carriage
Knightsbridge
Exhibition   Princes Gardens

Fifth Floor

One-O-One

Knightsbridge

Road

Sloane

St.

Haikin St.

BELGRAVE
SQ.

The Capital

The Levin

Knightsbridge

Brompton

Galoupet

HANS
PL.

Street

Belgrave

Pl.

5

VICTORIA AND
ALBERT MUSEUM

Egerton House

Pont

CADOGAN
PL.

Cadogan Lane

Eaton

Pl.

Road

NATURAL
HISTORY
MUSEUM

Good Earth

Racine

Cassis

Aubaine

Road

Walton

Toto's

LENNOX
GARDENS

Sloane

CADOGAN
SQ.

Sloane

Row

Elizabeth St.

King's

BELGRAVIA & VICTORIA (Plan IV)

The Pelham

South
Kensington

Brompton

Joe's

Daphne's

Admiral
Codrington

Ilia

CADOGAN

Le Cercle

St.

St.

Chester

Ebury Street

Road

Number
Sixteen

Bibendum
Oyster Bar

Bibendum

Awana

Draycott

The Botanist

Row

Aster
House

Rd

Poissonnerie
de l'Avenue

Cadogan

Chelsea Brasserie

SLOANE SQ.

Bourn

Sloane Sq.

Chester

Ebury Street

Eighty-
Six

Sydney

Rasoi

Sloane

Lower

St.

Pimlico

Road

Colombier

Fulham

Street

Cale

Geales

Tom's Kitchen

CHELSEA

Manicomio

Chelsea

Bridge

6

Builders Arms

Smith St.

Phoenix

St. Leonard's Terr.

Road

Road

Church St.

Cadogan Arms

King's

Oakley

Radnor Walk

Shawfield St.

Flood Street

Redburn St.

TEDWORTH
SQ.

Hospital

NATIONAL
ARMY MUSEUM

THE ROYAL
HOSPITAL

7

Bluebird

Old Church Street

Pig's Ear

Flood Street

Royal

Foxtrot Oscar

Gordon Ramsay

Embankment

Chelsea
Bridge

Painted Heron

St.

Chelsea

Embankment

Chelsea

North

Walk

Battersea
Bridge

THAMES

Albert
Bridge

Carriage   Drive   North

Drive

Carriage

Carriage

Battersea church Road

Battersea

Bridge

Parkgate Road

Worfield
Street

Albert
Bridge

Carriage Drive West

BATTERSEA PARK

Battersea Park
Lake

Drive

East

8

Drive   South

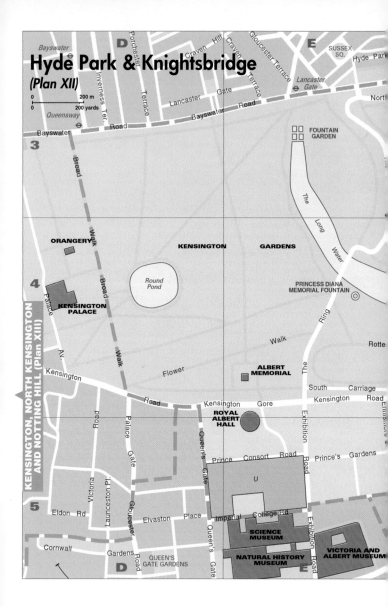

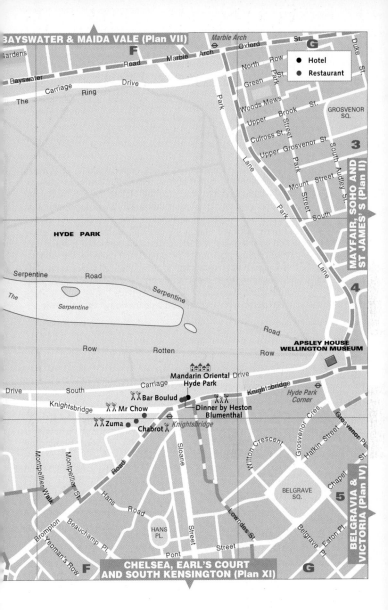

Admiral Codrington

Modern European

F6

17 Mossop St
✉ SW3 2LY
✆ (020) 7581 0005
www.theadmiralcodrington.com

⊖ South Kensington.
Closed 25-26 December

Carte £23/43

The Admiral Codrington is a smart, dependable affair as befits an establishment named after a hero of the Battles of Trafalgar and Navarino. What was once the HQ of the Sloane Ranger movement is now known for the quality of its food, although it still attracts a pretty smart crowd. The main bar and terrace are quite subdued during the day but get busy in the evening when all the eating is done in the neat, comfortable restaurant with its sliding glass roof. The menu can't quite decide whether this is a pub or a restaurant and so covers all bases from chilli salt squid to roast beef and coq au vin to fish and chips, with baguettes available at lunch. Service can sometimes lack a little personality but the young team do get the job done.

Aubaine

French ✗

E5

260-262 Brompton Rd.
✉ SW3 2AS
✆ (020) 7052 0100
www.aubaine.co.uk

⊖ South Kensington

Carte £22/52

This was the first of the bourgeoning Aubaine brand and it is easy to understand the appeal. A country style aesthetic is coupled with functionality and flexibility, so that a brisk morning coffee trade is followed by brunch, then a more structured lunch and dinner. Influences are European but the kitchen has its feet firmly set in France. Highlights include well-timed scallops and a decent rib-eye. Desserts are presented on a tray, to remind you this is also a place where one can pick up bread and pastries for home. The midday lunching ladies give way to a more mixed crowd in the evenings and service is young and eager. If you've got an appetite, then you may find it pricier than you expected but it's an easy place to like.

Awana

Malaysian XXX

85 Sloane Ave.
✉ SW3 3DX
✆ (020) 7584 8880
www.awana.co.uk

⊖ South Kensington
Closed 25-26 December, 1 January and
dinner 24 December –
booking essential

Menu £15 (lunch) – Carte £24/58

A/C
☼
VISA
MC
AE
D

The rich culinary diversity of Malaysia is presented here at Awana; a restaurant which manages the trick of looking smart and stylish, while staying relaxed and informal. It has also proved to be quite a hit with the Chelsea locals so it's worth booking in advance. Service does depend somewhat on the enthusiasm of your particular waiter, but if you choose to sit at the Satay Bar at the end of the room, you'll find the chef behind the counter takes very good care of you. To fully experience all the different cultures that influence Malaysian cooking, consider ordering the 'Malaysian Journey' menu, which comes with wine pairings; the highlights are the satay, roti canai, beef rendang and the prawn and chicken wonton soup.

Bangkok

E6

Thai X

9 Bute St
✉ SW7 3EY
✆ (020) 7584 8529
www.bankokrestaurant.co.uk

⊖ South Kensington
Closed 24 December-
2 January and Sunday

Carte £19/26

A/C
VISA
MC

Bangkok has been going strong for years and, for that, we should all be grateful. It is an honest, unpretentious neighbourhood restaurant and one of the first in the capital to offer Londoners a taste of Thailand in the days before gap years, package holidays and our discovery of woks. The menu's not overlong; starters include quite a few soups but the beef and chicken satay are particularly good. Main courses are helpfully divided into beef, pork and chicken; highlights include the beef with crispy Thai basil, while the noodles are very light and moreish. The prices are decidedly unKensington-like and the ladies go about their service with organised efficiency. The multitudinous following ensures there's always a bubbly atmosphere.

Bar Boulud

French ✗✗

F4

66 Knightsbridge   ⊖ Knightsbridge
✉ SW1X 7LA
✆ (020) 7201 3899
www.barboulud.com

Menu £20 (lunch and early dinner) – Carte £25/48

A/C
📺
🎭
☀
VISA
MC
AE
①

Lyon-born Daniel Boulud built his considerable reputation in New York and these two cities now inform the menu here at his London outpost. Order a plate of excellent charcuterie while you look at the menu; sausages are a highlight and there are plenty of classic French dishes, from fruits de mer to coq au vin, but it's the burgers that steal the show. Designed by Adam Tihany, the restaurant makes the best of its basement location which was previously used by the Mandarin Oriental Hotel as a storeroom. Don't think you'll be in exile if they lead you to a table around the corner: it's a good spot and you'll be facing the open kitchen. Service is fast and furious; prices are sensible and the place is noisy, fashionable and fun.

Bibendum

French ✗✗✗

E6

Michelin House, 81 Fulham Rd.   ⊖ South Kensington
✉ SW3 6RD   Closed 24-26 December and 1 January
✆ (020) 7581 5817
www.bibendum.co.uk

Menu £30 (lunch) – Carte £36/63

A/C
🎪
☀
VISA
MC
AE

Bibendum is now well into its twenties but very little has changed over those years, which is why it remains a favourite restaurant for so many. Matthew Harris' cooking continues to produce the sort of food that Elizabeth David would adore – it's mostly French but with a subtle British point of view. The set lunch menu has now been joined by a small à laCarte selection; evening menus are handwritten and the roast chicken with tarragon for two remains a perennial presence. Side dishes can bump the final bill up further than expected but the food is easy to eat and satisfying. The striking character of Michelin's former HQ, dating from 1911, is perhaps best appreciated at lunch when the sun lights up the glass Bibendum - the Michelin Man.

Bibendum Oyster Bar

Seafood

Michelin House, 81 Fulham Rd.
⊠ SW3 6RD
✆ (020) 7589 1480
www.bibendum.co.uk

⊖ **South Kensington**
Closed 24-26 December and 1 January
– (bookings not accepted)

Carte £21/35

The plateau de fruits de mer, for two, is the house speciality here. It includes crab, langoustines, prawns, oysters, winkles and whelks and will leave anyone satisfied and, when the sun is shining, pleased with the world in general. You'll find other appealing classics, from potted shrimps to egg mayonnaise, assorted salads and, predictably enough, a selection of oysters. The accessible wine list includes 460ml pots. It is all served in a relaxed continental-style café, with a mosaic floor and colourful ceramic tiles depicting the early days of French motoring – as befits any establishment located in the former foyer of Michelin House. The crustacea stall and florist at the front of the building attract plenty of passers-by.

Bistro K

French

117-119 Old Brompton Rd.
⊠ SW7 3RN
✆ (020) 7373 7774
www.bistro-k.co.uk

⊖ **Gloucester Road**
Closed Sunday and Monday

Menu £15 (lunch) – Carte £36/46

They call themselves a 'restaurant and lounge bar', so why use the word 'bistro' in their name? Perhaps they intended to distance themselves from the overtly ceremonial Ambassade de L'Ile, which previously occupied this spot, although it does suggest a level of informality that isn't entirely the case here: there are plenty of suited managers and the cooking is surprisingly delicate. The kitchen is clearly a skilled one and the cooking is underpinned by sound French techniques but is unafraid of adding the odd twist. The 'lounge bar' part of their name is represented by the type of music they play; a fact mildly baffling to their more mature customers, who don't realise that the restaurant is trying to target a younger crowd.

Bluebird

E7

350 King's Rd.
✉ SW3 5UU
✆ (020) 7559 1000
www.bluebird-restaurant.co.uk

⊖ Sloane Square

Menu £25 – Carte £26/49

[A/C]

The last refurbishment may have softened the huge space a little but Bluebird still delivers the atmosphere and excitement one expects from such a large industrial space. A former garage built in 1923, it houses everything from a wine store and café to a food shop and private members club, with the restaurant as the centrepiece. The kitchen champions British produce and highlights its provenance, be it Herdwick mutton, Cumbrian beef or Goosnargh chicken. It also features British cheeses along with seasonal fruit and veg. That being said, not all the dishes are so Anglo-centric: there are assorted pasta choices and the occasional French classic. Sunday roasts and a children's menu ensure that all bases are covered.

[VISA]

[MC]

[AE]

Bombay Brasserie

Indian ✗✗✗✗

D6

Courtfield Rd.
✉ SW7 4QH
✆ (020) 7370 4040
www.bombaybrasserielondon.com

⊖ Gloucester Road
Closed 25-26 December – booking advisable at dinner

Menu £22 (lunch) – Carte £31/43

[A/C]

Going strong since 1982, The Bombay Brasserie has always been one of the smartest Indian restaurants around, but in 2009 it emerged with a brand new look which revitalised the whole place. Plushness abounds, from the deep carpet and huge chandeliers of the large main room to the show kitchen of the conservatory and the very smart bar. The staff also got a new look with their burgundy waistcoats, but they continue to offer charming and professional service. The menu wasn't forgotten either and was overhauled by Hemant Oberoi. They replaced the predictable with the more creative, while at the same time respecting traditional philosophies; influences are a combination of Bori, Parsi, Maharashtrian and Goan cuisine.

[VISA]

[MC]

[AE]

The Botanist

F6

Modern European 🍴

7 Sloane Sq
✉ SW1W 8EE
☎ (020) 7730 0077
www.thebotanistonsloanesquare.com

⊖ Sloane Square
Closed 25-26 December

Carte £31/51

A/C
☼
VISA
MC
AE

Unlike say New Yorkers, Londoners seemingly prefer their bars separate from their restaurants, which is a shame as The Botanist demonstrates how well the two can coexist. You enter first into the bar and, by osmosis, its general bustle adds to the convivial atmosphere of the adjoining bright and warm restaurant. The place always appears full of people who 'get' what a restaurant should feel and sound like. The menu mixes cheffy descriptions like 'escabeche' with more prosaic words like 'pie' so expect a choice that includes terrines, fish from Billingsgate or more ambitious numbers like pigeon with Puy lentils. Dishes are unfussy in appearance – always a sign of a confident kitchen – and deliver on flavour.

Builders Arms

E6

British 🍴🍺

13 Britten St
✉ SW3 3TY
☎ (020) 7349 9040
www.geronimo-inns.co.uk

⊖ South Kensington.

Carte £22/34

A/C
☼
VISA
MC
AE

The Builders Arms is very much like a packed village local – the only difference being that, in this instance, the village is Chelsea and the villagers are all young and prosperous. The inside delivers on the promise of the smart exterior but don't expect it to be quiet as drinkers are welcomed just as much as diners. In fact, bookings are only taken for larger parties but just tell the staff that you're here to eat and they'll sort you out. The cooking reveals the effort that has gone into the sourcing of some decent ingredients; the rib of beef for two is a perennial favourite. Dishes are robust and satisfying and are not without some flair in presentation. Wine is also taken seriously and their list has been thoughtfully put together.

Bumpkin

British ✗

D6

102 Old Brompton Rd.
⊠ SW7 3RD
✆ (020) 7341 0802
www.bumpkinuk.com

⊖ Gloucester Road

Carte £30/37

A/C

⟐

☼

VISA

MC

AE

Their slogan is "for city folk who like a little country living", which is exactly the reason why many of the moneyed in this prosperous neighbourhood bought weekend retreats. This Bumpkin follows the success of the Notting Hill branch and they've largely repeated the formula by creating a restaurant with a pub-like informality that champions British produce. The rear room, with its large open-plan kitchen, is the more fun of the two and service is spirited and friendly. Quarterly printed menus double as placemats, with additional daily specials on the board. Expect lots of pies, burgers using Welsh Black beef and hotpots, with the simpler dishes often being the best ones. Weekend brunches and Sunday roasts are very popular.

Cadogan Arms

British 🍺

E7

298 King's Rd
⊠ SW3 5UG
✆ (020) 7352 6500
www.thecadoganarmschelsea.com

⊖ South Kensington.
Closed 25-26 December – booking
advisable at dinner

Carte £24/33

A/C

☼

VISA

MC

AE

The Martin brothers seem to have the King's Road covered, with The Botanist dominating the Sloane Square end and The Cadogan Arms doing its thing at the other. The tiled entrance step reads 'luncheon, bar and billiards' which sounds appealingly like a lost afternoon, and it is clear that this is still a proper, blokey pub. The upstairs billiard tables are available by the hour and, while you eat, you'll feel the beady eyes of the various stuffed and mounted animals on the walls staring at you. The cooking is appropriately gutsy; juicy Aberdeen Angus rib-eye, golden-fried haddock, Dexter Beef and Welsh lamb are all staples of the menu. Starters and desserts are a little showier – perhaps something for the ladies? Staff catch the mood just so.

Cambio de Tercio

D6

163 Old Brompton Rd.
✉ SW5 0LJ
✆ (020) 7244 8970
www.cambiodetercio.co.uk

⊖ Gloucester Road
Closed 25 December

Carte £30/54 s

A/C
⟨⊡⟩
🕸
⟨𝄞⟩
☀
VISA
MC
AE
①

The concept works well: choose 3 or 4 tapas each from the left side of the menu and they'll arrive in an orderly fashion so that sharing can be done at a leisurely pace. But if you feel that the tapas size just doesn't hit the spot or you haven't liked sharing since childhood then the dishes on the right hand side are pretty much the same except they come in regular main course size. Definitely start with Iberica ham and include the spicy patatas bravas and the sticky and rich oxtail in red wine. The chef uses his toys to good effect with the more contemporary desserts. Lots of vintages from Vega Sicilia and Pingus wines feature, along with Alion and Roda. Service gets better the more you visit. They also own the tapas bar across the road.

Le Cercle

F6

1 Wilbraham Pl.
✉ SW1X 9AE
✆ (020) 7901 9999
www.lecercle.co.uk

⊖ Sloane Square
Closed 25 December,
Sunday, Monday and bank holidays

Menu £15 (lunch) – Carte £28/31

A/C
VISA
MC
AE
①

Knowing this is owned by the same team as Club Gascon may lead to the raising of false hopes, as this is an altogether different operation. Le Cercle positions itself as a fashionable stop on the celebrity circuit and has the unsmiling receptionist and the managers with Secret Service ear pieces to prove it. Lunch sees a bewildering mix of business types and senior local ladies but what is certain is that it all comes alive at dinner; and its drapes and high ceiling do give it a fairly striking look. Where it does follow the same theme as its City sister is in the menu format, whereby you order three or four small dishes per person from the various sections. Dishes are nicely balanced and the French flavours pronounced.

Capote y Toros

D6

157 Old Brompton Road
✉ SW5 0LJ
✆ (020) 7373 0567
www.cambiodetercio.co.uk

⊖ Gloucester Road
Closed Sunday and Monday –
(dinner only)

Carte £19/32

A/C
⊗⊗
VISA
MC
AE
①

From the owners of not-quite-next-door Cambio de Tercio comes the compact and vividly coloured Capote y Toros which celebrates sherry, tapas and ham. Named after the matador's cape and his foe, there are enough bullfighting references to satisfy enthusiasts of Hemingway proportions, including a large wall of photos. However, it is sherry that takes centre stage and there's a huge variety and choice on offer. Those as yet unmoved by this most underappreciated of wines should start by trying 5 varieties in a 'flight'. Meanwhile, the menu revolves around about 25 dishes; try 3 per person. The Iberico ham is excellent and the octopus will make the queuing worthwhile – bookings aren't taken. Sherry is also used extensively in the cooking.

Cassis

E5

232-236 Brompton Rd.
✉ SW3 2BB
✆ (020) 7581 1101
www.cassisbistro.co.uk

⊖ South Kensington
Closed 25 December

Menu £20 (weekday lunch) – Carte £26/51

A/C
⊗⊗
☼
VISA
MC
AE
①

Brompton Road may never have featured in a Cézanne painting but Marlon Abela's paean to all things Provençal does a good job in bringing the colours of southern France to South Kensington. Pots of thyme on each table add aromatic hints of the Garrigue to the crisply stylish and contemporary room, which certainly has more substance than one usually encounters in somewhere calling itself a bistro. Kick off with one of their house cocktails and order some 'petites bouchées' such as the classic barbajuans or pissaladière; these can then be followed up by an authentic bouillabaisse or daube of beef. While Provençal wines do feature on the wine list, there's greater choice from the better known regions. You'll feel as though you've been on holiday.

Chabrot

French ✗

9 Knightsbridge Grn
✉ SW1X 7QL
☎ (020) 7225 2238
www.chabrot.co.uk

⊖ Knightsbridge

Carte £23/39

[A/C]
[🐾]
[☀]
[VISA]
[MC]
[AE]

In 2011 Thierry Laborde, formerly of Le Gavroche, got together with three friends – a sommelier, a restaurant manager and a florist – to open Chabrot, a bistro that couldn't be more French if it wore a beret and sang 'La Mer'. The kitchen looks to the SW of France and the Basque country for most of its inspiration. Sharing a board of Basque charcuterie is a good way to start and there are plenty of hearty offerings like roast foie gras as a main course, along with snails, octopus skewers and veal-stuffed cabbage. Add a few daily specials and a plat du jour and there should be something to everyone. If you really can't decide on what to order, the tables are so close you can simply take a peek at what your neighbour has chosen.

Chelsea Brasserie

French ✗✗

7-12 Sloane Sq.
✉ SW1W 8EG
☎ (020) 7896 9988
www.sloanesquarehotel.co.uk

⊖ Sloane Square
Closed Sunday dinner

Menu £25 (lunch and early dinner) – Carte £33/40

[A/C]
[🎭]
[VISA]
[MC]

If you're not going on to either the Royal Court or Cadogan Hall theatres then it may be best to alert your waiter; they are clearly so used to getting their customers fed and watered before curtain up that they sometimes find it hard to shift down a gear later on. It's no surprise that it is so busy early evening because their theatre menus represent excellent value. The menus, like the waiters, are mostly French born with some intercontinental experience. Vegetarians get plenty of choice and carnivores should be satisfied with the selection from the grill. The cooking has a breezy confidence and hits the spot. The front section of the restaurant attached to the bar is more fun, while tables at the back are quieter.

Chelsea Ram

British

D8

32 Burnaby St.
⊠ SW10 0PL
℡ (020) 7351 4008
Carte £22/26 s

⊖ Fulham Broadway.
Closed Sunday dinner

A/C

VISA

M©

It's easy to see why the Chelsea Ram is such a successful neighbourhood pub: it's somewhat secreted position means there are few casual passers-by to upset the peace, the locals appreciate the relaxed and warm feel of the place and the pub provides them with just the sort of food they want. That means proper pub grub, with highlights being things on toast, like chicken livers or mushrooms, and the constant presence of favourites like The Ram burger or haddock and leek fishcake; prices are fair and portions large. They do take bookings but somewhat reluctantly, as they always want to keep a table or two for that spontaneous visit. The Chelsea Ram's winning formula is that it's comfortable just being what it is – a friendly, reliable local.

Chutney Mary

Indian

D8

535 King's Rd.
⊠ SW10 0SZ
℡ (020) 7351 3113
www.realindianfood.com

⊖ Fulham Broadway
Closed dinner 25 December –
(dinner only and
lunch Saturday-Sunday)

Menu £22 (weekdays) – Carte £38/53

A/C

VISA

M©

AE

①

If you can't find it, ask a cabbie, as the precise location of Chutney Mary is reputed to form part of 'The Knowledge'. This long-standing Indian restaurant has always been more West End sophisticate than local eatery and was at the vanguard when Indian restaurants came of age in London. Silk wall hangings from Jaipur are the latest addition to the decoration which gets regularly refreshed, while the conservatory remains a favoured spot. The cooking has become slightly lighter recently and the flavours more subtle. Newer dishes include 'dabba gosht' made with lamb, halibut in a mustard sauce and steamed bream in a banana leaf, but kebabs and tandoor and grilled dishes remain popular. Wine from the glass-fronted cave plays a large part.

Le Colombier

E6

145 Dovehouse St.   ⊖ South Kensington
✉ SW3 6LB
✆ (020) 7351 1155
www.le-colombier-restaurant.co.uk

Menu £27 (lunch) – Carte £32/51

VISA
MC
AE

Le Colombier is as warm and welcoming as it is honest and reliable and thereby offers proof that being a good neighbourhood restaurant takes more than just being in a good neighbourhood. French influences abound, from the accents of the staff and the menu content to the inordinate amount of double cheek kissing that occurs – most of the customers appear to know one another or feel they should like to know one another. In summer, when the full-length windows fold back, the terrace is the place to sit although the under-floor heating ensures the place is equally welcoming in winter. Oysters, game in season, veal in various forms and regional cheeses are the highlights, as are the classic desserts from crêpe Suzette to crème brûlée.

Daphne's

Italian XX

E6

112 Draycott Ave.   ⊖ South Kensington
✉ SW3 3AE   Closed 25-26 December –
✆ (020) 7589 4257   booking essential
www.daphnes-restaurant.co.uk

Menu £20 (lunch and early dinner) – Carte £30/40

A/C
VISA
MC
AE
①

One wonders if theatrical agent Daphne Rye opened her eponymous restaurant as a means of keeping her resting actors busy. Forty years on and Daphne's is a chic Chelsea institution; there's even a branch in Barbados for those who can't live without their vongole on holiday. The narrow room is Tuscan in its look and the best seats are those at the front by the large windows. The many regulars clearly like the reassurance of familiarity so the kitchen sticks largely to a tried and tested assortment of Italian classics but prepared with greater care than one usually expects in an Italian restaurant with a 'celebrity' following. The lunch menu is good value and the occasional new dish, like salt-baked sea bass, gets in under the radar.

CHELSEA, SOUTH KENSINGTON, EARL'S COURT, HYDE PARK & KNIGHTSBRIDGE ▶ PLANS XI–XII

Dinner by Heston Blumenthal 🕸

British 🗶🗶🗶

F4

66 Knightsbridge ✉ SW1X 7LA
☎ (020) 7201 3833
www.dinnerbyheston.com

⊖ **Knightsbridge**
Closed Christmas

Menu £28 (weekday lunch) – Carte £45/60

A/C
📷
🔗
☀
VISA
MC
AE
①

Mandarin Oriental Hyde Park

The most eagerly anticipated opening in 2011 was Heston Blumenthal's mischievously named restaurant at the Mandarin Oriental Hyde Park. The reason it was the hottest ticket in town was hopefully because it was seen as the very embodiment of the increasing pride we now feel in our native cuisine, or it could just have been because he's on the telly a lot. The large, light room has quirky touches, like wall sconces shaped as jelly moulds, but the main focus is on the open kitchen, with its oversized watch mechanics powering the spit to roast the pineapple that goes with the Tipsy Cake (c.1810). The menu reads like a record of British kitchen triumphs, with the date of origin attached to each dish and a fashionably terse list of its parts; on the reverse you can read more. A kitchen brigade of 45 works with calm efficiency, meticulous attention to detail and intelligence to produce food that looks quite 'simple' but tastes sublime. Expect no 'molecular' alchemy; this is all about respect for, and a wonderful renewal of, British food, with just a little playfulness thrown in.

First Course
- Mandarin meat fruit.
- Roast scallops, cucumber ketchup and borage.

Main Course
- Spiced pigeon with ale and artichokes.
- Roast turbot, cockle ketchup and leaf chicory.

Dessert
- Tipsy cake with spit roast pineapple.
- Brown bread ice cream with salted butter caramel and malted yeast syrup.

Eight over Eight

E7

392 King's Rd
✉ SW3 5UZ
✆ (020) 7349 9934
www.rickerrestaurants.com

⊖ **Gloucester Road**
Closed 25-28 December

Carte £24/50

[A/C]
[✿]
[☼]
[VISA]
[MC]
[AE]
[◑]

A major fire at the back end of 2009 meant that Eight over Eight stayed shut for most of 2010, but anyone who missed it too much during this period needed only to nip up to Notting Hill to find another one of Will Ricker's fashionable Asian restaurants. From the day it reopened it has been full, so maybe its customers are more loyal than anyone thought; they are certainly a handsome bunch and many of them seem to know one another. The restaurant is largely unchanged; it just feels a little plusher and is better lit. Wisely, they didn't change the menu either; its influences stretch across a number of countries in South East Asia and dishes are designed for sharing. Highlights are the creamy curries and anything that's crispy.

Eighty-Six

Modern European ✗✗

E6

86 Fulham Rd, (1st Floor)
✉ SW3 6HR
✆ (020) 7052 9620
www.86restaurant.co.uk

⊖ **South Kensington**
Closed Sunday and Monday –
(dinner only)

Menu £41

[A/C]
[♥]
[VISA]
[MC]
[AE]
[◑]

If you want proof that the economic meltdown barely troubled the inner reaches of Chelsea then come along to this converted Georgian townhouse, as it's not just its name that evokes the carefree days of the '80s. Catering to those who know their Verbier from their Verdelho, it mixes three decorative styles – baroque, rococo and bling – to create a glamorous, gilded jewel for SW3's young movers and shakers. Upstairs from the cocktail bar is the dining room, where you'll find an over-eager service team and a dinner menu that roams around Europe. Here, the kitchen's strengths lie more in the simpler, more rustic dishes, especially those that make use of British ingredients and rare breeds such as Tamworth pork or Galloway beef.

CHELSEA, SOUTH KENSINGTON, EARL'S COURT, HYDE PARK & KNIGHTSBRIDGE ▶ PLANS XI-XII

Eleven Park Walk

Italian XXX

11 Park Walk
✉ SW10 0AJ
✆ (020) 7352 3449
www.11parkwalk.co.uk

⊖ South Kensington
Closed 25 December

Carte £34/58

A/C
📺
📅
☼
VISA
MC
AE

It was obvious to most that Aubergine was a restaurant that had clearly run out of gas; although its place in London's culinary history is assured. Walls were knocked down, tiles imported and lighting improved to create its far more handsome replacement, Eleven Park Walk. A smart, more mature Chelsea set quickly latched on to this sophisticated Italian and the effusive Roberto has been quick to identify regulars; his team of servers go about their business with equal vigour. The menu traverses Italy and dishes are generous in both size and flavour, but the kitchen appears to handle the Sardinian specialities with added care. The menu can get quite pricey but is balanced by a wine list that offers plenty of choice for under £25.

Henry Root

French X

9 Park Walk
✉ SW10 0AJ
✆ (020) 7552 7040
www.thehenryroot.com

⊖ South Kensington
Closed 25-27 December – booking
advisable

Menu £13 (lunch) – Carte £24/34

☂
A/C
🎱
☼
VISA
MC
AE

It was from his flat in Park Walk that satirist William Donaldson skewered many of the good and the great of his day through the letters of his eccentric alter ego, Henry Root. Now this little restaurant in the same street has adopted his name, which is surely a far better tribute than any blue plaque. The decoration is an appropriately curious mix of styles so expect everything from Jimi Hendrix photos to a stuffed salmon. The menu is appealingly divided into nibbles, salads, small plates, main courses and charcuterie. Terrines and ballotines are done well, as are traditional offerings like coq au vin or sea bass with cucumber and beetroot. Puddings often include a couple delivered from the nursery end of dessert-making.

Ilia

Italian ✕✕

96 Draycott Ave.   ⊖ South Kensington
✉ SW3 3AD
✆ (020) 7225 2555
www.ilia-london.com

Carte £29/47

[A/C]
[⟨·⟩]
[☼]
[VISA]
[MC]
[AE]

There must be worse philosophies to adopt in business than "give the customers what they want". The owner of this restaurant did precisely that by transforming his French restaurant by the name of 'Papillon' into an Italian one called 'Ilia'. It, in turn, offers its customers an almost bewildering array of dishes which are arranged under a dozen or so headings. This makes ordering quite an ordeal but at least the cooking is capably executed and everyone will find something that appeals. Support for the kitchen comes from the ebullient manager who spends much of his time proclaiming the freshness of his ingredients. The best tables are by the French windows at the front and the room has a light, cool and fresh feel.

Joe's

Modern European ✕✕

126 Draycott Ave   ⊖ South Kensington
✉ SW3 3AH   Closed 25 December, Easter Sunday
✆ (020) 7225 2217   and dinner Sunday-Monday
www.joseph.co.uk

Menu £17 (lunch) – Carte £24/37

[A/C]
[VISA]
[MC]
[AE]
[①]

Back in the '80s when the only thing bigger than the hair were the shoulder pads, Joe's was the place to be seen. Three decades later, it is once again a fashionable hang-out but this time a less excitable one with better food. The concise fortnightly changing menu is understated but at the same time appealingly intriguing. The cooking is fresh and vibrant and comes with Mediterranean overtones. Daily changing pulses and diminutive desserts give some clues as to the target audience, while midweek breakfasts and weekend brunches will power-up shoppers for the day ahead. Tables just past the bar are best for people-watching; those beyond are suited for anyone wanting to escape those prying eyes. Service is engaging but relaxed.

L'Etranger

I n n o v a t i v e ✗✗

36 Gloucester Rd.
✉ SW7 4QT
☎ (020) 7584 1118
www.circagroupltd.co.uk

⊖ Gloucester Road
Booking essential

Menu £24 (lunch) – Carte dinner £41/53

A/C

Messing around with classic French cooking is considered sacrilegious in certain parts of France but L'Etranger has escaped the tyranny of tradition by locating itself in South Kensington, London's own little Gallic ward. It offers an eclectic mix off French dishes that are heavily influenced by Japan, so a veal chop will come with wasabi sauce and salmon is poached in sake. Not every dish has a Nipponese constituent but it certainly makes for an original experience. The room is dark and moody and better suited to evenings, while service is a little more formal than it need be. The clientele is a mix of well-heeled locals and homesick French and Japanese émigrés, who also appreciate the depth and breadth of the impressive wine list.

VISA

M©

AE

Fifth Floor

M o d e r n E u r o p e a n ✗✗✗

109-125 Knightsbridge
✉ SW1X 7RJ
☎ (020) 7235 5250
www.harveynichols.com

⊖ Knightsbridge
Closed Easter Sunday,
25 December and Sunday dinner

Carte £35/55

A/C

If there is one thing that's never lacking on the fifth floor at Harvey Nicks, it's atmosphere. From the busy shop to the stylish bar and here in the elegant restaurant with its tent-like ceiling, there's seemingly plenty of fun to be had and lots of dressing up to do. The food is your standard modern European with the occasional Asian fling and, while fish appears to be a strength, the kitchen does have a tendency to occasionally add an unnecessary extra flavour that detracts from the overall dish. It's a shame that service can sometimes be a little too swift for its own good, as you can feel as though staff are more concerned with the time of your departure than in ensuring that you're having a good time.

VISA

M©

AE

①

Foxtrot Oscar

Traditional ✗

79 Royal Hospital Rd.
✉ SW3 4HN
☎ (020) 7352 4448
www.gordonramsay.com

⊖ Sloane Square
Closed 25 December –
booking essential

Menu £22 (lunch) – Carte £26/33

A/C
☀
VISA
MC
AE

There are always plenty of locals in Foxtrot Oscar, which is not something you can say about many of Gordon Ramsay's restaurants. The fact that this is probably his least known is perhaps a factor. The burgundy walls and black and white photos give it an almost '80s bistro feel and there's also a downstairs, which is actually quite a nice spot and not merely an overflow. The lunch menu is appealing priced; the dinner à laCarte is more mixed. Your best bet is to skip the starters and head for something braised or slow-cooked which should satisfy anyone's hunger. Another good choice is the Foxtrot burger, which arrives on a board, accompanied by tomato relish and some enormous chips. Regulars are well looked after.

Galoupet

Asian influences ✗✗

13 Beauchamp Pl
✉ SW13 1NQ
☎ (020) 7036 3600
www.galoupet.co.uk

⊖ Knightsbridge
Closed 25 December

Carte £35/50

A/C
☀
VISA
MC
AE
①

Peer through the window of this Georgian townhouse and you'll think you're looking at some sort of futuristic dispensary. The 'Enomatic' wine dispensers are a clue that wine plays an important part here; indeed, the owners have a vineyard in Provence. Their rosé is a refreshing rose-petal scented little number and all the wines on the constantly evolving list are available by the glass, even Krug – well, this is Beauchamp Place after all. Wine suggestions also accompany each of the dishes which fuse the East with the Mediterranean and, in a nod to the current fashion, are also available in smaller sizes. Although some combinations work better than others, the food offers pleasant contrasting textures and comes with a refreshing vitality.

Geales

Seafood 🍴

F6

1 Cale St.
✉ SW3 3QT
✆ (020) 7965 0555
www.geales.com

⊖ South Kensington
Closed 25-26 December,
1 January and Monday lunch

Carte £28/36

A/C
🛋
☼
VISA
MC
AE

Good fish and chips shouldn't just be the preserve of visiting tourists who are hoping to catch up on new episodes of the Benny Hill Show while they're here. We all need reminding of their appeal sometimes and, for this, there is Geales. Don't be fooled by the "Established 1939" sign outside, as this branch opened in 2010. It occupies the site of Tom Aikens' short-lived chippy but the extraction system has clearly improved as there has been no uprising by locals worried about frying fumes permeating their Colefax and Fowler. The place is charmingly decorated, cosy and warmly run and the menu successfully mixes the classics with the more modern, so there's fried haddock along with soft shell crab tempura. Puds are wholesome and homemade.

Good Earth

Chinese 🍴🍴

E5

233 Brompton Rd.
✉ SW3 2EP
✆ (020) 7584 3658
www.goodearthgroup.co.uk

⊖ Knightsbridge
Closed 23-31 December

Menu £12/30 – Carte £21/36

A/C
☼
VISA
MC
AE

The Brompton Road branch of this small chain has been a reliable constant for many a year and is suitably authentic on all levels: the service is brisk, the menu lengthy, cooking is dependable and desserts are not worth bothering with. There is no particular bias, save for a few Sichuan dishes, but they do use plenty of higher-end ingredients like scallops and Dover sole. Included among the set menus is the Lobster Dinner, a reminder of the restaurant's location and target market. More unusual dishes are often introduced but it's the old favourites and classic combinations that sell. Unlike most restaurants spread over two floors, here the basement level is actually the busier and more popular choice than the ground floor.

Gordon Ramsay ✿ ✿ ✿

French ✕✕✕✕

68-69 Royal Hospital Rd.
✉ SW3 4HP
☎ (020) 7352 4441
www.gordonramsay.com

⊖ **Sloane Square**
Closed Christmas, Saturday and
Sunday – booking essential

Menu £45/90

A/C

VISA

M/C

A/E

◍

Gordon Ramsay Holdings

Head Chef Clare Smyth's influence appears to stretch beyond the kitchen: it was her idea to add orchids to the room and this has given it a lighter, fresher look, although the David Collins interior still exudes calm. This composure is essential as the restaurant is as busy as ever, which means securing a reservation can still be a fairly tortuous experience; bookings are taken three months in advance but it is worth trying your luck at the last minute. Clare Smyth had a challenging task because, along with showcasing her lighter style of cooking in the 'seasonal inspiration' menu, she also had to deliver on the Gordon Ramsay classics, such as the ravioli of lobster and langoustine, the braised pig's trotter and the Best End of lamb – and these are the dishes that many of the regulars order time and time again. Fortunately, she succeeded and her instinctive feel for and understanding of harmonious flavours is clearly evident. Jean-Claude is a constant presence in the room and if you're a returning guest then he will probably remember you.

First Course

- Ravioli of lobster, langoustine and salmon with a lemongrass and chervil velouté.
- Pressed foie gras with peppered Madeira jelly.

Main Course

- Best End of lamb and a navarin of spring vegetables.
- Roasted turbot with asparagus, morels and wild garlic risotto.

Dessert

- Granny Smith parfait a blackberry foam, honeycomb and cider sorbet.
- Bitter chocolate cylinder, coffee granité and ginger mousse.

Lots Road Pub & Dining Room

D8

Traditional 🍺

114 Lots Rd
✉ SW10 0RJ
☎ (020) 7352 6645
www.lotsroadpub.com

⊖ Fulham Broadway.

Carte £20/30

[A/C]
☼
[VISA]
[MC]
[AE]

Lots Road Pub and its customers are clearly happy with one another as the it has introduced a customer loyalty scheme, whereby anyone making their fifth visit is rewarded with a discount. Lunch is geared more towards those just grabbing a quick bite but dinner sees a choice that could include oysters, mussels or a savoury tart; the Perthshire côte de boeuf is the house speciality. There are also pies and casseroles, in appropriate pub-like sizes, and even salads for those after something light. Service remains bright and cheery, even on those frantic Thursday nights when the pub offers 'Thursday Treats' with wine tasting and nibbles. The only disappointment is the somewhat ordinary bread for which they make a not insubstantial charge.

Manicomio

F6

Italian ✗

85 Duke of York Sq., King's Rd.
✉ SW3 4LY
☎ (020) 7730 3366
www.manicomio.co.uk

⊖ **Sloane Square**
Closed 1 January, 24-26
and 31 December

Carte £31/43

[hT]
[A/C]
☼
[VISA]
[MC]
[AE]

If anywhere encapsulates King's Road's journey from counterculture hub to retail playground it is Duke of York Square and its outlets. Among these is Manicomio, a glossy Italian restaurant which doesn't need to rely solely on weary shoppers as it also draws visitors from the Saatchi Gallery next door, a fact that shows just what an inspired location this was. Its success is also helped by an accessible menu, offering a greatest hits of easy-to-eat Italian food. Cooking is undertaken with care and the simplest dishes are the best ones, although prices do reflect the Chelsea postcode. Service remains sufficiently perky for one to forgive occasional moments of forgetfulness. The terrific front terrace fills quickly in nearly all seasons.

Marco

Traditional ✗✗

Stamford Bridge, Fulham Rd.
✉ SW6 1HS
✆ (020) 7915 2929
www.marcorestaurant.org

⊖ Fulham Broadway
▶ **Plans XVIII**
Closed 2 weeks July-August, 25 December,
Sunday and Monday –
booking advisable – (dinner only)

Carte £31/59

A/C
VISA
MC
AE

A section of Manchester United fans was once derided as being prawn sandwich eaters; London expectations being what they are, at Chelsea's ground you get a brasserie from Marco Pierre White. Some will inevitably cry foul and shed a tear for football's working class roots; others will cheer for this evidence of our growing culinary maturity. Both sides, though, should applaud the menu, which offers classics galore such as grilled Dover sole, assorted roasts and Scottish steaks. This being a polyglot club means other nationalities are also represented, in this case a bit of Italy and France, and more sophisticated fare such as foie gras terrine or duck confit is available. Puddings are a particular highlight.

Medlar

E7

Modern European ✗✗

438 King's Rd
✉ SW10 0LJ
✆ (020) 7349 1900
www.medlarrestaurant.co.uk

⊖ Sloane Square
Closed Sunday dinner and Monday

Menu £25/38

A/C
VISA
MC
AE

Of the many restaurant openings in 2011, Medlar was one that stood out, precisely because it wasn't trying to be different or original. There is no 'concept' to explain here, just two young owners who have quietly opened a super neighbourhood restaurant. David and his front of house team get the tone of the service just right – it's warm but not intrusive – while Joe, in the kitchen, concentrates on complementing flavours. He is an alumnus of Chez Bruce and there are clear similarities: it's a set menu, the ingredients are largely British and the cooking has a French base. But a year spent in Sydney has also lent his food added brightness and vitality. The restaurant has a crisp and composed feel that puts customers at ease.

Mr Chow

F4

Chinese 🍴🍴

151 Knightsbridge
✉ SW1X 7PA
☎ (020) 7589 7347
www.mrchow.com

⊖ **Knightsbridge**
Closed 1 January, 24-26 December,
Easter Monday dinner and
Monday lunch

Carte £38/57

AC
🕐
☀
VISA
MC
AE
◑

Chinese food, Italian waiters, swish surroundings, steep prices and immaculately coiffured regulars: it's an unusual mix that clearly works because Mr Chow has already celebrated his fortieth birthday. Even if you're not recognisable, you'll get a friendly welcome and the champagne chariot will be wheeled towards you. The laminated menu is long but clearly divided between sections entitled 'from the sea', 'from the land' and 'from the sky'; chickens will be pleased to find themselves in this last category. The cooking is far better than you expect, with genuine care shown. The desserts are thoroughly European and come on a trolley, with tarts the speciality. Your final bill won't be clearly itemised but this doesn't seem to bother anyone.

One-O-One

F4

Seafood 🍴🍴🍴

101 Knightsbridge
✉ SW1X 7RN
☎ (020) 7290 7101
www.oneoonerestaurant.com

⊖ **Knightsbridge**

Menu £22 (lunch) – Carte £55/75

AC
☀
VISA
MC
AE
◑

Walking past the Sheraton Park Tower hotel, one of London's less majestic buildings, you'd never know there was a restaurant behind those heavy net curtains, and a rather good one to boot. Granted, the room size and shape mean an animated atmosphere remains elusive and staff, pleasant though they are, have little presence. But the food is good and that food is mostly fish. They've found a balance between offering a traditional à laCarte menu and a list of 'petits plats', 6 of which, taken together, will satisfy the fiercest of appetites. Much of the produce comes from Brittany and Norway; the latter gives us the King crab legs which are the stars of the show. The kitchen is not afraid of adding a little playfulness to its classical base.

Painted Heron

Indian 🍴🍴

112 Cheyne Walk
✉ SW10 0DJ
✆ (020) 7351 5232
www.thepaintedheron.com

⊖ Gloucester Road
Closed 25 December –
(dinner only and lunch
Saturday-Sunday)

Menu £20/35 – Carte £30/38

They call their style "modern Indian" which, in essence, means the kitchen's influences come from across the land; from Kashmir and Rajasthan to Kerala and Goa. Fish, largely from Hastings, is handled dextrously and seasonal game often features on the menu, whether that's the tandoor pigeon breasts, the partridge with red chilli paste or grouse in a southern stew. Flavours tend to be well-defined and balanced. The room is bigger than you think and has quite a formal feel, thanks largely to the style of service from the young team, but it's broken up into nooks and crannies and hence quite intimate. The open courtyard is an attractive feature and, despite its tiny entrance and tucked away location, the restaurant always appears to be busy.

Pasha

Moroccan 🍴🍴

1 Gloucester Rd.
✉ SW7 4PP
✆ (020) 7589 7969
www.pasha-restaurant.co.uk

⊖ Gloucester Road
Closed 25-26 December

Menu £20/30 – Carte £27/33

If the prosaic surroundings of Gloucester Road leave you in need of more colourful fillip to your love-life then try buying into the whole Pasha experience: the exotic scent of incense and the rich, romantic and velvety décor should be enough to arouse anyone's ardour. Downstairs is the place to be, in one of the semi-private booths in particular, where rose petals are strewn seductively over the tables and service is appropriately sweet-natured. Choose from one of the 'feast' menus and the food will keep on coming, including kemia (Moroccan small plates), tagines and sweet pastries. By the end your more corpulent figure may leave you feeling less romantically inclined so be thankful to the belly dancers for buying you some time.

Phoenix

F6

23 Smith St.
✉ SW3 4EE
☎ (020) 7730 9182
www.geronimo-inns.co.uk/thepheonix

⊖ Sloane Square.
Closed 25 December

Carte £21/34

The same menu is served throughout and, while the bar has plenty of seating and a civilised feel, head to the warm and comfortable dining room at the back if you want a more structured meal or you're impressing a date. Blackboard specials supplement the menu which keeps things traditional: fish on a Friday, a pasta of the day and the likes of fishcakes or sausage and mash with red onion jam. For lunch, you'll find some favourites for late-risers, like eggs Benedict and, in winter, expect the heartening sight of crumbles or plum pudding. Wines are organised by their character, with nearly 30 varieties offered by the glass. The side dishes can bump up the final bill but The Phoenix remains a friendly and conscientiously run Chelsea local.

Pig's Ear

E7

35 Old Church St
✉ SW3 5BS
☎ (020) 7352 2908
www.thepigsear.com

⊖ Sloane Square.

Carte £15/25

This Chelsea pub may not look much like a foodie spot from the outside, or indeed from the inside, but it does have a refreshing honesty to it. Lunch is in the rough-and-ready ground floor bar, decorated with everything from 'Tintin' pictures to covers of 'Sounds' newspaper. There's a decent choice of 5-6 main courses and a wine list on a blackboard. With its wood panelling and dressed tables, the upstairs dining room provides quite a contrast, but the atmosphere is still far from starchy. Here the menu displays a little more ambition but cooking remains similarly earthy and the wine list has plenty of bottles under £30. The kitchen knows its way around an animal: slow-cooked dishes such as pork cheeks are done particularly well.

Poissonnerie de l'Avenue

E6

82 Sloane Ave.
⊠ SW3 3DZ
☏ (020) 7589 2457
www.poissonneriedelavenue.com

⊖ South Kensington
Closed Easter and
25-26 December

Menu £30 (lunch) – Carte £31/48

A/C
🗘
🕯
☼
VISA
MC
AE
①

There is something heartening about dining in a restaurant that is older than its waiters. Poissonnerie de l'Avenue began life in 1946 but the owner is still to be found greeting his customers – many of whom look as though they've been coming since the doors first opened – as old friends, as indeed many are. This is a restaurant all about traditional hospitality and it's easy to understand its longevity. The wood-panelled room has an air of luxury; service is well-organised and the cooking is done 'properly'. The menu is a large affair: expect about 18 starters with everything from oysters to smoked salmon and the same number of seafood and fish main courses. The well-groomed clientele hardly blink when handed the inevitably large bill.

Racine

E5

239 Brompton Rd
⊠ SW3 2EP
☏ (020) 7584 4477
www.racine-restaurant.com

⊖ South Kensington
Closed Christmas

Menu £18 (lunch and early dinner) – Carte £30/55

A/C
🗨
☼
VISA
MC
AE

Racine is as authentic a French brasserie as you can get at this end of the tunnel. The accents are thick; the baguettes are fresh and the room's wood and leather have that reassuring lived-in look. Some of the clientele, who are a mature and confident bunch, give the impression that they come here on a weekly basis and it's easy to understand why: along with the authentically prepared classics, such as steak tartare, tête de veau or fruits de mer, are plenty of other dishes that hit the spot, along with well priced lunch and early evening menus. Try to avoid the tables in the middle of the room because, on windier days, you'll find yourself assailed by the occasional gust of wind, whenever somebody opens the front door.

Rasoi ✿

F6

Indian ✗✗

10 Lincoln St
✉ SW3 2TS
✆ (020) 7225 1881
www.rasoirestaurant.co.uk

⊖ Sloane Square
Closed 25-26 December
and Saturday lunch

Menu £27/59 – Carte £59/85

A/C
🛋
☼
VISA
MC
AE

Rasoi

Part of the appeal of Vineet Bhatia's Rasoi is that it's found in an archetypal Chelsea townhouse and that the atmosphere inside is usually far warmer and more intimate than anything one usually experiences in an Indian restaurant. This is often despite, rather than because of, the staff, who bring a mix of nationalities and varying degrees of competency to the operation. Proof that most people are really here for the food comes in the fact that the 'gourmand' menu is by far the most popular choice; it has been reduced from an unwieldy nine courses to a more manageable seven. The cooking is inventive and the kitchen proves that Indian food can be just as open to interpretation as other cuisines. But what makes it all work is the quality of the ingredients used and the deft, controlled spicing. Tea drinkers will find much to savour in the range and the ritual. Sit in the bigger room at the back which has more personality than the one at the front; larger parties should consider one of the more opulent private rooms upstairs.

First Course	*Main Course*	*Dessert*
• Tandoori lobster with chilli and wasabi, lentil and lobster soup. • Street food chaats.	• Smoked rack of lamb with biryani khichdi. • Almond tikki.	• Chocolate craving platter. • Marmalade rasmalai.

Tendido Cero

D6

174 Old Brompton Rd.
✉ SW5 0BA
☎ (020) 7370 3685
www.cambiodetercio.co.uk

⊖ Gloucester Road
Closed 25 December

Carte £30/34

A/C
☼
VISA
MC
AE
①

Abel Lusa has got things pretty sewn up at this end of Old Brompton Road: on one side of the road he owns Cambio de Tercio and Capote y Toros and opposite he has Tendido Cero, a warmly decorated tapas bar adorned with paintings of matadors. On offer is an appealing mix of familiar hot and cold tapas, from padron peppers and Pata Negra ham to boquerones and assorted croquetas, but there are also a few unusual choices, like a mini 'hamburger' made with sardines. Further highlights include Galician octopus, white bean stew with chorizo and pork cheeks with potato purée. Lunchtimes are relatively quiet affairs; it is at night when the place comes alive and the pace hots up. Service is more about efficiency than personality.

Tom's Kitchen

E6

27 Cale St.
✉ SW3 3QP
☎ (020) 7349 0202
www.tomskitchen.co.uk

⊖ South Kensington

Carte £29/50

☼
VISA
MC
AE

The locals may not have taken to his fish and chip shop but they do seem to like his kitchen. This is a restaurant with a thoroughly sound plan: it's open from early in the morning until late at night and offers satisfying comfort food in relaxed surroundings. The tiled walls and open kitchen work well and there's an upstairs room for the overspill. With its shepherd's pie, sausage and mash, and belly of pork, the menu wouldn't look out of place in a pub; although, as the eponymous Tom is Tom Aikens, a few luxury ingredients like foie gras do sneak in. Bread, olives and side dishes can push up the final bill but it's a friendly place with a stress-free atmosphere. There's a less convincing second branch in Somerset House.

Toto's

Italian 𝕏𝕏𝕏

F5

Walton House, Walton St.
✉ SW3 2JH
☏ (020) 7589 0075

⊖ Knightsbridge
Closed 25-27 December –
booking essential at dinner

Menu £23 (lunch) – Carte £35/47

Toto's has been a Chelsea landmark around these parts for donkey's years. Its somewhat hidden location and old school service make you feel part of a club and you'll be dining with plenty of locals – lots of smartly dressed people of a certain age displaying varying degrees of tonsorial ingenuity. The room is not as big as one thinks as there's a mirrored wall at one end but there is also a gallery. The menu is familiar and despite the odd unseasonal ingredient, the cooking is very satisfying. The pasta course, such as black spaghetti with squid and clams, will be a highlight while main courses such as the lamb cutlets with pecorino also hit the spot. It ain't cheap but, if you're concerned about price, then you're in the wrong place.

Zuma

Japanese 𝕏𝕏

F5

5 Raphael St
✉ SW7 1DL
☏ (020) 7584 1010
www.zumarestaurant.com

⊖ Knightsbridge
▶ **Plan XII**
Closed Christmas

Carte £50/70

This stylish Knightsbridge restaurant with its contemporary Japanese food has proved to be a hit with the glittering and the glitterati and is ideally located for those seeking a little respite from the strain of shopping or being photographed doing so. The place is certainly catching in its design, with a plethora of granite, stone, marble and wood creating a restaurant that successfully blends east with west. Choose from a variety of seating options, from the bustle of the main dining area to the theatre afforded by the sushi counter. The menu offers up an intriguing mix of the traditional with the ultra modern, all expertly crafted and delicately presented. Lovers of sake will find over thirty varieties available.

Kensington · North Kensington · Notting Hill

It was the choking air of 17C London that helped put **Kensington** on the map: the little village lying to the west of the city became the favoured retreat of the asthmatic King William III who had Sir Christopher Wren build **Kensington Palace** for him. Where the king leads, the titled follow, and the area soon became a fashionable location for the rich. For over 300 years, it's had no problem holding onto its cachet, though a stroll down Kensington High Street is these days a more egalitarian odyssey than some more upmarket residents might approve of.

The shops here mix the everyday with the flamboyant, but for a real taste of the exotic you have to take the lift to the top of the Art Deco Barkers building and arrive at the Kensington Roof Gardens, which are open to all as long as they're not in use for a corporate bash. The gardens are now over seventy years old, yet still remain a 'charming secret'. Those who do make it up to the sixth floor discover a delightful woodland garden and gurgling stream, complete with pools, bridges and trees. There are flamingos, too, adding a dash of vibrant colour.

Back down on earth, Kensington boasts another hidden attraction in **Leighton House** on its western boundaries. The Victorian redbrick façade looks a bit forbidding as you make your approach, but step inside and things take a dramatic turn, courtesy of the extraordinary Arab Hall, with its oriental mosaics and tinkling fountain creating a scene like something from *The Arabian Knights.* Elsewhere in the building, the Pre-Raphaelite paintings of Lord Leighton, Burne-Jones and Alma-Tadema are much to the fore. Mind you, famous names have always had a hankering for W8, with a particular preponderance to dally in enchanting **Kensington Square,** where there are almost as many blue plaques as buildings upon which to secure them. William Thackeray, John Stuart Mill and Edward Burne-Jones were all residents.

One of the London's most enjoyable green retreats is **Holland Park,** just north of the High Street. It boasts the 400 year-old Holland House, which is a fashionable focal point for summer-time al fresco theatre and opera. Holland Walk runs along the eastern fringe of the park, and provides a lovely sojourn down to the shops; at the Kyoto Garden, koi carp reach hungrily for the surface of their pool, while elsewhere peacocks strut around as if they own the place.

Another world beckons just north of here – the seedy-cum-glitzy environs of **Notting Hill.** The main drag itself, Notting Hill Gate, is little more than a one-dimensional thoroughfare only enlivened by second hand record shops, but to its south are charming cottages with pastel shades in leafy streets, while to the north the appealing **Pembridge Road** evolves into

S. Ollivier / MICHELIN

the boutiques of Westbourne Grove. Most people heading in this direction are making for the legendary Portobello Road market – particularly on Saturdays, which are manic. The market stretches on for more than a mile, with a chameleon-like ability to change colour and character on the way: there are antiques at the Notting Hill end, followed further up by food stalls, and then designer and vintage clothes as you reach the Westway. Those who don't fancy the madding crowds of the market can nip into the Electric Cinema and watch a movie in supreme comfort: it boasts two-seater sofas and leather armchairs. Nearby there are another two film-houses putting the hip into the Hill – the Gate, and the Coronet, widely recognised as one of London's most charming 'locals'.

Hidden in a mews just north of **Westbourne Grove** is a fascinating destination: the Museum of Brands, Packaging and Advertising, which does pretty much what it says on the label. It's both nostalgic and evocative, featuring thousands of items like childhood toys, teenage magazines…and HP sauce bottles.

267

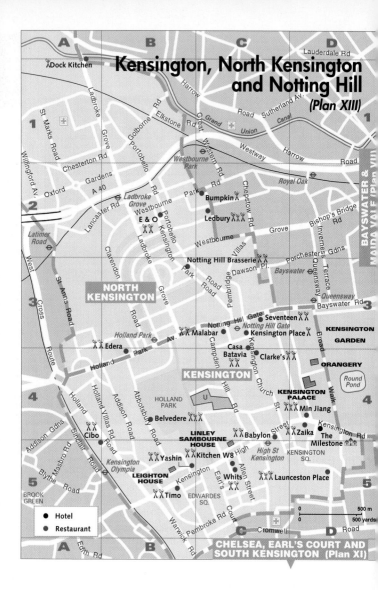

Kensington, North Kensington and Notting Hill (Plan XIII)

- Dock Kitchen
- Bumpkin
- Ledbury
- E & O
- Notting Hill Brasserie
- Seventeen
- Malabar
- Kensington Place
- Edera
- Casa Batavia
- Clarke's
- Min Jiang
- Belvedere
- Zaika
- Cibo
- Babylon
- The Milestone
- Yashin
- Kitchen W8
- Whits
- Launceston Place
- Timo

- Hotel
- Restaurant

0   500 m
0   500 yards

NORTH KENSINGTON

KENSINGTON

KENSINGTON GARDEN

ORANGERY

Round Pond

KENSINGTON PALACE

HOLLAND PARK

LINLEY SAMBOURNE HOUSE

LEIGHTON HOUSE

EDWARDES SQ.

BROOK GREEN

KENSINGTON SQ.

BAYSWATER & MAIDA VALE (Plan VIII)

CHELSEA, EARL'S COURT AND SOUTH KENSINGTON (Plan XI)

268

Babylon

C4

99 Kensington High St
(entrance on Derry St) ✉ W8 5SA
✆ (020) 7368 3993
www.roofgardens.virgin.com

⊖ High Street Kensington
Closed 24-30 December,
1-2 January and Sunday dinner

Menu £23 (lunch) – Carte £33/47

The challenge is to find the entrance, which is secreted on the right as you walk down Derry Street; then it's the lift up to the 7th floor and suddenly you're surrounded by trees. There's no doubting that this is quite a spot and while the gardens just below may not be 'hanging' they are an understandably appealing place for a party. The restaurant is a long, narrow affair whose contemporary décor reflects the leafy outdoors and the terrace takes some beating in summer. Influences on the menu remain largely within Europe and the cooking shows a degree of perkiness and ambition. The lunchtime set menu is priced to appeal to local businesses while the à la carte can get a little expensive. The wine list plants its flag firmly in the New World.

Belvedere

B4

Holland House, off Abbotsbury Rd.
✉ W8 6LU
✆ (020) 7602 1238
www.belvedererestaurant.co.uk

⊖ Holland Park
Closed Sunday dinner

Menu £20 (weekday lunch) – Carte £28/44

Built in the 17C as the summer ballroom to the Jacobean Holland House, The Belvedere sits in a stunning position in Holland Park. It's hard to believe you're still in London but check the location first as signposts within the park are a little elusive. The ground floor is the more glittery, with mirrors, glass balls and a small bar area. Upstairs is more traditional in style and leads out onto the charming terrace, which is well worth booking in summer. Service remains decidedly formal. The menu covers all bases from eggs Benedict to even the occasional Thai offering, but it's worth sticking to the more classical, French influenced dishes as these are kitchen's strength. Produce is well-sourced and dishes nicely balanced. France dominates the wine list.

Bumpkin

C2

209 Westbourne Park Rd ⊖ Westbourne Park
✉ W11 1EA
✆ (020) 7243 9818
www.bumpkinuk.com

Carte £29/37

[A/C]
[⊡]
[☼]
[VISA]
[MC]
[AE]

How refreshing to find a restaurant's name that sums up its spirit instead of merely repeating its street number or using the name of an obscure vegetable. Bumpkin, whose slogan is 'for city folk who like a little country living', champions British produce in quasi-rustic surroundings with a pub-like informality. Young, keen staff run around with 'Country Girl' or 'Country Boy' emblazoned on their T-shirts and the noisy open kitchen adds to the fun. The menu avoids being too earnest and focuses on using first-rate ingredients sensibly; the best dishes are the simplest ones, such as a 'Cow Pie' of which Desperate Dan would surely approve. Be sure to sit in the main room rather than in the corridor of uncertainty between it and the front bar.

Casa Batavia

C3

135 Kensington Church St ⊖ Notting Hill Gate
✉ W8 7LP   Booking advisable
✆ (020) 7221 7348
www.casabatavia.com

Menu £22 (lunch) – Carte £24/37

[A/C]
[⊡]
[⊙]
[☼]
[VISA]
[MC]
[AE]

In 2011 two friends from different backgrounds came together to open this intimate Italian restaurant on busy Kensington Church Street. The affable Paolo Boschi has been a recognisable figure on the London restaurant scene for many years, while Nicola Batavia established his reputation as a gifted chef in Turin in the late '90s. Here at Casa Batavia, Nicola oversees the menu and has installed one of his protégés as chef, while Paolo ensures that the service team are on their toes. The more refined cooking of Piedmont is the major influence on the menu, in such specialities as Castelmagno cheese with chestnut honey; potted rabbit with hazelnuts; pig's cheek with polenta and dried fruits; and, of course, panna cotta.

Cibo

A4-5

3 Russell Gdns
✉ W14 8EZ
☎ (020) 7371 6271
www.ciborestaurant.net

⊖ **Kensington Olympia**
Closed 1 week Christmas
and bank holidays

Menu £25 – Carte £23/37

Some of the sparkle may have dimmed since Cibo opened in 1989 but its band of local followers remain committed in their enthusiasm for this friendly Italian restaurant. The interior looks a tad weary these days but the quirky pictures celebrating the naked female form are still there and the imported hand-painted crockery is a nice touch. The ever-popular platter of grilled seafood dictates that the menu pretty much changes on a daily basis, although certain dishes can never be changed; some regulars can even guess who's in the kitchen that day by the degree of spicing. Service is friendly if a touch chaotic at times and while the opening front façade is a boon in summer, it can be draughty in winter, so ask for a table at the back.

Clarke's

C4

124 Kensington Church St
✉ W8 4BH
☎ (020) 7221 9225
www.sallyclarke.com

⊖ **Notting Hill Gate**
Closed Christmas-New Year,
Sunday dinner and bank holidays –
booking advisable

Menu £41 (dinner) – Carte £33/46

By constantly searching for the next big thing, many diners miss out on London's more dependable and worthy restaurants such as Clarke's, which has been a reassuring presence on Kensington Church Street since 1984. Regulars, of whom there are many, prefer the ground floor, although the tables downstairs benefit from the delicious aromas arising from the surprisingly serene open kitchen. The cooking remains true to Sally Clarke's founding principles of excellent ingredients and simple preparation and owes much to the influence of Alice Waters at Chez Panisse in San Francisco. There is a small, weekly changing à la carte plus 'Sally's Dinner Menu', a nicely balanced set price menu. The wine list has also been thoughtfully compiled.

Dock Kitchen

A0

Portobello Dock, 342-344
Ladbroke Grove ⊠ W10 5BU
✆ (020) 8962 1610
www.dockkitchen.co.uk

⊖ **Ladbroke Grove**
Closed last week August,
24 December-5 January
and Sunday dinner

Menu £19 (lunch) – Carte £26/37

VISA
MC
AE

What started as a pop-up restaurant became a permanent feature in this former Victorian goods yard and the space is shared with designer Tom Dixon, some of whose furniture and lighting is showcased here. The open kitchen dominates one end of the room where steel girders and exposed brick add to the industrial aesthetic. The similarities to Moro, River Café and Petersham Nurseries are palpable, not just in the refreshing lack of ceremony and the fashionable crowds that flock here, but also in the cooking, where quality ingredients are a given and natural flavours speak for themselves. The chef's peregrinations also inform his cooking; look out for his themed set menus which could be Sardinian one week, Moroccan the next.

E&O

B2

14 Blenheim Cres.
⊠ W11 1NN
✆ (020) 7229 5454
www.rickerrestaurants.com

⊖ **Ladbroke Grove**
Closed 25-26 December
and 1 January

Menu £19 (lunch) – Carte £23/54

A/C
⟨⟩
☼
VISA
MC
AE
①

Once you've sidestepped the full-on bar of this Notting Hill favourite, a step from Portobello Road, you'll find yourself in a moodily sophisticated restaurant packed with the beautiful and the hopeful. The room is understatedly urbane, with slatted walls, large circular lamps and leather banquettes, while noise levels are at the party end of the auditory index. Waiting staff are obliging, pleasant and often among the prettiest people in the room. E&O stands for Eastern and Oriental and the menu journeys across numerous Asian countries, dividing itself into assorted headings which include dim sum, salads, tempura, curries and roasts. Individual dishes vary in size and price so sharing, as in life, is often the best option.

Edera

B4

148 Holland Park Ave. ⊖ Holland Park
✉ W11 4UE
☎ (020) 7221 6090
www.edera.co.uk

Carte £37/54

A/C
⟨⟩
☼
VISA
MC
AE

The last makeover made Edera warmer and more comfortable and, while it actually holds up to 75 people, it still manages to feel quite intimate. On a typical night it seems as though the vast majority of customers have been before, that they know one another and probably walked here. In comparison, the staff are a youthful bunch, but they are well-marshalled and quietly efficient. The menu is quite broad and portions are on the generous side so if you're having a pasta dish you may struggle with a fourth course. The list of daily specials is wisely printed so you don't have to try to memorise the waiter's recital; there is a Sardinian element to the cooking, with bottarga omnipresent, and the ingredients are first-rate.

Kensington Place

Modern European ✗

C3

201-209 Kensington Church St. ⊖ Notting Hill Gate
✉ W8 7LX
☎ (020) 7727 3184
www.kensingtonplace-restaurant.co.uk

Closed Sunday dinner
and Monday lunch

Menu £20/25

A/C
⟨⟩
VISA
MC
AE
①

It must have been quite difficult for the D&D group to re-establish Kensington Place, especially as Rowley Leigh, its well-known former chef, now operates in nearby Bayswater. One thing they have got right is the menu; they dispensed with an à la carte and in its place introduced a competitively priced set menu which offers plenty of choice. There are some supplements for the few dishes using pricier ingredients but these can be easily avoided. The cooking is modern and quite dainty at times and desserts are done well. Service is still speedy and copes easily with the numbers when it needs to. The addition of cushions has succeeded in softening the acoustics so it's also easier to have a conversation these days.

Kitchen W8 ✿

Modern European 🍴🍴

11-13 Abingdon Rd
⊠ W8 6AH
☎ (020) 7937 0120
www.kitchenw8.com

⊖ High Street Kensington
Closed bank holidays

Menu £20 (lunch) – Carte £33/47

A/C
☀
VISA
MC
AE

Kitchen W8

Rebecca Mascarenhas, doyenne of south west London's restaurant scene, and Philip Howard, luminary chef of The Square, joined forces and considerable amounts of experience to open Kitchen W8 in a Kensington side street. Perhaps the only thing they didn't get quite right is the name as it implies a level of casualness that is just not present – this is quite a smart and comfortable restaurant with structured and relatively formal service. However, it does have a palpable neighbourhood feel and it helps that Abingdon Road has always played host to a good smattering of restaurants. Prices too are relatively restrained, particularly when one considers the quality of the ingredients and what equivalent restaurants with a W1 postcode would charge. Dishes appear quite simple on the plate and are refreshingly free of showiness, but the flavours do have depth and it is clear that this is a kitchen with skill and ambition; it displays a lightness of touch when one is required but also knows when to add a little oomph.

First Course

- Sauté of lamb sweetbreads and tongue with garlic, parsley and morels.
- Organic salmon rillette with watercress mousse and minted Jersey Royals.

Main Course

- Fillet of halibut with wild garlic and meat vinaigrette.
- Vintage Ayrshire rib-eye with field mushrooms, watercress and chips.

Dessert

- Salted chocolate parfait with malt ice cream.
- Financier of new season English raspberries with raspberry ripple ice cream.

Launceston Place

Modern European 🍴🍴🍴

D5

1a Launceston Pl.
✉ W8 5RL
✆ (020) 7937 6912
www.launcestonplace-restaurant.co.uk

⊖ Gloucester Road
Closed 24-30 December, Monday
lunch and dinner bank
holiday Mondays

Menu £22/45

Launceston Place forms part of the D&D group and is largely
unrecognisable from its former days. The last, much needed
reincarnation made the walls darker, the lighting moodier
and the ambition more evident but the best thing it that the
appealing neighbourhood feel has not been lost, even with
service that takes itself seriously. Tristan Welch, who previously
worked with Marcus Wareing, is the confident young chef at
the helm and his cooking is original but also well-grounded
and balanced. He's also a keen champion of home-grown
produce: about 80% of the ingredients come from within the
British Isles and he's planning to increase this figure further. Try
the Tasting Menu which is priced not far north of the à la carte.

Malabar

Indian 🍴🍴

C3

27 Uxbridge St.
✉ W8 7TQ
✆ (020) 7727 8800
www.malabar-restaurant.co.uk

⊖ Notting Hill Gate
Closed 1 week Christmas –
(buffet lunch Sunday)

Menu £25 s – Carte £26/41 s

One of the reasons why Malabar has been going strong since
1983 is that it keeps on top of its appearance, as, it seems,
do most of its Notting Hill customers. These days the front
has a sleek, understated look; the interior is a fashionable grey
and the staff do their bit by dressing in black. What doesn't
change is the quality of the food, from the breads to the piping
hot thalis. The favourites remain but the seafood section has
been beefed up with the addition of a monkfish curry and a
whole gilt-head bream; and just because the tandoori dishes
sit beside the starters on the menu, don't assume they come
in starter sizes. The excellent value Sunday buffet lunch, when
children under 12 eat for free, still packs them in.

Ledbury ✿✿

Modern European XXX

127 Ledbury Rd.
⊠ W11 2AQ
✆ (020) 7792 9090
www.theledbury.com

⊖ **Notting Hill Gate**
Closed 24-26 December, August bank
holiday and Monday lunch

Menu £34/70

The Ledbury

The Ledbury's Australian head chef, Brett Graham, is one of the more intelligent chefs around and his passion for quality ingredients really shines through. He is constantly on the lookout for new supplies and suppliers and knows what to do when he gets them. Hebridean lambs arrive whole and are then butchered, with every part of the beast used; game is also one of the kitchen's strengths – Brett is a keen shot. The kitchen is also firmly grounded in technique so that whenever a slightly unusual flavour or a little tease is introduced, it is done merely to enhance the dish. This is bravado cooking but without affectation. Even though the chef also has an involvement in The Harwood Arms, he does so without ever taking his eye off the ball here. Along with The Ashes, let's hope he's staying on this side of the world for a while. The room is elegant without being overdressed and the serving team are well organised and professional but they never forget that fundamentally this is a neighbourhood restaurant, albeit a rather good one.

First Course

- Buffalo milk curd, truffle toast and onion broth.
- Raviolo of rabbit, wild mushrooms, prune cooked in Lapsang Souchong and brown bread sauce.

Main Course

- Loin and shoulder of lamb, black sugar and glazed aubergine.
- Fillet of cod with pumpkin polenta, shellfish emulsion and yuzu.

Dessert

- Whipped ewe's milk yoghurt with berries, verbena meringues and beignets.
- Brown sugar tart with Muscat grapes and stem ginger ice cream.

Min Jiang

D4

Royal Garden Hotel (10th Floor),   ⊖ High Street Kensington
2-24 Kensington High St. ⊠ W8 4PT
☏ (020) 7361 1988
www.minjiang.co.uk

Menu £17/50 – Carte approx. £48

Named after the Min River in Sichuan province, this restaurant on the 10th floor of the Royal Garden hotel is an offshoot of the original in Singapore. The speciality is Beijing duck; its glistening skin is carved at the table and one then has the difficult task of choosing how to have the second serving from the six options available. The cuisine covers all provinces, most of which have representatives in the chef's ranks. Other signature dishes include prawns Gong Bao with plenty of chillies and braised pork belly with Chinese buns. The room is a stylish one, with vases influenced by the Ming Dynasty and photos of assorted Chinese scenes. Tables 11 and 16 offer the best views of Kensington Palace and Gardens below.

Notting Hill Brasserie

B3

92 Kensington Park Rd   ⊖ Notting Hill Gate
⊠ W11 2PN
☏ (020) 7229 4481
www.nottinghillbrasserie.com

Menu £20 (weekday lunch) – Carte £43/61

The word 'brasserie' in the title suggests that one can expect a level of informality but this is actually quite a smart restaurant, housed within a row of Edwardian townhouses, although the last makeover did make it warmer and brighter. Staff are clued up and capable, although the younger members of the team have an eagerness and enthusiasm that's sometimes lacking in their more senior colleagues. The style of cooking is also far more elaborate than the name suggests. There is plenty of choice, portions are on a heartening scale and the kitchen is clearly technically skilled, but sometimes there are too many flavours on the plate fighting for supremacy. The lunch menu is a scaled down model of dinner. Nightly live jazz adds to the mood.

Seventeen

C3

Chinese 𝕏𝕏

17 Notting Hill Gate
✉ W11 3JQ
✆ (020) 7985 0006
www.seventeen-london.co.uk

⊖ Notting Hill Gate

Menu £12/21 – Carte £18/45

AC
☼
🕸
VISA
MC
AE
DC

Burdening itself with an instantly forgettable name may not have helped its cause but still, this stylish Chinese restaurant should be attracting more locals as it offers something a little different in this part of town. Things are all very moody and cool inside, with candlelight and Chinese artefacts adding to the charm. The ground floor is a dimly lit, intimate space and there's further seating downstairs, along with a bar and an attractively screened private room. Authentic Sichuan and Shanghainese dishes provide the highlights, such as pork lung slices in chilli sauce, Sichuan-style fish and Chongqing chicken. The chef is from Mainland China and also offers delicacies from other regions, such as Dung Po pork, a Hangzhou speciality.

Timo

B5

Italian 𝕏𝕏

343 Kensington High St.
✉ W8 6NW
✆ (020) 7603 3888
www.timorestaurant.net

⊖ High Street Kensington
Closed Christmas, Sunday and bank
holidays – booking advisable

Menu £18 (lunch and early dinner) – Carte £30/40

AC
VISA
MC
AE

Step with purpose towards the entrance of Timo, otherwise you might find yourself being dazzled by the neon of the neighbouring Iranian shops or by the sales pitch of their enthusiastic owners. Once inside this comfortable and comforting Italian restaurant, head past the 'corridor' of tables and up to the more relaxing area at the back, with its deep banquette seating and effective lighting. The smart team deliver professional and conscientious service under the watchful eye of the owner, who knows his regulars and ensures they are looked after. The menu, supplemented by a few daily specials, offers a broad selection of recognisable specialities from across all regions and the cooking is neat, reliable and soundly executed.

Whits

Modern European XX

21 Abingdon Rd. ⊖ High Street Kensington
✉ W8 6AH Closed 1 week August, Sunday
✆ (020) 7938 1122 and Monday – (dinner only)
www.whits.co.uk

Menu £24 – Carte £31/40

A/C
VISA
MC
AE

Privately owned restaurants with a couple at the helm are becoming something of a rarity but there is a certain kind of service one only gets from an owner of a restaurant; it is usually a combination of concern, confidence, pride and sincerity. Eva at Whits is a case in point – she's one of life's natural hosts who puts all customers at ease and the relaxed atmosphere is the restaurant's great strength. Her partner Steve's cooking certainly doesn't pull any punches; combinations are tried-and-tested, techniques are classic and flavours bold and upfront. The presentation on the plate is somewhat elaborate but diners all leave eminently satisfied, thanks to some generous portioning. There's a good value set menu alongside the à la carte.

Yashin

B5

Japanese XX

1A Argyll Rd. ⊖ High Street Kensington
✉ W8 7DB Closed first and third Monday in month,
✆ (020) 7938 1536 25 and 31 December, and 1 January
www.yashinsushi.com – booking essential

Carte £41/90

A/C
☼
VISA
MC
AE

Two experienced sushi chefs joined forces to create this contemporary restaurant with its crisp, appealing black and white theme. Their worthy ambition to wean diners off fermented soya bean is reflected in their grammatically challenging but charmingly equitable slogan: "without soy sauce…but if you want to". There are three omakase choices offering 8, 11 or 15 pieces of sushi selected by the chefs and served together. The quality of the fish is clear and originality comes in the form of minuscule garnishes adorning each piece and the odd bit of searing. Service is knowledgeable and endearing but be sure to ask for a counter seat as one of the joys of sushi comes from watching the dextrous knife skills and the deft handling of the fish.

Zaika

D4

Indian �

1 Kensington High St.
✉ W8 5NP
✆ (020) 7795 6533
www.zaika-restaurant.co.uk

⊖ High Street Kensington
Closed 25-26 December, 1-2 January
and Monday lunch

Menu £25 (lunch) – Carte £30/45

A/C
☼
VISA
MC
AE
①

The smell of incense hits you immediately and is one clue that the days of this being a bank are long gone. To further disguise its previous function, the room is decorated in a theatrical way, with plenty of drapes, ornaments and lots of colour to counteract the high ceiling and all that rather imposing wood panelling. Lunch here is more about offering attractively priced set menus; at dinner everything goes up a notch and the majority of diners go for the 'Gourmand' menu, which comes with the option of wine pairings. There is certainly some originality to the sophisticated Indian cooking, and the kitchen uses plenty of quality British produce like Herdwick lamb and Scottish scallops, but sometimes the spicing can lack a degree of subtlety.

Remember, stars
(✿✿✿...✿) are awarded
for cuisine only! Elements
such as service and décor
are not a factor.

Greater London

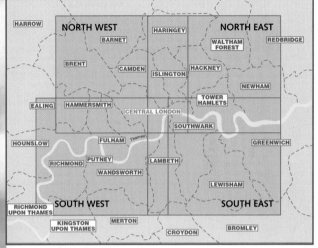

D. Chapuis/MICHELIN

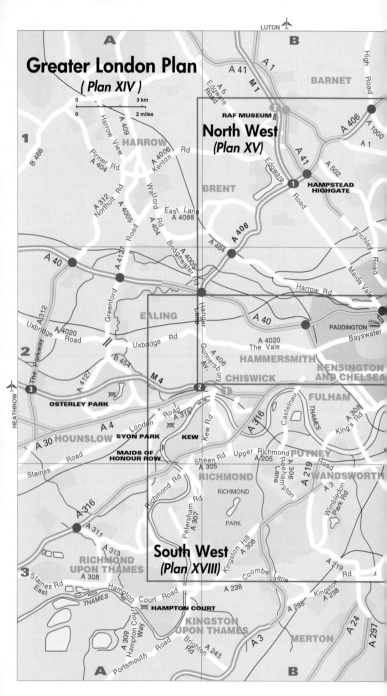

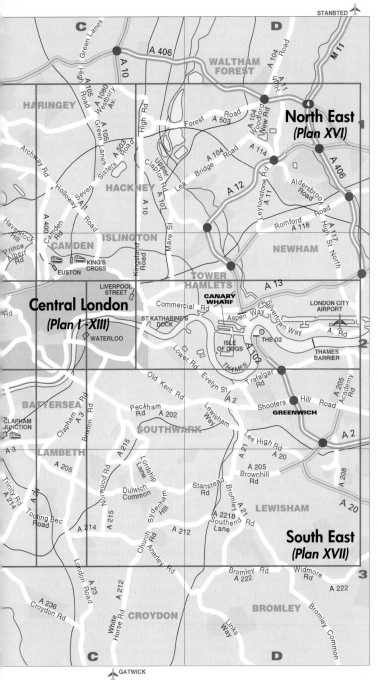

North-West London

Heading north from London Zoo and Regent's Park, the green baton is passed to two of the city's most popular and well-known locations: Hampstead Heath and Highgate Wood. In close proximity, they offer a favoured pair of lungs to travellers emerging from the murky depths of the Northern Line. Two centuries ago, they would have been just another part of the area's undeveloped high ground and pastureland, but since the building boom of the nineteenth century, both have become prized assets in this part of the metropolis.

People came to seek shelter in **Hampstead** in times of plague, and it's retained its bucolic air to this day. Famous names have always enjoyed its charms: Constable and Keats rested their brush and pen here, while the sculptors Henry Moore and Barbara Hepworth were residents in more recent times. Many are drawn to such delightful places as Church Row, which boasts a lovely Georgian Terrace. You know you're up high because the thoroughfares bear names like Holly Mount and Mount Vernon. The Heath is full of rolling woodlands and meadows; it's a great place for rambling, particularly to the crest of **Parliament Hill** and its superb city views. There are three bathing ponds here, one mixed, and one each for male and female swimmers, while up on the Heath's northern fringes, **Kenwood House,** along with its famous al fresco summer concerts, also boasts great art by the likes of Vermeer and Rembrandt. And besides all that, there's an ivy tunnel leading to a terrace with idyllic pond views.

Highgate Wood is an ancient woodland and conservation area, containing a leafy walk that meanders enchantingly along a former railway line to **Crouch End,** home to a band of thespians. Down the road at Highgate Cemetery, the likes of Karl Marx, George Eliot, Christina Rossetti and Michael Faraday rest in a great entanglement of breathtaking Victorian over-decoration. The cemetery is still in use – most recent notable to be buried here is Alexander Litvinenko, the Russian dissident.

Next door you'll find **Waterlow Park,** another fine green space, which, apart from its super views, also includes decorative ponds on three levels. Lauderdale House is here, too, a 16C pile which is now an arts centre; more famously, Charles II handed over its keys to Nell Gwynn for her to use as her North London residence. Head back south from here, and **Primrose Hill** continues the theme of glorious green space: its surrounding terraces are populated by media darlings, while its vertiginous mass is another to boast a famously enviable vista.

Of a different hue altogether is **Camden Town** with its buzzy edge, courtesy of a renowned in-

S. Ollivier/ MICHELIN

die music scene, goths, punks, and six earthy markets selling everything from tat to exotica. Charles Dickens grew up here, and he was none too complimentary; the area still relishes its seamy underside. A scenic route out is the **Regent's Canal,** which cuts its way through the market and ambles to the east and west of the city. Up the road, the legendary Roundhouse re-opened its arty front doors in 2006, expanding further the wide range of Camden's alt scene.

One of the music world's most legendary destinations, the **Abbey Road** studios, is also in this area and, yes, it's possible to join other tourists making their way over that zebra crossing. Not far away, in Maresfield Gardens, stands a very different kind of attraction. The Freud Museum is one of the very few buildings in London to have two blue plaques. It was home to Sigmund during the last year of his life and it's where he lived with his daughter Anna (her plaque commemorates her work in child psychiatry). Inside, there's a fabulous library and his working desk. But the pivotal part of the whole house is in another corner of the study – the psychiatrist's couch!

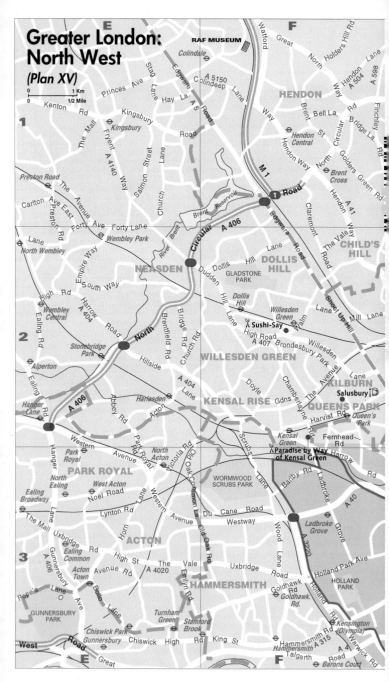

Greater London: North West

(Plan XV)

RAF MUSEUM

0 — 1 Km
0 — 1/2 Mile

HENDON

COLINDALE

Watford Great

North Holders Hill Rd

Hendon Lane

A 504

A 598

Princes Ave

Stag Lane

Edgware Road

A 5150

Colindeep Lane

Way

Brent St

Bell La.

Bridge La.

Finchley La.

Kenton Rd

Hay La.

A 5

Kingsbury

Hendon Central

Golders Green Rd

The Mall

Fryent

A 4140

Kingsbury

Road

Hendon Way

North Circular

Brent Cross

A 41

Preston Road

The Avenue

Salmon Street

Church Lane

M 1

Road

Hendon

Claremont Road

The Vale

Carlton Ave East

Preston Rd

Forty Ave

Forty Lane

River Brent

Brent Reservoir

A 406

Edgware Road

CHILD'S HILL

Lane

North Wembley

Wembley Park

Circular

Dollis Hill

DOLLIS HILL

Shoot Up Hill

Empire Way

NEASDEN

Dudden Hill Lane

GLADSTONE PARK

Walm Lane

High Rd

South Way

Dollis Hill Lane

Willesden Green

North Circular

Mill Lane

Wembley Central

Harrow Road

A 404

Brentfield Rd

Church Rd

△ Sushi-Say

High Road

A 407

Brondesbury Park

Willesden

The Avenue

KILBURN

Stonebridge Park

North

Bridge Rd

WILLESDEN GREEN

Chamberlayne

Lane

Alperton

Hillside

A 404

Lane

Doyle

KENSAL RISE

Gdns

Salusbury

QUEENS PARK

Ealing Rd

Harlesden

Acton

Queen's Park

Hanger Lane

A 406

Abbey Rd

Park Royal

Scrubs Lane

Kensal Green

Harvist Rd

Fernhead Rd

Western

North Acton

Victoria Rd

△ Paradise by Way of Kensal Green

Harrow

Rd

Park Royal

Avenue

Old Oak Common La.

Barby Rd

Ladbroke

PARK ROYAL

North Ealing

West Acton

Noel Road

WORMWOOD SCRUBS PARK

A 40

Ealing Broadway

Horn Lane

Western Avenue

Du Cane Road

Westway

Wood Lane

Ladbroke Grove

A 3220

The Mall

Lynton Rd

ACTON

Uxbridge Road

Holland Park Ave

Uxbridge Rd

Gunnersbury Ave

Ealing Common

High St

A 4020

The Vale

Emlyn Rd

HAMMERSMITH

Goldhawk Rd

Holland Rd

HOLLAND PARK

Acton Town

A 406

Avenue Rd

Goldhawk Rd.

Pope's Lane

Bollo Lane

GUNNERSBURY PARK

Chiswick Park

Turnham Green

Stamford Brook

Rd

King St

Kensington (Olympia)

Gunnersbury

Chiswick High

Hammersmith

A 315

West

Road

Great

Talgarth

A 4

Warwick Rd

Hammersmith

Barons Court

288

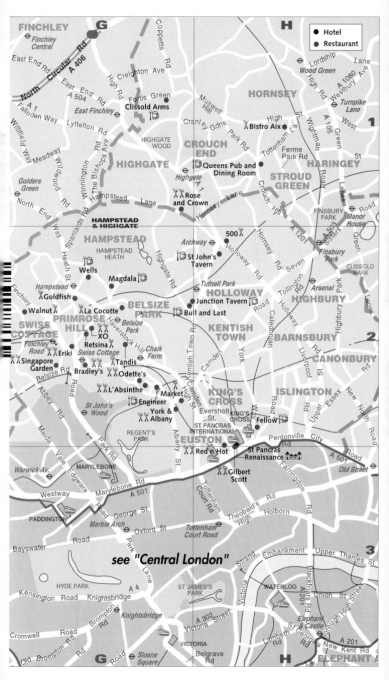

FINCHLEY

Finchley
Central

G

H

● Hotel
● Restaurant

HORNSEY

Lordship
Wood Green Lane

Finchley Central
East End Rd
North Circular Rd A 406
East End Rd
A 504
East Finchley
A 1
Falloden Way
Lyttelton Rd
Wildwood Rd
Meadway
Golders
Green
North End Way
Wildwood Rd
Winnington Rd
The Bishops Ave
Spaniards Rd
Hampstead Lane

Coppetts Rd
Creighton Ave
High Rd
Fortis Green
Clissold Arms
Cranley Gdns
HIGHGATE WOOD
HIGHGATE
Highgate

Muswell Hill
Park Rd
High St
CROUCH END

High St
Tottenham Lane
Bistro Aix

Ferme Park Rd

HARINGEY

A 105

Turnpike Lane
West

Queens Pub and
Dining Room

STROUD GREEN

Crouch Hill

A 1080 Westbury Ave

HAMPSTEAD & HIGHGATE

HAMPSTEAD
HAMPSTEAD HEATH

Hornsey Lane
Rose and Crown

A 1201

FINSBURY PARK
Manor House

Wells
Magdala

Heath St
Highgate Rd

Archway
500

Holloway Rd

Finsbury Park

Manor House

CLISSOLD PARK

Hampstead
Goldfish
Walnut

SWISS COTTAGE
Finchley Road
Eriki
Singapore Garden

PRIMROSE HILL
La Cocotte
XO
Retsina
Swiss Cottage
Tandis
Bradley's
Odette's
L'Absinthe

St John's Tavern

Tufnell Park

HOLLOWAY

Junction Tavern
Bull and Last

BELSIZE PARK
Belsize Park
Haverstock Hill
Chalk Farm

KENTISH TOWN

Seven Sisters Rd
Tollington Rd

Arsenal

HIGHBURY

BARNSBURY

Holloway Rd

Caledonian Rd

CANONBURY

Highbury Park

Liverpool Rd

Belsize Rd

Abbey Rd

St John's Wood

Engineer
Market
York & Albany

Camden Rd

York Way

ISLINGTON

Upper St

Essex Rd

New North Rd

Maida Vale
Warwick Av.

MARYLEBONE

Park Rd

REGENT'S PARK

Albany St

Euston Rd

Camden High St

KING'S CROSS
Eversholt St
KING'S CROSS
ST PANCRAS INTERNATIONAL
EUSTON
Red n Hot
Pentonville Rd

Fellow

City Rd

A 501 Old Street

Westway
Edgware Rd

Marylebone Rd
A 501

George St

PADDINGTON
Marble Arch
Bayswater Road

Oxford St
Park Lane

Tottenham Court Rd

Theobald's Rd
Holborn

Farringdon Rd

St Pancras
Renaissance

Gilbert Scott

A 501

see "Central London"

HYDE PARK
Kensington Road Knightsbridge

Brompton Rd

Knightsbridge
A 302 Victoria Street

VICTORIA

Strand

ST JAMES'S PARK

Embankment Upper Thames St

WATERLOO
A 201

Blackfriars Rd

Union St

Elephant & Castle

A 201

Cromwell Road
Old Brompton Rd

Sloane Square

Victoria Rd
Belgrave Rd

Lambeth Rd

St Georges Rd

New Kent Rd

ELEPHANT &

G

H

500 😊

H2

Archway
782 Holloway Rd ✉ N19 3JH
☎ (020) 7272 3406
www.500restaurant.co.uk

⊖ Archway
Closed 2 weeks summer, 2 weeks
Christmas-New Year and lunch Monday-
Thursday – booking essential

Carte £21/25

☼
VISA
Ⓜ©
ΑΕ

Named after the cute little Fiat and that couldn't be more appropriate because here is a restaurant that is small, fun, well-priced and ideal for London. The owner is an ebullient fellow who takes an active role in the service, as does the chef who likes to see the look of satisfaction on his customers' faces. Their shared passion is evident in the cooking: homemade breads and pastas are very good; the fluffy gnocchi with sausage ragu delivers a kick; the tender veal chop is a winner and the rabbit is the house special. The menu, which has occasional Sardinian leanings, changes regularly and the sheet of daily specials includes great little snacks to have with a drink. Black and white photos of old Holloway are the only incongruity.

St John's Tavern

H2

Archway
91 Junction Rd ✉ N19 5QU
☎ (020) 7272 1587
www.stjohnstavern.com

⊖ Archway.
Closed 25-26 December and 1 January
– booking advisable at dinner –
(dinner only and lunch Friday-Sunday)

Carte £24/33

🏠
☼
VISA
Ⓜ©
ΑΕ

Too many diners arrived expecting Clerkenwell's St John restaurant – hence the addition of 'tavern' to the name of this pub, which has long been a beacon of hope on drab old Junction Road. The dark colours and fireplace in the dining room may make it look like somewhere for a winter's night but staff keep things light and perky throughout the year. The menu changes daily and the open kitchen puts some thought into the vegetarian choices, be they the courgette and cheddar tart or the squash and halloumi parcels; but they also know how to fire up the heat when cooking a pork chop or rib-eye. The wine list is sensibly priced, with enough carafes to make up for the 125ml glasses, although Black Sheep bitter is a popular alternative.

Retsina

Greek 𝕏

G2

Belsize Park
48-50 Belsize Ln ✉ NW3 5AR
☎ (020) 7431 5855
www.retsina-london.com

⊖ **Belsize Park**
Closed 25-26 December,
1 January, Monday lunch
and bank holidays

Menu £20 (lunch) – Carte £20/47

A/C

☼

VISA

MC

Having outgrown their previous address on Regent's Park Road, the family owners moved to these larger premises in Belsize Park and the locals appear mighty grateful that they did. As in Greece, the place is all about two things: good food and pleasant service. The menu is unapologetically traditional and all the old favourites are there, from dolmades to soutzoukakia, kleftiko to stifado but the grill and the souvla are the stars of the show and the meats are gloriously juicy and tender. House specialties such as suckling pig or shoulder of lamb must be ordered 24 hours in advance. The dining room is split over two floors and is simply kitted out with tiles and Athenian artefacts. Service and atmosphere are both relaxed and friendly.

Tandis

Persian 𝕏

G2

Belsize Park
73 Haverstock Hill ✉ NW3 4SL
☎ (020) 7586 8079
www.tandisrestaurant.com

⊖ **Chalk Farm**
Closed 25 December

Carte £20/30

A/C

☼

VISA

MC

AE

Haverstock Hill's maturing restaurant scene has now acquired a little exoticism thanks to Tandis and its enticing Iranian cooking. The appeal of this contemporary looking restaurant stretches way beyond the Iranian diaspora – plenty of locals also appear to have been seduced as soon as they tasted the traditional flat bread baked in a clay oven. A varied selection of invigorating 'koresht' stews and succulent 'kababs' form the mainstay of the menu but other specialities such as 'sabzi polo' and the rich and complex flavours of 'kashke bademjaan' are well worth exploring. Finish with some of their fine teas and a 'faloodeh', where rose water sorbet is matched with a sour cherry syrup. The best seats are to be found at the back.

XO

Asian ✗✗

Belsize Park
29 Belsize Ln. ✉ NW3 5AS
☎ (020) 7433 0888
www.rickerrestaurants.com/xo

⊖ Belsize Park
Closed 25-26 December
and 1 January

Menu £15 (lunch) – Carte £23/33

AC
☀
VISA
MC
AE
①

Who knew Belsize Park was so trendy? Apart from estate agents, obviously. This branch of Will Ricker's small chain of glossy pan-Asian restaurants may not be quite as frenetic as the others but it still attracts plenty of shiny happy people, many of whom are holding hands. It follows the same theme as the others: a busy front bar that serves decent cocktails, behind which is the slick, uncluttered restaurant in shades of lime. The menu trawls through most of Asia; start with some warm edamame while reading through it. Highlights include the ever-popular crispy squid and the tender and tasty Indonesian lamb rendang curry but tempura is done with too heavy a hand. Sharing is the key, especially as those who come in large parties get the booths.

Market ☺

British ✗

Camden Town
43 Parkway ✉ NW1 7PN
☎ (020) 7267 9700
www.marketrestaurant.co.uk

⊖ Camden Town
Closed 25 December-3 January ,Sunday
dinner and bank holidays – booking
essential

Carte £25/34

AC
VISA
MC
AE
①

The name is spot on because this is all about market fresh produce, seasonality and cooking that is refreshingly matter of fact, with big, bold flavour and John Bull Britishness. Dishes come as advertised, with no pointless ornamentation, and you can expect to find the likes of brawn, ox tongue fritters and devilled kidneys alongside stews and shepherd's pie in winter, followed by proper puddings, not desserts. But be sure to have lamb or beef dripping on toast as a pre-starter – it'll leave you licking your lips for the next few hours. The exposed brick walls, zinc-topped tables and old school chairs work very well and the atmosphere is fun without ever becoming too excitable. The terrific prices entice in plenty of passers-by.

York & Albany

Modern European ✗✗

Camden Town   ⊖ Camden Town
127-129 Parkway ⊠ NW1 7PS   Booking essential
✆ (020) 7388 3344
www.gordonramsay.com/yorkandalbany

Carte £25/38

It's hard to believe that this 1820s John Nash coaching inn lay virtually derelict before Gordon Ramsay Holdings resuscitated and relaunched it. The terrific front bar offers a more civilised environment than is usually the case in Camden and leads into the restaurant at the back. Don't come expecting pub grub: the cooking here is quite neat and refined in its makeup, but without being fussy, and is designed to be enjoyed as three courses. The menu is not overly long and keeps its influences mostly within Europe. If you want to watch how it's all done then ask for a table in the lower ground floor where you'll find the open kitchen. Service can still be a little hit and miss but the overall atmosphere and look of the place add extra appeal.

Bistro Aix

French ✗

Crouch End   Closed 1 January –
54 Topsfield Par., Tottenham Ln. ⊠ N8 8PT   (dinner only and
✆ (020) 8340 6346   lunch Saturday-Sunday)
www.bistroaix.co.uk

Carte £23/32

Contemporary artwork, antique dressers and glass-filled cabinets lend an authentic Gallic edge to this local bistro whose subtle lighting and warm atmosphere also clearly appeal to Crouch Enders of a romantic disposition. The American owner runs a popular place and offers a big menu whose highlights are the more traditional French choices such as onion soup and steak frites. Desserts are also done well and the individual Tarte Tatins are a constant presence. Those willing to venture out at the beginning of the week are rewarded with a good value early evening set menu. Service is earnest but can become slightly distracted during busier times; ask for a table at the back to avoid a bracing draft whenever the front door opens.

NORTH-WEST ▶ PLAN XV

Queens Pub and Dining Room

British 🍺

H1

Crouch End

26 Broadway Par. ✉ N8 9DE
✆ (020) 8340 2031
www.thequeenscrouchend.co.uk

Carte £24/29

From the original mahogany panelling to the beautiful stained glass windows and ornate ceiling, this pub offers a striking example of Victoriana. Originally built as a hotel, its dining room is particularly attractive and is separated from the bar by a glass door; those looking for a little more intimacy should ask for a table on the raised section. The open kitchen recognises that the locals want classic pub food in this environment and doesn't disappoint. The blackboard acknowledges the pub's main suppliers and the menu evolves seasonally, with traditional British comfort food being the main attraction. Along with the specials, look out for their autumn 'Sausage and Ale' festival – what can compete with Toad in the Hole and a pint?

Bull and Last

British 🍺

G2

Dartmouth Park

168 Highgate Rd ✉ NW5 1QS
✆ (020) 7267 3641
www.thebullandlast.co.uk

⊖ Tufnell Park.
Closed 24- 25 December –
booking essential

Carte £27/33

The Bull and Last understands absolutely what makes a good foodie pub and top of that list would be a menu that reflects the time of year and the weather outside: come on a snowy December night – when you'll be greeted by the aroma of cloves and mulled wine – and you can dine on pumpkin soup, mutton broth and apple strudel. The menu changes with every service and even the nibbles, such as lamb fritters and sweet anchovies, reveal the cleverness of the kitchen. The chefs also know their way around an animal: the charcuterie boards of terrines, parfaits and rillettes are well worth ordering. This Victorian pub, spread over two floors with a slightly quieter upstairs, has plenty of charm and character and is always busy so booking is vital.

Red N Hot

Euston

37 Chalton St ✉ NW1 1JD
📞 (020) 7388 0808
www.rednhotgroup.com

⊖ Euston
Closed 25 December

Carte £15/19

The clue is in the name – this is all about the fiery pepper, so if you fancy Chinese food but also want something different then Red N Hot should fit the bill. Formerly called 'Snazz Sichuan', it was set up by an émigré from Sichuan and forms part of the New China Club which includes a members' club and an art gallery. If you don't already know that Sichuan cooking is hot then you soon will. Again, more clues lie in the name of dishes, like 'hot and numbing beef jerky' - so you can't say you weren't warned. And don't be fooled into thinking that a cold dish will be any less fiery. The ingredients are also a little different: stir-fried kidney, pig's blood mix, fried intestines and pig's ear in chilli oil; hotpots feature at lunch.

Clissold Arms

Fortis Green

105 Fortis Green ✉ N2 9HR
📞 (020) 8444 4224
www.clissoldarms.co.uk

⊖ East Finchley.

Carte £18/30

Such is the growing reputation of The Clissold Arms that it may soon be better known for the quality of its cooking than its more long-standing claim to fame – that of having played host to The Kinks' first gig. Come at lunch and the menu and atmosphere make you feel you're in a proper pub, where you can expect classics like fishcakes or steak sandwiches. At dinner it all looks more like a restaurant, with loftier prices and slightly more ambitious, but still carefully prepared, dishes. The place is a lot bigger than you expect and, while staff could do with a little more guidance, it's often busy with locals grateful to have somewhere other than chain restaurants in their neighbourhood. The decked terrace has recently been extended.

La Cocotte

French 🍴

G2

Hampstead
85b Fleet Rd ✉ NW3 2QY
📞 (020) 7433 3317
www.la-cocotte.co.uk

⊖ **Belsize Park**
Closed Sunday dinner,
Monday and lunch Tuesday-Thursday

Menu £13 (lunch) – Carte £21/31

A/C
VISA
MC
AE

First an Italian restaurant tried its luck here and now it is the turn of the French. With its tricolour above the door, onions and garlic hanging in the window and classic red checked tablecloths, one's initial impression is of cliché overload but this is countered by the presence of the affable, self-deprecating French owner. The menu provides a checklist of robust and capably prepared bourgeois classics, from terrines and rillettes to steak frites, but what sets it apart – and the clue is in the name – are the small, shallow iron pots of slow-cooked ingredients. These are a must, especially on a wintery night, and leave one feeling warmed and satisfied. The ground floor is the lively spot; upstairs is a little more intimate.

Goldfish

Asian 🍴

G2

Hampstead
82 Hampstead High St ✉ NW3 1RE
📞 (020) 7794 6666
www.restaurantprivilege.com

⊖ **Hampstead**

Carte approx. £40

VISA
MC
AE

For some reason Hampstead has never been the easiest place in which to open a restaurant but it looks like Goldfish may be one to buck the trend. This sweet place calls its cooking 'modern Chinese' but really the kitchen looks to influences from across Asia. The à la carte menu is lengthy but highlights include anything involving crab, the fish dishes and some of the chef's own creations, such as the rich Mocha ribs. Prices at lunch are very reasonable, especially the dim sum which pulls in plenty of punters at weekends. The place is divided into three little rooms which all have their own style. Staff have their hearts in the right place and they remember their regulars, of whom there are growing numbers.

Magdala

G2

Hampstead

$\ominus$ Belsize Park.

2A South Hill Park ✉ NW3 2SB

📞 (020) 7435 2503

www.the-magdala.com

Carte £22/30

The Magdala is divided into three: on the right-hand side is the locals bar – you can eat here but not many do as it's a little dark and you'll feel like an impostor. Just go left, grab a seat anywhere and you'll be served. The third part of the operation is the upstairs, used as an extension at weekends or for hosting the monthly comedy club or fortnightly quiz. There's nothing on the menu to frighten the horses: there are burgers, sausages, paella and charcuterie plates or meze to share. However, the cooking is undertaken with greater care than you expect and you end up feeling as though you're in a country pub miles from the city. The owner certainly found a novel solution to the problem of keeping her chef – Reader, she married him.

Wells

G2

Hampstead

$\ominus$ Hampstead.

30 Well Walk ✉ NW3 1BX

📞 (020) 7794 3785

www.thewellshampstead.co.uk

Carte £28/38

The Wells is named after Chalybeate Well which, in 1698, was given to the poor of Hampstead – it's about 30 yards away, next to that BMW. Equidistant between Heath and High Street, this handsome pub is split in two: downstairs is the busier, more relaxed part of the operation, while upstairs you'll find a formally dressed dining room. Apart from a couple of extra grilled dishes downstairs, the two areas share a menu, which is cleverly balanced to satisfy all appetites from spirited dog walker to leisurely shopper. Salads or seared scallops can be followed by sea bass, assorted pasta or duck confit; puds are good and they do a decent crumble. Add a commendable range of ales and wines and you have a pub for all seasons.

Rose and Crown

G1

Highgate
86 Highgate High St.   ✉ N6 5HX
☎ (020) 8340 0770
www.roseandcrownhighgate.co.uk

⊖ **Archway**
Closed Sunday dinner
and Monday lunch

Menu £15/18 – Carte £26/34

☂

VISA

MC

An attractive white façade, illuminated at night, highlights what was once a pub but is now most definitely a restaurant. There's some 18C cornicing still there but the theme is now contemporary and all black and white. The bar remains but is now where you sit deliberating over the menu and the dining tables are smartly laid. This may all give the impression of a formal restaurant but in fact the atmosphere is relaxed and inclusive, thanks largely to the confident and genial staff. The influences on the kitchen are mostly European, although the original touches are not quite as daring as they suggest. Overall the cooking is soundly executed and the prices more than fair, especially on the weekly changing set menu.

Paradise by way of Kensal Green

F2

Kensal Green
19 Kilburn Ln.   ✉ W10 4AE
☎ (020) 8969 0098
www.theparadise.co.uk

⊖ **Kensal Green.**
(dinner only and lunch
Saturday and Sunday)

Carte £21/36

A/C

□

☼

VISA

MC

◌

Their slogan is 'they love to party at Paradise' and, frankly, who can blame them? This is so much more than just a pub, it's a veritable fun palace – upstairs plays host to everything from comedy nights to film clubs and you can even 'host your own roast' with friends in a private room. If you're coming in to eat then grab a squashy sofa in the Reading Room off the bar and share some of the terrific snacks; or sit in the dining room where the cooking is showy but satisfyingly robust. Whether it's potted meats, terrines, chateaubriand or poached turbot, it's clear that this is a very capable kitchen. The atmosphere throughout is great and helped along in no small way by a clued-up team who know their food.

L'Absinthe

French ✗

G2

Primrose Hill
40 Chalcot Rd ✉ NW1 8LS
☎ (020) 7483 4848
www.labsinthe.co.uk

⊖ Chalk Farm
Closed August,
Christmas and Monday

Menu £13 (lunch) – Carte £22/34

AC
⌂
88
☼
VISA
MC
AE

L'Absinthe has succeeded on a site where so many tried and failed because it gives the locals exactly what they have clearly always wanted: a classic French bistro run with integrity and enthusiasm. It offers the sort of food that really hits the spot at the end of a working day: beef bourguignon, duck confit, steak frites or some fresh skate, with a crème brûlée to follow. The place has an authentic air too, with its Belle Époque posters and staff who are either French or can at least do a convincing accent. Don't be put off if they give you a table downstairs – even if you are the first down there, it'll soon fill up with regulars. The other great strength is the wine list: the owner merely charges corkage on the retail price.

Engineer

British ✗🍺

G2

Primrose Hill
65 Gloucester Ave ✉ NW1 8JH
☎ (020) 7722 0950
www.the-engineer.com

⊖ Chalk Farm.
Closed 1 week Christmas

Carte £26/44

⌂
☼
VISA
MC

Although speculation remains as to the identity of the original engineer, what is certain is that this is a great local, which is at the heart of the local community. It's divided equally between bar and dining room, with a terrific garden terrace to boot; and it's always busy, with occasional live music on Sundays adding to the fun. The reverse of the menu name checks the suppliers – always a reassuring act – and there are usually a couple of vegetarian options along with a separate menu of the day's specials. The steak and fabulous baker fries are a constant and cooking is wholesome and generally gutsy. The wine list is printed within old cartoon annuals; wines are decently priced and divided up according to their character.

Odette's

G2

Primrose Hill
130 Regent's Park Rd. ✉ NW1 8XL
✆ (020) 7586 8569
www.odettesprimrosehill.com

⊖ Chalk Farm
Closed 1 week Christmas

Menu £20 (lunch and early dinner) – Carte £31/51

It's amazing what a window can do: they installed a big one at the front of the restaurant and it opened the whole place up and made it feel far more welcoming. Locals used to regard Odette's as being a little bit standoffish but service is now a lot chattier and the atmosphere more relaxed, which in turn makes it feel more a part of the community. The cooking is also a little less complicated than it was and is all the better for it, although there is still depth to the dishes. Flavours are robust and braised dishes a highlight; the chef-owner also displays a passion for his Welsh roots. The lunch and early evening menus are a steal and change every fortnight; there are also tasting and vegetarian menus alongside the à la carte.

Salusbury

F2

Queens Park
50-52 Salusbury Rd. ✉ NW6 6NN
✆ (020) 7328 3286
www.thesalusbury.co.uk

⊖ Queen's Park.
Closed 25-26 December
and Monday lunch

Carte £20/30

The Salusbury was never one to worry unduly about its looks: its appeal lay simply in the quality of its cooking. Now a refit has smartened it up somewhat but the imperturbable atmosphere is unchanged and the service is as youthful and sprightly as ever. The pub comes divided in two, with a bar on one side and a dining room in sage green, with a subtle Edwardian feel, on the other. The kitchen has a pronounced Italian accent and the menu is divided according to cooking method so that under the 'roast' section you might find whole sea bream in a salt crust and under 'fried', crispy squid with lemon; dishes are as big in flavour as they are in size. Much of their produce is also available to buy in their shop next door.

Gilbert Scott

H2-3

British ✗✗

St Pancras
Euston Rd ✉ NW1 2AR
✆ (020) 7278 3888
www.thegilbertscott.co.uk

⊖ King's Cross St. Pancras

Carte £32/70

[A/C]

[VISA]

[MC]

[AE]

Britain's less than stellar reputation for the quality of its food won't change until more people come and see what's cooking in our kitchens, so snaring those tourists as soon as they step off the Eurostar is no bad thing. Run under the aegis of Marcus Wareing and named after the architect who designed this Gothic masterpiece of a hotel in 1873, the restaurant has the splendour of a Grand Salon but the buzz of a busy brasserie. More significantly, the kitchen celebrates our culinary heritage by trumpeting both our native produce and regional specialities. In amongst the Eccles cakes, Manchester tart, Cullen skink and Glamorgan sausages are also dishes like 'soles in coffins' and 'Tweed kettle' that prove someone's done some research.

Bradley's 🐵

G2

Modern European ✗✗

Swiss Cottage
25 Winchester Rd. ✉ NW3 3NR
✆ (020) 7722 3457
www.bradleysnw3.co.uk

⊖ Swiss Cottage
Closed Saturday lunch
and Sunday dinner

Menu £18/25 – Carte £30/40

[A/C]

[VISA]

[MC]

[AE]

Simon Bradley has been steadily going about his business for nigh on 20 years and has engendered such loyalty in his regulars that many of them wouldn't countenance a visit to a competitor until it had been going for at least a couple of years. Whilst there is an appealing and nicely balanced à la carte, the real draw here are the very well priced set menus. This affordability is achieved by proper 'cheffing' such as braising beef and buying less fashionable and underused fish like ling to create dishes with clear, complementary flavours. Simon is also a proper neighbourhood restaurateur: he can often be found at the local farmers' market and is now also responsible for the catering at the splendid Hampstead Theatre around the corner.

Eriki

G2

Swiss Cottage
4-6 Northways Par, Finchley Rd ✉ NW3 5EN
☎ (020) 7722 0606
www.eriki.co.uk

⊖ Swiss Cottage
Closed Saturday lunch

Menu £20 (dinner) – Carte £27/35

AC
☼
VISA
MC
AE

Eriki eschews tired old standards and instead offers a diverse and contrasting gastronomic tour around all parts of India, from Goan curries to Punjabi-style prawns, Hariyali scallops to Lucknowi lamb. The cooking is fresh and invigorating; vegetarians will be in clover and the breads are good. The cutlery is imported from Rajasthan and the carved tables and heavy chairs add a sense of permanence. The staff are a pleasant bunch, although this vibrantly coloured restaurant can go from quiet to full in a matter of moments so get your order in quickly. Eriki is so much more than your typical neighbourhood Indian restaurant, a fact not lost on its many regulars. The only negative is the less than inspiring view of drab old Finchley Road.

Singapore Garden

G2

Swiss Cottage
83 Fairfax Rd. ✉ NW6 4DY
☎ (020) 7328 5314
www.singaporegarden.co.uk

⊖ Swiss Cottage
Closed 24-28 December

Menu £30 (dinner) – Carte £31/52

AC
🕐
☼
VISA
MC
AE

Avoid the more generic dishes on the menu at this long-standing Swiss Cottage favourite and head instead to the back page of Singaporean and Malaysian specialities or to the separate list of seasonal dishes such as the 'grandma pork belly'. Squid blachan with sugar snap peas and plenty of chilli is a fresh and fiery number; Chiew Yim soft shell crab is full of flavour and Daging curry of tender beef and coconut is satisfying and filling. The staff are a happy and helpful lot; its female members wear traditional costumes, their male counterparts, bow ties. The room is comfortable and the clientele are a smart and mature bunch. The moped-riders keeping warm outside testify to its popularity in the local home delivery market too.

Junction Tavern

Tufnell Park
101 Fortess Rd ✉ NW5 1AG
☎ (020) 7485 9400
www.junctiontavern.co.uk

⊖ **Tufnell Park.**
Closed 24-26 December
and 1 January

Carte £23/31

Over the years, Tufnell Park has appealed to young urban professionals because, along with its pretty Victorian terraces, it has a belligerent edge to add a little credibility. The Junction Tavern fits in well. The menu changes daily and portion size has been slightly reduced to give more balance to the menu as a whole; the cooking remains unfussy and relies on good flavours. There's plenty of choice, from light summer dishes such as grilled sardines and seared tuna to the more robust rib-eye and pork belly. Staff are a chatty bunch who know their beers – they offer weekly changing guest ales and hold a popular beer festival; the 'pie and a pint' choice remains a favourite. Commendably, they also offer tap water without being prompted.

Walnut

West Hampstead
280 West End Ln., Fortune Grn. ✉ NW6 1LJ
☎ (020) 7794 7772
www.walnutwalnut.com

⊖ **West Hampstead**
Closed Sunday
and Monday –
(dinner only)

Carte £24/38

'Local. Seasonal. Sustainable' proclaims the menu at this convivial local restaurant. This is no empty slogan: the chef-owner also outlines in print the 'Walnut ethos' which includes working with good-practice suppliers, recycling and energy-saving – even the staff all walk or cycle to work. More importantly, he understands what people want from a local restaurant: at least some part of the menu changes daily and his classical background and honest approach means that the emphasis is on flavours rather than presentation; fish and game are handled particularly well and the crusty breads are homemade. The well-meaning service can sometimes struggle to keep up but the warmth and integrity of the place make one surprisingly forgiving.

Sushi-Say

F2

Willesden Green
33B Walm Ln.
✉ NW2 5SH
✆ (020) 8459 2971

⊖ Willesden Green
Closed 2 weeks August, 25-26 December,
1 January, Wednesday after bank holidays,
Monday and Tuesday – (dinner only and
lunch Saturday-Sunday)

Menu £20/42 – Carte £17/42

☼

VISA

ⓂⒸ

One of the delights of Willesden Green must surely be this long-standing Japanese restaurant which has never looked back since being revamped in 2007 and which is nearly always full. As the name suggests, sushi is the reason why many come and a seat at the counter, watching owner Mr Shimizu's expertise with his knife, is the place to be; if you're tempted to supplement your selection with some creamy uni or rich, warmed unagi then just ask him and he'll oblige. If you prefer other styles of Japanese cookery then you'll find plenty of choice; it's often worth considering the monthly specials menu; the yakitori is particularly good and there's a well-priced selection of sake and shochu. Mrs Shimizu leads her team with alacrity and efficiency.

Good food without spending a fortune? Look for the Bib Gourmand ⊛.

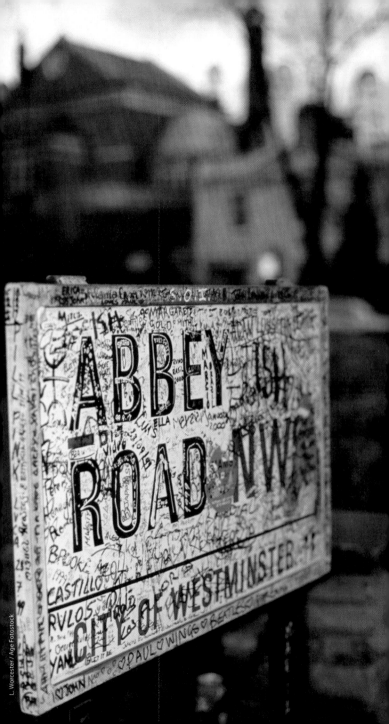

North-East London

If northwest London is renowned for its leafy acres, then the area to its immediate east has a more urban, brick-built appeal. Which has meant, over the last decade or so, a wholesale rebranding exercise for some of its traditionally shady localities. A generation ago it would have been beyond the remit of even the most inventive estate agent to sell the charms of Islington, Hackney or Bethnal Green. But then along came Damien Hirst, Tracey Emin et al, and before you could say 'cow in formaldehyde' the area's cachet had rocketed.

Shoreditch and **Hoxton** are the pivotal points of the region's hip makeover. Their cobbled brick streets and shabby industrial remnants were like heavenly manna to the artists and designers who started to colonise the old warehouses twenty years ago. A fashionable crowd soon followed in their footsteps, and nowadays the area around **Hoxton Square** positively teems with clubs, bars and galleries. Latest must-see space is Rivington Place, a terrific gallery that highlights visual arts from around the world. Nearby are Deluxe (digital installations), AOP (photographic shows) and Hales (Spencer Tunick's acres of gooseflesh… etc).

Before the area was ever trendy, there was the Geffrye Museum. A short stroll up Hoxton's **Kingsland Road**, it's a jewel of a place, set in elegant 18C almshouses, and depicting English middle-class interiors from 1600 to the present day. Right behind it is St. Mary's Secret Garden, a little oasis that manages to include much diversity including a separate woodland and herb area, all in less than an acre. At the southern end of the area, in Folgate Street, Dennis Severs' House is an original Huguenot home that recreates 18 and 19C life in an original way – cooking smells linger, hearth and candles burn, giving you the impression the owners have only just left the place. Upstairs the beds remain unmade: did a certain local artist pick up any ideas here?

When the Regent's Canal was built in the early 19C, **Islington's** fortunes nose-dived, for it was accompanied by the arrival of slums and over-crowding. But the once-idyllic village managed to hold onto its Georgian squares and handsome Victorian terraces through the rough times, and when these were gentrified a few years ago, the area ushered in a revival. **Camden Passage** has long been famed for its quirky antique emporiums, while the slinky Business Design Centre is a flagship of the modern Islington. Cultural icons established themselves around the Upper Street area and these have gone from strength to strength. The **Almeida** Theatre has a habit of hitting the production jackpot with its history of world premieres, while the King's Head has earned itself a

C. Eymenier / MICHELIN

reputation for raucous scene-stealing; set up in the seventies, it's also London's very first theatre-pub. Nearby, the Screen on the Green boasts a wonderful old-fashioned neon billboard.

Even in the 'bad old days', Islington drew in famous names, and at Regency smart **Canonbury Square** are the one-time homes of Evelyn Waugh (no.17A) and George Orwell (no.27). These days it houses the Estorick Collection of Modern Italian Art; come here to see fine futuristic paintings in a Georgian villa. To put the history of the area in a proper context, head to St. John Street, south of the City Road, where the Islington Museum's shiny new headquarters tells the story of a colourful and multi-layered past.

Further up the A10, you come to **Dalston,** a bit like the Islington of old but with the buzzy Ridley Road market and a vibrant all-night scene including the blistering Vortex Jazz Club just off Kingsland Road. A little further north is **Stoke Newington,** referred to, a bit unkindly, as the poor man's Islington. Its pride and joy is Church Street, which not only features some characterful bookshops and eye-catching boutiques, but also lays claim to Abney Park Cemetery, an enchanting old place with a wildlife-rich nature reserve.

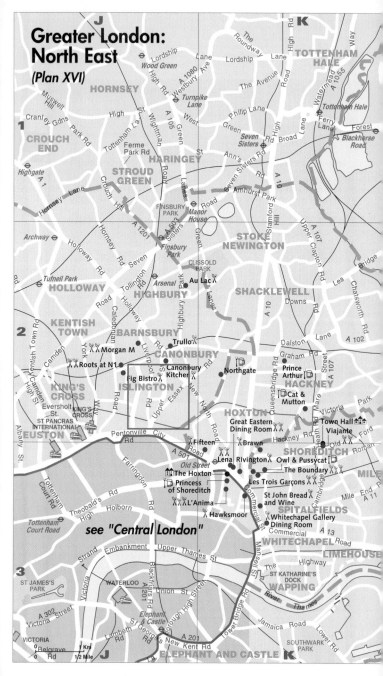

Greater London: North East
(Plan XVI)

J K

CROUCH END
HORNSEY
HARINGEY
STROUD GREEN
Highgate
Archway
Tufnell Park
HOLLOWAY
HIGHBURY
KENTISH TOWN
BARNSBURY
CANONBURY
ISLINGTON
KING'S CROSS
EUSTON
ST PANCRAS INTERNATIONAL
KING'S CROSS

TOTTENHAM HALE
Tottenham Hale
Blackhorse Road
Seven Sisters
FINSBURY PARK
Manor House
Finsbury Park
CLISSOLD PARK
Arsenal
Au Lac ✕
STOKE NEWINGTON
SHACKLEWELL
HACKNEY
Prince Arthur
Cat & Mutton
Northgate
HOXTON
SHOREDITCH
Town Hall
Viajante
Morgan M ✕✕
Roots at N1 ✕✕
Trullo ✕
Canonbury Kitchen
Fig Bistro

Great Eastern Dining Room ✕✕
Fifteen ✕
Brawn ✕
Lena Rivington ✕
Owl & Pussycat
The Hoxton
The Boundary ✕✕✕
Princess of Shoreditch
Les Trois Garçons ✕✕
L'Anima ✕✕
St John Bread and Wine ✕
Hawksmoor ✕
Whitechapel Gallery Dining Room ✕
SPITALFIELDS
WHITECHAPEL
LIMEHOUSE
MILE

see "Central London"

ST JAMES'S PARK
WATERLOO
VICTORIA
Elephant & Castle
ST KATHARINE'S DOCK
WAPPING
SOUTHWARK PARK

ELEPHANT AND CASTLE

0 ___ Km
0 ___ 1/2 Mile

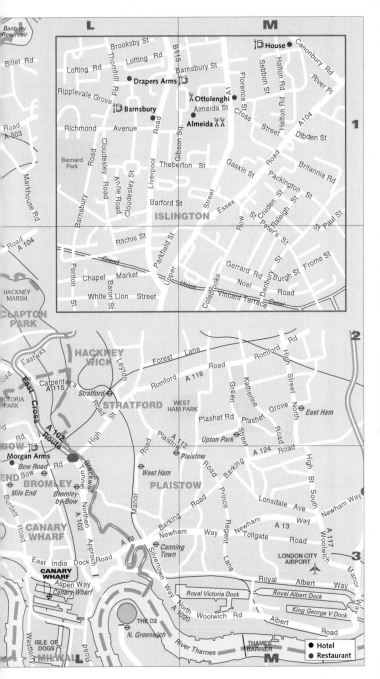

Fig Bistro

Modern European ✗

J2

Barnsbury

169 Hemingford Rd. ✉ **N1 1DA**
✆ (020) 7609 3009
www.figbistro.co.uk

⊖ **Caledonian Road**
Closed 25-26, 31 December,
1 January and Sunday dinner –
(dinner only and Sunday lunch)

Carte £19/31

It's often the case that when a chef-owner opens a second restaurant he tries to give the impression that he's still also at the stove in his original premises. Owner-chef Christoffer Hruskova, now ensconced at North Road, is far too honest for such subterfuge and flagged up the simpler cooking style here by adding 'bistro' to the name. That being said, he may now be slightly underselling things here, as the flavoursome dishes still display a degree of polish in both execution and presentation. The compact, slightly frayed room may also lack the clutter and clamour of a bistro but it has definitely become more accessible – just check out the popularity of Sunday brunch. This welcoming, charmingly run little place deserves its success.

Morgan M

French ✗✗

J2

Barnsbury

489 Liverpool Rd. ✉ **N7 8NS**
✆ (020) 7609 3560
www.morganm.com

⊖ **Highbury & Islington**
Closed 24-30 December, Monday, Sunday
dinner and lunch Tuesday and Saturday

Menu £29/43

Boldly patterned wallpaper and retro lighting have added some warmth to this converted pub which has firmly established itself in this corner of Islington. The M stands for Meunier, a proud Frenchman from the Champagne region, and his classic, full-flavoured cooking continues to appeal to a refreshingly varied group of customers. The menu can appear a little bewildering at first, as it offers à la carte, seasonal and 'Garden' choices - with some overlap - but portions are generous and all come with plenty of extra little dishes. The predominantly French wine list is accessibly priced. A little more personality from the suited managers wouldn't go amiss, especially during the early evening while the restaurant is still filling up.

Roots at N1

J2

Indian ✗✗

Barnsbury
115 Hemingford Rd ✉ N1 1BZ
✆ (020) 7697 4488
www.rootsatn1.com

⊖ **Caledonian Road**
Closed 25-26 December and Monday
– booking essential – (dinner only)

Menu £23 – Carte £25/39

A/C
VISA
M©

Three friends from India came to London, worked at Benares for three years, then went their own ways. But they kept in touch and their shared dream came true when together they opened this restaurant in a converted Victorian pub in Barnsbury. The most startling and refreshing aspect of this warm, friendly operation is the unusually short menu, which changes every two months. Around a dozen dishes are offered, many of which are available in two sizes, along with a few vegetables dishes and four desserts. This means everything is prepared to order, and tastes accordingly. The tandoori lamb chops and the lamb shank Rogan Josh quickly established their own fan clubs, the breads are terrific and the refreshing kulfi provides a great finish.

Morgan Arms

L3

Gastropub 🍴🍺

Bow
43 Morgan St ✉ E3 5AA
✆ (020) 8980 6389
www.capitalpubcompany.com/The-Morgan-Arms

⊖ **Bow Road**
Closed 25 December

Carte £24/34

🍽
A/C
☼
VISA
M©
AE

This former boozer's clever makeover respects its heritage while simultaneously bringing it up to date. The bar's always busy while the dining area is more subdued. You'll find the kitchen keeps its influences mostly within Europe but also understands just what sort of food works well in a pub. The daily changing menu usually features pasta in some form and staples like whitebait - which come devilled in this instance - assorted tarts and the perennial favourite, fishcakes accompanied by a poached egg. What's more, prices are kept at realistic levels which makes this pub appealing to those who live nearby and who like a little spontaneity in their lives. Look out for the occasional themed evening and charity auction.

Canonbury Kitchen

Italian ✗

J2

Canonbury
19 Canonbury Ln ✉ N1 2AS
✆ (0207) 2269 791
www.canonburykitchen.com

⊖ **Highbury & Islington**
Closed Monday – (dinner only and lunch Saturday-Sunday)

Carte £24/31

A/C
☼
VISA
MC
D

Inserting the word 'kitchen' into the name of one's restaurant is becoming more and more common as it instantly evokes images of simple food and unpretentious dining. That certainly applies to Canonbury Kitchen, which comes with an appropriately light, fresh look, thanks to its exposed brick walls, high ceiling and painted floorboards. With seating for just forty it also feels like the very epitome of a neighbourhood restaurant. Owner Max and his team provide gently reassuring service and the kitchen – on-view at the far end – sensibly keeps things simple. That includes an ever-popular fritto misto made with cuttlefish and octopus, pan-fried hake with herbs, and a lemon tiramisu with limoncello replacing the marsala.

House

Modern European ✗

M1

Canonbury
63-69 Canonbury Rd ✉ N1 2DG
✆ (020) 7704 7410
www.thehouse.islington.com

⊖ **Highbury & Islington.**
Closed Monday except bank holidays

Carte £20/30

☂
☼
VISA
MC
AE

The front terrace is certainly an appealing feature in summer but, thanks to its warm atmosphere and candlelit tables, The House is just as welcoming on a winter's night. The regulars relaxing around the bar exude a general sense of localness and on the whole they prefer the sort of food that goes well with a pint; it's others who come looking for something a little special on the menu. The kitchen is intelligent enough to appreciate these two different markets in equal measure, so puts just as much effort into a shepherd's pie or a burger as it does with the sea bass or partridge. Weekends are busy, especially the breakfasts, but check first as The House often holds wedding receptions for those who've got hitched at Islington Town Hall.

Trullo 😊

Italian 🍴

J2

Canonbury
300-302 St Paul's Rd.   ✉ N1 2LH
📞 (020) 7226 2733
www.trullorestaurant.com

⊖ **Highbury & Islington**
Closed 23 December-2 January,
Sunday dinner and Monday –
booking essential – (dinner only
and lunch Saturday-Sunday)

Carte £25/32

A/C
VISA
MC

The owners' CVs read like a checklist of eateries known for their relaxed atmospheres and uncomplicated cooking, including Moro, St John, and the River Café, so it is no surprise to find delicious Italian cooking here in this friendly restaurant, filled every day with noisily contented diners. The menu, small in size and content, changes daily so don't be surprised when something runs out. Expect great antipasti, such as pumpkin and chilli fritti, as well as flavoursome dishes cooked on the charcoal grill – and all at terrific prices. Trullo is named after the conical-shaped buildings of southern Italy, used primarily by farm workers for meeting and eating, which seems most appropriate for somewhere exuding such contentment.

Cat & Mutton

British 🍺

K2

Hackney
76 Broadway Mkt.   ✉ E8 4QJ
📞 (020) 7254 5599
www.catandmutton.co.uk

⊖ **Bethnal Green.**
Closed 25-26 December
and Sunday dinner

Menu £15 (dinner) – Carte £24/34

VISA
MC

The Cat & Mutton has been a fixture here since the 1700s, when it was a drover's inn quenching the thirst of farm workers bringing their livestock down from East Anglia. The streets round here might still frighten out-of-towners and the pub may now look a little frayed around the edges but step inside, look past the rough and ready character, and the young staff will make you feel reassuringly welcome. The open kitchen adds a little theatre to proceedings and the relatively concise menu changes often. The cooking is straightforward but is also undertaken with more care than you expect. Their beef is organic and in the evening steaks stand out amongst the more elaborate dishes. It's upstairs for quiz nights and art classes.

Lena

K3

Italian ✕✕

Hackney

66 Great Eastern St.   ✉ EC2A 3JT
✆ (020) 7739 5714
www.lenarestaurant.com

⊖ **Old Street**
Closed 25 December, 1 January
and Sunday lunch

Menu £14 (lunch) – Carte £21/34

A/C
VISA
MC
AE
D

If you want customers to know that your Italian restaurant is authentic, then naming it after your mother is a good start. Eclectically decorated to befit its fashionable Shoreditch postcode, it uses leather, plastic, woods and ceramics to create the sort of high-maintenance shiny interior that one instantly either loves or hates. Jazz enthusiasts will find much to enjoy here, particularly the live weekend jazz in the stylish bar downstairs. The cooking looks to southerly regions of Italy for influences, especially around Naples and the Amalfi coast. Dishes have a bracing freshness to them, although the dessert selection is a little more predictable. Breads, pastas and ice creams are all homemade.

Prince Arthur

K2

British 🍺

Hackney

95 Forest Rd.   ✉ E8 3BH
✆ (020) 7249 9996
www.theprincearthurlondonfields.com

⊖ **Bethnal Green.**
Closed 25-26 December –
(dinner only and
lunch Saturday-Sunday)

Carte £26/41

A/C
☼
VISA
MC
AE

Those who judge by first impressions will probably walk on by as this slightly scruffy corner pub would struggle to entice anyone on looks alone. To be honest, the inside isn't much keener on the eye, apart from the stuffed animals and the postcard collection, but then this isn't about appearances, more about good food and convivial company. Sit anywhere in the U-shaped room and the amiable staff will be quick to come over. The menu reads appealingly: smoked salmon, terrines, fish and chips, sausage and mash – but the cooking is done with unexpected care and more than a little skill; fish from Billingsgate is handled particularly deftly. Just thinking about the deep-fried jam or cherry sandwich for dessert will be enough to seal an artery.

Au Lac

Vietnamese ✗

J2

Highbury
82 Highbury Park   ⊠ N5 2XE
✆ (020) 7704 9187

⊖ Arsenal
Closed 1-2 January and 24-26
December – (dinner only and
lunch Thursday-Friday)

Carte £10/23

A/C
☼
VISA
MC

Au Lac may look a little ordinary from the outside, but that just adds to its appeal. Run enthusiastically by two brothers – one's in the kitchen, the other's out front – it provides proof of why Vietnamese cooking is considered one of Asia's healthiest cuisines: it involved lots of quick stir-frying, uses plenty of fresh herbs like mint and basil and keeps vegetables crisp. Specialities here include 'Pho' noodle soup with rare beef and chargrilled sea bass with banana leaves but they also regularly introduce new dishes on the menu. Portions are on the more-than-generous side so sharing is necessary and, while there are a few Chinese dishes on the menu to attract the less adventurous, it's best to stick to what they do best.

Fifteen London

Italian ✗

K3

Hoxton
15 Westland Pl.   ⊠ N1 7LP
✆ (020) 3375 1515
www.fifteen.net

⊖ Old Street
Closed 24-26 December –
booking essential

Menu £30 (lunch) – Carte dinner £29/48

A/C
☼
VISA
MC
AE

This is the original branch of Jamie Oliver's charitable 'Fifteen' restaurants and it's already on its ninth intake of trainees. Their programme lasts for 18 months and they receive schooling in all departments of the restaurant while being closely monitored by the experienced full-time staff. There are two operations here: the buzzy ground floor trattoria and a slightly more formal basement restaurant. The Italian cooking bears the unmistakeable signature of Jamie Oliver and the students are clearly being taught that most valuable of lessons: buy the best quality, seasonal ingredients and don't mess them about too much. This laudable project makes worrying about the occasional lapse seem somewhat mean-spirited.

Great Eastern Dining Room

K3

Hoxton   ⊖ Old Street
54 Great Eastern St   ✉ EC2A 3QR   Closed Saturday lunch and Sunday
✆ (020) 7613 4545
www.rickerrestaurants.com

Menu £20 (lunch and early dinner) – Carte £22/39

[AC]
[VISA]
[MC]
[AE]
[D]

Will Ricker's flourishing group of hip restaurants came into its own here in Great Eastern Street and coincided with Hoxton's own emergence onto the fashion radar. The format here is similar to the others in the group: the bar, given equal billing as the restaurant, occupies most of the front section and it's usually so packed even a sardine would think twice. The noise spills into the restaurant, adding a lively vibe to the place. It's all great fun. The kitchen's influences spill across South East Asia, with dim sum, curries, roasts and tempura all carefully prepared. Helpfully, the reverse of the menu carries a glossary of Asian culinary terms. The serving team are a sassy and well-informed bunch.

Almeida

M1

Islington   ⊖ Angel
30 Almeida St.   ✉ N1 1AD   Closed Sunday dinner and Monday lunch
✆ (020) 7354 4777
www.almeida-restaurant.co.uk

Menu £19/34 – Carte £35/55

[AC]
[icon]
[icon]
[VISA]
[MC]
[AE]

If you're not here for a pre-theatre bite before going to the Almeida theatre opposite then try not to arrive around 7-7.30pm as you'll find yourself in the midst of an almighty exodus which leaves the restaurant in a degree of disarray and the waiters looking shell-shocked. They then dim the lights and take a deep breath but it's usually a while before the atmosphere builds again. Prices at this crisply decorated restaurant are more realistic these days, especially at lunch when the room really benefits from the two large windows. The menu's French influence is a little less pronounced but dishes still use intelligent combinations, like venison with pumpkin and lamb with artichoke. Look out for some interesting regional French wines.

Barnsbury

L1

Islington
209-211 Liverpool Rd ✉ N1 1LX
☎ (020) 7607 5519
www.thebarnsbury.co.uk

⊖ **Highbury & Islington.**
Closed 24-26 December –
(dinner only and lunch Friday-Sunday)

Carte £20/35

The young owner may have a background in some of London's more fashionable dining establishments, but he's turned The Barnsbury back into a proper local pub as he felt it had become too much like a restaurant. That being said, the food is still done well and the menu is appealing, with tarts, salads, potted shrimps and mussels jostling for attention alongside Toulouse sausages, risottos and steaks served with the ubiquitous triple-cooked chips; the homemade puds are especially good. Lunch trade is not big in these parts so the midday menu is more limited. Chandeliers fashioned from wine glasses are dotted around the place and add character; but do sit in the more atmospheric front bar rather than the dining area at the back.

Drapers Arms 😊

L1

Islington
44 Barnsbury St ✉ N1 1ER
☎ (020) 7619 0348
www.thedrapersarms.com

⊖ **Highbury & Islington.**
Booking advisable at dinner

Carte £24/32

Unless meeting the in-laws, your best bet is to stay on the ground floor of this handsome Georgian pub, as the more demure surroundings of the upstairs dining room, with its powder blue walls and flickering candlelight, are slightly at odds with the muscular nature of the cooking. This is the sort of food that prompts the rolling up of sleeves and the generous pouring of wine. Snail and chorizo soup, game terrine, Barnsley chop and onglet: flavours here pack a veritable punch and the kitchen recognises a decent ingredient when it sees one. The owners never forget that this is a pub and so prices are kept at sensible levels. Even the wine list plays its part by offering most of its largely French and Spanish selection for under £30.

Northgate

Mediterranean 🍺

K2

Islington
113 Southgate Rd ✉ N1 3JS
☎ (020) 7359 7392

⊖ Dalston Kingsland (rail).
Closed 1 January –
(dinner only and lunch Saturday-Sunday)

Carte £20/29

The Northgate is decked out in the usual gastropub aesthetic of mismatched furniture and local artists' work for sale on the walls; at the back you'll find tables laid up for dining and an open kitchen. You'll also find an extraction fan that's so strong you can feel its tug. Staff are pretty laid back, at times almost to the point of somnolence; go with a similarly relaxed frame of mind to avoid irritation. Where the pub scores is in the food: there's a strong Mediterranean influence on the vast blackboard. You'll find merguez and chorizo sausages, assorted pastas, a bit of Greek and some French – all in generously sized portions with the emphasis on flavour. Finish with something a little closer to home like treacle tart.

Ottolenghi

Mediterranean ✗

M1

Islington
287 Upper St. ✉ N1 2TZ
☎ (020) 7288 1454
www.ottolenghi.co.uk

⊖ Highbury & Islington
Closed 25-26 December, dinner Sunday
and bank holidays – booking essential

Carte £20/45

Coming with friends and sharing is the key at Ottolenghi. It's primarily a deli, with tempting salads and piles of meringues in its window, but morphs into a little restaurant at night, with communal tables, speedy but sociable service and a fun atmosphere. Dishes come either 'from the counter', where a waitress will go and dish up for you – so be nice – or 'from the kitchen' which involves some heating up. The menu changes daily and influences come from all parts of the wider Mediterranean: this is all about good fresh ingredients yielding plenty of flavour – and Veggies will be in clover. Three dishes per person are too many, yet two are not enough, so sharing is the key. The desserts are especially good and if you think you know salad, think again.

Fellow

Modern European 🍴🍺

H2

King's Cross
24 York Way ✉ N1 9AA
☏ (020) 7833 4395
www.thefellow.co.uk

⊖ King's Cross St Pancras.
▶ **Plan XV**
Closed 25 December
and Sunday dinner

Carte £26/33

A/C
📷
VISA
MC
AE

It was just a matter of time before a few decent pubs opened around the rapidly developing area of King's Cross. The Fellow is one of the busiest, attracting a youthful and local clientele; it also manages to give the impression it's been here for years. Eating happens on the dark and atmospheric ground floor, with drinkers heading upstairs to the even more boisterous cocktail bar. The menu is quite a sophisticated little number but the kitchen is up to the task. Start with ham hock terrine or potted crab, followed by roast rump of lamb or grilled haddock with champ. Desserts such as apple tart display a lightness of touch. The serving team are a bright, capable bunch. There is an outdoor terrace but you'll be surrounded by smokers.

L'Anima

Italian 🍴🍴🍴

K3

Shoreditch
1 Snowden St. ✉ EC2A 2DQ
☏ (0207) 4227 000
www.lanima.co.uk

⊖ Liverpool Street
Closed 25 December, Saturday lunch,
Sunday and bank holidays –
booking essential

Menu £37 (lunch) – Carte £35/63

A/C
VISA
MC
AE

L'Anima is an extremely handsome restaurant that looks as though it should be located somewhere slightly more glamorous than the edge of The City. A glass wall separates the bar from the restaurant, where you find limestone walls, impeccably laid tables, white leather chairs and clever lighting; ask for one of the tables on the raised section at the back. The mood is sophisticated and the look smart and stylish. The chef may come from Calabria but his team have arrived from all parts of Italy. His menu is appealing and balanced, offering a mix of classic and less familiar dishes; and there's a helpful glossary of terms for the unfamiliar. The emphasis is on flavour and most dishes deliver that in spades. Service is smooth but also personable.

Boundary

French XXX

K3

Shoreditch
2-4 Boundary St.   ✉ E2 7DD
✆ (020) 7729 1051
www.theboundary.co.uk

⊖ **Old Street**
Closed Sunday dinner – (dinner only
and lunch Saturday-Sunday)

Menu £25 (lunch) – Carte £28/56

[A/C]
🎱
VISA
M©
AE
①

When the management team took over his restaurant group,
many thought Sir Terence Conran's days of opening restaurants
were over. Not a bit of it, because he was soon back with a
bang with Boundary. As is his way, he has taken an interesting
building, in this case a large warehouse and former printworks,
and turned it into a veritable house of fun. From the top, you
have a roof terrace with an open fire; Albion is a ground
floor 'caff' alongside a shop and bakery, and Boundary is the
French-inspired 'main' restaurant below. The room is stylish,
good-looking and works well, while the kitchen serves up
reassuringly familiar cross-Channel treats, including fruits de
mer. The fourth part of the equation are the comfy, individually
designed bedrooms.

Princess of Shoreditch

Traditional 🍴🍺

K3

Shoreditch
76-78 Paul St.   ✉ EC2A 4NE
✆ (020) 7729 9270
www.theprincessofshoreditch.com

⊖ **Old Street.**
Closed 24-26 December

Menu £18 (lunch) – Carte £25/32

☼
VISA
M©
AE

The old girl may change hands now and then but she remains as
popular as ever. The ground floor is your proper pub; drinkers
are the mainstay but they get an appealing and appropriate
menu where platters of sausage, charcuterie and cheese are the
highlights, along with pies of the cottage or pork variety. For
more mellow surroundings follow the fairy lights up to a warm,
candlelit room. Here, the menu displays greater ambition.
The cooking is more European in its influence and, despite
the occasional affected presentation, it's clear the kitchen
has confidence and ability. Flavours are good, techniques are
sound and parfaits are a real highlight. The pub prides itself on
the friendliness of its staff and upstairs is no different.

Rivington Grill

British ✗

K3

Shoreditch
28-30 Rivington St. ✉ EC2A 3DZ
✆ (020) 7729 7053
www.rivingtonshoreditch.co.uk

⊖ **Old Street**
Closed 25-26 December

Carte £26/48

AC
☼
VISA
MC
AE
D

A converted warehouse surrounded by design studios, galleries and printing premises means not only that this place is popular with artistically inclined types but that it also shows work itself, including a Tracey Emin neon "Life without you, never". However, it is also close to The City so head left when you enter as larger groups tend to occupy the tables on the right. The British menu will fill you with patriotic fervour – if this was what John Major had meant when he referred to 'back-to-basics' there wouldn't have been such derision. There's a section 'on toast' and oysters are a speciality; there are pies, chops and faggots, even fish fingers and bubble and squeak. There are also plenty of bottles under £30 and special offers for weekend lunches.

Sunday brunch plans?
Look for the 🍴 !

South-East London

Once considered not only the wrong side of the tracks, but also most definitely the wrong side of the river, London's southeastern chunk has thrived in recent times courtesy of the Docklands Effect. As the gleaming glass peninsula of **Canary Wharf** (ironically, just north of the Thames) sprouted a personality of its own – with bars, restaurants, slinky bridges and an enviable view, not to mention moneyed residents actually putting down roots – the city's bottom right hand zone began to achieve destination status on a par with other parts of London. You only have to stroll around the glossy and quite vast **Limehouse Basin** – a slick marina that was once a hard-grafting East End dock – to really see what's happened here.

Not that the area hasn't always boasted some true gems in the capital's treasure chest. **Greenwich,** with fabulous views across the water to the docklands from its delightfully sloping park, has long been a favourite of kings and queens: Henry VIII and Elizabeth I resided here. The village itself bustles along with its market and plush picturehouse, but most visitors make their way to the standout attractions, of which there are many. The **Royal Observatory** and the Meridian Line draw stargazers and hemisphere striders in equal number, while the palatial Old Royal Naval College is a star turn for lovers of Wren, who designed it as London's answer to Versailles. On the northern edge of Greenwich Park, the **National Maritime Museum** has three floors of sea-faring wonders; down by the pier, the real thing exists in the rather sorry-looking shape of the **Cutty Sark,** devastated by fire in 2007. Up on the peninsula, the O2 Arena's distinctive shape has become an unmistakable landmark, but if you fancy a contrast to all things watery, the Fan Museum on Crooms Hill has more handheld fans (over 3,000 of them) than anywhere else on earth. Strolling south from Greenwich park you reach **Blackheath,** an alluring suburban village, whose most striking feature is the towering All Saints' Church, standing proud away from the chic shops and restaurants.

Of slightly less spectacular charms, but a real crowd-pleaser nevertheless, is **Dulwich Village,** hidden deeper in the southeastern enclaves. It's a leafy oasis in this part of the world, with a delightful park that boasts at its western end, next to the original buildings of the old public school, the Dulwich Picture Gallery. This will soon reach its 200th birthday, and its pedigree is evident in works by the likes of Rembrandt, Rubens, Van Dyck and Canaletto. Half an hour's walk away across the park is the brilliant Horniman Museum, full of natural history and world culture delights – as well as a massive aquarium that seems to take up much of southeast London.

GREENWICH MARKET

ERECTED· MDCCCXXXI·

C. Eymenier / MICHELIN

A bit further east along the South Circular, there's the unexpected gem of Eltham Palace, originally the childhood home of Henry VIII with a magnificent (and still visible) Great Hall. What makes it unique is the adjacent Art Deco mansion built for millionaires in the 1930s in Ocean Liner style. It's the closest you'll ever get to a setting fit for hog roast and champagne. Heading back towards London, a lifestyle of bubbly and banquets has never really been **Peckham**'s thing, but it boasts a couple of corkers in the shape of the South London Gallery with its zeitgeist-setting art shows, and the Peckham Library, a giant inverted 'L' that after a decade still looks like a lot of fun to go into.

Back in the luxury flat-lands of the **Docklands, Wapping** has become an interesting port of call, its new-build architecture mixing in with a still Dickensian feel, in the shape of glowering Victorian warehouses and Wapping New Stairs, where the bodies of pirates were hanged from a gibbet until seven tides had showered their limp bodies. You can catch a fascinating history of the whole area in the nearby Museum in Docklands.

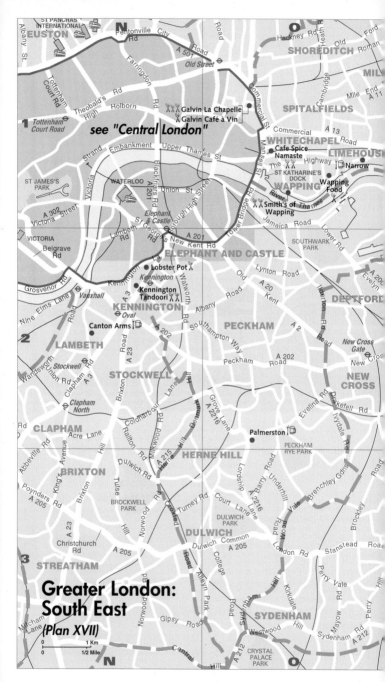

Greater London: South East

(Plan XVII)

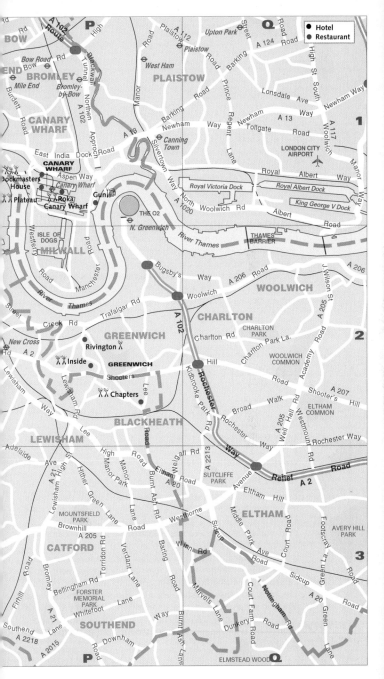

Legend
- ● Hotel
- ● Restaurant

BOW
END
BROMLEY
Bow Road
Mile End
Bromley-by-Bow
Burdett Road
CANARY WHARF
East India Dock Road
Dockmasters House
Plateau
Roka
Canary Wharf
Canary Wharf
Aspen Way
Westferry Road
ISLE OF DOGS
MILLWALL
Manchester Road
River Thames
Creek Rd
New Cross
GREENWICH
Rivington
Inside
GREENWICH
Shooters
Chapters
Lee
Lewisham Rd
LEWISHAM
Adelaide
Ave
Lewisham High St
Hither Green
Manor Park
MOUNTSFIELD PARK
Brownhill
A 205
CATFORD
Torridon Rd
Verdant Lane
Bellingham Rd
FORSTER MEMORIAL PARK
Whitefoot
Lane
Firthill
Southend
A 2218
A 2015
SOUTHEND
Downham
Way
Burnt Ash Lane

A 102
Route
Blackwall Tunnel
Northern Approach
A 102
A 13
Manor Road
Silvertown Way
Canning Town
North Woolwich Rd
A 1020
THE O2
N. Greenwich
River Thames
Bugsby's Way
Woolwich
Trafalgar Rd
A 102
Charlton Rd
Hill
CHARLTON
CHARLTON PARK
Charlton Park La.
Kidbrooke Park Rd
Rochester Way
Broad
Rochester
Way
BLACKHEATH
High Road
Manor Road
Eltham Road
A 20
Burnt Ash Rd
Gall Rd
A 2213
SUTCLIFFE PARK
Avenue
Eltham Hill
Westhorne
Baring Road
Winn Rd
Marvels Lane
Burnt Ash Lane
Dunkery Road
Court Farm Road
Nottingham Rd
A 20
ELMSTEAD WOOD

PLAISTOW
Upton Park
Plaistow Road
A 112
Plaistow
West Ham
Barking Road
Newham Way
Prince Regent Lane
Newham Way
A 13
Tollgate Road
LONDON CITY AIRPORT
Royal Albert Way
Royal Victoria Dock
Royal Albert Dock
King George V Dock
Woolwich Rd
Albert Road
THAMES BARRIER
A 206 Road
WOOLWICH
A 205
J. Wilson St
A 206
WOOLWICH COMMON
Academy Road
A 207
Shooter's Hill
ELTHAM COMMON
Well Hall
Westmount
Rochester Way
A 205
Relief Road
A 2
ELTHAM
Middle Park Ave
Court Road
Sidcup
A 20
AVERY HILL PARK
Footscray La.
Green Lane
Road

Street
High St South
Newham Way
A 124
Lonsdale Ave
A 117 Woolwich
Manor Way

1

2

3

P

Q

325

Brawn 🏠

K3

Bethnal Green
49 Columbia Rd. ✉ E2 7RG
✆ (020) 7729 5692
www.brawn.co

⊖ **Bethnal Green**
▶ **Plan XVI**
Closed Sunday dinner
and bank holidays

Carte £21/28

[A/C]
[VISA]
[MC]

After the success of Terroirs, the owners wisely decided against trying to duplicate it and instead created this terrific neighbourhood restaurant in a Victorian former furniture warehouse, away from the West End. It's simply kitted out, with Formica tables and white brick walls with local artists' work. The name really captures the essence of the cooking perfectly: it is rustic, muscular and makes particularly good use of pig. Order about three dishes per person, such as prosciutto or rillettes, mussels or prawns from the 'plancha' section; something raw like Tuscan beef; and something slow-cooked like duck confit. It's all immeasurably satisfying and the polite young staff are genuinely proud of the menu and happily proffer advice.

Chapters 🏠

P2

Blackheath
43-45 Montpelier Vale ✉ SE3 0TJ
✆ (020) 8333 2666
www.chaptersrestaurants.com

Closed 2-3 January

Carte £19/35

[🏠]
[A/C]
[☀]
[VISA]
[MC]
[AE]
[①]

Down at Chapters it appears to be the '80s all over again: the champagne flows, the cocktails are shaken and everyone knows everyone else. If ever there was a change of concept that worked it was here: out went the serious, in came just the sort of place you'd want to come to after a hard day's work. The bar is always packed; the restaurant has an ersatz industrial feel and the menu is reassuringly familiar with a roll-call of classics that include fish and chips and belly of pork. The most expensive dishes are also the most popular – the assorted meats cooked over charcoal in the Josper oven. It's an all-day operation and they take as much care with breakfast as they do with dinner, while service is ably performed by a nimble team.

Viajante ✿

Bethnal Green
Patriot Sq. (entrance on
Cambridge Heath Rd) ✉ E2 9NF
☎ (020) 7871 0461 **www**.viajante.co.uk

⊖ Bethnal Green
▶ **Plan XVI**
Closed lunch Monday-
Tuesday and bank holidays –
booking essential

Menu £28/65

A/C
☼
VISA
MC
AE

Viajante

Bethnal Green's converted Victorian town hall is the unlikely
setting for Portuguese chef Nuno Mendes' highly innovative
style of cooking. Despite the presence of large, looming
lampshades, there's still a whiff of civic functionality about the
restaurant – although the chairs are comfier than they look.
But it's all about the food here and the sight of chefs working
away with tweezers in the very open kitchen tells you it'll be
a little different. Don't be entirely fooled by their swan-like
serenity, however: there's another kitchen downstairs where
the donkey work is done. The choice is between 6, 9 or 12
courses; so, if you haven't got the time, don't bother. Each
delicate and diminutive course provides a blast of flavour and
textures are enjoyably contrasting. Dishes are highly inventive
and sometimes playful in their make-up and presentation, but
ingredients match and there's no recourse to using unusual
combinations. Inevitably, some dishes work better than others,
but when taken as a whole, one cannot fail to be impressed.

First Course	*Main Course*	*Dessert*
• Cod and potatoes with egg yolk and saffron. • Braised salmon skin and fried aubergine.	• Pork secretos with artichokes and hot potato gel. • Sea bass toast, garlic kale and São Jorge cheese.	• White chocolate with grapefruit and lemon. • Frozen maple panna cotta with shiso granité and green apple.

Dockmaster's House

Indian

P1

Canary Wharf
1 Hertsmere Rd ✉ E14 8JJ
✆ (020) 7345 0345
www.dockmastershouse.com

⊖ Canary Wharf
Closed Christmas, Sunday,
Saturday lunch and bank holidays
– booking advisable

Menu £20 (lunch and early dinner) – Carte £28/40

On the edge of Canary Wharf and in the shadow of its skyscrapers sits this striking three-storey Georgian house which has been given a contemporary overhaul. There are two contrasting dining rooms: one in the original part of the house with all the period features; the other more modern and shiny and encased in a glass extension. There's a funky basement bar, plus rooms upstairs and a garden for private parties. The Indian food adds modern twists to its conventional foundations. The menu is more seasonally based than many but it is also more expensive. The saffron prawns are good, the grilled section is worth exploring and there are interesting teas; but a little less pretentiousness all round wouldn't be a bad thing.

Gun

Gastropub 🍺

P1

Canary Wharf
27 Coldharbour ✉ E14 9NS
✆ (020) 7515 5222
www.thegundocklands.com

⊖ Blackwall (DLR)
Closed 25-26 December

Menu £18 (lunch) – Carte £28/49

The 18C Gun may have had a 21C makeover but that doesn't mean it has forgotten its roots: its association with Admiral Lord Nelson, links to smugglers and ties to the river are all celebrated in its oil paintings and displays of assorted weaponry. The dining room and the style of service are both fairly smart and ceremonial, yet The Gun is a pub where this level of formality seems appropriate. Dockers have now been replaced by bankers, the majority of whom rarely venture beyond the 35-day aged steak. This is a shame as the menu cleverly combines relatively ambitious dishes such as game or John Dory with more traditional local specialities like eel and oysters. Even the dessert menu offers a mix, from soufflés to stewed plums.

Plateau

Modern European ✗✗

P1

Canary Wharf   ⊖ Canary Wharf
Canada Place (4th floor), Canada Square ⊠ E14 5ER   Closed
℘ (020) 7715 7100   25 December,
www.plateaurestaurant.co.uk   1 January and Sunday

Menu £28 – Carte £39/55

In a building that wouldn't look out of place in Manhattan is a restaurant that harks back to a time when bankers ruled the world. This striking 1970s retro designed room is an impressive open-plan space and its dramatic glass walls and ceilings make the surrounding monolithic office blocks seem strangely attractive. There are two choices: the Grill where, as the name suggests, the choice is from rotisserie meats and classic grilled dishes, or the formal restaurant beyond it, which comes with more comfortable surroundings. Here, the range is more eclectic and dishes are constructed with more global influences. They also come in ample sizes, though, so ignore the enthusiastic selling of the side dishes.

Quadrato

Italian ✗✗✗

P1

Canary Wharf   ⊖ Canary Wharf
Westferry Circus ⊠ E14 8RS
℘ (020) 7510 1999
www.fourseasons.com/canarywharf

Menu £39 – Carte £37/53

Grumbling that a restaurant within a Four Seasons Hotel in Canary Wharf is a little too corporate in its look is like protesting about all the grockles in a Torquay tea room. Granted, most customers are tied and jacketed, but it is still a comfortable, well run room whose size is made more manageable by its subdivision into four smaller sections – but do ask for a table either facing the exposed glass-fronted kitchen or overlooking the terrace and river. The kitchen helps itself to plenty of luxury ingredients and uses them in dishes that reflect styles and flavours from all parts of Italy; portions are generous and clearly much care goes into the preparation. Sunday brunches draw in the crowds from an easterly direction.

Roka Canary Wharf

Japanese ✗✗

P1

Canary Wharf
4 Park Pavilion (1st Floor) ✉ E14 5FW
☎ (020) 7636 5228
www.rokarestaurant.com

⊖ Canary Wharf
Closed Christmas –
booking essential

Carte £35/65

AC
VISA
MC
AE
DC

London's second Roka restaurant sits in the shadow of Canary Wharf Tower, still the UK's tallest building, and the first thing to hit you, once you've actually found the entrance, is a wall of sound. This is a big, open and perennially busy affair, with tightly packed tables which are usually occupied by large groups of City folk – and is not somewhere for a quiet dinner à deux. The menu follows the format of the Charlotte Street branch by offering a wide selection of mostly contemporary Japanese dishes. The easiest option is to head straight for one of the tasting menus which offer a balanced picture of what the food is all about. The robata grill is the centrepiece of the kitchen's operation – the lamb chops are particularly good.

Palmerston

Traditional 🍺

O2

East Dulwich
91 Lordship Ln ✉ SE22 8EP
☎ (020) 8693 1629
www.thepalmerston.net

⊖ East Dulwich (rail).

Menu £16 (lunch) – Carte £25/32

☼
VISA
MC
AE

It's not just for the locals – those passing through for a visit to the Horniman Museum or Dulwich Picture Gallery must also be pleased to have somewhere so welcoming in which to extend their stay in SE22. You can sit anywhere, although there is a section at the back with wood panelling and a mosaic floor which they call 'the dining room'. The menus tend to evolve on a monthly basis, with influences ranging from the Med to Asia. The bread is good, which usually augurs well and, refreshingly, the dishes come with just the ingredients described on the menu. Add a well-priced weekday menu and a host of engaging young staff and it's little wonder the pub attracts such a wide range of ages, which in turn creates a pleasant atmosphere.

Inside

P2

Modern European ✗✗

Greenwich
19 Greenwich South St. ✉ SE10 8NW
✆ (020) 8265 5060
www.insiderestaurant.co.uk

⊖ Greenwich (DLR)
Closed 24 December-2 January,
Sunday dinner and Monday

Menu £18 (weekday lunch)/23 – Carte dinner £21/26

A/C
VISA
MC
AE

The advantage of having an unremarkable façade is that it dampens unrealistic expectations. Indeed, 'Inside' was so named because the chef and his fellow owners had very little money when they opened, so wisely concentrated on the interior. With seating for just under forty, the room is tidy, comfortable and uncluttered, although it does take a few diners to generate an atmosphere. On offer is an appealingly priced set menu, elements of which change every fortnight. Dishes are attractively presented, relatively elaborate in their makeup and clearly prepared with care; most of the influences come from within Europe but staples do include the chicken and coriander spring rolls. There's also a decent choice of wine for under £25.

Rivington Grill

P2

British ✗

Greenwich
178 Greenwich High Rd. ✉ SE10 8NN
✆ (020) 8293 9270
www.rivingtongreenwich.co.uk

⊖ Greenwich (DLR)
Closed 25-26 December,
Monday and lunch
Tuesday-Wednesday

Carte £25/39

It's open from breakfast until late and the menu changes every two weeks so they can introduce seasonal specials; the 'on toast' section is a local favourite and includes Welsh rarebit or devilled kidneys. Steaks are from Scotland; the prosperous can upgrade their fish and chips to lobster and chips; the puds are satisfyingly rich. The wine list is sensibly priced and includes beers and Somerset brandies. It's spread over two floors, with the ground floor being the more casual; it attracts a younger, hipper crowd than the Shoreditch branch and has a more local feel; it also gets swamped with look-alikes whenever there's a pop siren playing the O2 arena. Tables of up to four people can get a discount at the next door cinema.

331

Kennington Tandoori

Indian ✗✗

N2

Kennington
313 Kennington Rd ✉ SE11 4QE
✆ (020) 7735 9247
www.kenningtontandoori.com

⊖ Kennington
Booking advisable

Menu £18/28 – Carte £22/40

Known affectionately as KT, the Hoque family's long-standing Indian restaurant was reinvigorated a couple of years ago when their son Kowsar took over. He brought the look up-to-date and then set about raising the standards all round. The result is that he now has a very pleasant neighbourhood restaurant that is clearly a cut above the norm. The menu is made up of recognisable classics and old favourites but the kitchen's skill is evident in the execution. Vegetarian dishes stand out and everything is made from scratch, from the chutneys to the kulfi. Mind you, many of the regulars, who make up the vast majority of customers – and include plenty of cricket fans and politicians – don't even bother with the menu and just ask for their 'usual'.

Lobster Pot

French ✗

N2

Kennington
3 Kennington Ln. ✉ SE11 4RG
✆ (020) 7582 5556
www.lobsterpotrestaurant.co.uk

⊖ Kennington
Closed 24 December-3 January,
Sunday and Monday

Carte £38/53

Ignore the fairly shabby exterior, dive straight in and you'll think you've stumbled onto a French film set. Fish tanks, portholes, the cries of seagulls and the hoots of ferries…the place has the lot and it's hard to avoid getting caught up in the exuberance of it all. It's no surprise that it's also all about fish. The chef-owner, from Vannes in Brittany, goes to Billingsgate each morning and he knows what he's doing: his menu is classical and appetising, with fruits de mer, plenty of oysters, a lobster section and daily specials on the blackboard. Be sure to make room for the crêpes, which are great. It's not cheap but it is an experience. Underlining the family nature of the business, the son has opened a brasserie next door.

Narrow

01

Limehouse
44 Narrow St ✉ E14 8DP
☎ (020) 7592 7950
www.gordonramsay.com

⊖ Limehouse (DLR).
Booking essential

Menu £22 (lunch) – Carte £24/36

Despite receiving some negative publicity a while back, when it was revealed that certain dishes in Gordon Ramsay's pubs are prepared in a central kitchen, The Narrow does not seem to be any less frenetic. This 'logistical cooking', as they describe it, is used for dishes requiring a lengthy cooking process, such as the slow-roasted pork belly or beef braised in Guinness. However it gets there, the food on the plate is tasty, seasonal and laudably British, be it devilled kidneys, Morecambe Bay brown shrimps, a chicken pie or a sherry trifle. What is also certain is that no other London pub has better views, as one would expect from a converted dockmaster's house; just be sure to request a table in the very appealing conservatory.

Galvin Café a Vin ☺

01

French

Spitalfields
35 Spital Sq. (entrance on Bishops Sq.) ✉ E1 6DY
☎ (020) 7299 0404
www.galvinrestaurants.com

⊖ Liverpool Street
Closed
25 December

Carte £24/30

In the same building as La Chapelle, but with a separate entrance around the corner, is this simpler but no less professionally run operation from the Galvin brothers. The room may not have the grandeur of next door but what is does offer is classic French bistro food at very appealing prices. Snails, confit of duck and rum baba are all here — tasty and satisfying dishes to evoke memories of French holidays and have you reaching for the Gauloises. So, if you want the fillet or the loin, go next door; if you're happy with the leg or bavette then come here. The place is loud, fun and friendly, and the atmosphere is helped along by a cheerful team and a thoughtfully compiled wine list which is also well-priced.

Galvin La Chapelle ✿

01

Spitalfields
35 Spital Sq. ⊠ E1 6DY
✆ (020) 7299 0400
www.galvinrestaurants.com

⊖ Liverpool Street
Closed dinner 24-26 December
and 1 January

Menu £26 (lunch)/30 (early dinner) – Carte £32/51

Galvin La Chapelle

These days, it is rare to walk into a restaurant in London and be taken back with the grandeur and sheer scale of a room. However, this venture from the Galvin Brothers, who have already proved themselves expert restaurateurs, is one that will dazzle the most jaded of diner. The Victorian splendour of St Botolph's Hall, with its vaulted ceiling, arched windows and marble pillars, lends itself effortlessly to its role as a glamorous restaurant. There are tables in booths, in the wings or in the middle of the action and those who like some comfort with their food will not be disappointed. It is also a fitting backdrop to the cooking, which is, in essence, bourgeois French but with a sophisticated edge, which means it is immensely satisfying. There are no unnecessary fripperies, just three courses of reassuringly familiar combinations with the emphasis on bold, clear flavours. Add in a service team who are a well-drilled, well-versed outfit and you have somewhere that will be part of the restaurant landscape for years to come.

First Course	*Main Course*	*Dessert*
• Lasagne of crab with velouté of girolles. • Velouté of broad beans with smoked duck and pea shoots.	• Tagine of pigeon with aubergine purée and harissa sauce. • Tranche of calves liver, Lyonnaise onions, bacon and pommes mousseline.	• Chilled Valhrona chocolate fondant, banana and yoghurt ice cream and fresh honeycomb. • Toasted hazelnut parfait, lime confiture.

Hawksmoor

Beef specialities ✗

01

Spitalfields
157 Commercial St. ✉ E1 6BJ
✆ (020) 7247 7392
www.thehawksmoor.com

⊖ Shoreditch
▶ **Plan XVI**
Closed 1 week Christmas and Sunday
dinner – booking essential

Carte £40/60

A/C
VISA
MC
AE

Hawksmoor was a 17C architect and student of Sir Christopher Wren so you could expect this steakhouse to be found in a building of note rather than in this modern edifice of little aesthetic value. Inside is equally unremarkable but no matter because this place is all about beef and, more specifically, British beef which has been hung for 35 days. It comes from Longhorn cattle raised by the Ginger Pig Co in the heart of the North Yorkshire Moors and the quality and depth of flavour is exceptional. Just choose your preferred weight – go for 400g if you're hungry. Starters and puds don't come close in quality but again, no matter, because when you've got some fantastic red meat in front of you, all you need is a mate and a bottle of red wine.

Owl & Pussycat

British 🍺

K3

Spitalfields
34 Redchurch St ✉ E2 7DP
✆ (020) 3487 0088
www.owlandpussycatshoreditch.com

⊖ Shoreditch.
▶ **Plan XVI**
Closed 25-26 December,
1 January and bank holidays

Carte £25/43

☀
VISA
MC
AE

As they did with The Fellow in King's Cross, the owners like to open pubs at the embryonic stage of a neighbourhood's gentrification. This was a run down East End boozer called The Crown which now has a raggedly modish look, with ironic touches of Victoriana to match the Edward Lear name. The ground floor is for drinkers and snackers; dining is done upstairs, where a concise but constantly changing and appealingly stout British menu is offered in the evening. Pork terrines, a crayfish cocktail or even oysters and Guinness may be followed by a Barnsley chop or a proper pie. Their puds, like lavender rice pudding and rhubarb crumble, are the kind that should be compulsory in all pubs. Bread and filtered water are provided gratis.

St John Bread and Wine 🐶

K3

Spitalfields
94-96 Commercial St ✉ E1 6LZ
☎ (020) 7251 0848
www.stjohnbreadandwine.com

⊖ Shoreditch
▶ **Plan XVI**
Closed Christmas-New
Year and bank holidays

Carte £23/29

AlC
☼
VISA
MC
AE
O

Less famous but by no means less loved than its sibling, this English version of a classic comptoir is the sort of place we would all like to have at the end of our road. Just the aroma as you enter is enough to get the appetite going. As the name suggests, this is a wine shop and a bakery but also a local restaurant. The menu changes twice a day and depends on what's in season; the Britishness of its ingredients and its promotion of forgotten recipes will enthuse everyone, not just culinary genealogists. But it's not all man-food like roast pig spleen or 'raw Angus'; there are lighter dishes such as plaice with samphire; and the Eccles cakes are a must. From breakfast to supper, certain dishes are only ready at certain times, so do check first.

Les Trois Garcons

K3

Spitalfields
1 Club Row ✉ E1 6JX
☎ (020) 7613 1924
www.lestroisgarcons.com

⊖ Shoreditch
▶ **Plan XVI**
Closed 23 December-3 January,
Saturday lunch, Sunday dinner
and bank holidays

Menu £22/47

AlC
⟨̇⟩
VISA
MC
AE

The surrounding streets may be somewhat drab but the three friends (hence the name) who own this former pub are also antique dealers (hence the eccentric and exuberant decoration that resembles a theatrical props department). There are stuffed animals, beads, handbags and assorted objets d'art; heavy velvet curtains ensure that the lighting is dim and atmospheric. The kitchen, meanwhile, uses fairly classical French cooking techniques and flavour combinations, although the majority of ingredients are British. Menus change seasonally and presentation on the plate is neat and appetising. The early-in-the-week set menu is good value; the à la carte somewhat expensive. Service can occasionally veer from the efficient to the over-confident.

Canton Arms 🐸

N2

Stockwell
177 South Lambeth Rd ✉ SW8 1XP
☎ (020) 7582 8710
www.cantonarms.com

⊖ Stockwell.
*Closed Christmas-New Year,
Monday lunch, Sunday dinner
and bank holidays*

Carte £19/27

🌂
VISA
🅜🅒
⊙

Its appreciative audience prove that the demand for fresh, honest, seasonal food is not just limited to smart squares in Chelsea or Islington. The oval-shaped bar dominates the room, with the front half busy with drinkers and the back laid up for diners, although it's all very relaxed and you can eat where you want. The kitchen's experience in places like the Anchor & Hope and Great Queen Street is obvious on their menu which features rustic, earthy British food, of the sort that suits this environment so well. Lunch could be a kipper or tripe and chips; even a reinvented toasted sandwich. Dinner sees a short, no-nonsense menu offering perhaps braised venison or grilled haddock, with daily specials like steak and kidney pie for two.

Smith's of Wapping

O1

Wapping
22 Wapping High St ✉ E1W 1NJ
☎ (020) 7488 3456
www.smithsbrasserie.com

⊖ Wapping
*Closed Sunday dinner –
booking advisable*

Menu £25 (lunch) – Carte £33/60

A/C
VISA
🅜🅒
AE

Having been providing seafood to the burghers of Essex for over 50 years, the Smith family have finally got around to opening a second branch. In 2011 they joined forces with a local restaurateur to open this large, contemporary brasserie looking out over the bobbing houseboats on the river and providing great views of Tower Bridge. The menu is a lengthy but appealing read and the kitchen is unapologetically traditional in its approach. Subsequently the best dishes are old favourites like deep-fried calamari from Cornwall, whole dressed Scottish crab or Dover sole meunière, served on or off the bone. Lobster thermidor is proving equally popular and they'll cook your fish however you wish. They also do a decent pudding.

Wapping Food

01

Wapping
Wapping Wall ✉ E1W 3SG
℘ (020) 7680 2080
www.thewappingproject.com

⊖ **Wapping**
Closed 24 December-3 January,
Sunday dinner and bank holidays

Carte £25/41

What does a former theatre director with a passion for food do when looking for a change? She buys a disused Victorian former hydraulic power station, spends two years doing it up and then opens it as the Wapping Project, a bringing together of a restaurant and an art gallery. The two functions marry perfectly: you sit among the old turbines and enjoy robust dishes fashioned from what suppliers have brought in that day. This could be mackerel with fennel, a ham hock terrine, Brecon lamb shank or panna cotta; all served by an enthusiastic team who know their onions. To make the most of your visit, be sure to take in the artwork before or after your meal; it could take the form of an installation, an exhibition or a performance.

Cafe Spice Namaste ☺

01

Whitechapel
16 Prescot St. ✉ E1 8AZ
℘ (020) 7488 9242
www.cafespice.co.uk

⊖ **Tower Hill**
Closed 25 December-2 January,
Saturday lunch, Sunday
and bank holidays

Carte £27/33

Cyrus Todiwala's contribution to Indian cuisine and the hospitality industry was recognised in 2010 when he was appointed an OBE. Café Spice Namaste opened back in 1995 and was where the dining public first became aware of his ability. The bright decoration of this former magistrate's court may not be quite so effervescent these days but the food remains just as fresh and vibrant. Many of the ingredients used are from within the British Isles and the cooking influences are spread across India; the Parsee specialities are particularly memorable. There's a plethora of menus to look through but don't hesitate to ask Cyrus' wife Pervin for guidance; she's a charming hostess who runs a tight ship and keeps an eye on everything.

Whitechapel Gallery Dining Room

Italian influences ✗

K3

Whitechapel
77-82 Whitechapel High St. ⊠ E1 7QX
✆ (020) 7522 7896
www.whitechapelgallery.org/dining-room

⊖ Aldgate East
▶ **Plan XVI**
Closed Christmas-New Year,
Monday and dinner Sunday
and Tuesday – booking advisable

Carte £24/30

A/C

VISA

M/C

AE

D

Angela Hartnett oversees things here in her role as a consultant chef and she's made some positive changes. Out went the set menu and in came greater flexibility that is far more appropriate to an informal gallery setting. The menu is divided into 'nibbles', 'small plates' and 'bigger plates' and most of the dishes are of European provenance, with the Med supplying plenty of influences, in dishes like rump of lamb with Niçoise salad. The Whitechapel Gallery was founded in 1901 and is best known for exhibiting Picasso's 'Guernica'. It underwent a major refit in 2009, when it expanded into the former library next door and created this very sweet restaurant. It's a bright, well-lit room, with tightly packed tables.

Bib Gourmand ☻
indicates our inspectors'
favourites for good value.

South-West London

Meandering like a silver snake, **The Thames** coils serenely through south-west London, adding definition to the area's much-heralded middle-class enclaves and leafy suburbs. It's the focal point to the annual **university boat race** from **Putney** to **Mortlake,** and it serves as the giant glass pond attractively backing countless bank-side pubs. This area has long been regarded as the cosy bourgeois side of town, though within its postcode prowls the lively and eclectic **Brixton,** whose buzzing street markets and lauded music venues such as the Academy and the Fridge add an urban lustre and vibrant edge.

In most people's minds, though, south-west London finds its true colours in the beautiful terrace view from the top of **Richmond Hill,** as the river bends majestically through the meadows below. Or in the smart **Wimbledon Village,** its independent boutiques ranged prettily along its own hill, with the open spaces of the Common for a back garden. Or, again, in the Italianate architecture that makes **Chiswick House** and grounds a little corner of the Mediterranean close to the Great West Road.

Green space is almost as prolific in this zone as the streets of Victorian and Edwardian villas. **Richmond Park** is the largest royal park in the whole of London and teems with kite flyers, cyclists and deer – though not necessarily in that order. From here, round a

southerly bend in the river, delightful grounds surround **Ham House,** which celebrated its 400th birthday in 2010, although not so excessively as during the seventeenth century when it was home to Restoration court life. Head slightly north to **Kew Gardens** and its world famous 300 acres can now be viewed from above – the treetop walkway, opened in 2008, takes you 60 feet up to offer some breath-taking views. Just across the river from here is another from the historical hit-list: **Syon Park,** which boasts water meadows still grazed by cattle, giving it a distinctly rural aspect. Syon House is considered one of architect Robert Adam's finest works; it certainly appealed to Queen Victoria, who spent much of her young life here. Up the road in bourgeoning Brentford, two unique museums bring in hordes of the curious: the Musical Museum includes a huge Wurlitzer theatre organ (get lucky and watch it being played), while almost next door, the Kew Bridge Steam Museum shows off all things steamy on a grand scale, including massive beam engines which pumped London's water for over a century.

Hammersmith may be known for its bustling Broadway and flyover, but five minutes' walk from here is the Upper Mall, which has iconic riverside pubs and Kelmscott House, the last home of artistic visionary William Morris: down in the basement and coach house are

D. Chapuis / MICHELIN

impressive memorabilia related to his life plus changing exhibitions of designs and drawings. From here, it's just a quick jaunt across **Hammersmith Bridge** and down the arrow-straight Castelnau to the Wetland Centre in Barnes, which for ten years has lured wildlife to within screeching distance of the West End. **Barnes** has always revelled in its village-like identity – it juts up like an isolated peninsula into the Thames and boasts yummy boutiques and well-known restaurants. The Bulls Head pub in Lonsdale Road has featured some of the best jazz in London for half a century.

In a more easterly direction, the urbanised areas of **Clapham** and **Battersea** have re-established themselves as desirable places to live over the last decade. **Clapham Common** is considered prime southwest London turf, to the extent that its summer music festivals are highly prized. It's ringed by good pubs and restaurants, too. Battersea used to be famous for its funfair, but now the peace pagoda in the park lends it a more serene light. And if you're after serenity on a hot day, then a cool dip in the wondrous **Tooting** Lido is just the thing.

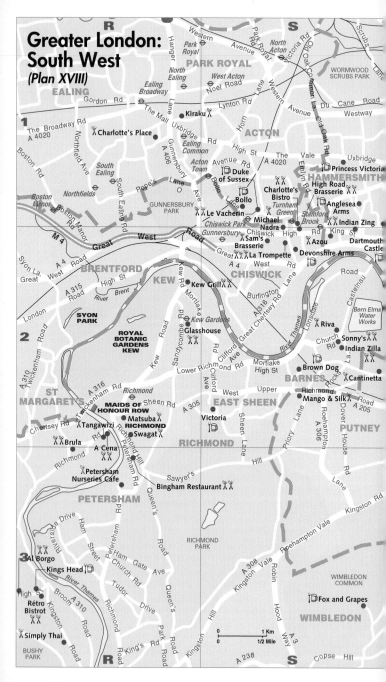

Greater London: South West
(Plan XVIII)

EALING

PARK ROYAL

North Acton

West Acton

WORMWOOD SCRUBS PARK

Ealing Broadway

ACTON

Kiraku ✗

Charlotte's Place ✗

South Ealing

Princess Victoria

Duke of Sussex

HAMMERSMITH

Charlotte's Bistro ✗✗

High Road Brasserie ✗✗

Bollo ✗

Le Vacherin ✗

Anglesea Arms

GUNNERSBURY PARK

Michael Nadra ✗

Indian Zing ✗✗

Sam's Brasserie ✗

Azou ✗

Dartmouth Castle

BRENTFORD

La Trompette ✗✗✗

Devonshire Arms

CHISWICK

Kew Grill ✗✗

KEW

SYON PARK

ROYAL BOTANIC GARDENS KEW

Kew Gardens ✗

Glasshouse ✗✗

Riva ✗

Sonny's ✗

Indian Zilla ✗✗

Brown Dog

BARNES

Cantinetta ✗

ST MARGARET'S

EAST SHEEN

Mango & Silk ✗

Victoria

PUTNEY

MAIDS OF HONOUR ROW

Tangawizi ✗

Matsuba ✗

RICHMOND

Swagat ✗

A Cena ✗✗

Brula ✗✗

Petersham Nurseries Cafe ✗

Bingham Restaurant ✗✗

PETERSHAM

RICHMOND PARK

Al Borgo ✗✗

Kings Head

Rétro Bistrot ✗

RICHMOND PARK

WIMBLEDON COMMON

Fox and Grapes

Simply Thai ✗

BUSHY PARK

WIMBLEDON

0   1 Km
0   1/2 Mile

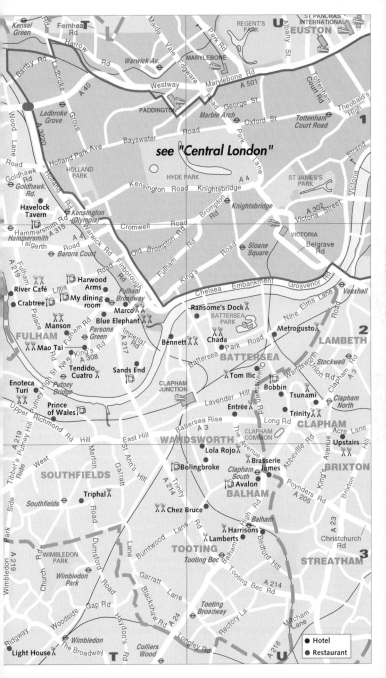

see *"Central London"*

● Hotel
● Restaurant

343

Bollo

Traditional 🍺

Acton Green   ⊖ Chiswick Park.
13-15 Bollo Ln. ✉ W4 5LR
☎ (020) 8994 6037
www.thebollohouse.co.uk

Carte £20/31

The Bollo is a large, handsome Victorian pub whose glass cupola and oak panelling give it some substance and personality in this age of the generic pub makeover. Tables and sofas are scattered around in a relaxed, sit-where-you-want way and the menu changes as ingredients come and go. The kitchen appeals to its core voters by always including a sufficient number of pub classics like the Bollo Burger, the haddock or fishcakes. But there is also a discernible southern Mediterranean influence to the menu, with regular appearances from the likes of chorizo, tzatziki, bruschetta and hummus. This is a pub where there's always either a promotion or an activity, whether that's the '50% off a main course' Monday or the Wednesday quiz nights.

Duke of Sussex

Mediterranean 🍺

Acton Green   ⊖ Chiswick Park.
75 South Par. ✉ W4 5LF   Closed dinner 25 December
☎ (020) 8742 8801   and Monday lunch
www.realpubs.co.uk

Carte £23/28

Perhaps it's part of the plan but the Duke of Sussex seems like a typical London pub, even from the front bar, but step through into the dining room and you'll be in what was once a variety theatre from the time when this was a classic gin palace, complete with proscenium arch, glass ceiling and chandeliers. If that wasn't unusual enough, you could then find yourself eating cured meats or fabada, as the menu has a strong Spanish influence. Traditionalists can still get their steak pies and treacle tart but it's worth being more adventurous and trying the sardines, the paella and the crema Catalana. This is a fun, enthusiastically run and bustling pub and the kitchen's enthusiasm is palpable. On Mondays it's BYO; Sunday is quiz night.

Le Vacherin

French ✕✕

Acton Green
76-77 South Par. ✉ W4 5LF
✆ (020) 8742 2121
www.levacherin.com

⊖ Chiswick Park
Closed 25 December and Sunday dinner
– (dinner only and lunch Saturday-Sunday)

Menu £20 (weekdays)/35 – Carte £20/40

A/C
VISA
MC
AE
①

Le Vacherin calls itself a bistro but, with its brown leather banquette seating, mirrors and belle époque prints, it feels more like a brasserie, and quite a smart one at that. The most important element of the operation is the appealing menu of French classics which rarely changes, largely because they don't need to but also because the regulars wouldn't allow it. The checklist includes oeufs en cocotte, escargots, confit of duck and crème brûlée. Beef is something of a speciality, whether that's the côte de boeuf, the rib-eye or the chateaubriand. Portions are sensible, flavours distinct and ingredients good. The only thing missing in terms of authenticity are some insouciant French staff and a little Piaf playing in the background.

SOUTH-WEST ▶ PLAN XVIII

Avalon

Gastropub 🍺▯

Balham
16 Balham Hill ✉ SW12 9EB
✆ (020) 8675 8613
www.theavalonlondon.com

⊖ Clapham South.
Closed 25-26 December and 1 January
– booking advisable

Carte £25/30

🌿
A/C
'◌'
☀
VISA
MC
AE

So Avalon really does exist…and it comes in the shape of a huge, atmospheric pub topped with an illuminated sign that makes it hard to miss on Balham Hill. Sir Edward Coley Burne-Jones prints add a suitably mythical edge to the aesthetic of the long bar and here you can order the sort of snacks that go well with a pint. Head through to the tiled and characterful rear dining room for their seasonal menu which is of the sort to appeal to a broad constituency. You'll find everything from a pie of the day and steaks to dishes of a more Mediterranean persuasion like whole grilled bream with caponata or gnocchi with porcini mushrooms. Once the team warm up, service is pleasant and the large summer terrace at the back is a great feature.

Brasserie James

Modern European ✗

U3

Balham
47 Balham Hill ✉ SW12 9DR
✆ (020) 8772 0057
www.brasseriejames.com

⊖ **Clapham South**
Closed 23-30 December

Carte £28/36

If you have the courage to open your own restaurant, especially in times of economic anxiety, then no one will begrudge your naming it eponymously. Craig James is a former chef in the Conran/D&D empire and he has brought his experience to bear in the more relaxed environs of a neighbourhood joint. It's on a site previously home to a Pakistani restaurant that was itself quite a local institution and he's given it a top-to-toe revamp. There's something for everyone on the menu, from seasonal oysters and the popular moules à la crème, to daily fish from the market, quality meats, pasta and good old-fashioned puds. There are good value set price menus; brunch at weekends and sensibly priced wines by the bottle, glass or carafe.

Harrison's

Mediterranean ✗

U3

Balham
15-19 Bedford Hill ✉ SW12 9EX
✆ (020) 8675 6900
www.harrisonsbalham.co.uk

⊖ **Balham**
Closed 24-28 December

Carte £30/39

Following the success of Sam's Brasserie in Chiswick, owner Sam Harrison took over what was Soho House Bar and Grill and turned it into another all-day brasserie. It provides a lesson for all neighbourhood restaurants in the importance of being a focal point for the local community: it is open from breakfast until late and is as welcoming to those just in for a coffee as those wanting a three course meal. The food is uncomplicated, fresh and satisfying, whether that's a cheeseburger, tuna Niçoise, Cumberland sausages or a fishcake. Brunch is served at weekends; they offer a kids' menu, as well as a good value weekday set menu; and there's a decent wine selection. It's hardly surprisingly the locals have embraced the place.

Lamberts

Traditional ✖

U3

Balham
2 Station Par. ✉ SW12 9AZ
✆ (020) 8675 2233
www.lambertsrestaurant.com

⊖ Balham
Closed 24-26 December, 1 January,
Sunday dinner and Monday – (dinner
only and lunch Saturday-Sunday)

Menu £20 (midweek) – Carte £27/34

A/C
VISA
MC

Mr Lambert and his eponymous restaurant have succeeded by offering the locals exactly what they want: relaxed surroundings, hospitable service and tasty, seasonal food. The menu is updated each month and small suppliers have been sought out. The cooking is quite British in style and has a satisfying wholesomeness to it; Sunday's ribs of Galloway beef or legs of Salt Marsh lamb are hugely popular. Equal thought and passion have gone into the commendably priced wine list, which includes some favourites offered in 300ml decanters. Other nice touches include filtered water delivered gratis and velvety truffles brought with the coffee. The owner's enthusiasm has rubbed off on his team, for whom nothing is too much trouble.

Brown Dog 🐶

Gastropub 🍽🍺

S2

Barnes
28 Cross St ✉ SW13 0AP
✆ (020) 8392 2200
www.thebrowndog.co.uk

⊖ Barnes Bridge (Rail)
Closed 25-26 December

Carte £20/30

VISA
MC
AE

Thankfully, changes of ownership don't appear to mean much here – perhaps you really can't teach an old dog new tricks – because The Brown Dog remains a terrific neighbourhood pub and the locals clearly love it just the way it is. Mind you, this pretty Victorian pub is so well hidden in the maze of residential streets that it's a wonder any new customers ever find it anyway. The look fuses the traditional with the modern and service is bubbly and enthusiastic. Jugs of iced water arrive without prompting and the cleverly concise menu changes regularly. A lightly spiced crab salad or pint of prawns could be followed by a succulent rump of lamb, while puddings not only display a terrific lightness of touch but are also very commendably priced.

Indian Zilla

S2

Indian ✗✗

Barnes

2-3 Rocks Ln. ⊠ SW13 0DB
✆ (020) 8878 3989
www.indianzilla.co.uk

Menu £15 (lunch) – Carte £27/36

A/C
📷
☼
VISA
MC
AE
◑

Judging by the crowds, Barnes' locals are clearly delighted that their district was chosen as the third location for this bourgeoning little group, following on from the success of Indian Zing and Indian Zest. The bright restaurant has a lovely buzz to it and the young, eager-to-please service team are very attentive. The new-wave Indian cooking is surprisingly light yet full of flavour, with many of the dishes using organic ingredients. Whilst a few old favourites are offered, it is the more delicate options that really stand out, such as lobster Balchao and specialities from the owner's home province of Maharashtra, like vegetable Bhanvala. The breads are super as is the lemon and ginger rice, and be sure to end with the Tandoori figs.

Riva

S2

Italian ✗

Barnes

169 Church Rd. ⊠ SW13 9HR
✆ (020) 8748 0434

Closed 3 weeks August,
10 days Christmas-New Year,
Saturday lunch and bank holidays

Carte £32/56

A/C
☼
VISA
MC
AE

Customer loyalty is the sine qua non of any successful restaurant; those seeking guidance on how to build it should get down to Barnes and learn from Andrea Riva. His secret is to shower so much attention on his regulars that all other diners sit imagining the day when they will be treated in the same way – when he will tell them what he's going to cook especially for them. That could be some milk-fed lamb, game, suckling pig or risotto; all expertly rendered using tip-top, seasonal ingredients. While you wait for graduation, you'll be served by a friendly young female team and still get to enjoy some gutsy, flavoursome food. Andrea is also a keen wine collector so if you can talk oenology it could improve your chances of joining the club.

Sonny's

Modern European ✗✗

Barnes

Closed Sunday dinner and
bank holidays

94 Church Rd ✉ SW13 0DQ
✆ (020) 8748 0393
www.sonnys.co.uk

Menu £17/20 (midweek) – Carte £23/35

A/C
🕰
VISA
MC
AE

When restaurants try to be all things to all people, they usually come a cropper, but Sonny's has successfully managed the task of being a deli, bar-café and restaurant and, as such, has firmly established itself as a much valued local landmark. It has also reinvested regularly over the years so that its upkeep is unimpeachable; and the owner's private art collection has added to its personality. The restaurant menu is full of seasonal goodness, like pot-roasted pheasant to warm the bones in winter or tortellini of crab for lighter months. This being Not-the-West-End means portions are generously sized and there's a very smartly priced set menu for midweek. Meanwhile, staff display a warmth and confidence that belie their youthful looks.

Bennett

British ✗✗

Battersea

🚇 Clapham Junction (rail)
Closed Sunday dinner

7-9 Battersea Sq. ✉ SW11 3PA
✆ (020) 7223 5545
www.bennettsbrasserie.com

Carte £29/36

🏠
VISA
MC
AE

It makes sense that if yours is one of the first restaurants to open in an area not overly-encumbered by competition, then you'll want it to do more than just lunch and dinner. Bennett, so called because that was the name etched on the wall from the time when it was a coal merchant's, also serves breakfast and afternoon tea and even doubles as a wine shop. The brasserie is quite a smart number, with further seating at the marble-topped bar. The menu continues the theme of appealing to a broad constituency by offering everything from brasserie classics and a large seafood selection to traditional British staples and nursery favourites. The cooking delivers what it promises and you can spend as much or as little as you want.

Bolingbroke

British 🍺

U3

Battersea
174 Northcote Rd ✉ SW11 6RE
✆ (020) 7228 4040
www.thebolingbroke.com

⊖ Clapham Junction (rail).
Closed 25-28 December

Carte £21/34

The influx of professionals with young families is such that this end of Northcote Road is now known as 'Nappy Valley'. A Cath Kidston shop? Check. Artisan food markets? Check. Antique emphoria? Check. Now it's time for a decent pub and here's where The Bolingbroke comes in. Its glass roof makes the fairly small dining room feel bigger, although the romantically inclined should ask for the table under the stairs. The menus change weekly, with more choice at dinner. British influences lead the way, from the asparagus and cheddar tart, to the lamb shoulder and apple crumble. Steaks and burgers are perennials but you'll also find additional Euro stars like ravioli and a Niçoise salad. Unsurprisingly, there's also a children's menu.

Chada

Thai 🍴🍴

U2

Battersea
208-210 Battersea Park Rd. ✉ SW11 4ND
✆ (020) 7622 2209
www.chadathai.com

Closed Sunday and bank holidays –
(dinner only)

Carte £19/43

Chada, whose positively resplendent façade marks it out on Battersea Park Road, is still going strong after 20 years, although it doesn't face huge competition. A striking carved Buddha dominates the simply dressed room but check out the owner's gilded headdress, displayed in a cabinet, which she uses for festivals. This may never be the busiest restaurant around but the welcome is always warm, the service polite and endearing and the Thai cooking satisfying and keenly priced. The menu is still a very long affair but it's easy to navigate through and the seafood selection is an undoubted highlight. Several dishes can be made with a choice of chicken, duck, prawn or vegetables; portions are generous and presentation is appealing.

Entrée

U2

Battersea
2 Battersea Rise ✉ SW11 1ED
✆ (020) 7223 5147
www.entreebattersea.co.uk

⊖ Clapham Junction (rail)
Closed 24-28 December –
(dinner only and lunch
Saturday-Sunday)

Carte £29/36

A/C
☼
VISA
MC
AE

The name doesn't quite fit as it implies a devotion to all things French and a degree of pretentiousness that is thankfully absent. In reality they have gone more for a casual bistro look which, along with an intimate basement bar and weekend pianist, appears to have hit the right note with the locals. The style of food is a little harder to categorise: the attractively priced menu offers a selection of French classics together with dishes of a more modern European persuasion, as well as other choices that could be considered as being more from the '80s. It is this third section which actually provides some of the highlights, such as the scallop and crab lasagne. Haunch of venison and the ubiquitous pork belly are also popular choices.

Lola Rojo

U3

Battersea
78 Northcote Rd ✉ SW11 6QL
✆ (020) 7350 2262
www.lolarojo.net

⊖ Clapham Junction (rail)
Closed 25-26 December –
booking essential

Menu £9 (weekday lunch) – Carte £22/31

Northcote Road hosts a plethora of restaurants but few are as fun as this lively Spanish eatery. There's no denying the layout is a little cramped but the all-white look, dotted with splashes of red, makes it feel fresh. The owner-chef comes from Valencia so paella is a sure thing but other Catalan specialities are worth seeking out, such as the tomato bread, the creamy spinach with pine nuts, various salt-cod and shellfish dishes and, to finish, crema Catalana. Despite the volume of customers the kitchen delivers dishes promptly and consistently while the serving team just about keep up; 3 or 4 tapas per person should do it and there's an affordable wine list to lift the mood even more. It's little wonder the locals can't get enough.

Metrogusto

U2

Italian ✗

Battersea
153 Battersea Park Rd. ✉ SW8 4BX
✆ (020) 7720 0204
www.metrogusto.co.uk

⊖ **Battersea Park** (rail)
Closed 25-26 December,
Easter and Sunday dinner

Carte £21/35

[A/C]
[VISA]
[MC]
[AE]

Ambro Ianeselli is one of London's most affable restaurateurs and his move from Islington back to his original Battersea base resulted in moans in the north and cheers in the south. This was once a pub and he's kept it uncluttered, although Metrogusto followers will recognise some of his modern art collection. They will also notice he's gone back to basics: the menu starts with 'morsels' such as delicious sweet and sour Sicilian aubergines, which can be followed by goat's cheese ravioli with a great walnut sauce or a generous helping of pappardelle with veal ragout and a decent panna cotta to finish. The food is simple and satisfying, matched with a fair range of wines from his homeland and his never-ending hospitality.

Ransome's Dock

U2

British ✗

Battersea
35-37 Parkgate Rd. ✉ SW11 4NP
✆ (020) 7223 1611
www.ransomesdock.co.uk

Closed Christmas, August bank
holiday and Sunday dinner

Carte £24/37

[⛱]
[🎿]
[VISA]
[MC]
[AE]
[①]

It's not just honest cooking and a great wine list that are responsible for the impending 20 year anniversary: owners Martin and Vanessa Lam's passion and palpable enjoyment have also contributed to the success. Their menu is underpinned by seasonality and careful sourcing: duck is from Devon; lamb from Elwy Valley; beef from Cornwall and fish from Essex day boats. They also know their butchery and have most beasts delivered whole, so you may find gutsy dishes like braised shin on the lunch menu. Martin is equally passionate about wine; not only is his wine list far-reaching and well-priced but he also hosts winemaker dinners. The converted warehouse has a relaxed feel and the terrace overlooking the canal is a great spot in summer.

Tom Ilić

Traditional 🍴

Battersea
123 Queenstown Rd. ✉ SW8 3RH
✆ (020) 7622 0555
www.tomilic.com

Closed Christmas, 1 week summer,
Monday, Sunday dinner
and Tuesday lunch –
booking essential

Menu £20/22 – Carte £29/38

A/C
VISA
MC
AE
①

Serbian Tom Ilić came to the UK 20 years ago, took a job as a dish washer before a planned career in engineering, developed an interest in food and now has his own restaurant. He chose the site formerly occupied by The Food Room and turned it into an unpretentious, neighbourly place with closely set tables and a semi-open kitchen. It's also in an area of Battersea that's played host to a few famous restaurants in its day. His menu is written in a refreshingly straightforward way. There's plenty of offal featured as well as lots of pork, something of a beloved national dish for Serbs. Flavours are far from shy but his cooking also displays a certain graft and clear respect for the ingredients; prices are kept realistic.

Upstairs

Modern European 🍴🍴

Brixton
89b Acre Ln. ✉ SW2 5TN
✆ (020) 7733 8855
www.upstairslondon.com

⊖ Clapham North
Closed 24 December-9 January, 8-18 April,
19 August-4 September, Sunday and
Monday – (dinner only)

Menu £32

VISA
MC
AE

At the risk of upsetting the locals - who clearly like the idea of having a hard-to-find, and thus almost secret, restaurant in their neighbourhood - you'll need to look for the buzzer on the side door next to the Opus coffee shop if you want to go Upstairs. You'll still be a little unsure as you climb the dark staircase, at least until you're greeted by the hospitable manager who'll offer you a drink in the bar; dining is then done on the next floor up. The set menu is a short but nicely balanced affair, with just three choices per course plus the occasional special; its also represents unquestionably decent value for money. The food is prepared with understanding and seasonal relevance; it is easy to eat, uncomplicated and flavoursome.

Charlotte's Bistro ⬤

S1

Modern European ✕✕

Chiswick
6 Turnham Green Terr ✉ W4 1QP
✆ (020) 8742 3590
www.charlottes.co.uk

⊖ **Turnham Green**
Booking advisable

Menu £16/26 (early dinner) – Carte £28/31

A/C

☀

VISA

MC

AE

Unlike some desirable London neighbourhoods, Chiswick has always had plenty of restaurants, so locals never feel the need to venture too far from home for dinner. This little sister to nearby Ealing's Charlotte's Place provides them with another pleasantly unpretentious option. A large bar takes up most of the front section and then it's a few steps up to the bright dining room with a glass roof. The menu changes regularly and has a European accent, with such dishes as crab and celeriac tian, cod brandade, pan-fried halloumi, rolled leg of lamb and fishcakes. There's also a nice little cheese menu. Wines are listed by character and include bottles from some small producers. Service and prices are equally friendly.

Devonshire Arms

S2

Modern European 🍺

Chiswick
126 Devonshire Rd ✉ W4 2JJ
✆ (020) 8742 2302
www.devonshirearmspub.com

⊖ **Turnham Green.**
Booking advisable

Carte £20/25

☂

☀

VISA

MC

Those behind the Drapers Arms in Islington are now at the helm of this roomy, characterful neighbourhood pub and they've given it a makeover true to its Edwardian roots. The front room is the cosier spot and is dominated by the central bar which allows plenty of space for drinkers. The menu changes twice daily and dishes are vibrant and appealing, courtesy of the French and Mediterranean influences. Starters vary from a half pint of prawns to a pigeon breast salad, grilled bavette or Cornish mackerel with broad bean relish. There's a thoughtfully compiled wine list of around 70 bins with a good selection by the glass and carafe. The relaxed yet friendly service provided by the young team add further to the pleasant local atmosphere.

High Road Brasserie

Traditional ✗

S2

Chiswick
162 Chiswick High Rd. ⊠ W4 1PR
☏ (020) 8742 7474
www.highroadhouse.co.uk

⊖ Turnham Green
Booking essential

Menu £16 (lunch) – Carte £20/42

It's usually so busy you'll have trouble getting in the door – quite literally sometimes, as the entrance is often crowded with evening drinkers or lunchtime pushchairs. This modern take on the brasserie certainly has the look, with its mirrors, panelling and art deco lighting; turn right for the more comfy seating. Staff are used to being busy and get the job done, although without much time for pleasantries. What is surprising is that, despite the volume of customers, the kitchen is able to deliver a good standard of accurately cooked classics including steak frites, duck confit, grilled lobster or whole sea bass, along with salads and sandwiches. The bill can rise quickly as sides are required, but there's a good value daytime menu.

Michael Nadra

Modern European ✗✗

S1-2

Chiswick
6-8 Elliott Rd. ⊠ W4 1PE
☏ (020) 8742 0766
www.restaurant-michaelnadra.co.uk

⊖ Turnham Green
Closed Sunday dinner and Monday

Menu £24/35

Tucked away from the more excitable restaurants on the High Street, Michael Nadra has been quietly and steadily going about the business of creating a very good restaurant. The result is that there are enough regulars now appreciating his cooking for him to have the confidence to finally put his own name above the door. Seafood remains an important part of his repertoire – crab tempura and monkfish with salmon mousse remain perennial favourites – but he now offers more meat dishes and there's a greater degree of sophistication to his cooking. Along with the fixed price menu is a very reasonable 7 course tasting menu, with suggested wine pairings. The restaurant has an intimate, local feel which is helped along by friendly staff.

Sam's Brasserie

Mediterranean ✗

S2

Chiswick
11 Barley Mow Passage ✉ W4 4PH
✆ (020) 8987 0555
www.samsbrasserie.co.uk

⊖ Turnham Green
Closed 23-28 December

Menu £17 (weekday lunch)/19 (weekday dinner)
Carte £29/35

A/C
☀
VISA
MC
AE

The building was once a Sanderson wallpaper mill and the industrial feel works well in this bustling brasserie environment. An added helping of hipness comes courtesy of the artwork from local resident, and occasional diner here, Sir Peter Blake. Look out too for the regular Soul and Jazz evenings. Dining is on two levels; the mezzanine is the quieter one, while the larger room looks into the kitchen and has plenty of bustle. The modern brasserie food is prepared with more care and expertise that one expects when one considers the size of the operation and, with a wine list offering over half its bottles for under £30, it's no surprise that the place gets busy. Service is efficient but could be a little more communicative.

Bobbin

Traditional 🍺

U2

Clapham
1-3 Lillieshall Rd ✉ SW4 0LN
✆ (020) 7738 8953
www.thebobbinclapham.com

⊖ Clapham Common

Carte £19/27

🌂
VISA
MC
AE
①

You'll find the Bobbin in a quiet residential street which, combined with its warm service, cosy bar and the Wednesday Quiz night, makes it feel like a proper local. You can eat in the bar or in the conservatory, from a menu which changes every six weeks and offers a choice of five starters and five mains. The charcuterie boards are great for sharing but vegetarians are also looked after, with the likes of leek, nettle and artichoke cannelloni. The kitchen sticks to using what's in season and, refreshingly, they don't feel they have to name-check every supplier to prove it. This pub may never set the world on fire yet that's part of its charm: they seem to have got everything right and are just, well, bobbin' along nicely.

La Trompette ✾

S2

Chiswick
5-7 Devonshire Rd ✉ W4 2EU
☎ (020) 8747 1836
www.latrompette.co.uk

⊖ Turnham Green
Closed 24-26 December –
booking essential

Menu £26/40

La Trompette

Chiswick now makes regular appearances in those 'don't you wish you lived here?' features that bulk up the weekend papers, thanks largely to its impressive number of restaurants and cafés. Chief among them is La Trompette, although many of its local regulars presumably hope its reputation doesn't spread too far, otherwise they'll never get a table. The interior is stylish and comfortable but also warm and relaxing, and there's usually a buzzy atmosphere. The menu may be a single sheet of A4 but everyone will find something on it that appeals. Dishes come and go as the seasons pass and, while there's a clear classic base, there are also other European influences exerted. Sauces are clearly a strength of the kitchen and there's refreshing lack of frippery to the dishes when they arrive at the table. The wine list is a weighty, leather-bound tome which offers a remarkably varied selection in both geography and price. The serving team's competence and friendliness enhances the experience still further.

First Course

- Scallops with pea purée and Bayonne ham.
- Duck confit tortellini with creamed hispi cabbage, button mushrooms, bacon and mustard foam.

Main Course

- Corn-fed chicken with morel ragout, shallots, broad beans and macaroni.
- Loin of cod and salt cod croquette with lemon butter emulsion.

Dessert

- Strawberry shortbread and sorbet with Chantilly cream.
- Chocolate fondant with rum poached banana and milk chocolate sorbet.

Trinity

Clapham
4 The Polygon ✉ SW4 0JG
✆ (020) 7622 1199
www.trinityrestaurant.co.uk

⊖ **Clapham Common**
Closed 24-30 December,
Monday lunch and Sunday dinner

Menu £20 (lunch) – Carte £31/47

A/C

VISA

MC

AE

①

Trinity is smarter and a little more formal than your average neighbourhood restaurant and residents of Clapham Old Town have clearly taken to it, especially as it means they don't have to schlep up to the West End for a 'proper' night out. The cooking is suitably sophisticated, with the kitchen adding some innovative combinations to what is a fairly classical base. Offal dishes are often the highlight and the pig's trotter on toasted sourdough has become a signature dish. The lunch menu is simpler in style and content but is priced very appealingly. To underline its neighbourhood credentials, the restaurant also offers cookery classes. In summer, ask for a table by the windows, which open up to add a little continental colour.

Tsunami

Clapham
Unit 3, 5-7 Voltaire Rd ✉ SW4 6DQ
✆ (020) 7978 1610
www.tsunamirestaurant.co.uk

⊖ **Clapham North**
Closed 24-26 December –
(dinner only and lunch Saturday-Sunday)

Carte £23/45

A/C

☼

VISA

MC

As fun, noisy and as lively as ever, particularly at weekends when it stays open until 2am, Tsunami continues to pull in plenty of Clapham locals, many of whom make the effort to scrub up nicely for this good looking Japanese restaurant with its popular club-like bar. The menu's focus is on modern fusion food but there is also an extensive selection of nigiri, sashimi and sushi rolls. Sharing is actively encouraged which is wise as some of the dishes are really quite substantial. Tempura is suitably light and allows the ingredient to shine, while steamed fish dishes such as the sea bass are often the highlight. Desserts are light and refreshing and presentation is appealing. There is another branch in Charlotte Street.

Charlotte's Place

R1

Ealing
16 St Matthew's Rd. ✉ W5 3JT
☎ (020) 8567 7541
www.charlottes.co.uk

⊖ **Ealing Common**
Closed 26 December-4 January

Menu £16/26 (early dinner) – Carte £28/32

It's been a sweet shop, a transport café and a private club but found its niche as an honest and warmly run local restaurant. The ground floor offers views over the Common so is popular at lunch; downstairs is ideal for couples who only have eyes for each other. The à la carte offers ample choice and the cooking is largely British, with smoked fish, traditional Sunday lunches and homely puddings done well; there are also one or two Mediterranean influences and the beef onglet is a constant. There is a small cover charge but it covers bread and unlimited filtered water rather than being an accountant's wheeze for squeezing more money out of the customers. As we went to print the restaurant was planning to move to another site in Ealing.

Kiraku

R1

Ealing
8 Station Par., Uxbridge Rd. ✉ W5 3LD
☎ (020) 8992 2848
www.kiraku.co.uk

⊖ **Ealing Common**
Closed 10 days
Christmas-New
Year, 10 days August, Tuesday
following bank holidays and Monday

Carte £17/33

Ayumi and Erica became so frustrated with the lack of a decent local Japanese restaurant that they decided to open one themselves; and now it is not just the bourgeoning Japanese community who flock to this cute little place. It's modestly styled and enthusiastically lit, but service is very charming. Look out for the blackboard menu and its daily changing dishes. Zensai, or starters, include the popular Agedashi dofu; these can then be followed by assorted skewers, noodles and rice dishes. Fish is purchased daily and their sushi now displays a more modern touch; Bara Chirashi is the house speciality. Be sure to end with matcha ice cream or green tea sponge cake. The restaurant's name means 'relax and enjoy' and it's hard not to.

Mango & Silk 😊

Indian 🍴

S2

East Sheen
199 Upper Richmond Rd. West ⊠ SW14 8 QT
☎ (020) 8876 6220
www.mangoandsilk.co.uk

Closed 25 December and Monday – (dinner only and buffet lunch Sunday)

Carte £20/23

VISA
M©
AE

Mango and Silk welcomes you to "the mystic and exotica of classic Indian dining in a serene and peaceful surrounding" and you can't argue with that. Owner Radhika Jerath is a natural and charming hostess but, more importantly, she has persuaded Udit Sarkhel back to the stove. His reputation was sealed from the day he opened his eponymous restaurant in Southfields and his menu provides an exhilarating culinary tour of India. His cooking displays a lightness of touch, expert spicing and a respect for ingredients; the Hyderabadi Chicken Sixers are a speciality. That window on the kitchen works both ways: he likes to see his customers enjoying themselves. The prices are terrific and those are his paintings on the wall.

Victoria

British 🍺

S2

East Sheen
10 West Temple Sheen ⊠ SW14 7RT
☎ (020) 8876 4238
www.thevictoria.net

⊖ Mortlake (Rail).

Carte £28/30

VISA
M©
①

Many pubs claim to be genuine locals – The Victoria is the real deal: it sponsors local clubs and the chef is patron of the local food festival; he also holds cookery workshops at the school next door. This is a beautifully decorated pub, with a restored bar with a wood burning stove and plenty of nooks and crannies; a few steps down and you're in the more formal conservatory overlooking the terrace. The cooking is modern British with the odd international note. Warm homemade bread could be followed by Scotch egg with roast beetroot, cod with a white bean stew and, to finish, blood oranges with rhubarb sorbet. Produce is local where possible: veg is from Surrey and honey from Richmond. Service is engaging and there are simple bedrooms available.

Blue Elephant

T2

Fulham
4-6 Fulham Broadway ✉ SW6 1AA
☎ (020) 7385 6595
www.blueelephant.com

⊖ Fulham Broadway
Closed 24-27 December
and 1 January – booking essential

Menu £20/37 – Carte £42/60

This London institution shows what imagination and unrestrained ambition can lead to. There are plants and streams, pergolas and bridges and the place is about the size of a film set with a healthy budget - you half expect Indiana Jones to come through the undergrowth, machete in hand. It's sensibly divided into smaller sections so you'll have just as good a time if you're a table of two or have come with nine friends. Granted, the service can get stretched but the staff are a pleasant bunch. Dishes are a mix of classics from across Thailand and contemporary creations. The ingredients are good and the curries a strength. There's a cabinet by reception selling their own branded goods and recipes to remind you this is now a global chain.

Manson

T2

Fulham
676 Fulham Rd. ✉ SW6 5SA
☎ (020) 7384 9559
www.mansonrestaurant.co.uk

⊖ Parsons Green
Closed 25-26 December and
Sunday dinner – booking advisable

Menu £18 (lunch and early dinner) – Carte £26/36

Manson is the second project from the team who brought us The Sands End. This time they have created a restaurant rather than a pub, but it too appears to have been an instant hit with the locals. Smoked mirrors and 1930s French street lamps give it a slightly lived-in, Left Bank aesthetic and the breezy service keeps things moving along nicely. However, there is a slight disparity between the relaxed look and feel of the place and the sophistication of its cooking. That's not to say the food is fussy or overblown, but is does display more ambition and creativity than one usually finds in Fulham. Excellent homemade breads kick things off and along with the refined dishes are a few more straightforward offerings like côte de beouf.

Harwood Arms ✿

T2

Fulham
Walham Grove ⊠ SW6 1QP
✆ (020) 7386 1847
www.harwoodarms.com

⊖ **Fulham Broadway.**
Closed 26-29 August, 25-28
December, 1 January and Monday
lunch – booking essential

Carte £30/34

A/C
✿✿
☼
VISA
MC
AE

Michelin

Its reputation may have spread around London like wildfire but what many visitors find most reassuring is how unaffected the Harwood Arms has remained. This is still a proper local pub, just one that happens to serve really good food; Tuesday is quiz night and it's packed when Chelsea are playing at home. The reason for its success is largely down to the shared passion of the three owners. Accordingly, it comes as no surprise that, despite the change in the kitchen in 2011, there has been no discernible deviation in the standard of the food. The cooking remains very seasonal and properly British; faggots, nettle soup, beef cheeks and Hampshire lamb all make regular appearances. There is obvious skill in the cooking but none of the dishes ever seem out of place in this relaxed environment – it's cooking that's all about carefully matched ingredients and great flavours, and not about technique and ego. The wine list has clearly been complied by someone who knows their food and the bar snacks are pretty good too.

First Course

- Rabbit, prune and bacon faggots with celeriac purée.
- Poached salmon with cucumber sandwiches on rye and gin jelly.

Main Course

- Glazed duck leg and Douglas fir sausage with beetroot tart.
- Cornish cod with cauliflower purée, brown shrimps, chanterelles and samphire.

Dessert

- Chilled rice pudding, strawberries and Grasmere gingerbread.
- English strawberry jam tart with clotted cream ice cream.

Mao Tai

Chinese ✕✕

T2

Fulham
58 New Kings Rd., Parsons Green ✉ SW6 4LS
✆ (020) 7731 2520
www.maotai.co.uk

⊖ **Parsons Green**
Closed 25-27
December –
(dinner only and Sunday lunch)

Carte £31/55

Fulham residents clearly expect a certain standard from their local Chinese restaurant as they've remained loyal to Mao Tai for years. The modern menu uses influences from across China, ranging from Shanghai dumplings to Sichuan duck. Dim sum is also served at dinner and other Asian countries get a look-in too; the cooking is crisp and the natural flavours of the ingredients are apparent. It's not just the food that's a cut above the average: the restaurant is divided into two stylish rooms, with the front section being a little more animated as that's where the cocktail bar is found. Be aware of over-ordering as the final bill can easily mount up, but that's probably not too much of a concern for the locals.

My dining room

French ⛾

T2

Fulham
18 Farm Ln ✉ SW6 1PP
✆ (020) 7381 3331
www.mydiningroom.net

⊖ **Fulham Broadway**

Menu £14/20 – Carte £21/37

'My dining room' is the archetypal gastropub of our day: yes, there's a bar with an open fire and a smattering of locals, but the bar's modern, the fire is gas and the locals are in suits. Head through 'The Lounge' and you'll get to a smart dining room, all silver and velvet, with John Garrett photos on the walls. Again, the menu is not that of your typical boozer: the kitchen displays a classical education and throws in a few French influences with their tartiflettes and cassoulets; there are even modern touches like foie gras with apple crumble. Add an impressive selection of wine by the glass and it's perhaps no surprise to learn that the owner is actually French. Al Murray's Pub Landlord wouldn't know where to look.

Sands End

British 🍺

T2

Fulham
135-137 Stephendale Rd. ✉ SW6 2PR
☎ (020) 7731 7823
www.thesandsend.co.uk

⊖ **Fulham Broadway**
Closed 25-26 December –
booking advisable

Carte £32/42

Sands End is probably not the best known part of London, or indeed Fulham, but no doubt its residents prefer it that way so they can keep their eponymous pub to themselves. It's a cosy, warm and welcoming one, with a central bar offering some nifty homemade snacks, but try resisting because the main menu – which changes every few days – is pretty appealing itself. There's a distinct British bias which amounts to more than merely name-checking the birthplace of the ingredients. Winter dishes like braised lamb neck or roast partridge with Savoy cabbage are particularly pleasing and West Mersea oysters a good way of starting things off. There's a well-chosen and equally equitably priced wine list that sticks mostly to the Old World.

Tendido Cuatro

Spanish 🍴

T2

Fulham
108-110 New Kings Road ✉ SW6 4LY
☎ (020) 7371 5147
www.cambiodetercio.co.uk

⊖ **Parsons Green**

Carte £21/49

Any resemblance to their other restaurants in Old Brompton Road is entirely intentional: here too the front panels burst open in summer to reveal a warm interior where vivid colours are used with wild abandon. The main difference is that, along with tapas, the speciality is the Valencian classic, paella. Using bomba rice, the choice varies from seafood to quail and chorizo; cuttlefish ink to vegetarian. They are designed for two but that assumes a more than eager appetite, especially if you've had a couple of small dishes as a run-up. The tapas is nicely varied, from refreshing baby anchovies to crisp pigs ears. Service is spirited and the room comes alive later in the evening as the locals return from work and wander over.

Anglesea Arms

British 🍴🍺

S1

Hammersmith
35 Wingate Rd. ✉ W6 0UR
✆ (020) 8749 1291
www.anglesea-arms.com

⊖ Ravenscourt Park
Closed 25-27 December –
(bookings not accepted)

Carte £20/52

The Anglesea Arms proves that you can update a pub while still respecting its heritage. Its windows are etched with the inviting words 'Pies and Hams' and 'Stout and Oysters' and above the door is 'Mon Mam Cymru', Mother of Wales, as the Isle of Anglesey is known. The wood-floored, wood-panelled bar has a cluttered, lived-in feel and gets very crowded, so if you're in for eating head for the brighter rear dining room, with its part-glass ceiling and exposed kitchen. The blackboard menu might change between services and can be a little unbalanced with lots of starters, fewer mains and a limited number of puddings but the cooking is robust and has a strong British bias, with the likes of pig's head terrine, smoked eel and game featuring.

Azou 🐶

North African 🍴

S2

Hammersmith
375 King St. ✉ W6 9NJ
✆ (020) 8563 7266
www.azou.co.uk

⊖ Stamford Brook
Closed 25 December, 1 January and bank
holidays – booking essential – (dinner only
and lunch Saturday-Sunday)

Carte £23/35

You'll probably walk past the first time and not notice this unassuming little place but, once visited, you won't walk past again. Inside is all silks, lanterns and rugs but it is also very personally run; the owner will often pop out from his kitchen to offer guidance – and his advice is well worth listening to. The cooking skips across North African countries – order some Algerian olives while you choose from the wide choice of main courses. Understandably, most of the regulars come here for a tajine, especially the Constantine with its tender lamb and tri le-steamed couscous. Highlights to start include the terrific baba ganoush with homemade bread and fresh briouat. It's the perfect food to share as the dishes come in large portions.

Crabtree

Modern European 🍴🍺

T2

Hammersmith   ⊖ Barons Court
4 Rainville Rd. ⊠ **W6 9HA**
✆ (020) 7385 3929
www.thecrabtreeW6.co.uk

Carte £24/34

On a sunny day few things in life beat being by the river in a
London pub and The Crabtree certainly makes the most of its
location. Its beer garden, with its barbeque-style menu, can
hold up to 200, while the dining room boasts its own terrace
overlooking the river – and if you haven't yet booked for lunch
on Boat Race day then you're probably already too late. A
variety of ploys are used to fill the equally large interior of
this Victorian beauty, from BYO Mondays to quiz nights on
Tuesdays. For lunch the selection varies from ciabatta sarnies
to shepherd's pie; the evening menu is more adventurous.
The kitchen does things properly – parfaits and terrines are
highlights and fish is perfectly timed – but vegetarians are also
looked after.

Dartmouth Castle

Mediterranean 🍴🍺

S1

Hammersmith   ⊖ Hammersmith
26 Glenthorne Rd. ⊠ **W6 0LS**   Closed 24 December-2 January and
✆ (020) 8748 3614   Saturday lunch
www.thedartmouthcastle.co.uk

Carte £18/31

The view one way is of offices, the other, smart Victorian
terraced houses, so this pub has to satisfy a wide variety of
customers and their differing needs – and it does so with
aplomb. Plenty just come in for a drink but you can eat on
either of the two floors, although the ground floor has the
better atmosphere, despite its somewhat over-enthusiastic
lighting; just order at the bar and leave them your credit card.
The Mediterranean exerts quite an influence on the large
menu, whose prices are more than fair. Pasta appears to come
in two sizes – big or even bigger – and the antipasti dish for
two is great for sharing over a bottle of wine. Sandwiches use
ciabatta, and desserts like tiramisu or panna cotta finish things
off nicely.

Havelock Tavern

T1

Traditional 🍺

Hammersmith
57 Masbro Rd., Brook Grn. ✉ W14 0LS
✆ (020) 7603 5374
www.havelocktavern.com

⊖ **Kensington Olympia**
Closed 25-26 December –
(bookings not accepted)

Carte £21/30 s

Head straight for the bar where smiley, somewhat dishevelled looking staff will organise a drink, open a tab and add your name to the list of those waiting for a table, which are allocated on a first-come-first-served basis. This actually appears to add to the atmosphere as everyone is forced to rub shoulders in the bar first, where you'll find bowls of pistachios and olives while you wait. The blackboard menu changes with each service and cooking is on the stout side so you're better off sharing a nibble like chipolatas and mustard or pickled quail egg, before choosing a pie or steak; only if your appetite is really healthy will you have room for crumble and custard. The busier the place gets, the better the service.

Indian Zing

S1-2

Indian ✕✕

Hammersmith
236 King St. ✉ W6 0RF
✆ (020) 8748 5959
www.indianzing.co.uk

⊖ **Ravenscourt Park**
Closed dinner 25 December

Menu £15 (lunch) – Carte £25/35

Despite opening a couple more restaurants, none of the zing appears to have gone out of this keenly run Indian neighbourhood favourite. Chef-owner Manoj Vasaikar flits between them and remains committed to seeing his customers satisfied, so much so that he has been known to send out an extra dish on the house if he feels an order is not sufficiently balanced. While he is from Bombay, his cooking seeks inspiration from all over India; from sweet fish dishes to drier North Indian dishes or spicier Madras specialities. Effort is also made to match wines with the food and the list even offers a couple of choices from India. The restaurant is colourfully decorated while the serving team are keen if a little disorganised at times.

River Café ⁸³

T2

Hammersmith
Thames Wharf, Rainville Rd ✉ W6 9HA
📞 (020) 7386 4200
www.rivercafe.co.uk

⊖ **Barons Court**
Closed Christmas, Sunday
dinner and bank holidays –
booking essential

Carte £49/78

River Café

They should run a shuttle service from local catering colleges to
the River Café so that the students can learn the secret of good
cooking: good ingredients. There's a vigour and honesty to the
kitchen and, with the chefs all on view as they go about their
work, there seems to be more of a relationship here between
cook and customer than is found in most restaurants. The big
wood-fired oven really catches the eye and the restaurant
seems to attract a wonderfully mixed bunch of customers,
united in their appreciation of what makes a restaurant tick.
That includes charming service: on looks alone, the team can
rival those in glossier and glitzier restaurants but they break
ranks here by actually smiling and caring about their customers.
The menu is still written twice a day and head chef Sian Wyn
Owen brings an added sparkle to the cooking. Things taste just
the way you want them to taste. Ordering a pasta dish ought
to be made compulsory and the Chocolate Nemesis dessert
should be a recognised treatment for depression.

First Course

- Crab linguini.
- Chargrilled squid
  with fresh red chilli
  and rocket.

Main Course

- Sea bass baked in
  salt with salsa verde.
- Wood-roasted veal
  chop with rosemary
  and lemon, Italian
  spinach and pan-
  fried girolles.

Dessert

- Chocolate Nemesis.
- Panna cotta with
  grappa and baked
  nespole.

The Glasshouse ✿

R2

Kew
14 Station Par. ✉ TW9 3PZ
☎ (020) 8940 6777
www.glasshouserestaurant.co.uk

⊖ **Kew Gardens**
Closed 24-26 December and 1 January

Menu £26/40

A/C
🍇
☼
VISA
MC
AE

The Glasshouse

There are some restaurants where the style of food matches the setting perfectly and The Glasshouse is one such example. Despite opening on the eve of the new millennium, the bright and open interior still feels fresh and contemporary. Meanwhile, the seasonally informed cooking is as crisp and vibrant as ever. A seamless change of head chef has seen no drop in the general standard and the flavours are allowed to shine on each dish. The menu is a lesson in balance and the cooking is predominantly modern European but the kitchen is not averse to slipping in a few tastes of the East. Offal remains something of a highlight and wines are shrewdly recommended and graciously served. The service team are imbued with an unflappable confidence which, in turn, relaxes the room, although most of the customers appear to already have the imperturbable demeanour of those who know their food and recognise a decent restaurant when they see one. Reservations for weekends, when lunches are largely family affairs, need to be made about a month in advance.

First Course

- Sashimi of sea bass, wasabi mayonnaise and shrimp beignet.
- Pan-fried lamb sweetbreads and tongue with root vegetables and mustard.

Main Course

- Roast pollock, wild garlic velouté, morels and leeks.
- Raw spicy beef with pommes Sarladaise, quail eggs, rocket, truffle dressing and parmesan.

Dessert

- Lemon tart with custard ice cream.
- Apple sundae with candied pecan nuts and crème fraîche.

Kew Grill

R2

Kew
10b Kew Grn. ⊠ TW9 3BH
📞 (020) 8948 4433
www.awtrestaurants.com

⊖ **Kew Gardens**
Closed Monday lunch –
booking essential

Menu £15 (weekday lunch) – Carte £29/49

A/C
☀
VISA
MC
AE

Busy, relaxed and fun are the hallmarks of this Antony Worrall Thompson neighbourhood joint specialising in meats. Top quality steaks come with a choice of a sauce or butter; there are daily specials like shepherd's pie or duck confit and even a section dedicated to AWT's pork. There are seasonal dishes like haunch of venison; fish-eaters and Veggies are catered for and children aren't forgotten either. The cooking is heart-warming and unfussy, the aged beef really is excellent and the nursery puds will finish you off. The concise wine list offers a good selection by the carafe. It's all done in quite a narrow room with something of a country feel; the friendly staff help the atmosphere along nicely.

Cantinetta

S2

Putney
162-164 Lower Richmond Rd
(Entrance on Pentlow St) ⊠ SW15 1LY
📞 (020) 8780 3131
www.cantinetta.co.uk

⊖ **Putney Bridge**
Closed Sunday dinner and
Monday lunch in winter

Menu £16/18 – Carte £21/32

🛖
A/C
VISA
MC
AE

The Phoenix occupied this spot for many years until it finally burnt itself out. A series of pop-up restaurants then followed until seasoned restaurateur Rebecca Mascarenhas opened this relaxed, modern day trattoria. The bright room opens onto a much sought-after terrace and the bar is a great spot for a light bite at lunch. The menu represents decent value and the cooking delivers on flavour, whether that's the deep-fried anchovies with carpione dressing, the Ligurian classic 'trofie al pesto' or market fresh fish with lentils. The bread basket is worth its price and includes wonderfully light focaccia. Add a well chosen wine list with lesser known grape varieties and some spirited service and you have a very appealing local spot.

Enoteca Turi

Italian ✗✗

T2

Putney
28 Putney High St. ✉ **SW15 1SQ**
☎ (020) 8785 4449
www.enotecaturi.com

⊖ **Putney Bridge**
Closed 25-26 December,
1 January, Sunday and lunch
bank holiday Mondays

Menu £20 (lunch) – Carte £32/40

AC
⊡
☸
VISA
MC
AE
①

Originally from Puglia, Giuseppe Turi celebrated 20 years in 2010 as Putney's favourite Italian restaurateur. In that time hardly a day has gone by without his restaurant bursting with chat and buzz – this really is a local institution. He began life in London as a sommelier in the city's grandest hotels and so the grape plays an important role here: the menu matches wines with the dishes, the list has over 300 bins, he hosts regular food and wine evenings and the cellar hosts larger parties. The cooking is undertaken with a clear passion and the flavours pack a punch, which points to more northerly influences; dishes are satisfying and authentic. The restaurant is divided into three - the roomier front section is the best place to sit.

Prince of Wales

British 🍺

T2

Putney
138 Upper Richmond Rd ✉ **SW15 2SP**
☎ (020) 8788 1552
www.princeofwalesputney.co.uk

⊖ **East Putney**
Closed 23 December-
1 January and Monday lunch
except bank holidays

Carte £27/43

☼
VISA
MC
AE
①

You'll feel the warmth as soon as you enter. The bar, whose walls are lined with tankards, is usually packed with a mix of drinkers and diners, perhaps enjoying homemade Scotch eggs or fish with triple-cooked chips; you'll feel as though you just want to join in the fun. There is a quieter space behind the bar but if you want something completely different then go down a few steps and you'll find a grand and lavishly kitted out baronial-style dining room. The daily changing menu is full of seasonality and diversity. Oysters, Asian salads or charcuterie can be followed by beef Bourguignon or some terrific game, and there's usually a great selection of ice creams to finish. Sunday lunch is a family affair, with spit-roast chicken a speciality.

Bingham Restaurant

R3

Richmond
61-63 Petersham Rd. ✉ TW10 6UT
✆ (020) 8940 0902
www.thebingham.co.uk

⊖ **Richmond**
Closed first week January
and Sunday dinner

Menu £26/55

🛖
🚗
A/C
VISA
⓲
AE
①

The Bingham always feels part of the local community and has lots of supporters in the neighbourhood who use it for a variety of different occasions. Perhaps its location, within a relatively unremarkable looking building, does it a favour as the restaurant has something of a 'hidden jewel' feel about it and the décor is surprisingly swish and comfortable. Come on a warm summer's day and you could find yourself having lunch on the balcony terrace, looking out over a garden and the Thames – and you don't get that everywhere. The cooking is contemporary and displays some original touches, however, dishes don't always deliver the flavours promised by the impressive presentation.

Matsuba

R3

Richmond
10 Red Lion St ✉ TW9 1RW
✆ (020) 8605 3513

⊖ **Richmond**
Closed 25-26 December,
1 January and Sunday

Carte £40/45

A/C
VISA
⓲
AE

Matsuba is a small, family-run place that is so understated it's easy to miss – look out for the softly lit sign above the narrow façade. The interior is equally compact and low-key, with just a dozen or so tables along with a small counter at the back with room for four more. In fact the biggest thing in the room is the menu, which offers a comprehensive tour through most recognisable points in Japanese cooking. The owners are Korean so you can also expect to see bulgogi, the Korean barbecue dish of marinated meat that comes on a sizzling plate. All the food is fresh and the ingredients are good; lunch sees some very good value set menus. The service is well-meaning and it's hard not to come away thinking kind thoughts.

Petersham Nurseries Café ✿

Italian influences ✗

R3

Richmond
Church Ln (off Petersham Rd)
✉ TW10 7AG
✆ (020) 8605 3627 **www**.petershamnurseries.com

Closed 24-29 December and Monday
– booking advisable – (lunch only)

Carte £45/61

Michelin

Don't even think about driving here – this plot of paradise should only be reached via a stroll along the river and across the fields – and allow time to wander around the nursery, because if you want to really appreciate lunch here then you have to buy into the Sunday supplement loveliness of it all. The Café is a moveable feast: it's on the terrace on summer days and in a greenhouse the rest of the time and the well-meaning service comes from grown-up versions of the Famous Five. Skye Gyngell's kitchen epitomises the 'less is more' maxim of the modern kitchen: it simply works with the best seasonal produce and lets natural flavours shine. Amalfi lemons are used for the jugs of lemonade and a glass of prosecco with rose syrup makes for the perfect aperitif. The menu is not overlong and there is an earthiness and vibrancy to the food that seems so right when you're eating among plants and flowers. It may not come cheap but neither do ingredients of this quality. And don't wear the Manolo Blahniks – unless he's started designing wellies – as there's nothing but soil underfoot.

First Course
- Crab salad with nam jim sauce and mixed cress.
- Linguine with lemon, sage and tipico.

Main Course
- Sea bass fillet with spinach, fresh chilli and preserved lemon dressing.
- Wood pigeon with wild garlic and borlotti beans.

Dessert
- Chocolate mousse with ginger caramel and Jersey cream.
- Almond tart with raspberries and crème fraîche.

Swagat

Indian ✗

Richmond

86 Hill Rise ✉ TW10 6UB

✆ (0208) 9407 557

www.swagatindiancuisine.co.uk

⊖ Richmond

Closed 25-26 December, 1 January and

Sunday – (dinner only)

Menu £30 – Carte £22/34

[A/C]
☼
[VISA]
[MC]

Richmond's nascent restaurant scene was given a boost by the arrival of Swagat, which translates as 'welcome'. With just 14 tables, it's best to book otherwise you'll find yourself in a queue with the locals. Its popularity is down to the attentive, very well-meaning service and the likeable menu, which aims to promote healthy eating by using less oil and more subtle spicing. You'll find plenty of classics but try the less recognisable dishes, like chicken Chettinad from southern India. Fortnightly changing specials add further interest, as do the moist breads, fresh chillies and the complimentary poppadoms and chutneys. Prices are also appealing and allow vegetarian dishes to be ordered as main courses or accompaniments.

Princess Victoria

Traditional 🍴🍺

Shepherd's Bush

217 Uxbridge Rd. ✉ W12 9DH

✆ (020) 8749 5886

www.princessvictoria.co.uk

⊖ Shepherd's Bush

Closed 24-28 December

Menu £13 (lunch) – Carte £21/34

[☂]
[A/C]
[⊗]
☼
[VISA]
[MC]
[AE]

London has a wealth of fine Victorian gin palaces but few are as grand as The Princess Victoria. From the friezes to the etched glass, the portraits to the parquet floor, the last restoration created a terrific pub. Mind you, that's not all that impresses: there's a superb, wide-ranging wine list, with carafes and glasses providing flexibility; enticing bar snacks ranging from quail eggs to salt cod croquettes; a great menu that could include roasted skate wing or homemade pork and herb sausages; and, most importantly, cooking that's executed with no little skill. Those with proclivities for all things porcine will find much to savour – charcuterie is a passion here and the board may well include pig's cheeks and rillettes.

Triphal 🐾

Southfields

201 Replingham Rd ✉ SW18 5LY
☎ (020) 8870 0188
www.triphalindianrestaurant.com

⊖ **Southfields**
Closed 25-26 December,
1 January and Monday

Carte £15/19

A/C
☼
VISA
MC

When the Indian restaurant Sarkhel's closed a few years back, it left a big hole in this neighbourhood, but those still mourning its passing should be delighted that a worthy successor has been found in the form of Triphal. Created on a shoestring by three partners, two of whom are chefs with some impressive addresses on their CVs, this is a sweet little place making real efforts. The decoration may have been largely inherited from the previous occupants but the cooking is fresh and full of vitality. The menu is concise and includes a broad palate of regional Indian dishes, although, as both chefs are from Goa, the fish curries are often a highlight. In further echoes of Sarkhel's, the prices represent excellent value.

Al Borgo

Teddington

3 Church Rd. ✉ TW11 8PF
☎ (020) 8943 4456
www.alborgo.co.uk

Closed Sunday and bank holidays

Carte approx. £35

VISA
MC
AE

Aside from being home to Ted, love rival to Ernie the Fastest Milkman in the West, Teddington has rarely featured in the national consciousness – but a few more restaurants like Al Borgo may start to change people's perceptions. This refreshingly unpretentious Italian eatery, owned and keenly run by Brescia born Marco and his partner Nikola, exudes warmth and bonhomie in the way that only a true neighbourhood restaurant can. The menu cleverly appeals to both traditionalists and those a little more adventurous. The focaccia is homemade, as is the pasta; try the tagliolini with scallops or the pumpkin tortelli with sage. Special seasonal offerings such as a black truffle menu prove popular and there's a great value lunch menu too.

Kings Head

Modern European 🍺

R3

Teddington
123 High St ✉ TW11 8HG
☎ (020) 3166 2900
www.whitebrasserie.com

Menu £14/16 – Carte £19/26

Britain has its pubs and France its brasseries; The King's Head does its bit for the entente cordiale by combining both. Raymond Blanc's team has given this Victorian pub a tidy makeover and, although there might not be much character left, they have created a suitably warm environment. The brasserie at the back is run by a pleasant, enthusiastic team and the menus offer all comers plenty of choice. Classic brasserie dishes such as Toulouse sausages and beef stroganoff come with a satisfyingly rustic edge, while the dual-nationality element is maintained through the inclusion of a ploughman's board alongside the charcuterie. Steaks on the charcoal grill are popular and families are lured in by the decent kiddies menu.

Rétro Bistrot

French ✗✗

R3

Teddington
114-116 High St ✉ TW11 8JB
☎ (0208) 9772 239
www.retrobistrot.co.uk

Closed first 2 weeks August, first 10 days January, Sunday dinner and Monday

Menu £14/23 – Carte £23/41

There's substance as well as style to this classic French bistrot. The kitchen brigade were once teammates at the much missed Monsieur Max, so they know their way around a French menu. Moules marinière, coq au vin, foie de veau and crème brûlée – all the classics of bourgeois cuisine are here and all are prepared with innate skill and understanding. Lunch and early evening menus are a steal, and the service team display equal commitment to the cause as cheeks are kissed and cries of "bon appétit" ring out. The mix of fabrics, exposed brick walls, simple tables and art for sale creates a very genial environment. The best seats are in the room at the back with the partially open kitchen, which adds aroma and a little more noise.

Simply Thai 😊

R3

Teddington
196 Kingston Rd. ✉ **TW11 9JD**
✆ (020) 8943 9747
www.simplythai-restaurant.co.uk

Closed 25-26 December and Monday
– (dinner only)

Menu £25 – Carte £23/34

AC
☼
VISA
MC

The delightful owner, Patria Weerapan, made her television debut on Gordon Ramsay's 'The F Word'. Her restaurant wasn't exactly quiet beforehand, but now her long term future here seems assured. Decoratively it's as modest inside as the unassuming façade suggests but everyone comes here for the food and forgives the occasional delay. She cooks everything fresh, from a bewilderingly large menu; dishes themselves are quite small so order one dish more than you think you need, which shouldn't be too difficult as the prices are far from high. Along with the new creations that are often being added to the menu are the favourites like spicy sweet pork, fishcakes, a refreshing trout salad and crisp deep-fried soft shell crab.

A Cena

R2

Twickenham
418 Richmond Rd. ✉ **TW1 2EB**
✆ (020) 8288 0108
www.acena.co.uk

⊖ **Richmond**
Closed 25-26 December,
Sunday dinner and Monday lunch

Carte £30/36

AC
VISA
MC
AE

A Cena is a little unusual for an Italian restaurant insofar as the owners and the chef are all Brits, but their passion for all things Italian is palpable. More relevantly, they have wholeheartedly embraced the Italian ethos of using fresh produce, cooked carefully, in simply presented dishes. The menu, written in both languages, is constantly evolving. Not all dishes exude the appropriate zing but pasta dishes are usually a highlight. The place looks a little deceptive from the outside as it's not as small as it appears: avoid the tables at the front and head for the more open-plan rear area from where you can see what's going on. The restaurant's local popularity had led to the opening of a nearby foodstore and bakery.

Brula

French ✗✗

Twickenham
43 Crown Rd., St Margarets ✉ TW1 3EJ
✆ (020) 8892 0602
www.brula.co.uk

Closed 26-30 December and Sunday dinner
– booking essential

Menu £18 (lunch) – Carte £22/36

VISA
MC
AE

Brula is already well past its tenth birthday and this relative longevity can be put down to a combination of reliable cooking, sensible prices and personable service. This pretty Victorian building has been both a pub and a butcher's shop in the past but now thoroughly suits its role as an authentic looking bistro. France remains at the heart of the cooking but over the past couple of years influences from Spain and Italy have started to appear on the menu, which is priced per dish rather than per course as it once was. Cooking is also more exact in its execution. The cheeses and the thoughtfully arranged wine list remain exclusively French. The friendly and helpful service also extends to those using one of the private rooms.

Tangawizi

Indian ✗

Twickenham
406 Richmond Rd., Richmond Bridge
✉ TW1 2EB
✆ (020) 8891 3737
www.tangawizi.co.uk

⊖ Richmond
Closed 25-26 December
and 1 January – (dinner only
and Sunday lunch)

Carte £15/31

A/C
☼
VISA
MC
AE

Rich in colour and vitality, Tangawizi - meaning 'ginger' in Swahili – is another in the new breed of Indian restaurants. That means thoughtful design with clever use of silks and saris, attentive and elegant staff but, above all, cooking that is original, fresh and carefully prepared. North India provides much of the influence and although the à la carte menu offers plenty of 'safe' options, there are gems such as the roasted then stir-fried 'liptey' chicken. Diners should, however, head for the 'specials' section where the ambition of the kitchen is more evident. Lamb is another house speciality and is marinated to ensure it arrives extremely tender. For cooking this good, the prices are more than fair.

Chez Bruce ✿

French

Wandsworth
2 Bellevue Rd ✉ SW17 7EG
✆ (020) 8672 0114
www.chezbruce.co.uk

⊖ **Tooting Bec**
Closed 24-26 December and 1 January
– booking essential

Menu £28 (weekday lunch)/45

A/C
VISA
MC
AE

Chez Bruce

Not only did Chez Bruce weather the choppy waters of recession better than most but it finally expanded into the old deli next door. What this meant for its merry band of dependable followers was nothing more than 'business as usual', as Chez Bruce has had a successful formula for years. That means flavoursome and uncomplicated food, sprightly service, sensible prices and an easy-going atmosphere. Matthew Christmas is the head man in the kitchen, having worked closely with Bruce Poole for over 10 years. His cooking provides an object lesson in the importance of flavours and balance: dishes are never too crowded and natural flavours are to the fore. The base is largely classical French but comes with Mediterranean tones, so expect words like parfait, pastilla, brandade and confit. The menu offers an even-handed selection, with a choice of around seven dishes per course. Cheese is always worth exploring and coffee comes with shortbread at lunch and terrific palmiers at dinner.

First Course

- Rare grilled tuna à la Niçoise, fennel purée and anchovy beignet.
- Quail with Coronation dressing, cucumber and almonds.

Main Course

- Rump and shoulder of lamb with spring vegetables, creamed potato and rosemary.
- Roast cod with olive oil mash, Provençale tomato and gremolata.

Dessert

- Hot chocolate pudding with praline parfait.
- Raspberry and almond tart with crème fraîche sorbet.

Fox and Grapes 😊

S3

Wimbledon
9 Camp Rd. ✉ SW19 4UN
✆ (020) 8619 1300
www.foxandgrapeswimbledon.co.uk

⊖ **Wimbledon**
Closed 25 December –
booking advisable

Menu £20 (lunch) – Carte £26/38

A/C
☼
VISA
MC

Claude Bosi first made his mark in Ludlow where, along with his Hibiscus restaurant, he also had a pub. When he moved to London the plan was to open a pub again once his restaurant was established and this he duly did in 2011. Cedric, his brother, runs the show and one look at the menu confirms their credentials as honorary Brits: this is proper pub food. Their prawn cocktail is hugely popular, as is the Cumberland sausage with mash, the ale battered hake and Angus sirloin. Scotch egg is made with wild boar, and junket makes an appearance, which makes you forgive their sneaking in the odd Gallic touch like snails and some of the over-formality. Thankfully, the pub's bigger than it looks as it's very popular. It also has three cosy bedrooms.

Light House

T3

Wimbledon
75-77 Ridgway ✉ SW19 4ST
✆ (020) 8944 6338
www.lighthousewimbledon.com

⊖ **Wimbledon**
Closed 25-26 December,
1 January and Sunday dinner

Menu £15 (lunch) – Carte £23/32

VISA
MC
AE

The façade may have been smartened up but one's first impression is of being in a branded operation. Fortunately, that notion is quickly dispelled by the quality of the food. While they still have the odd Thai dish, it is in Italy where the majority of the menu and the kitchen's strength lie, with a roll call of favourites that include tagliatelle, gnocchi, saltimbocca and panna cotta. The food is wholesome and confident, with plenty of bold flavours and prices at lunch and early evening are attractive, which ensures that it is often very busy. The result is that the young team can sometimes struggle to keep up, but they remain admirably calm and cheery. As this was once a shop selling lights and fittings, it is fittingly well lit.

Where to **stay**

▶ *These 50 recommended hotels are extracted from the Great Britain & Ireland 2012 guide, where you'll find a larger choice of hotels selected by our team of inspectors.*

Thierry Burot/Fotolia.com

Andaz Liverpool Street

M2

40 Liverpool St.
✉ EC2M 7QN
✆ (020) 7961 1234
www.andazdining.com

⊖ Liverpool Street

264 rm – †£144/516 ††£372/600, ☕ **£22 – 3 suites**
†○**1901** *(See restaurant listing)*

The 'Andaz' brand (which apparently means "personal style" in Hindi) belongs to Hyatt, and this former railway hotel, which once went by the less ambiguous name of the Great Eastern, was the London prototype before its export to New York and L.A. The idea is to create luxury hotels with a less structured and more informal feel. In practical terms this mostly means that instead of a reception desk you have staff wandering around the nearest thing they have to a lobby, armed with laptops. The hotel may not be quite as hip as they imagine but it does provide a comfortable and contemporary environment that has a palpable sense of individualism. The crisply dressed bedrooms use a slick red, white and black palette and mod cons are comprehensive and largely concealed. Those wanting to be fed and watered will find themselves almost overwhelmed by the choice: there's the traditional George pub, a cosy Japanese, a lively brasserie, a stylish seafood bar and the eye-catching 1901 restaurant.

Arch

F2

50 Great Cumberland Pl
✉ W1H 7FD
✆ (020) 7724 4700
www.thearchlondon.com

80 rm – ♦**£258/1,020** ♦♦**£258/1,020,** ☕ **£19.50 – 2 suites**

⊖ Marble Arch

The Arch

If God is in the detail, then The Arch shows touches of the divine. Fashioned out of a row of seven terraced houses and a couple of mews cottages, the hotel has been thoughtfully put together by people who have clearly stayed in a lot of places and who know what it takes to make them comfortable. For starters, the bedrooms offer an impressive list of extras such as HD TVs and internet radios; beds have oversized duvets so there's no nocturnal wrestling required to secure one's half; there are complimentary soft drinks and coffee; and some of the larger rooms not only have a TV in the bathroom but also have a pillow in the tub to make the watching of it more comfortable. The public areas are relatively compact but are smartly designed. The restaurant, which doubles as a champagne bar and is named after the dialling code from the '50s, has an easy-going menu, with a kitchen that makes good use of its wood fired oven. The Martini bar has discreet call buttons to summon service and interesting pieces of art are scattered liberally around the hotel.

Aster House

3 Sumner Pl.
⊠ SW7 3EE
✆ (020) 7581 5888
www.asterhouse.com

13 rm – †£96/180 ††£162/300

Michelin

If you made a mathematical calculation to find the best location for a tourist in London, then chances are the X would mark a spot somewhere near Aster House on Sumner Place. You've got all the best museums within strolling distance; Hyde Park mere minutes away; all the famous shops and, above all, you're staying in a charming Victorian house in a typical Kensington street where people actually live rather than in a faceless hotel district. Mr and Mrs Tan keep the house commendably shipshape and are enthusiastic hosts. The bedrooms at the front of the house benefit from larger windows while those at the back are quieter and overlook the garden, but all boast fairly high ceilings and room to breathe. Wi-fi is available without charge in all the rooms, while L'Orangerie, a first floor conservatory looking down over Sumner Place, doubles as the breakfast room and guests' sitting room. Prices are also kept within the parameters of decency so bookings need to be made plenty of time in advance.

Athenaeum

 G4

116 Piccadilly ⊖ Hyde Park Corner
✉ W1J 7BJ
✆ (020) 7499 3464
www.athenaeumhotel.com

153 rm – †£240 ††£720,☕ £27.50 – 11 suites

Athenaeum

The Athenaeum has such a high number of regular guests who treat it as a home from home, that before the hotel undertook its latest refurbishment, it conducted a lengthy survey to find out what they wanted. Gone is the country house style of old and in its place has come a refreshing new look which blends all the latest mod cons with pastel shades and floor to ceiling windows. In these days of hidden charges, it's refreshing to find a hotel where the price of the room includes wi-fi, soft drinks from the mini-bar and a daily paper. The restaurant menu is appealingly down-to-earth and offers a decent selection of easy-to-eat classics with an English bent and the bar holds over 270 whiskies from around the world. Another striking feature of the hotel is its 'Living Wall', which is basically a vertical garden; this can be admired from the lounge, which does a brisk trade in afternoon tea. There are apartments for longer stays and those with children will appreciate the Kids' Concierge who will organise relevant activities.

MAYFAIR ▶ PLAN II

Berkeley

G4

Wilton Pl.   ⊖ Knightsbridge
✉ SW1X 7RL
✆ (020) 7235 6000
www.the-berkeley.co.uk

189 rm – ♦£588/708 ♦♦£708, ☕ £29 – 25 suites
🍴**Marcus Wareing at The Berkeley and Koffmann's**
(See restaurant listing)

The Berkeley

You'd have thought that having Marcus Wareing's luxury restaurant on one side of the hotel would be enough, but the hotel then coaxed Pierre Koffman out of retirement and his restaurant now provides the bookend on the other side. In the middle you have the Blue Bar which is as cool as the name suggests and, on the other side of the lobby, the Caramel Room whose target audience is obvious when you consider that tea is called "Prêt-à-Portea" and the biscuits look like mini handbags. The most unique area of the hotel must be the 7th floor, with its rooftop pool, treatment rooms and personal training services to satisfy the most slavishly health-conscious traveller. By using a number of different designers, bedrooms have been given both personality and a sense of individualism; the most recent have softer, calmer colours and a lighter, more contemporary feel while the classic rooms feel richer, thanks to their deeper, more intense colours. All the rooms are immaculately kept and several of the suites have their own balcony.

Bermondsey Square

 M5

Bermondsey Sq, Tower Bridge Rd
✉ SE1 3UN
✆ (020) 7378 2450
www.bermondseysquarehotel.co.uk

⊖ London Bridge

79 rm – ♦£130/250 ♦♦£130/600,⊇ £11

Bermondsey Square

The only people in Bermondsey busier than its restaurateurs and designers appear to be the estate agents, who all materialised overnight, at the exact moment that everyone noticed just how trendy Bermondsey had become. In fact, Bermondsey Square alone offers more entertainment than any number of high streets in London. Standing at its heart is the Bermondsey Square Hotel and, although there's something mildly municipal about its look from the outside, it is, like many places around here, not quite what is seems. For a start, there are some idiosyncratic designery touches scattered around the building and the open-plan ground floor has a suitably relaxed air. The bar merges into Alfie's, their accessible restaurant, which makes good use of produce from nearby Borough Market. Meanwhile, the bedrooms have something of a raffish feel, especially on the top floor with its black walls and black carpets which must require almost round-the-clock vacuuming. One of the largest rooms is 'Lucy' which comes with its own deck, complete with a hot-tub.

BERMONDSEY ▶ PLAN X

Blakes

D6

33 Roland Gdns.
⊠ SW7 3PF
✆ (020) 7370 6701
www.blakeshotels.com

⊖ Gloucester Road

33 rm – ♦£234/594 ♦♦£390/654,☕ £19.50 – 8 suites

🍴
🚲
🛎
((•))
SAT
VISA
MC
AE
①

Blakes

To see Blakes at its best, one needs to up the financial ante and go for one of the stylish deluxe rooms with their towers of cushions, flowing drapes and luxury bathrooms. Room 5 comes all in white, which means it occupies the housekeeping department more than any other; Room 7 covers such an impressive acreage that entry-level bedrooms can suffer by comparison. The hotel was created by Anouska Hempel in the early '80s and remains a favoured pit-stop for those riding the celebrity circuit. All mod cons are there in the rooms but are just camouflaged and concealed – Anouska was clearly not too fond of TVs and other electronic paraphernalia as they must have got in the way of the overall design effect. Downstairs is a slick and stylish affair, from the dark and mysterious Chinese Room and bar to the intimate restaurant with its Asian-influenced menu. There's a charming courtyard at the back and since these days the hotel is a little more welcoming to those who aren't staying, it now offers afternoon tea.

Brown's

H3

Albemarle St ⊖ Green Park
✉ W1S 4BP
✆ (020) 7493 6020
www.roccofortehotels.com

105 rm – ♦£264/582 ♦♦£354/858, ☕ £29.50 – 12 suites

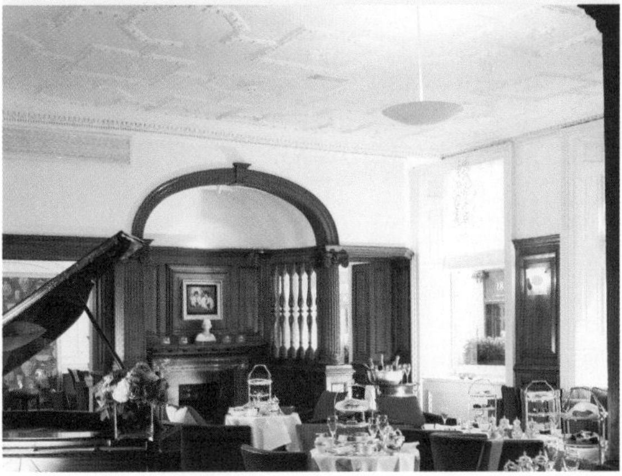

Brown's

Opened in 1837 by James Brown, Lord Byron's butler, Brown's has a long and distinguished history and has been the favoured hotel of many a visiting dignitary: it was here that Alexander Graham Bell first demonstrated his telephone and The Kipling Suite is just one named after a former guest. It reopened in 2005 after a full face-lift, with Olga Polizzi personally overseeing the design and her blending of the traditional with the modern works well. The bedrooms have personality and reflect the character of the hotel, albeit with all of today's required gadgetry. One thing that has remained constant is the popularity of the afternoon teas – the selling point, apart from the pianist, is that the waiter replenishes all stands and pots without extra charge. The wood-panelled restaurant took slightly longer to bed in and now goes by the name of Hix at The Albemarle; the menu features British comfort food. The Donovan Bar is probably the hotel's best feature and celebrates the distinguished work of British photographer Terence Donovan.

The Capital

22-24 Basil St.
✉ SW3 1AT
✆ (020) 7589 5171
www.capitalhotel.co.uk

⊖ Knightsbridge

49 rm – ♦**£294/420** ♦♦**£294/420**, ☕ **£19.50 – 1 suite**

The Capital

The Capital is one of London's most enduringly discreet and comfortable hotels and is thoroughly British in its feel. It is owned by David Levin, who opened it in 1971, and it is this continuity which has lead directly to there only being five head chefs in 40 years. The restaurant is as elegant as ever, with a menu filled with classic British dishes and an extensive wine list that includes selections from the Levins' own winery in the Loire. Bedrooms remain classically chic and the contemporary embellishments are restrained and in keeping with the general atmosphere. Each floor is slightly different and uses designs from the likes of Mulberry, Ralph Lauren and Nina Campbell. What has always raised The Capital to greater heights than similarly styled hotels has been the depth and detail of the service. No one can walk through the small lobby without being greeted and the concierge is old-school in the best sense of the word and can arrange anything for anyone.

Charlotte Street

12

15 Charlotte St.
✉ W1T 1RJ
✆ (020) 7806 2000
www.charlottestreethotel.co.uk

48 rm – 🛉£288 🛉🛉£396, ☕ **£20 – 4 suites**

⊖ Goodge Street

Firmdale

Expect the lobby and bar to be full of men with man-bags and horn-rimmed specs, for Charlotte Street is the hotel of choice for those in the advertising industry. But even if you've never pitched, promoted or placed a product and are just after a stylish, contemporary hotel in a street thronged with bars and restaurants then get on the mailing list here. Oscar is the busy bar and restaurant that spills out onto the street in summer; its sunny contemporary European menu and vivid mural brighten it in winter. Film Club is on Sunday evening: dinner followed by a film in the downstairs screening room. Those after some quiet can nab one of the sofas in the Drawing room or Library. The bedrooms are, as with all hotels in the Firmdale group, exceptionally well looked after. Every year, three or four are fully refurbished and one thing you'll never see is a bit of dodgy grouting or a scuff mark. They are all decorated in an English style but there is nothing chintzy or twee about them. Bathrooms are equally immaculate and the baths face little flat screen TVs.

BLOOMSBURY ▶ PLAN V

393

Claridge's

Brook St
✉ W1K 4HR
✆ (020) 7629 8860
www.claridges.co.uk ⊖ Bond Street

143 rm – ♦£792 ♦♦£792/936, ☑ £31.50 – 60 suites
🍴**Gordon Ramsay at Claridge's** *(See restaurant listing)*

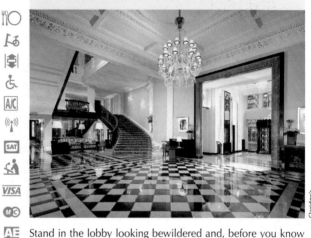

Claridge's

Stand in the lobby looking bewildered and, before you know it, a liveried member of staff will appear promptly before you to enquire after your well being; Claridge's may have a long and very illustrious history but it recognises that reputations are forged because of service rather than longevity. That being said, no modern, purpose-built hotel could afford the extravagance of having such wide corridors or such ornate decoration. The art deco is perhaps the hotel's most striking decorative feature and it's kept suitably fresh and buffed. Despite its long and glittery past, Claridge's has never been in danger of being a museum piece; the David Collins designed bar attracts a more youthful crowd and The Foyer, with its eye-catching light sculpture, proves that afternoon tea need not be a stuffy or quaint affair. The Gordon Ramsay restaurant continues to pull in the punters and the people-watchers. Further bedrooms and other guest facilities are to be added over the next few years and the challenge will be to make this extension as seamless as possible.

MAYFAIR ▶ PLAN II

Connaught

Carlos Pl.   ⊖ Bond Street
✉ W1K 2AL
✆ (020) 7499 7070
www.the-connaught.co.uk

95 rm – 🛉£660 🛉🛉£780/1,104, ⊑ £30 – 26 suites
🍴○**Hélène Darroze at The Connaught** *(See restaurant listing)*

The Connaught

The restored, refurbished and rejuvenated Connaught still retains a sense of effortless serenity and exclusivity – but has now been discovered by a new generation. These sprightlier guests should take the stairs up to their room, that way they'll see the largest mahogany staircase in the country. The bedrooms are now more contemporary in style; they have wooden floors, leather worked into the soft furnishings and come with larger marble bathrooms; some overlook a small oriental garden, others peer down on mews houses. All rooms have full butler service, use linen specially woven in Milan and toiletries from Daylesford. The Coburg Bar honours the hotel's original name and its seats are so deep it's a wonder anyone ever leaves. In contrast, the Connaught Bar attracts a more youthful clientele. Hélène Darroze oversees the restaurant with her refined French cooking and Espelette is an all-day venue just off the lobby that offers a weekly changing list of classic French and British dishes. If you need anything, just ask one of the hotel's 300 members of staff.

MAYFAIR ▶ PLAN II

Covent Garden

10 Monmouth St.
✉ WC2H 9HB
✆ (020) 7806 1000
www.coventgardenhotel.co.uk

56 rm – †£300 ††£426, ☕ **£21 – 2 suites**

⊖ Covent Garden

Firmdale

The Covent Garden Hotel has always been hugely popular with those of a theatrical bent, whether cast or audience member, not least because of its central location, a mere saunter away from the majority of playhouses and productions. The hotel was once a French hospital – the words 'Nouvel hopital et dispensaire francais' are still etched into the brickwork – but the style is essentially British. Mannequins, soft fabrics and antique furniture are juxtaposed with crisp lines and contemporary colours to create a very stylish and comfortable environment. The first floor residents-only wood-panelled sitting room is a delight and so is occasionally used by a visiting grandee for a backdrop to an interview; the presence of an honesty bar adds further to the appeal. The Screening Room holds weekend dinner-and-a-film nights, while Brasserie Max feels much more like a proper restaurant than a mere addendum; its menu is appealingly accessible and afternoon tea is a popular event.

Dorchester

G4

Park Ln.
✉ W1K 1QA
✆ (020) 7629 8888
www.thedorchester.com

Hyde Park Corner

196 rm – †£378/798 ††£510/798, ☕ £31.50 – 54 suites
🍴**Alain Ducasse at The Dorchester and China Tang**
(See restaurant listing)

The Dorchester

The focus here recently has been on improving still further the quality of service and this is most apparent in The Promenade: it may look as though it is an extension of the lobby but try walking through and you won't get far without being welcomed enthusiastically by a member of staff. Afternoon tea here remains a huge draw but they also now offer more of an evening service, to the accompaniment of a jazz trio who replace the day-shift pianist. Suites are always snapped up quickly and it is easy to see why: all have their own personality, from the three elegant rooftop suites which have their own outside terraces, to the Lionel Messel suite on the 7th floor, which has seemingly hosted virtually every visiting idol and has now been listed. There's an impressive choice of restaurant, after you've had a Martini in the bar: they've added more grilled dishes to the menu in The Grill, which seems logical; China Tang sets the standard for stylish dining in a Chinese restaurant and Alain Ducasse provides luxury surroundings to match the food.

MAYFAIR ▶ PLAN II

Draycott

26 Cadogan Gdns.
⊠ SW3 2RP
☏ (020) 7730 6466
www.draycotthotel.com

⊖ Sloane Square

24 rm – ♦£168/312 ♦♦£282/312, ☕ £20.95 – 11 suites

Draycott

The sitting room is one of the best things about The Draycott, especially when the light streams in from the garden outside. It also has a well stocked bar and offers guests complimentary tea at 4pm, champagne at 6pm and hot chocolate at 10pm. This is a discreet little townhouse, decorated more like a country house. The bedrooms have plenty of personality themselves; six have fireplaces and all have an Edwardian feel to their decoration. Each is named after an acting legend about whom you'll find a biography or assorted pictures within the room, be it Vivien Leigh or John Gielgud. The breakfast room is called the Peter O'Toole Room; the name was apparently chosen in a staff competition although he's not a man one would necessarily associate with an early morning meal. Not many hotels have individual guest books in each room and write the names of the occupants on cards outside the door, but The Draycott has always done things 'properly' and its sincere hospitality ensures a very healthy number of returning guests.

Dukes

H4

35 St James's Pl.
✉ SW1A 1NY
📞 (020) 7491 4840
www.dukeshotel.com

⊖ Green Park

84 rm – †£270 ††£420,⌣ £24 – 6 suites

Dukes

As St James's is one of the more traditionally British parts of London, what with all those gentlemen's clubs, wine merchants and tailors, it is no surprise to find that a hotel like Dukes has been a constant presence here for over 100 years. But that is not to say this is some sort of crusty old museum piece: its most recent refurbishment gave it a fresh and brighter feel and introduced more modern elements without losing any of the character. For example, the pretty little sitting room, popular for afternoon tea, opens out into a small Zen-inspired garden. The bar is quite clubby and was apparently one of Ian Fleming's old haunts and the basement dining room, with its international menu, actually looks out at street levels thanks to the vagaries of local topography. Breakfast is served until the thoroughly louche hour of 11am. Bedrooms are comfortable and discreet and bathrooms are kitted out in marble. This is still the sort of hotel where you can leave your shoes outside the door for cleaning. It is also surprisingly peaceful, when you consider the central location.

ST JAMES'S ▶ PLAN II

Egerton House

17-19 Egerton Terr.
✉ SW3 2BX
℘ (020) 7589 2412
www.egertonhousehotel.com

⊖ South Kensington

27 rm – †£336/408 ††£420/732,⊋ £29.50 – 1 suite

Egerton House

In challenging economic times hotels can either panic and cut staff and slash rates – a course of action which usually ends in ruin – or they can hold their nerve and provide greater value for their guests. Anyone wondering what more a hotel can do should get along to Egerton House. This is a townhouse whose decorative style is at the lavish end of the scale; the fabrics are of the highest order and the colours neatly coordinated. The ground floor Victoria and Albert Suite comes with its own little decked terrace and a row of filled decanters for company. All the rooms are slightly different; the marble bathrooms are very neat and the hotel has made the best use of limited space – ask for one of the quieter rooms at the back overlooking the little garden. What really makes this little place stand out, though, is the service and the eager attitude of the staff. Lots of hotels spout tosh about being 'a home from home' but here they do make a genuine effort to make their guests feel part of things by, for example, arranging complimentary admission to events at the V&A.

Four Seasons

Hamilton Pl, Park Ln
✉ W1J 7DR
☎ (020) 7499 0888
www.fourseasons.com

⊖ Hyde Park Corner

148 rm – ♥£690 ♥♥£714,☕ £30 – 45 suites

Four Seasons

These days competition is pretty fierce at the luxury end of the hotel market so, to stay ahead of the game, contenders need to do more than just tinker with the cosmetics. The Four Seasons, which was the group's first hotel outside the US, closed for a couple of years and in that time was stripped right back, before being put together again. The result is that Park Lane now has a hotel that's really raised the bar in the comfort stakes. The bedrooms, trimmed with plenty of walnut, sycamore, marble and shiny steel, are particularly striking and come with all the latest wizardry like self-regulating ambient heating. They also occupy impressive square footage, as do the suites, the number of which has been greatly increased. Dining is a flexible feast – Amaranto is divided into a three areas: a bar, restaurant and lounge and you can eat what you want, where you want it, and that includes on the secluded outdoor terrace. The stunning top-floor spa, with its fantastic views, caps off this hotel's dazzling renaissance.

MAYFAIR ▶ PLAN II

The Gore

D5

190 Queen's Gate   ⊖ Gloucester Road
✉ SW7 5EX
✆ (020) 7584 6601
www.gorehotel.com

50 rm – ♦£174/198 ♦♦£174/528, ☲ £17.50

The Gore

Being the nearest hotel to the Royal Albert Hall makes The Gore a popular choice for performers as well as attendees and the bright, casual bistro is always busier early and late in the evening than it ever is at 8pm. The hotel clearly stands out at the top of Queen's Gate with its fluttering Union flag and gleaming brass plaque and who needs a fitness room when you've got Kensington gardens just yards away. If you were in any doubt that this is the part of London most closely associated with Queen Victoria, then just step through the door because the walls are covered with pictures and paintings relating to her reign. But, despite the plethora of antiques and all that Victoriana, this is a hip little hotel with a large element of fun attached. Rooms like Miss Fanny and Miss Ada are as camp as they sound; the Tudor Room has a secret bathroom and minstrel's gallery, and many of the bathrooms give meaning to the expression 'sitting on the throne'. Bend down in the rooms and you might find a card saying "Look, we've cleaned here too".

Goring

H5

15 Beeston Pl, Grosvenor Gdns
✉ SW1W 0JW
✆ (020) 7396 9000
www.thegoring.com

62 rm – ♦£492/570 ♦♦£550, ☕ £25 – 7 suites

The Goring

Not only did The Goring celebrate its centenary in 2010, but it is still owned by the family who built it. Jeremy Goring, the great-grandson of the founder, is now at the helm and this lineage is clearly welcomed by the staff – many of whom have been working at the hotel for years – as well as being appreciated by regular guests, who benefit from the excellent service. The hotel still has a pervading sense of Britishness, which designers like Nina Campbell fully respected when they were asked to update its look. There has been a clever introduction of new technology, from the TVs that rise from the desk to the touch panels that control everything but, reassuringly for those less familiar or enamoured with the modern world, one can still get a proper key with which to open one's bedroom door. The ground floor restaurant is a bright, discreet and comfortable affair and its menu celebrates Britain's own culinary heritage; the bar is colonial in its feel and the veranda overlooks the hotel's surprisingly large back garden.

VICTORIA ▶ PLAN IV

Halkin

G5

5 Halkin St
✉ SW1X 7DJ
✆ (020) 7333 1000
www.halkin.como.bz

⊖ Hyde Park Corner

35 rm – ♦£312/540 ♦♦£312/660, ☕ **£28.50 – 6 suites**
¶○**Nahm** *(See restaurant listing)*

Halkin

The Halkin is still looking pretty sharp considering it opened nearly 20 years ago as one of London's first boutique hotels. It's certainly more discreet than its sibling, The Metropolitan, which attracts a livelier and feistier crowd, although guests here can use its spa. Apart from the relatively recent addition of a small gym, there is not much in the way of public areas, save for the small but perfectly formed bar area next to the lobby, and Nahm, the hotel's acclaimed and inventive Thai restaurant. The hotel is really all about the bedrooms, which are neatly set out and cleverly thought through. The touch pad operation makes everything seem so effortless but the technology never reaches baffling proportions. All rooms have silk covered walls and marble bathrooms with lots of natural minerals and the Nahm menu is also available as room service. Staff are in abundance and appear to stay for a long time, which improves standards of service no end and pleases the regulars. They also all wear Armani, so no pressure there, then.

Hart House

51 Gloucester Pl
✉ W1U 8JF
☎ (020) 7935 2288
www.harthouse.co.uk

15 rm ☕ – ♦£98/115 ♦♦£150/175

⊖ Marble Arch

Michelin

Hart House has been in the same family for nearly 40 years and while the owner may not spend as much time in the hotel as he used to, he's got enough friendly staff running the place in his absence. Equally importantly, he's also still writing the occasional cheque, as the recent introduction of new LCD TVs would testify. The hotel wouldn't win any design awards but what you get, for a fair price, is clean and tidy accommodation in a late Georgian terrace house that's in a useful central location: it's just a short walk from Oxford Street and Hyde Park and less than a ten minute cab ride from Paddington for those who've taken the Heathrow Express. Gloucester Place may be a fairly busy thoroughfare but the bedrooms on the front have sufficient double glazing; there are family rooms available as well as rooms on the ground floor. Ceilings get lower the higher you climb, reflecting the time when the house's staff had their quarters at the top of the house. The only public area is the small, basement breakfast room but the hotel still manages to have a sociable, international atmosphere.

REGENT'S PARK & MARYLEBONE ▶ PLAN V

Haymarket

1 Suffolk Pl.
✉ SW1Y 4HX
☏ (020) 7470 4000
www.haymarkethotel.com
⊖ Piccadilly Circus

47 rm – †£312 ††£564, ☕ **£20 – 3 suites**

Firmdale

It's hard to believe that The Haymarket hotel opened back in 2007 – you would think it no more than a few months ago, which is testament to its housekeeping department. The hotel is a stylish, hip place, fashioned out of a grand John Nash Regency building that had been a gentleman's club and office before being gutted by a fire. Art and an eclectic collection of furniture now run through it; the lobby, conservatory and library are immaculately decorated and set the tone. No two rooms are the same but all come with dressed mannequins – the motif of the Kemp's hotels – and custom-made furniture. Those on the front could be used to advertise double-glazing but for extra quiet, ask to overlook the inner decked courtyard. The location couldn't be better: theatre-land is literally just outside – indeed, the hotel adjoins the Haymarket Theatre – and all that London offers is a short stroll away. If that isn't enough, there's a very swish swimming pool downstairs, just for residents. Brumus is the spacious restaurant serving easy, Italian food.

Hazlitt's

6 Frith St
✉ W1D 3JA
📞 (020) 7434 1771
www.hazlittshotel.com

27 rm – ♦£222 ♦♦£282 – 3 suites

⊖ Tottenham Court Road

Hazlitt's

Along with its central Soho location, one of the best features of Hazlitt's has always been its intimate and chummy atmosphere, which even the addition of eight rooms in 2009 failed to disrupt. The building dates from 1718 and was named after the essayist and critic William Hazlitt, whose home it was. Appropriately, it still attracts plenty of writers today, but while there is much character to be found in all the bedrooms - from the wood panelling and busts to the antique beds and Victorian fixtures - you do also get free wi-fi. Duke of Monmouth is the most striking of the newer rooms: it's spread over two floors and has its own terrace with a retractable roof. Madam Dafloz, named after another of Soho's former roguish residents, is also appealing, with a sultry, indulgent feel. The Library, with its 24/7 honesty bar, is the hotel's only communal area and was slightly enlarged when the newer rooms were added. This is also one of the few hotels where breakfast in bed really is the only option – and who is going to object to that?

SOHO ▶ PLAN 11

The Hempel

31-35 Craven Hill Gdns.
✉ W2 3EA
✆ (020) 7298 9000
www.the-hempel.co.uk

⊖ Queensway
Closed 24-27 December

44 rm – ♦£214/310 ♦♦£241/310, ☲ £22.50 – **6 suites**

The Hempel

It's no surprise that The Hempel stands out in this part of town – on any given day you can walk past tourists with faces that tell of the disappointment and distress caused by staying in one of the terrible local hotels. This hotel remains true to the principles of its original designer, Anouska Hempel, who, in the late '90s, created a crisp, minimalist environment in a blizzard of white; the maintenance man must get through gallons of white emulsion to keep it looking fresh. Room 107 boasts one of the highest ceilings in London; there's a suspended bed in 110 and those who prefer black should ask for 405. As newer design-led hotels have sprouted up, so everyone has had to raise their game – The Hempel is no exception and these days is not quite so self-satisfied which, in turn, makes it feel more welcoming. The restaurant was moved to the ground floor and the menu changed to a more British affair. Its former space downstairs is now used as an art gallery and for private parties.

The Hoxton

K3

81 Great Eastern St.

✉ EC2A 3HU

☎ (020) 7550 1000

www.hoxtonhotels.com

⊖ Old Street

208 rm – 👤£70/358 👥£70/358, ☕ £12

The Hoxton

A hotel run for the convenience of its guests rather than the management is a concept not as prevalent as one would think, but The Hoxton is one with an inherent understanding of what paying customers want. For a start they offer plenty of freebies, from newspapers and internet access on Apple Macs to 'Pret Lite' breakfasts and even an hour's free phone calls per day. Then there's the convenience of the rakish and relaxed Hoxton Grill, where all-day dining is positively encouraged; you can get a bacon sandwich for breakfast or a burger and a smoothie late at night. The young, good-looking, Converse-wearing staff may look indistinguishable from the customers but are a very helpful and refreshingly cheerful bunch. Bedrooms are quite compact – this isn't the sort of place where you tuck yourself away in your room anyway – but there are some nice touches, like the natty credit-card sized booklet which gives relevant information on the local area. The 'no rip-off' mantra even extends to a twice yearly auction when bedrooms are sold at crazy prices.

HOXTON ▶ PLAN XVI

K + K George

1-15 Templeton Pl.   ⊖ Earl's Court
⊠ SW5 9NB
✆ (020) 7598 8700
www.kkhotels.com

154 rm ☕ – ♦£140/300 ♦♦£150/336

K&K Hotels

Providing a model lesson on the importance of keeping on top of your product, The K+K hotel spent time during the recent economic turndown refurbishing all its bedrooms; they now boast fast internet, 320 thread count linen, American cherry wood panelling, flat screen TVs, full minibars, and under-floor heating in the bathroom; and the hotel is reaping the rewards. It occupies seven houses of a stucco fronted terrace; its interior in contrast to the period façade, is colourful and contemporary and fresh flowers and bowls of fruit are scattered around the lobby. The unexpectedly large rear garden, for which most hotels would give their eye teeth, has won local horticultural prizes and hosts breakfast on warm summer days. A simple menu is served in the bar but most guests take advantage of the central location and go out to eat. The hotel may be part of an international chain but there are plenty of staff on hand to add a personal touch and it also manages to feel part of the local community.

Knightsbridge

F5

10 Beaufort Gdns
✉ SW3 1PT
✆ (020) 7584 6300
www.knightsbridgehotel.com

⊖ Knightsbridge

44 rm – †£216/276 ††£384/774, ☕ £19

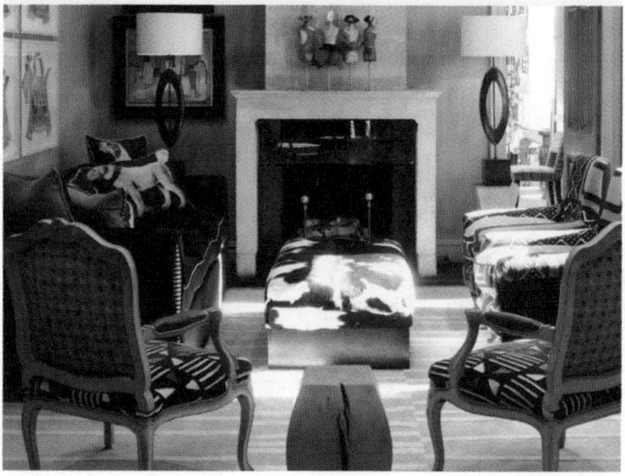

Firmdale

Firmdale Hotels all seem so quintessentially British that it'll be interesting to see what New Yorkers make of them now they have one of their own. The Knightsbridge, converted from a row of Victorian terrace houses in an attractive square, is another typical example of what they do so well: it proves style and comfort are not mutually exclusive and that a hotel can be fashionable without being fuzzy. The work of British artists, such as Carol Sinclair's slate stack and Peter Clark's dog collages sets the tone and the bedrooms are constantly being refreshed and rearranged. Those facing the square on the first floor benefit from floor to ceiling windows, while the Knightsbridge Suite stretches from the front to the back of the building. All rooms are so impeccably tidy and colour coordinated it'll make you question your own dress sense. The Library Room differs from many similarly named hotel sitting rooms by actually containing books, along with an honesty bar which holds everything from fruit and snacks to champagne and ice cream.

Lanesborough

Hyde Park Corner ⊖ Hyde Park Corner
⊠ SW1X 7TA
℡ (020) 7259 5599
www.lanesborough.com

83 rm – ♦£630 ♦♦£738, ⌂ £30 – **10 suites**
⫿○**Apsleys** *(See restaurant listing)*

The Lanesborough

Many of London's luxury hotels boast long and illustrious histories and have names that are recognised the world over. Having opened relatively recently in 1991, The Lanesborough still feels like something of a newcomer, but there is no doubt that it deserves its place among the top tier of London hotels. Constructed in 1733 as Viscount Lanesborough's country house, the building was perhaps better known as a hospital before it was converted into a hotel. The series of drawing rooms are smartly kitted out; the clubby library bar offers a vast selection of whiskies and cognacs and the Garden Room provides a hugely popular sanctuary for cigar smokers. Apsleys is their lavishly dressed Italian restaurant with superlative cooking. Bedrooms come in a rich and decorative Regency style and boast a host of extras, including laptops. There's a butler on each floor, on call 24 hours a day, and rooms are tripled-glazed. Ask for a room facing Hyde Park – you may not hear anything of the outside world but you can enjoy some pretty terrific views.

Langham

1c Portland Pl., Regent St.
✉ W1B 1JA
✆ (020) 7636 1000
www.langhamhotels.com

⊖ Oxford Circus

357 rm – ♦£239/499 ♦♦£239/499, ☕ £30 – 21 suites
🍴 **Roux at the Landau** *(See restaurant listing)*

Langham

The Langham was one of Europe's first purpose-built Grand hotels when it opened in 1865. Since then it has been owned by all sorts, including at one stage the BBC – they used it as their library and was where 'The Goon Show' was recorded. In 2009 it emerged from an extensive refurbishment programme that didn't provide much change from £80 million and it is now competing with the big boys once again. Pride of place must be the Palm Court, a twinkling ersatz art deco space, which serves light meals and afternoon teas. The Artesian bar is a stylish affair and does interesting things with gin; there's a small courtyard terrace named in honour of a BBC radio gardener and the striking restaurant is under the aegis of the Roux organisation. The bedrooms have personality and, for a change, the furniture is free-standing rather than fitted; the boldly decorated Club rooms are particularly distinctive. The health and fitness club is impressively kitted out and includes a swimming pool in what was once a bank vault.

The Levin

28 Basil St.
✉ SW3 1AS
☎ (020) 7589 6286
www.thelevinhotel.co.uk

12 rm – ♦£300/384 ♦♦£300/384

⊖ Knightsbridge

The Levin

Its bigger sister, The Capital, is a few strides down the road and may be better known, but The Levin still does the (Levin) family proud. Here you'll find a different decorative style but still the same level of care and enthusiasm in the service. The eye-catching fibre optic chandelier dominates the staircase, while the collection of Penguin paperbacks reminds you that this is a fundamentally British hotel. All 12 bedrooms are light and fresh-feeling; there are subtle nods in the direction of art deco in the styling but these are combined with a cleverly contemporary look which blends in well with the building. The best room is the top floor open-plan suite. Mini-bars are stocked exclusively with champagne - along with some helpful hints on how to prepare an assortment of champagne cocktails. In the basement you'll find Le Metro which provides an appealing, all-day menu with everything from quiche and salads to shepherd's pie and sausage and mash, along with selections from the family estate in the Loire.

Mandarin Oriental Hyde Park

F4

ⓗⓗⓗⓗ

66 Knightsbridge ✉ SW1X 7LA ⊖ Knightsbridge
✆ (020) 7235 2000
www.mandarinoriental.com/london

173 rm – 🛉£810 🛉🛉£900, ☕ £19.50 – 25 suites
🍴 **Dinner by Heston Blumenthal and Bar Boulud**
(See restaurant listing)

Mandarin Oriental Hyde Park

When the bewilderingly expensive new apartments next door went on sale things could finally quieten down in this part of town for a while. That said, during their construction there was also plenty of work being done on the hotel too. Bar Boulud, celebrated New York based chef Daniel Boulud's first European venture, occupies what was previously the hotel's housekeeping storeroom and proved a hit from day one. But that was nothing compared to the frenzy caused by Heston Blumenthal's enigmatically named restaurant with its thrilling menu of rediscovered and re-imagined British dishes. Meanwhile, the hotel continues to constantly upgrade and redecorate its bedrooms which all offer every imaginable luxury and extra. They are decorated in a classic English country house style and come in either beige and blue or red and gold – although the TVs do seem to be incongruously large. If evidence were still needed that the hotel is keen to remain one of the most luxurious in the capital, it comes in the fact that it recently spent a mere £1 million just on doing up its Royal Suite.

HYDE PARK & KNIGHTSBRIDGE ▶ PLAN XII

415

Mayflower

C6

26-28 Trebovir Rd.
✉ SW5 9NJ
☎ (020) 7370 0991
www.mayflowerhotel.co.uk

⊖ Earl's Court

43 rm – ♦£120/130 ♦♦£120/130,⊊ £10 – 4 suites

Mayflower

The Mayflower shares the same ownership as Twenty Nevern Square just around the corner and it too offers good value accommodation. It is also twice the size so the chances of actually getting a room are somewhat greater. Some of those rooms can be a little tight on space but this is also reflected in the room rates. Rooms 11, 17 and 18 are the best in the house and the general decoration is a blend of the contemporary with some Asian influence; some of the rooms have jet showers and others balconies. But what makes the hotel stand out is that the owner is nearly always on the property and his enthusiasm has been passed to his staff. This may not be a glitzy West End hotel but they really do make an effort to get to know their guests and help in anyway they can. There is no restaurant, but then it doesn't need one: there are plenty of places in which to eat that are no more than a vigorous stroll away. A plentiful breakfast is provided and, on summer days, can even be taken on the small terrace.

Metropolitan

G4

Old Park Ln
✉ W1K 1LB
☏ (020) 7447 1000
www.metropolitan.como.bz

⊖ Hyde Park Corner

147 rm – ♥£251/468 ♥♥£287/504, ☕ £28 – 3 suites
🍽 **Nobu** (See restaurant listing)

Metropolitan

The Metropolitan is inextricably linked to its über-cool hang-out, The Met Bar. If you've never managed to blag your way past the doorman at night you can now secure entry by grabbing yourself some 'Afternoon Delight': a healthy version of afternoon tea with low-fat cakes and breadless sandwiches. The Metropolitan Hotel is well over a decade old now; in design terms, there may be more contemporary competitors around but it continues to hold its own in the fashion stakes by letting its guests create their own atmosphere. The bedrooms are neutral in colour and gadgets are discreetly integrated; all get regular licks of paint or, following an overnight stay from the occasional wannabe rock star, a full redecoration. Plenty of rooms overlook the park but the more interesting views are those facing east over the rooftops. The spa promises plenty of holistic treatments while London's original Nobu on the first floor ensures a further sprinkling of stardust. Even better, the staff now provide good service instead of just standing at an angle, looking cool.

MAYFAIR ▶ PLAN II

The Milestone

D4

1-2 Kensington Ct. ⊖ High Street Kensington
W8 5DL
(020) 7917 1000
www.milestonehotel.com

56 rm – †£360/534 ††£420/594, ☕ £29.50 – 6 suites

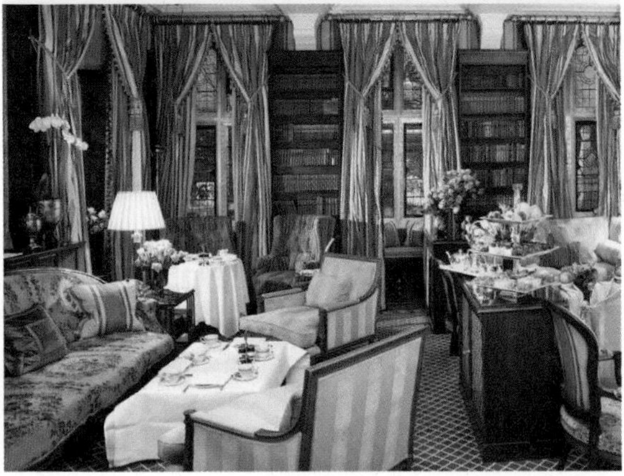

The Milestone

The Milestone proves that it is the service, not the space, which makes a hotel. With 100 members of staff for 57 bedrooms, it's odds-on you'll be well looked after; the hotel prides itself on keeping records of the whims and preferences of their regulars. Plenty of thought has gone into the design and decoration of the bedrooms which are undergoing a refurbishment. It's in the detail where you notice the extra effort: there's a little gift with the turn-down service and the bathrobes are seasonally adjusted so one gets a lighter robe in summer. The suites display greater levels of whimsy than the standard rooms – just check out the art deco inspired Mistinguett Suite, named in honour of the celebrated music hall entertainer, while Johnny Weissmuller would feel more at home in The Safari Suite. The sitting room is a comfy place, with a jaunty looking Noel Coward hanging above the fireplace. The Jockey bar is so named as this was where the horses were stabled in the days when this Victorian building was a private house. The dining room is an intimate, wood-panelled affair.

Number Sixteen

16 Sumner Pl.
✉ SW7 3EG
✆ (020) 7589 5232
www.numbersixteenhotel.co.uk

⊖ South Kensington

42 rm – ♦£156/210 ♦♦£258, ☕ £18.50

Firmdale

Number Sixteen opened back in 2001 and was the first one in Tim and Kit Kemp's Firmdale Group of hotels not to have its own restaurant. This actually suits it because it feels more like a private house than the others and, with repeat business standing at around 55%, they've clearly got it right. Attention to detail underpins the operation, whether in the individual styling of the bedrooms or the twice-daily housekeeping service. Breakfast is in the conservatory overlooking the little garden – don't miss the smoothie of the day – and is served until midday: welcome acknowledgement that not every guest has an early morning meeting. Firmdale also operates its own laundry service which explains how the bed linen retains such crispness. Rooms 2 and 7 have their own private patio terrace and all the first floor rooms benefit from large windows and balconies. The drawing room, with its plump sofa cushions and pretty butterfly theme, is a very charming spot and there's the added bonus of a nearby honesty bar.

One Aldwych

1 Aldwych
✉ WC2B 4RH
☏ (020) 7300 1000
www.onealdwych.com

⊖ Temple

93 rm – ♦£288/415 ♦♦£288/498, ☕ **£24 – 12 suites**
🍴**Axis** *(See restaurant listing)*

One Aldwych

Things have gone all green down at One Aldwych. The hotel is hoping to take a lead within the hospitality industry on matters environmental (without, of course, neglecting its duties as a luxury hotel) and has appointed a 'green team' to oversee and coordinate procedures. The swimming pool is chemical and chlorine free; bath products are organic; and the chocolate on your pillow has been replaced by a book called 'Change the World'. As far as guests are concerned though, it's business as usual, which means extremely comfortable bedrooms and plenty of polished staff. Fruit and flowers are changed daily in the rooms, which are awash with Bang & Olufsen toys and also come with Frette linen; deluxe rooms and corner suites are particularly desirable. There's a choice of restaurant: the first floor Indigo offers a light, easy menu while Axis boasts more personality and greater ambition in its cooking. The lobby of the hotel is perhaps its most well-known feature; not only does it double as a bar surprisingly successfully but it also changes its look according to the seasons.

The Pelham

15 Cromwell Pl
✉ SW7 2LA
☎ (020) 7589 8288
www.pelhamhotel.co.uk

⊖ South Kensington

51 rm – †£216/300 ††£324/399, ☐ **£17.50 – 1 suite**

The Pelham

It may no longer be part of the Firmdale group – it is owned by the people who have The Gore in Queensgate – but The Pelham retains that stylish look which comes from juxtaposing the feel of a classic English country house with the contemporary look of a city townhouse. Originally three houses, the hotel has a pleasing lack of conformity in its layout. Bold pastel colours, fine fabrics and a housekeeping department that could satisfy Howard Hughes combine to create bedrooms that are pristine, warm and comfortable. Spend too long in the panelled sitting room or library, with all those cushions, an honesty bar and a fridge full of ice cream and the world outside will seem positively frenzied. Downstairs you'll find Bistro Fifteen, a relaxed all-day affair which becomes a cosy and romantic dinner spot. Its menu is mostly centred on Europe with an extra Gallic element – a nod to the high number of French émigrés in the neighbourhood. There's a genuine helpfulness and an eagerness to please amongst the staff.

SOUTH KENSINGTON ► PLAN XI

Ritz

150 Piccadilly   ⊖ Green Park
⊠ W1J 9BR
✆ (020) 7493 8181
www.theritzlondon.com

116 rm – ▮£360/696 ▮▮£426/822, ⊑ £35 – 20 suites
🍴**Ritz Restaurant** *(See restaurant listing)*

The Ritz

Henry James considered that, "There are few hours in life more agreeable than the hour dedicated to the ceremony known as afternoon tea". Such is the popularity of Tea at the Ritz, which is served daily in the grand surroundings of the Palm Court, that the ceremony begins at 11.30 am – an hour before lunch is served in their restaurant – and doesn't cease until 7.30pm. Meanwhile, the rest of the hotel, built in 1906 in the style of a French chateau, remains in fine form thanks to constant re-investment by its owners, the Barclay Brothers. The William Kent Room must be the most ornate private dining room in London and the bedrooms are all immaculately kept. The Royal and Prince of Wales Suites both have enormous square footage and are often booked for long stays by those for whom the credit crunch is no more than a mild irritant. The Ritz Restaurant, with its dinner dances, lavish surroundings and brigades of staff, evokes images of a more formal but more glamorous age and the art deco Rivoli bar remains a veritable jewel.

The Rockwell

C5

181-183 Cromwell Rd.
SW5 0SF
(020) 7244 2000
www.therockwell.com

Earl's Court

40 rm – †£140/220 ††£200/260, ☕ £9.50

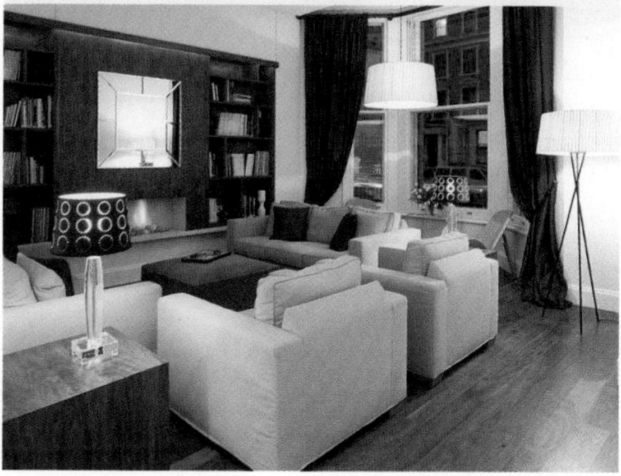

The Rockwell

The Rockwell is steadily establishing itself on the London hotel scene and is building up quite a loyal client base. They certainly get a lot of things right: the reception is manned 24/7 and staff are imbued with sufficient self-confidence to make eye-contact with their guests and offer help when needed; the housekeeping department also do an evening service of all the rooms. The lobby is a comfortable space, with its fireplace and generous scattering of newspapers. The hotel is made up of two Victorian houses; the best two rooms are the split level 104 and 105 and those on the lower ground floor have their own private patios. All rooms have showers rather than baths, and come with top-brand toiletries, mini bars and free internet – you can even borrow a laptop. Meals are relaxed affairs with plenty of favourites and decent cocktails. Freshly baked croissants and homemade breads are a feature of breakfast; sometimes served on the south-facing garden terrace which is the hotel's most appealing feature.

The Rookery

L2

12 Peters Ln, Cowcross St
✉ EC1M 6DS
✆ (020) 7336 0931
www.rookeryhotel.com

⊖ Barbican
Closed 24-26 December

32 rm – †£222/282 ††£246/282, ☕ £11.95 **– 1 suite**

A/C
((•))
VISA
MC
AE
①

The Rookery

The mere fact that the original opening of the hotel was delayed because the owner couldn't find quite the right chimney pots tells you that authenticity is high on the agenda here. Named after the colloquial term for the local area from a time when it had an unruly reputation, the hotel is made up of a series of Georgian houses whose former residents are honoured in the naming of the bedrooms. Its decoration remains true to these Georgian roots, not only in the antique furniture and period features but also in the colours used; all the bedrooms have either half-testers or four-poster beds and bathrooms have roll-top baths. Rook's Nest, the largest room, is often used for fashion shoots. However, with the addition of flat screen TVs and wireless internet access, there is no danger of the hotel becoming a twee museum piece. Breakfast is served in the bedrooms and there is just one small sitting room which leads out onto a little terrace - its mural of the owner herding some cows goes some way towards blocking out the surrounding sights of the 21C.

CLERKENWELL ▶ PLAN IX

St James's Hotel and Club

 H4

7-8 Park Pl.
✉ SW1A 1LS
☎ (020) 7316 1600
www.stjameshotelandclub.com

⊖ Green Park

50 rm – ✝£282/414 ✝✝£282/414, ⊑ £22 – 10 suites
🍽 **Seven Park Place**
(See restaurant listing)

St James's Hotel & Club

Dating from 1892, this building was a private club for many years and the hotel manages to retain something of that clubby spirit. It certainly feels as though it is run for the benefit of its guests rather than a balance sheet, and staff make genuine efforts to get to know the guests and their individual peculiarities. While the public areas are quite compact, the interior has been sympathetically modernised and features over 200 pieces of art, most of which are German works from the 1930s and '40s. Bedrooms are well-equipped and have smart, marble bathrooms; a few have small terraces and the Presidential Suite comes with an enormous one that can host up to 60 people. The restaurant is intimate and the cooking and service are undertaken with considerable expertise. The hotel's other great bonus is its location: this is the centre of central London but Park Place is also a cul-de-sac so it's quiet to boot. There's also a cut-through to Green Park where you'll find a pile of towels and water, placed there by the hotel for those who insist on running round it.

ST JAMES'S ▶ PLAN II

St Martins Lane

13

45 St Martin's Ln
✉ WC2N 3HX
✆ (020) 7300 5500
www.stmartinslane.com

⊖ Charing Cross

202 rm – ♦£258/594 ♦♦£258/594, ☕ £25 – 2 suites

St Martin's Lane

If you're uncomfortable with the idea of hotel staff calling you by your first name or have never considered working out in a gym wearing a pair of stilettos then St Martins Lane is probably not the hotel for you; nor you the right guest for them. Philippe Starck's design of the modern juxtaposed with the baroque creates an eye-catching lobby. The bedrooms are decorated in a blizzard of white, although you can change the lighting according to your mood. The views get better the higher you go but all have floor to ceiling windows. Thanks to the paparazzi, readers of the more excitable magazines will be familiar with Bungalow 8: Anne Sacco's London outpost of her hip New York club is a favoured hang-out for the already-famous, the would-be-famous and the related-to-someone-famous-famous. Asia de Cuba is Scarface meets Dr No: fiery Floridian Cuban mixed with teasing influence from across Asia – dishes are designed for sharing. The Light Bar is sufficiently hip and the Gymbox is a branded gym with a nightclub vibe – what else?

Sanderson

50 Berners St
⊠ W1T 3NG
☏ (020) 7300 1400
www.morganshotelgroup.com
⊖ Oxford Circus

150 rm – 🛏£270/654 🛏🛏£270/654, ☕ £23

Sanderson

When the doorman greets you with a "how ya doing?" you know this is not a hotel that stands on ceremony. The staff do now smile here, something that was all too rare in the early days when they were mostly recruited from model agencies and had a somewhat disdainful attitude towards the whole concept of service. The Sanderson has always worn its exclusivity with confidence but now there's some substance to it. The Philippe Starck designed bedrooms still impress, with their celestial whiteness, sleigh beds in the middle of the room and idiosyncrasies such as the framed print hung on the ceiling – its actually the same print in all the rooms, is called 'Pathway to Heaven' and is designed to encourage heavenly thoughts before sleep. Some bedrooms have their own treadmills while others boast small terraces; the top two suites have their own lifts. On the ground floor the Purple Bar has over 75 different vodkas, miniature chairs and a selective door policy; the Long Bar is more accessible and leads into Suka, their modern Malaysian restaurant.

Savoy

Strand
✉ WC2R 0EU
✆ (020) 7836 4343
www.fairmont.com/savoy

⊖ Charing Cross

221 rm – ♦£678 ♦♦£750, ☕ £30 – 47 suites
🍴 **Savoy Grill** *(See restaurant listing)*

The Savoy

It took longer than anyone expected, but finally, in late 2010, the grande dame of London hotels made her long-awaited entrance. The careful restoration took nearly three years but the best news for the hotel's legions of regulars was that many of the familiar Edwardian and art deco features were retained. There is no longer a front desk – just numerous staff waiting to greet you as soon as you enter. Afternoon tea is served in the Thames Foyer, which remains at the heart of the operation – although it now has a steel gazebo beneath a glass dome. Just off the Foyer is a new bar to complement the world famous American Bar: The Beaufort Bar occupies the space from where the BBC once broadcast, with a champagne bar on the original stage. The River Room's art deco splendour has been given a contemporary makeover and its windows looking out over the river open fully in summer. The luxurious bedrooms remain true to the hotel's origins and are split between Edwardian or art deco styles.

Soho

4 Richmond Mews   ⊖ Tottenham Court Road
✉ W1D 3DH
✆ (020) 7559 3000
www.sohohotel.com

85 rm – ☥£354 ☥☥£570, ⬛ £20 – 2 suites

Firmdale

It's almost as if they wanted to keep it secret. The hotel is on a relatively quiet mews – not something one readily associates with Soho – and, even as you approach, it gives little away. But inside one soon realises that, if it was a secret, it wasn't very well kept as it's always buzzing with people. Their guests' every dietary whim or food mood should find fulfilment in 'Refuel', the restaurant with its own bar as a backdrop. Whether your diet is gluten-free, vegetarian, vegan, carnivorous or organic you'll discover something worth ordering and, if you're off out, you'll find the early dinner menu a steal. It's also worth checking out the Film Club for a meal and a movie in the screening room. Upstairs and the bedrooms are almost celestial in their cleanliness. From jazzy orange to bright lime green, from crimsons to bold stripes, the rooms are vibrant in style and immaculate in layout; those on the top floor have balconies and terraces. Add infectiously enthusiastic service and it's little wonder the hotel has so many returning guests. And to think this was once an NCP car park.

Stafford

H4

16-18 St James's Pl.
✉ SW1A 1NJ
✆ (020) 7493 0111
www.kempinski.com/london

73 rm – ♦£330/492 ♦♦£443/660, ☕ £25 – **15 suites**

⊖ Green Park

Stafford

The Stafford has, for a few years, been a mix of the new and the more traditional. Recently, the owners have been busy injecting considerable amounts of money into its refurbishment; something which no doubt terrifies many of its loyal and longstanding guests who appear to like things just the way they are. Thanks to some judicious lighting, the lobby and lounge appear brighter and more inviting. The dining room now opens out more into the drawing room and has changed its name to the Lyttleton, after a family who once lived here, but it has wisely kept its traditional British menu. The relatively recently created suites in the Mews House, a converted office block in the rear courtyard of the hotel, are the most impressive of all the bedrooms. What will never change at The Stafford is the celebrated American Bar, which is festooned with an impressive collection of assorted ties, helmets and pictures and is one of the best in London for those who like their bars with chairs and without music.

ST. JAMES'S ▶ PLAN II

Twenty Nevern Square

C6

20 Nevern Sq.   ⊖ Earl's Court
✉ SW5 9PD
✆ (020) 7565 9555
www.twentynevernsquare.co.uk

20 rm – †£115/180 ††£220/250, ⌣ £9

Michelin

Booking well in advance is the key here, as this small but friendly hotel, with its quiet and leafy location in the typically Victorian Nevern Square, represents good value for money and gets booked up pretty quickly. The two best rooms are the Pasha and the more recently added Ottoman Suite and both have their own terrace, but all rooms are well looked after and given regular refits. Ten of the rooms overlook the gardens opposite but try to get one of the rooms on the top floor as these have more space. Hand-carved Indonesian furniture is found throughout and, together with the elaborately draped curtains, adds a hint of exoticism. You'll find gratis tea, coffee, water and a pile of daily newspapers laid on in the pleasant lounge beside the lovebirds, Mary and Joseph. Continental breakfast comes included in the room rate; it can be taken in the bedroom or the bright conservatory. The hotel's other great selling point is the genuine sense of neighbourhood one feels. Its sister hotel, the Mayflower, is around the corner.

Westbury

H3

Bond St — ⊖ Bond Street
✉ W1S 2YF
✆ (020) 7629 7755
www.westburymayfair.com

233 rm ☕ – 🚹£239/469 🚹🚹£239/469 – 13 suites

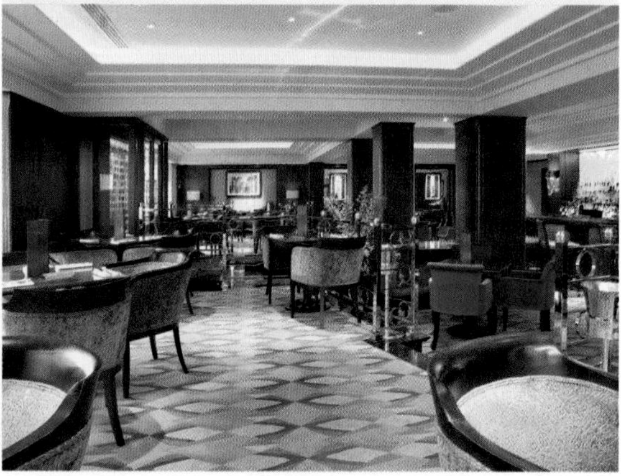

Westbury

They spent £25 million on The Westbury a few years ago but the owner didn't like the bathrooms so he had them replaced with Italian marble; rather like Premier League football clubs, it helps having an owner who is more concerned with quality than with balance sheets. The hotel was built in the 1950s and caused quite a commotion at the time with its New York sensibilities. Nowadays it benefits from having some of the most famous designer brands just outside the front door, while inside it's all very polished and comfortable. The celebrated Polo bar is elegantly decorated in Gucci and Fendi and the restaurant exudes an air of permanence and quiet professionalism. The bedrooms are sleek and comfy, and each floor is decorated with photos from that decade (for example, 1960s style icons adorn the 6th floor). The suites are particularly smart, especially those with art deco styling. The room service menu is also one of the most comprehensive you'll see - there are so many members of staff they have to be kept busy somehow.

Zetter

St John's Sq., 86-88 Clerkenwell Rd. ⊖ Farringdon
✉ EC1M 5RJ
✆ (020) 7324 4444
www.thezetter.com

72 rm – ♦£222 ♦♦£222/480, ☕ £9.50
⊗ Bistrot Bruno Loubet
(See restaurant listing)

The Zetter

The Zetter ticks all the boxes for a contemporary hotel - it's a converted Victorian warehouse in a hitherto neglected area of the city that's now having its time and is environmentally aware, with spring water bottled from its building's own well. Its restaurant, thanks to the reputation of chef Bruno Loubet, is busy pulling in the crowds; it has understated bedrooms offering everything from a huge array of music tracks to classic Penguin paperbacks and, to appreciate all these things, it attracts a clientele who know their wiis from their wi-fis. But what makes the place more than just another hip hotel is its friendly and hospitable staff who understand that the principles of hospitality remain the same, regardless of whether the hotel is trendy or traditional, and that coolness need not equate to aloofness. Across St. John's Square you'll find the more idiosyncratically decorated Zetter Townhouse, fashioned from two Georgian houses. Despite a very busy cocktail lounge, this is sadly used more as an overflow than a hotel in its own right.

FINSBURY ▶ PLAN IX

The Michelin Adventure

It all started with rubber balls! This was the product made by a small company based in Clermont-Ferrand that André and Edouard Michelin inherited, back in 1880. The brothers quickly saw the potential for a new means of transport and their first success was the invention of detachable pneumatic tyres for bicycles. However, the automobile was to provide the greatest scope for their creative talents. Throughout the 20th century, Michelin never ceased developing and creating ever more reliable and high-performance tyres, not only for vehicles ranging from trucks to F1 but also for underground transit systems and aeroplanes.

From early on, Michelin provided its customers with tools and services to facilitate mobility and make travelling a more pleasurable and more frequent experience. As early as 1900, the Michelin Guide supplied motorists with a host of useful information related to vehicle maintenance, accommodation and restaurants, and was to become a benchmark for good food. At the same time, the Travel Information Bureau offered travellers personalised tips and itineraries.

The publication of the first collection of roadmaps, in 1910, was an instant hit! In 1926, the first regional guide to France was published, devoted to the principal sites of Brittany, and before long each region of France had its own Green Guide. The collection was later extended to more far-flung destinations, including New York in 1968 and Taiwan in 2011.

In the 21st century, with the growth of digital technology, the challenge for Michelin maps and guides is to continue to develop alongside the company's tyre activities. Now, as before, Michelin is committed to improving the mobility of travellers.

MICHELIN TODAY

WORLD NUMBER ONE TYRE MANUFACTURER
- 70 production sites in 18 countries
- 111,000 employees from all cultures and on every continent
- 6,000 people employed in research and development

Moving
for a world

Moving forward means developing tyres with better road grip and shorter braking distances, whatever the state of the road.

CORRECT TYRE PRESSURE

RIGHT PRESSURE

- Safety
- Longevity
- Optimum fuel consumption

-0,5 bar

- Durability reduced by 20% (- 8,000 km)

-1 bar

- Risk of blowouts
- Increased fuel consumption
- Longer braking distances on wet surfaces

forward together
where mobility is safer

It also involves helping motorists take care of their safety and their tyres. To do so, Michelin organises "Fill Up With Air" campaigns all over the world to remind us that correct tyre pressure is vital.

WEAR

DETECTING TYRE WEAR

The legal minimum depth of tyre tread is 1.6mm.

Tyre manufacturers equip their tyres with tread wear indicators, which are small blocks of rubber moulded into the base of the main grooves at a depth of 1.6mm.

Tyres are the only point of contact between vehicle and road.

The photo below shows the actual contact zone.

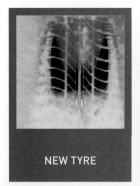

NEW TYRE

WORN TYRE
(1,6mm tread)

If the tread depth is less than 1.6mm, tyres are considered to be worn and dangerous on wet surfaces.

Moving forward
means sustainable mobility

By 2050, Michelin aims to cut the quantity of raw materials used in its tyre manufacturing process by half and to have developed renewable energy in its facilities. The design of MICHELIN tyres has already saved billions of litres of fuel and, by extension, billions of tonnes of CO2.

Similarly, Michelin prints its maps and guides on paper produced from sustainably managed forests and is diversifying its publishing media by offering digital solutions to make travelling easier, more fuel efficient and more enjoyable!

The group's whole-hearted commitment to eco-design on a daily basis is demonstrated by ISO 14001 certification.

Like you, Michelin is committed to preserving our planet.

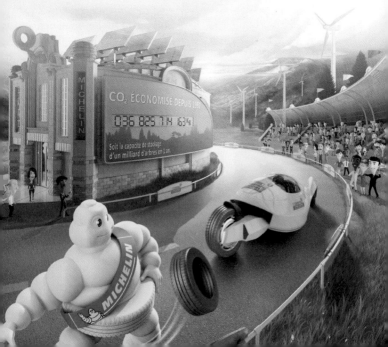

Chat with Bibendum

Go to
www.michelin.com/corporate/fr
Find out more about Michelin's
history and the latest news.

Michelin develops tyres for all types of vehicles. See if you can match the right tyre with the right vehicle…

Solution : A-6 / B-4 / C-2 / D-1 / E-3 / F-7 / G-5

Alphabetical list of Restaurants

Index **& Maps** ▶ **Alphabetical list of Restaurants**

Index of maps

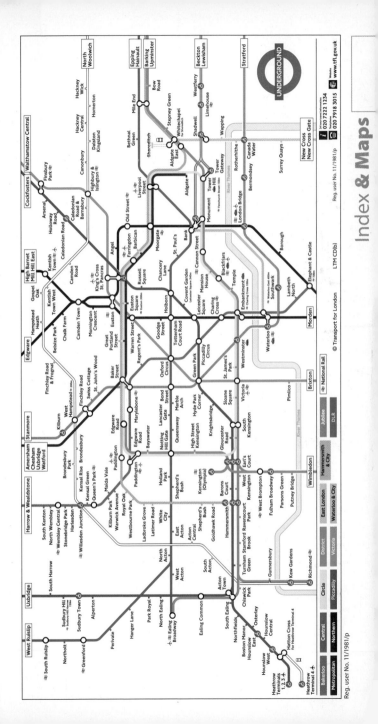

Index & Maps

UNDERGROUND

www.tfl.gov.uk
020 7222 1234
020 7918 3015

© Transport for London

LTM CD(b)

Reg. user No. 11/1981/p

Great Britain: Based on Ordnance Survey of Great Britain with the permission
of the Controller of Her Majesty's Stationery Office, © Crown Copyright 100000247.

Cover photography : Dinner by Heston Blumenthal

Manufacture française des pneumatiques Michelin

Société en commandite par actions au capital de 504 000 004 EUR
Place des Carmes-Déchaux – 63000 Clermont-Ferrand (France)
R.C.S. Clermont-Fd B 855 200 507

© Michelin, Propriétaires-éditeurs

Dépot légal octobre 2011
Printed in Italy : 09-2011
Printed on paper from sustainably managed forests
Compogravure : NORD COMPO à Villeneuve-d'Ascq (France)
Impression et brochage : LA TIPOGRAFICA VARESE, Varese (Italie)